THE CREED

BERARD L. MARTHALER, O.F.M.Conv.

TWENTY-THIRD PUBLICATIONS
Mystic, Connecticut

Twenty-Third Publications
P.O. Box 180
Mystic, CT 06355
(203) 536-2611

Cover design by George Herrick
Edited by Cyril Reilly
Interior design by John G. van Bemmel

Cover symbol: ©   Terra Sancta Guild
Broomall, Penn.

This copyrighted design by Terra Sancta Guild depicts the ancient Christian symbol of the fish. The Greek characters in the design spell the word "fish," while at the same time forming an acronym. The faith statement concealed within the characters translates in English to "Jesus Christ, Son of God, Savior."

Library of Congress Catalog Card Number 86-50891
ISBN 0-89622-222-5 (cloth)
ISBN 0-89622-320-5 (paper)

PREFACE

A Fresh Look at the Creed

"Creed" looks like a simple word that designates a rather straightforward statement of beliefs. It isn't and it doesn't.

The pages that follow are intended to show that while the Christian Creed is simple enough for the barely literate to grasp, it is worthy of study by professional scholars. And while this work is written for an audience more advanced than the former and not as informed as the latter, it assumes that everyone can profit from a fresh look at the Creed.

In October 1983, a group of some twenty theologians met in Rome under the auspices of the Commission on Faith and Order of the World Council of Churches. The purpose of the consultation was to clarify the authority, significance and use of the Nicene Creed in today's church. The theologians admitted they encountered "persistent difficulty" in carrying out their mandate, for reasons I shall explain below. In the midst of their frustration they concluded that the best way to overcome the obstacle would be by explicating the Nicene Creed in light of contemporary questions and in relationship to the Scripture witness of apostolic faith.[1]

Without any official mandate other than the responsibility of every Christian to enter into the ecumenical dialogue according to one's ability, I take up the challenge. This book represents my "explication" of the two great confessional statements of Western Christendom, the Ecumenical Creed promulgated by the Council of Constantinople in

A.D. 381—popularly known as the Nicene Creed—and the Apostles' Creed, which came into common use about the sixth century. Too many Christian issues in contemporary theology seem far removed from the basic doctrines of the church and farther still from the teachings of the New Testament. It is my purpose to show that the three—Scripture, Creed, and contemporary theology—are a package. They belong together and, when separated, each is in danger of being misunderstood.

For a long time I have been fascinated by the great number of commentaries on the Creed. From the ancient church we have, among others, the catechetical lectures attributed to St. Cyril of Jerusalem, St. Augustine's *Enchiridion*, and the introduction to the Apostles' Creed by Rufinus of Aquileia. The Creed was the centerpiece of medieval catechesis, and drew the attention of the best medieval theologians including Alexander of Hales, Bonaventure, and Thomas Aquinas. While Renaissance scholars such as Erasmus were questioning the apostolic origins of the Apostles' Creed, Protestant and Catholic authorities alike explained it article by article in their catechisms. In the modern period, church historians and patristic scholars, from the great Philip Schaaf in the United States to the Germans Adolf von Harnack, A. Seeberg, and Hans Lietzmann, and the English C. H. Turner, have studied every conceivable aspect of the origins, wording and early use of the Creed. Nor has the flow of commentaries abated in our time; one thinks of authors such as Karl Barth, Oscar Cullmann, Gustav Wingren, Josef Ratzinger, Wolfhart Pannenberg, and Henri de Lubac, to mention only a few. Finally, there is the magisterial study by J.N.D. Kelly, *Early Christian Creeds*, now in its third edition, the text that introduced many of us in the English speaking world to the richness of the creeds and is the source of much of the historical information about their development in the pages that follow.

It is precisely because the Creed is not as simple and straightforward as it seems that even the best minds in the church have thought it worthy of their attention. Some are attracted to the study of it because of historical and theological interest, some for pastoral reasons. The Creed has attracted renewed interest all about. We have already alluded to the attention it has received from the Commission on Faith and Order in the context of ecumenical relations. Within Roman Catholicism the new Rite of Christian Initiation of Adults has restored the ancient practice of handing over the Creed to the catechumens in a formal ceremony. The year 1981, the sixteenth centenary of the Council of Constantinople, which gave us the expression of the Nicene faith in classic form, was the occasion for a new look at the old formulas. In the centennial year there were the to-be-expected historical and theological investigations, and there were novel studies that showed the influence of phenomenology, linguistic analysis, and the social sciences.[2]

Theologians such as the late Karl Rahner have written extensively on "short formulas of faith" in an ongoing search for effective ways to translate the ancient beliefs into a modern idiom. Pope Paul VI's "Credo of the People of God," published in 1968, paraphrased and elaborated the text of the Nicene-Constantinopolitan Creed in an effort to combat modern errors. Individuals from many Christian traditions have published personal creeds, and several churches have commissioned statements of faith for use in congregational worship, in private devotion, and for purposes of study.[3]

Granted the need for creeds, why another book about them? Or to frame the question another way, what is different about this commentary on the Creed? As already noted, this book is in part inspired by ecumenical concerns. The World Council of Churches through the Commission on Faith and Order is making a concerted effort to bring Christians of all denominations to a common confession of the apostolic faith. Ecumenical planners suggest that an important first step (and every journey, no matter how long, begins with a first step) is to explain how various social and cultural factors gave rise to the development of creedal authority. They call for studies that go beyond textual criticism and mere exegesis. Commentaries that concentrate on doctrinal issues to the neglect of the liturgical context, not to mention the social and cultural factors, present only a partial picture. In an effort to bring all these elements together I draw on specialized works in biblical, liturgical, historical, and theological studies. For Christians to relate the Creed to today's questions, it is necessary to situate it in the life of the confessing church.

The Introduction, Parts I and II, sets the stage. The introduction relates the Creed to the New Testament kerygma; it describes various forms and functions of the Creed in the life of the church. The introductory sections also present the rationale for the division of the book into three parts. Efforts in and among the churches to agree on a common confession of faith have highlighted several issues that run through my study like subplots in a novel; so, I judged it worthwhile to round out the introduction with a chapter on the Creed in ecumenical dialogue.

The body of the book is a commentary on the contents of the Creed in light of today's questions. It is, in fact, a compendium that attempts to capture not only the meaning but the spirit and life of the Christian community as it has come to be embodied in Catholic tradition. Although I do not force the text of the ancient creeds into the categories of systematic theology, I do relate the Creed to fundamental theological issues. One of the major points of agreement that has emerged from the ecumenical consultations in recent years is that the Creed must be read in the context of the Scriptures, especially the New Testament. Therefore, I incorporate the insights of modern biblical scholarship wherever it seems appropriate to do so. I am conscious that my interest and training in cultural history is reflected in the narrative style, and has made the presentation more discursive than analytical. But by allowing the clauses of the Creed to create the outline for the chapters, I gained many fresh insights. The Christian Creed can be turned like a kaleidoscope to yield endless variety as the traditional doctrines are brought into relationship with one another, producing different patterns.

Unlike most works of this kind, this one waits until the very end to take up the chief concern of Christians and of this book—personal faith. In effect, I have laid out the beliefs of the church before raising the question of faith, though it is close to the surface throughout the book.

Rather than overburden the pages with footnotes—some people find them distracting—I have included documentation at the end of each chapter for readers who want to pursue particular issues at greater depth. Some statements, based on recent research, contradict older positions and thus need to be substantiated. Still a third kind of note provides information that fills out certain points but that is only incidental to the main argument in the text. And of course, readers who find notes unnecessary or diversionary will simply ignore any or all of them.

In my mind *The Creed* will be a success if it accomplishes two aims: provide fresh insight and clarity into the classic creeds so that they may be more appreciated, and contribute to the ecumenical venture by illustrating how Roman Catholics (or at least one Roman Catholic) bring the Creed into dialogue with Scripture and contemporary theological issues.

The work grew out of a course that I taught several times at the Catholic University of America and elsewhere. One-time students, now friends and professional colleagues, encouraged me to bring the material together in a book. The gradual evolution from lecture notes to manuscript to published book, moreover, would not have occurred were it not for the support and assistance they gave me. I should single out many people, beginning with a number of my Franciscan confreres, to whom I am especially indebted, but I mention the names of only a few. The Most Reverend Seely Beggiani, chor-bishop and rector of the Maronite Seminary in Washington, D.C., reviewed the manuscript in its formative stages. Dr. Robin Maas of Wesley Seminary in Washington, a friendly and thoroughly professional critic, made innumerable suggestions, most of which I followed, for the improvement of the text. Jane E. Regan, now of St. John's University, Collegeville, Minnesota, served variously as researcher, copy editor, and typist as she prepared the final draft of the manuscript for the typesetter. Edward J. Furton graciously prepared the index. And last but not least there is Laura Way, my longtime editorial assistant; over the years I have learned to value her professional advice and counsel, and my readers are the beneficiary of her untiring insistence on clarity.

I dedicate *The Creed* to all my former students who have taught me a great deal about theology, about ritual, about religious education, about church and, most important, about faith. I have written the work for them, and I have written the work for myself. In presenting the church's statement of beliefs—really a doxology—I witness to my own confession of faith.

Notes

1. Hans-Georg Link, *The Roots of Our Common Faith*. Faith and Order Paper No. 119 (Geneva: World Council of Churches, 1984), p. 18.

2. The *Irish Theological Quarterly* published a series of important articles on the Nicene Creed and the Council of Constantinople by way of commemorating the anniversary. See vol. 49 (1981), nos. 3 and 4.

3. Avery Dulles, "Foundation Documents of the Faith: Modern Creedal Affirmations," in *The Expository Times* 91 (1979–80):291–296.

CONTENTS

18: From Community to Ecclesiology   289

"We believe in [the] church"

19: The Marks of the Church   306

"One holy catholic and apostolic"

THE CREED

THE NICENE CREED

I believe in one God
the Father, the Almighty,
maker of heaven and earth,
of all that is seen and unseen.

We believe in one Lord, Jesus Christ,
the only Son of God,
eternally begotten of the Father,
God from God, Light from Light,
true God from true God,
begotten, not made, one in Being with the Father.
Through him all things were made.
For us and for our salvation
he came down from heaven:
by the power of the Holy Spirit
he was born of the Virgin Mary, and became man.

For our sake he was crucified under Pontius Pilate;
he suffered, died, and was buried.
On the third day he rose again
in fulfillment of the Scriptures;
he ascended into heaven
and is seated at the right hand of the Father.
He will come again in glory to judge the living and the dead,
and his kingdom will have no end.

We believe in the Holy Spirit, the Lord, the giver of life,
who proceeds from the Father and the Son.
With the Father and the Son he is worshiped and glorified.
He has spoken through the Prophets.
We believe in one holy catholic and apostolic Church.
We acknowledge one baptism for the forgiveness of sins.
We look for the resurrection of the dead,
and the life of the world to come. Amen.

THE APOSTLES' CREED

I believe in God, the Father almighty,
  creator of heaven and earth.

I believe in Jesus Christ, his only Son, our Lord,
  He was conceived by the power of the Holy Spirit
  and born of the Virgin Mary.
  He suffered under Pontius Pilate,
  was crucified, died, and buried.
  He descended to the dead.
  The third day he rose again.
  He ascended into heaven,
  and is seated at the right hand of the Father.
  He shall come again to judge the living and the dead.

I believe in the Holy Spirit,
  the holy catholic Church,
  the communion of saints,
  the forgiveness of sins,
  the resurrection of the body,
  and life everlasting. Amen.

INTRODUCTION

Part I
FORMS AND FUNCTIONS OF THE ANCIENT CREED

Part II
THE CREED IN ECUMENICAL DIALOGUE

INTRODUCTION

PART I

FORMS AND FUNCTIONS OF

THE ANCIENT CREED

According to an ancient legend, as the apostles were about to split and go their separate ways, they felt the need to agree on the contents of the message they would preach. The occasion is said to have been the origin of the "Apostles' Creed." One version of the story recalls the scene in John 20:29. It tells how each of the Twelve, inflamed with the Holy Spirit, made a personal contribution to the profession of faith:

> . . . Peter said, "I believe in God the Father almighty . . . maker of heaven and earth" . . . Andrew said "and in Jesus Christ His Son . . . our only Lord" . . . James said "Who was conceived by the Holy Spirit . . . born from the Virgin Mary" . . . John said "suffered under Pontius Pilate . . . was crucified, dead and buried" . . . Thomas said "descended into hell . . . on the third day rose again from the dead" . . . James said "ascended to heaven . . . sits on the right hand of God the Father almighty" . . . Philip said "thence He will come to judge the living and the dead" . . . Bartholomew said "I believe in the Holy Spirit" . . . Matthew said "the holy Catholic Church . . . the communion of saints" . . . Simon said "the remission of sins" . . . Thaddaeus said "the resurrection of the flesh" . . . Matthias said "eternal life."[1]

2

Even though the story had all the marks of a pious fiction, it won almost universal acceptance in medieval Europe. But only in Europe. Greek Christians, for example, knew nothing of a creed attributed to the apostles. By the fifteenth century, historians and theologians everywhere had begun to doubt that the apostles were the authors of any creed. Scholars could find no evidence in the New Testament that there existed a *fixed* list of doctrines in the first century. Nonetheless the legend continues to be told even now because it captures certain insights that are worth preserving, despite the fact that it also distorts the true nature and function of the Creed.

First, a word about insights. In the Roman liturgy we pray "for all who hold and teach the catholic faith that comes to us from the apostles" (Roman Canon). But there is also a sense in which faith is mediated to us by the community that traces its origins to the preaching of the Apostles. In another form of the Creed—the Ecumenical Creed promulgated by the Council of Constantinople and used in the Sunday liturgy—we confess our belief in ONE HOLY CATHOLIC AND *APOSTOLIC* CHURCH. We share the faith of the first Christian community; and in that sense our faith is that of the apostles. By attributing its contents to the Twelve acting under the inspiration of the Holy Spirit, the legend clearly implies that wherever Christians recite "the Apostles' Creed," they profess the same faith as that of the ancient church.

Before the Twelve thought of themselves as "apostles"—people with a mission—they were witnesses. They were eyewitnesses to the important events in Jesus' public life, notably the circumstances of his trial and execution. They heard him expound the Scriptures in the Temple precincts, they listened when he denounced the Pharisees and when he spoke of the reign of God. These firsthand experiences took on new meaning after Easter. Blessed with hindsight—not to mention being overpowered by the Spirit—the apostles began to see Jesus of Nazareth in a new light.

FROM KERYGMA TO CREED

On the first Pentecost, Peter "with the Eleven" was driven by an inner compulsion to proclaim what they had seen and heard and, yes, felt. The proclamation—in Greek, *kerygma*—was in fact a profession of faith. Peter definitively outlined the beliefs that were to become the fundamentals of Christianity: The "day of the Lord" foretold by the prophets is at hand; it has been ushered in by Jesus of Nazareth, a man sent by God; his credentials were his words and works. This Jesus, "by the set plan and purpose of God," was crucified and killed by the pagans, but death could not hold him. He fulfilled the vision of King David, who had predicted the resurrection of the Messiah. Peter continued,

> Therefore let the whole house of Israel know beyond any doubt that God has made both Lord and Messiah this Jesus whom you crucified. (Acts 2:36)

If one seeks a statement of what the apostles believed, it must be looked for in the *kerygma*. The "good news" of salvation—the gospel—was proclaimed again and again, and always it stressed the same general points: Jesus of Nazareth, of the lineage of David, had come as Son of God and Messiah; he announced the coming of the kingdom; he was crucified, died, and was buried; on the third day he rose again and was exalted to the right hand of God; he will come again to judge the living and the dead. Those who respond to the gospel, repent and are baptized, will receive the forgiveness of their sins and share in the life of the coming again. Even St. Paul, who got the story secondhand, followed the same outline in much of his preaching. One finds in his letters (as we shall see) many words and phrases that are echoed in the Creed. It is clear that Paul, the author, and his readers in the churches at Thessalonica, Corinth, Rome, and elsewhere shared a common faith.

The Pauline letters contain certain expressions that have the ring of slogans. Some seem to be verses from hymns, phrases from prayers or lines from the liturgy. "Jesus is Lord," is one example of a catchphrase that appears over and over in the Pauline Epistles. It sounds like a fragment of a creed. Brief formulas of this kind are found side by side with fuller and more detailed confessions of faith. The best-known example is the passage at the end of Paul's first letter to the Corinthians:

> I handed on to you first of all what I myself received, that Christ died for our sins in accordance with the Scriptures, rose on the third day. . . . (1 Cor 15:3-4)

Already in the apostolic age, Christians recognized that their beliefs regarding Jesus of Nazareth separated them from the mainstream of Judaism and gave them a distinctive identity. From the outset, Christianity owed its existence to a community intent on propagandizing its beliefs through preaching and teaching. Further, Paul makes it clear that its adherents were concerned to transmit authentic doctrine, untainted by personal opinion and sectarian interests. The author of the Epistle to the church at Colossae instructs his readers to grow "ever stronger in faith, as you were taught. . . . See to it that no one deceives you through any empty, human traditions, a philosophy based on cosmic powers rather than on Christ" (2:7–8). Elsewhere Paul exhorts his fellow believers to "stand firm. Hold fast to the traditions you received from us" (2 Thess 2:15). He insists that he handed on only what he had received (see 1 Cor 11:23 and 15:3).

It is true that nowhere in the Scriptures does one find an authoritative list of Christian doctrines, but almost all the beliefs that are professed in the so-called Apostles' Creed and other early confessions of faith—notably, the Ecumenical Creed of Nicea-Constantinople—have their roots in the New Testament.

THE ARTICLES OF FAITH

In recounting the old legend which recounted how the apostles, in order to ensure uniformity in preaching and teaching, compiled a creed, we granted that the story was weak on history but contained elements of truth and insights of lasting value. But it also has a negative side. The great French revisionist Henri de Lubac, S.J. complained that the legend imposed an artificial structure on the Creed, distorted its function and meaning.[2]

Twelve apostles, twelve articles of faith. The Apostles' Creed became a kind of syllabus for preachers and teachers, a catalog of divine truths to be explained, interpreted, and applied from pulpit and podium. Studied individually, apart from the whole, the meanings of the propositions are easily misrepresented both because they are often made to relay more factual information than in fact is the case and because at the same time they are divorced from the mystery of creation and redemption.

Medieval theologians emphasized the notion that the propositions are "articles" of faith. In Latin *articulus* is the word for "joint." It envokes a comparison with the skeletal structure of the human body. Just as the vertebrae of the spine are both divided and bonded by joints, so the Creed "articulates" what Christians believe, focusing on particulars while at the same time expressing their organic unity.

In stressing the wholeness of something, medieval scholars liked to classify its constituent parts in groups of seven. They discovered sevens everywhere. While emphasizing the intrinsic unity of the apostolic Creed, they saw it as composed of fourteen propositions grouped into two sections of seven each. The first seven deal with the Godhead and things eternal; the second seven deal with the humanity of Christ and his work in time. Thus Bonaventure:

> . . . the articles of faith which are the foundations of belief are concerned either with the Godhead, or with the humanity [of Christ]. Now the Godhead must be seen in the three Persons: the Father begetting, the Son begotten, and the Holy Spirit proceeding; and also in four operations: creation in the order of nature, re-creation in the order of grace, resuscitation for the restoration of life, and beatification through the imparting of glory. That is why the articles dealing with the Godhead are seven in number. Likewise, the humanity of Christ must be seen as conceived of the Holy Spirit, born of the Virgin, suffering on the cross, descending into hell, rising from the dead, ascending into heaven, and coming at the final judgment. That is why the articles dealing with the humanity of Christ are also comparable to the seven stars and the seven golden lampstands in the midst of which the Son of Man was seen. (Cf. Rev. 1:13,16).[3]

Following St. Augustine, St. Bonaventure and his contemporaries note that the whole of faith relates to these two points: the Trinity, which is the be-all and end-all of human existence, and the humanity of Christ, which reveals the way to union with the Godhead. As artificial as the division into seven is, it does come closer to capturing the theological significance of the Creed than does the legend about its apostolic origins. For in actual fact, the primitive form of the Creed, rooted in the baptismal rites, focuses on the Trinity and the Incarnation.

THE CREED AS PROFESSION OF FAITH

Matthew brings the gospel account to a climax with Jesus sending his followers out with instructions to "make disciples of all the nations. Baptize them in the name of the Father, and of the Son, and of the Holy Spirit" (Mt. 28:19).

The usual form of the Creed found today in liturgical texts and prayerbooks is said to be "declaratory." We have fragments of declaratory creeds that go back to the second century; by the fourth century they were in common use. The "interrogatory" form of the Creed, however, seems to be the most primitive. The declaratory creeds are framed as statements—assertions using the first person: "I believe" or "We believe." The interrogatory form of the Creed, by contrast, consists of a question or a series of questions addressed to an individual or group: "Do you believe that. . . ?" When the bride responds to the question, "Do you take this man for your lawful wedded husband?" the expected response is, "I do." In this example the substance of the marriage vows is in the question; the groom and bride declare their assent by a simple "I do" which in turn commits them to a way of life appropriate to married couples.

In the reform of Roman rites after Vatican II the interrogatory form of the Creed replaced the declaratory form in the baptismal liturgy. The renewed rite represents a conscious effort to retrieve the ancient rite of baptism as it was known in Rome about A.D. 200. In 215, St. Hippolytus, a rival of Pope Calixtus for leadership of the Roman church, compiled a sacramentary known in history as the *Apostolic Tradition*. It describes liturgical practice in the Eternal City at the beginning of the third century, including a detailed account of the catechumenate and of the rite of baptism. The profession of faith made by the candidate for baptism followed the interrogatory form:

> And [when] he [who is to be baptised] goes down into the water,
> let him who baptises lay hands on him saying thus:
>   Dost thou believe in God the Father Almighty?
> And he who is to be baptised shall say
>   I believe.
> Let him forthwith baptise him at once, having his hand laid
> upon his head. And after this let him say:
>   Dost thou believe in Christ Jesus, the Son of God,
>   Who was born of Holy Spirit and Virgin Mary,
>   Who was crucified in the days of Pontius Pilate,
>   And died,
>   And rose the third day living from the dead,
>   And ascended into the heavens,
>   And sat down at the right hand of the Father,
>   And will come to judge the living and the dead?
> And when he says: I believe, let him baptise him the second time

and again let him say:
> Dost thou believe in the Holy Spirit, in the Holy Church,
> And the resurrection of the flesh?

And he who is being baptised shall say: I believe. And so let him baptise him the third time.[4]

Whatever is to be said of other ways of expressing one's beliefs, the text at the end of Matthew's Gospel and the passage from St. Hippolytus highlight the Trinitarian theme fundamental to Christian faith. The Apostles' Creed, the Nicene formula of Constantinople, and similar confessions of faith do not simply assert belief in the triune God; they affirm it by making belief in the Father, Son, and Spirit serve as the basic structure. Henri de Lubac's main complaint against the ancient legend is that by singling out twelve propositions according to the number of apostles, the tripartite structure of the Creed is obscured and its Trinitarian theology lost sight of in prayer and catechesis.

Long ago that master catechist Martin Luther recognized the advantage of summarizing the entire Creed in three articles "according to the three persons in the Godhead." Three articles of faith, each with a certain intrinsic unity, is simply easier and plainer than twelve articles that read like a shopping list. "The first article," says Luther, "concerning the Father, explains creation; the second, concerning the Son, explains redemption; and the third, of the Holy Spirit, explains sanctification."[5]

The Catechism of the Council of Trent—also known as the "Roman Catechism"—published in 1565, is a belated response to Luther's catechisms. It begins by instructing pastors to inform the people that the Apostles' Creed "briefly comprehends" the doctrine of the mystery of the Trinity. It states that the first and essential truth to be believed by all "is a summary of the unity of the divine essence, of the distinction of three persons, and the actions which are peculiarly attributed to each." The Tridentine catechism proceeds, like Luther's, to acknowledge

> that the Creed seems to be divided into three principal parts, one describing the first Person of the divine nature, and the stupendous work of the creation—another, the second person, and the mystery of man's redemption—a third, comprising in several most appropriate sentences, the doctrine of the third Person, the head and source of our sanctification.[6]

Although the authors of the Roman Catechism were obviously aware of the Trinitarian structure of the creed, it did not influence their treatment. They proceeded to identify twelve articles and consider them one by one without much effort to explain them in the broader context of creation, redemption and sanctification. Given the lasting influence of the Tridentine Catechism on preaching and catechesis in the Roman church, it is little wonder that the doctrine of the Trinity came to be regarded as one mystery among many, rather than *the* mystery of salvation that underlies all of Christian teaching. When the salvific activity of Father, Son, and Spirit in the world is lost sight of, the Trinity becomes a puzzle for logicians rather than a mystery to be lived by Christians.

CREED AS NARRATIVE

The transition from the interrogatory form to the declarative form of the Creed was gradual. Historians cite evidence that by the fourth century declaratory forms were in use everywhere. The change signaled more than a simple transposition of sentence structure such as we make in beginning French when we move from the interrogative "est-ce-que" to a declarative form. J.N.Ð. Kelly says that declaratory creeds are "a by-product of the Church's fully developed catechetical system."[7] The original function of the Creed in its interrogatory form, integral to the rite of baptism itself, was a confession of personal faith. Declaratory creeds became a part of the preparatory instruction preceding baptism. They served as convenient summaries that made explicit the teaching that had been implicit, and perhaps only hinted at, during the time of the catechumenate. In Lent, as the day of baptism approached, the bishop "handed over" the Creed (the *traditio symboli*) and proceeded to comment on it phrase by phrase. The catechumens in turn were expected to learn it by heart so as to be able to "give it back" (the *redditio symboli*); that is, they were asked to recite it publicly to demonstrate that they were sufficiently grounded in the faith.

In the context of catechetical instruction the declaratory form of the Creed simply tells a story of creation and reconciliation. In terms of literary form it is a narrative much like the *shema* of ancient Israel. "Hear, O Israel: The Lord is our God, the Lord is one" (Dt 6:4), became Judaism's classical confession of faith. It is called *shema* from the opening word, "hear." The *shema* remains the customary call to prayer. It is a reminder to Israel of the favor Yahweh bestowed on his people. Though it took on a fixed form rather late in the history of

Judaism, the *shema* expresses the radical monotheism that gave the ancient Israelites their sense of identity as a people. Echoing that other popular Israelite acclamation, "The Lord is God; there is no other besides him" (Dt 4:35), it enshrines a communal conviction not as a timeless truth but as an affirmation of a particular relationship of the people of Israel to the God who is unique, the one and only Lord of the universe.[8]

A number of formulations in the Old Testament have the ring of declaratory creeds. Like the baptismal declarations of the Christians who are to come after, the early Israelite creeds are professions of faith ritualized in a liturgical setting. They tell the story of God's involvement in the events of Israel's history. One such summary—called by Gerhard von Rad, the great Old Testament scholar, a "cultic credo"—is found in the book of Deuteronomy. It is a classic example of a narrative interpretation of historical events that takes on a creedal function in the community created by those events:

> . . . you shall declare before the Lord, your God, "My Father was a wandering Aramean who went down to Egypt with a small household and lived there as an alien. But there he became a nation great, strong and numerous. When the Egyptians maltreated and oppressed us, imposing hard labor upon us, we cried to the Lord, the God of our fathers, and he heard our cry and saw our affliction, our toil and oppression. He brought us out of Egypt with his strong hand and outstretched arm, with terrifying power, with signs and wonders; and bringing us into this country, he gave us this land flowing with milk and honey. . . ." (26:5-9)

From the account in Deuteronomy and parallel texts, it seems that formulas similar to this were recited by Israelites when they brought the first fruits of the harvest as an offering to Yahweh at one of the hallowed shrines.

Another example of a cultic credo is found in Joshua 24:2-13. Associated with the renewal of the covenant at Shechem, it narrates Israel's entry into the land of Canaan under the leadership of Moses' successor, Joshua. "If the setting described there," writes Bernhard Lang, "is more than a literary fiction we must think in terms of a regular service involving a profession of faith."[9] The ritual not only reaffirmed Israel's commitment to the covenant; it was also the way in which new clans or tribes became members of the Israelite confederation. As tribes recited the narrative of Yahweh's involvement with the people of Israel, they professed their faith and appropriated for themselves Israel's traditions and beliefs. The rite consisted of two parts: 1) a priest or prophet recounted the history of Yahweh's dealings with his people from Abraham on and asked those present to commit themselves to this God; and 2) the tribes then responded (see Jos 24:16–17).

Other confessional statements that tell the saga of Israelite history are found in the Psalms (e.g. Ps 44:1–8; 78; 105; 106). These texts further illustrate the way in which, on important occasions, Israelites recalled past events and interpreted them according to a set pattern. They are synopses of the complex Israelite epic told in the Deuteronomic account that runs from Genesis through II Kings and are repeated and carried forward to post-exilic times by the author-editors of I and II Chronicles, Ezra and Nehemiah. As expressions of Israel's faith, these narratives were foundational to the renewal of the covenant between God and his people.

Similarly the baptismal creed, especially in its declaratory form, narrates the saving events that are the basis for the faith of the Christian community. The three parts of the Christian story tell of God's action in creation, in Jesus of Nazareth, and in the Spirit who continues to work in the life and history of the church. As with most stories, it has a beginning, middle, and end. The narrative function of the Creed is most evident in the second part, which tells of Jesus' heavenly origins, his birth, life, death, and resurrection. It recapitulates the main points of the *keyrgma* and makes it clear that everything else is interpreted in the light of the events which climaxed his earthly career.

CREED AS DOXOLOGY

The Creed, like the *shema*, serves both as a chant of praise (in Greek, *doxa*) and as a witness of faith. Christians confess before their Maker and their fellow human beings the wonders God has done for them. Although there are important differences between creeds and hymns, the two genres have much in common.[10] The Creed functions in the liturgy as a hymn of praise, just as many of the Hebrew Psalms praising the glorious deeds of Yahweh are also creedal statements. In the words of St. Paul, we confess with our lips what we believe in our hearts (see Rom 10:8–10; 2 Cor 4:13). Thus the public recitation of the Creed in the eucharistic liturgy is meant as both praise and testimony.

The prayer of the liturgy also became a personal acclamation of praise. St. Augustine urges that Christians recite it frequently: "Say the creed daily. When you rise, when you compose yourself to sleep, repeat your creed, render it to the Lord, remind yourself of it, be not irked to say it over."[11] "Render it to the Lord" suggests it is a prayer. "Remind yourself of it" suggests that the Creed is a statement of identity with a community and a commitment to a pattern of life. In jargon redolent of the social sciences the Creed has been called *an identity avowal*.[12] It refers to a new sense of meaning and purpose that one acquires from incorporation into Christ in baptism and from being a member of the Christian community. Although baptism is not repeated, the Creed is a constant reminder that we have made a commitment and have taken upon ourselves a network of new relationships to God and to the world. In summary form the Creed discloses who God is and what we are called to be as human beings. And like all good stories, which are in essence pointed narratives, it has the power to change the pattern of thought and behavior not only of individuals but of nations.

CREED AS THEOLOGICAL STATEMENT

The baptismal creeds of the second and third centuries enshrined the catholic faith that had come down from the apostles, but not all the churches expressed that faith in exactly the same words. Christians in Rome, in Africa, in Antioch, and in other regions seem to have had their own variations on the common theme. The fourth century, however, marks a transition to a new type and function of the Creed. This transition takes place on four fronts: 1) synods and councils introduce terms and phrases to elaborate points in the *keyrgma* and to ensure orthodoxy and uniformity of belief; 2) the wording of the Creeds, including the conciliar interpolation, become fixed at the same time that liturgical formulas become more uniform; 3) local creeds, notably in the Eastern churches, cede their places to the formulas that have the endorsement of ecumenical councils; and 4) the creeds once used chiefly in the baptismal liturgy come to be recited in the eucharistic liturgy as well.

It does not appear that the bishops at the councils of Nicea (325) and Constantinople (381) intended the creedal statements of the councils to displace the traditional confessions of faith used in baptism by the local churches, but that is what happened. The baptismal creeds that developed as acts of faith—confessional narratives—evolve into theological statements. They begin to function as tests of orthodoxy, with stress on particular words and phrases.

By 200, writers had already begun to speak of a "rule of faith." They were referring not so much to the creedal formula as to the faith underlying it. The official teaching of the church, expressed in narrative form and based on the *kerygma*, followed a distinctive outline. To moderns, who find most rules oppressive, a "rule of faith" seems like thought control. The early Christians, however, saw it in a positive light. They wanted some guidelines to ensure that the faith teaching being passed on to them was the authentic teaching of Christ himself. St. Paul was careful to hand on what he had received (1 Cor 15:3), and the author of the pastoral Epistles repeatedly hammered at the importance of sound doctrine (1 Tim 4:6; 6:20; 2 Tim 1:13–14). According to St. Irenaeus it is a prime responsibility of bishops, successors of the apostles, to safeguard the unity of the church and the authenticity of the gospel message by seeing to it that teaching conforms to the "rule of faith."

What was this "rule of faith"? All agreed that it was the "apostolically authorized deposit of doctrine which had been handed down in the Church from the beginning."[13] When forced to list specific beliefs, writers such as Irenaeus and Tertullian fell back on formulas that echoed the baptismal creeds. They cited the "rule of faith" against those whose teaching was a cause of dissension and schism in the church. The polemics and anti-heretical animus of the early church fathers notwithstanding, it was the positive aspect of the Creed that they emphasized.

It is true that in facing off against particular heresies the Christian communities inserted clauses and adjectives into the Creed to make its meaning more precise. As will be seen in the commentary on the individual phrases that follows, words were added to the Creed to combat certain errors and misleading interpretations. When one church found an appropriate phrase, often other churches picked it up. These clarifications were made without fanfare at the local level. It was a different matter, however, at the Council of Nicea in 325 when the bishops inserted the *homoousion* clause, "one in being with the Father." They needed a formula to condemn Arianism, which made the

Son lesser than the Father. Arius, an influential theologian in the church at Alexandria, had been able to twist the biblical texts to his own purposes. Simple and direct, the narrative form of the baptismal creed about the work of the Trinity was not subtle enough for the kind of issues raised by Arianism. Thus in an effort to state the church's faith more precisely regarding the relationship of the Father and Son, Nicea made some additions. Later the Council of Constantinople in 381 did likewise in trying to clarify the relationship of the Spirit to the other persons of the Trinity.

These insertions, made after much soul searching by the bishops, marked a dramatic change in the function of the Creed. Unlike the earlier additions made by local churches for particular purposes, those made at Nicea and Constantinople were binding on the universal church because they were mandated by ecumenical councils. Thus the Creed serves many purposes. Originally a simple confession of personal faith, it came to be used in the second and third centuries as a rule of thumb to guarantee sound doctrine, and finally it was turned into a theological statement that could be used as a formal test of orthodoxy. As C.H. Turner put it, "The old creeds were creeds for catechumens, the new creed was a creed for bishops."[14]

In the sixth century the Creed came to be recited in the eucharistic liturgy. In the East, bishops with monophysite leanings, afraid that the efforts of the Council of Chalcedon to affirm the integrity of Jesus's humanity would be misunderstood by the faithful, introduced the Creed of Constantinople into the eucharist to exalt the divinity of Christ.[15] The practice of reciting the Creed in the Latin Mass began in Spain (where, it should be noted, Byzantine influence on the liturgy was present). The immediate occasion was the conversion of the Visigoths, led by King Reccared, from Arianism to the Catholic faith. Thereupon the council of Toledo in 589 decreed that the Nicene faith be professed at every mass. Charlemagne extended the practice through the Frankish empire at the end of the eighth century as a defense against adoptionism (another form of the Arian heresy). It was another two centuries before the practice was introduced in Rome, and then only at the insistence of Henry II, the Holy Roman Emperor. The excuse that Romans gave for not reciting the Creed so often was that their church had never been affected by heresy and therefore they did not need to protest their orthodoxy in the Eternal City.

ATHANASIAN CREED

A word about one other confession of faith is in order here. It is sometimes called the "Athanasian Creed" after the bishop of Alexandria who spent his life fighting the errors of Arianism. St. Athanasius was for a long time thought—mistakenly—to be the Creed's author.[16] Today it is more commonly referred to by the opening word of the Latin text, *Quicumque*, "Whosoever would be saved. . . ." Another example of a declaratory creed, it consists of forty rhythmical sentences divided by reason of content into two rather distinct parts. The first part expounds the doctrine of the Trinity; the second, of the Incarnation. The latter part, in words that echo the Apostle's Creed, includes a list of the saving works of Christ. The *Quicumque* begins and ends with the assertion that it enunciates "the Catholic faith," which is necessary for salvation.

In the Middle Ages the *Quicumque* found its way into the Liturgy of the Hours at Prime. It was retained in the service books of a number of Protestant churches, notably the Lutherans and the Anglicans. In the Anglican book of Common Prayer it replaces the Apostles' Creed at Morning Prayer on certain days. In the new (1979) American edition of the Book of Common Prayer the *Quicumque* is no longer a part of the worship service but is found among "historical documents" appended to the end of the Anglican prayerbook. The Lutheran Prayer Book says, "Custom does suggest the liturgical use of the Athanasian Creed on the festival of the Holy Trinity." In the Roman breviary the *Quicumque* continued to be part of the Sunday office for Prime. In 1955, however, its use was restricted to the feast of the Holy Trinity, and currently it is not found in the breviary at all.

Quicumque is quite different from baptismal creeds in style and language. It is not a narrative, but an attempt to teach the theology of the councils of Nicea and Chalcedon—"the Catholic faith"—in a form that can be committed to memory. Its rhythmic cadence lends it to communal recitation. It incorporates the technical language of the councils (e.g., "person," "nature," "processions"), and as a carefully constructed theological statement it serves as a popular rule of faith. Its strong emphasis on the Trinity and the Incarnation is reflected in the commentaries of the medieval theologians who read a similar structure into the Apostles' Creed.

There is no question about the theology of the *Quicumque*, but is it a confession of faith? Like the other declaratory creeds whose three-fold structure was blurred by being divided and subdivided by cate-chists, preachers and theologians, its Trinitarian ground plan was obscured. The work of each of the persons lost its distinctiveness. That we came to a point when the Trinity was no longer central to the faith of Christians, that it made no difference in people's lives and even their prayer was in large part, according to de Lubac, the result of misunderstanding the basic structure and function of the Creed.

Ironically, the Athanasian Creed, echoing the additions made at Nicea and Constantinople to ensure Trinitarian orthodoxy, in the eyes of many obscured the Trinity. The new phrases were from the outset targets of theological controversies that rent the church. As debate focused with increasing bitterness on individual points, the ground plan of the Creed was lost sight of. Debate over the finer points in theology—which is not to say insignificant issues—deflected attention from the Trinity's role in the story of salvation.

In an effort to bring the central purpose of the Creed to the fore, that is, to emphasize its dual function as a profession of faith and doxology, the following chapters are grouped under the headings of three articles: Father, creator; Son, redeemer; and Spirit, sanctifier. It will become evident that while we distinguish the articles in the Creed, we cannot isolate them from one another any more than we can separate the works of the three persons in the Godhead. We attribute particular activities in the world to the Father, Son, and Spirit; but, as we hope to make clear, it is always the one God who creates, redeems, and makes holy.

Notes

1. Quoted in J.N.D. Kelly, *Early Christian Creeds*, 3rd ed. (Essex U.K.: Longman, 1972) p. 3. Henceforth *Creeds*.

2. This is the point of Henri de Lubac's important book *La foi chrétienne*, 2nd ed. (Paris: Aubier-Montaigne, 1970), described in the subtitle as "a study of the structure of the Apostles' Creed."

3. *Breviloquium*, pt. 5, c. 7, 6. The Works of St. Bonaventure, II: The Breviloquium (Paterson, N.J.: St. Anthony Guild Press, 1963), pp. 209–210.

4. Gregory Dix, ed., *The Apostolic Tradition of St. Hippolytus of Rome* (New York: Macmillan, 1937), pp. 36–37.

5. *Luther's Large Catechism*, pt. 2, n. 141, trans. J.N. Lenkner (Minneapolis: Augsburg Publishing Heuse, 1967), p. 79.

6. *The Roman Catechism*, trans. R.I. Bradley and E. Kevane (Boston: St. Paul Editions, 1985), p. 17.

7. Kelly, *Creeds*, p. 51.

8. Michael Wyschogrod, "The 'Shema Israel' in Judaism and the New Testaments," in H.G. Link, ed., *The Roots of Our Common Faith*. Faith and Order Paper No. 119 (Geneva: World Council of Churches, 1984), pp. 23–32.

9. "Professions of Faith in the Old and New Testaments," H. Küng and J. Moltmann, eds., *An Ecumenical Confession Faith*. Concilium 118 (New York: Seabury Press, 1979), p. 5.

10. Geoffrey Wainwright, *Doxology. The Praise of God in Worship, Doctrine, and Life* (New York: Oxford University Press, 1980), pp. 182–217. Henceforth *Doxology*.

11. Ser. 58, 11. Quoted in Kelly, *Creeds*, p. 370.

12. David B. Harned, *Creed and Personal Identity* (Philadelphia: Fortress Press, 1981), p. 19.

13. Kelly, *Creeds*, p. 98.

14. Quoted in Kelly, *Creeds*, p. 205.

15. Wainwright, *Doxology*, p. 186.

16. See J.N.D. Kelly, *The Athanasian Creed* (New York: Harper & Row, 1964).

INTRODUCTION
PART II

THE CREED IN ECUMENICAL DIALOGUE

It is not simply a matter of tactics that ecumenical discussions return inevitably to reconsider the ancient baptismal creeds as a basis for agreement among the divided churches. Those creeds stand as symbols of unity. The Apostles' Creed, in almost universal use in the West between the ninth and nineteenth centuries, emphasizes the ties that unite the believing community of today with that of New Testament times. The Ecumenical Creed, the Creed of Constantinople, expresses the common faith of East and West repeatedly affirmed by councils from Nicea I (325) to Nicea II (787). If Christians are to experience unity and witness to the faith they profess in baptism, they must reclaim their common heritage.

As far back as 1927 the World Conference on Faith and Order took up the topic "The Church's Common Confession of Faith." The initial presentation made by Bishop Charles Gore of the Church of England linked the discussion of the Creed to the earlier conference discussions on the Gospel and the church. Bishop Gore, acknowledging the differences within Christendom, noted that "at the time of the Great Schism and the later schisms of the Reformation this doctrine, . . . the doctrine of the Nicene Creed was the agreed point among all the divisions of Christendom."[1] Almost fifty years later the Assembly of the World Council of Churches meeting in Nairobi urged the member churches "to undertake a common effort to receive, reappropriate and confess together, as contemporary occasion requires, the Christian truth and faith, delivered through the Apostles and handed down through the centuries."[2] And Pope John Paul II, speaking to the Roman curia on the topic "The Reality, Progress and Problems of Christian Unity," stated, "Unity in the profession of faith is the fundamental element in manifestation of ecclesial communion."[3]

In response to the urging of the Nairobi Assembly, the Faith and Order group (now a commission within the World Council of Churches) initiated a project "Towards the Common Expression of the Apostolic Faith Today." The Commission on Faith and Order set three goals for the project:

1. the common *recognition* of the apostolic faith as expressed in the Ecumenical Symbol of that faith, the Nicene Creed;

2. the common *explication* of this apostolic faith in contemporary situations of the churches;

3. a common *confession* of the apostolic faith today.

Despite the fact that it represents a heritage shared by Christians of both East and West, a common recognition, explication, and confession of the Nicene Creed by the churches seems a long way off, for not all the churches regard creeds in the same light.

SUSPICION OF CREEDS

On the way to having the churches endorse the Nicene-Constantinopolitan Creed as the foundation for agreement and unity among the churches, the Commission on Faith and Order has focused attention on some perennial issues and has surfaced some new ones. While the Roman Catholic, the Orthodox, the Anglican churches, and most churches of the Reformation assign the ancient creeds a central and decisive role, some Christian bodies are suspicious of all creeds. Baptists, for example, are reluctant to make a formal endorsement of any creed. Although they "acknowledge the apostolic faith as contained in Scriptures and expressed in the Apostles' and Nicene Creeds," they voice reservations about their misuse. In England the Baptist Union has summarized the reasons for this reserve in five points.

1. Creeds are a human construction, bearing the marks of the age to which they belong, and, as compared with the authority of Scriptures, have a subordinate and secondary character.

2. They promote a legalistic outlook.

3. They intend to inhibit liberty of interpretation.

4. They become the source of division.

5. They appear to emphasize the faith as a body of doctrine at the expense of faith as a personal act.[4]

The Disciples of Christ and "free churches," less intent than Baptists to affirm historical continuity with the past, discard the creeds altogether for most of the same five reasons. Catholics, Orthodox, Anglicans, and Protestants in the mainstream of the Reformation tradition, recognizing the dangers alluded to in points two through five, hold generally to the position sketched in point one. To say, however, that the creeds are "a human construction" and that to assign them authority "subordinate" and "secondary" to the Scriptures does not mean they have no more significance than statements by individual bishops or the writings of great Christian luminaries.

Besides the general suspicion of creeds in some traditions, the Commission on Faith and Order surfaced other issues that demand attention as the churches attempt to come to some agreement on a common confession of the apostolic faith. Two issues in particular are not easily resolved: the language of the Nicene Creed, and the relation of baptism, eucharist, and ministry to the Creed. Although these topics are addressed in the pages that follow, it will be helpful at the outset to say a word about each in so far as it affects the effort to reappropriate the Nicene Creed as the common expression of Christian faith. A third issue, more specific, stems from the addition of the Latin phrase *filioque*—"and the son"—to the Ecumenical Creed. The *filioque*, a bone of contention between East and West since Charlemagne insisted that it be inserted into the Creed in the eighth century, will be discussed in the context of the third article (Chapter 19).

LANGUAGE

Even in churches where the ancient creeds continue to have a firm place in the liturgy, they have become targets of criticism because of their wording. Quarrels over the Apostles' Creed dating back to the last century provide telling examples. Some object that references to the virgin birth and the descent *ad inferos* have become obsolete in view of modern biblical criticism. Phrases like these and others, including the resurrection of the body, are said to be "mythological" and therefore to have lost their meaning for the modern mind.[5] Similarly, others argue that the "metaphysical" language of the Nicene Creed has made it inaccessible to contemporary Christians. Modern scientific awareness and shifts in philosophical outlook, it is said, have rendered the traditional language of faith unintelligible.[6]

Christians in the "young churches" of the Third World find difficulty with the language of the ancient creeds for other reasons. One surmises, however, that their difficulty lies more in cultural conflict than in a lack of faith. They accept the Christian Scriptures but are loath to embrace the early ecumenical councils and the Nicene Creed because they express an alien culture which they feel threatens their own. If people are to maintain their identity and dignity, they must retain continuity with their past. On the other hand, if they are to identify themselves as Christians they must also appropriate the church's history, assimilating Christian tradition within their own in a symbiosis that gives both traditions new life. It was thus that European culture came into being. Italic, Celtic, Germanic, and Slavic peoples embraced Christianity and learned to become bilingual, speaking the idiom of the ancient creeds and confessing the faith in their own tongues, in literature, art, music and many other ways. Cultural pluralism, a reality in the church from the beginning, does not rule out a common confession of faith, but it does complicate the problem.

The wording of the ancient creeds has become a stumbling block for still another group. Many American women complain that the Creed "appears to make use of language and imagery about God and the Incarnation that describes Christian realities in patriarchal terms."[7] More than the word "father" is at issue. Feminists fear that by calling God Father we legitimize, even absolutize, male chauvinism and all its pretensions. In broader terms, the issue of inclusive language brings the relationship of the Creed to Scripture under scrutiny. The Creed speaks of "Father" because that was Jesus' preferred way of referring to God in the gospel accounts. None of the early Christian writers thought of it as anything but an analogy—a metaphor—to describe the relationship first of Jesus and then derivatively of every Christian with God. "Father" affirms something more than Creator-creature relationship (as we shall see in addressing the first article of the Creed), but no one pretends that it establishes a parallel between God and human paternity. In fact (as will be evident when we come to the second article), to understand the Father-Son relationship in the Trinity in narrowly human terms is to misunderstand it. The Council of Nicea chose its words precisely to exclude the Arians, who drew such a parallel.

Discussions about the language of the ancient creeds have made Christians once more aware of the distinction between the *content* of the Creed and the language in which it is expressed. The sixteenth centenary of the Council of Constantinople provided the occasion for many scholars to take a new look at the text of the so-called Nicene Creed. Their research has led them to conclude that while it was the explicit intention of the bishops at Constantinople to reaffirm the faith of the Council of Nicea, they deliberately adopted a different formula. The point is not lost on church leaders engaged in ecumenical dialogue. Many argue that it should likewise be possible to formulate a creed that expresses the apostolic faith in modern language. But the task, as we shall see, is proving easier said than done.

CREED, SACRAMENTS, AND MINISTRY

The distinction between faith and the way in which it is expressed is important for another reason. The Creed taken by itself sketches only a partial picture, and a rather abstract one at that, of Christian beliefs. The Ecumenical Creed and the Apostles' Creed, the most ancient and authoritative confessions of faith, omit mention of important elements of Christian life. Missionary preaching, the eucharist, and ministry, as well as other practices and institutions about which the classic creeds are silent, must also be seen as expressions of the church's faith. The life of Christians, corporately and individually, give substance to the verbal formulas. Praxis has a bearing on the content of the traditional faith inherited from the apostles, proclaimed in the Scriptures, and confessed in the baptismal creed. Evangelization, liturgy, and prayer provide the ecclesial context without which any common confession of faith rings hollow.

It was not by mere coincidence that the Lima conference in 1982 issued statements both on baptism, eucharist, and ministry, and on the Nicene Creed. Seven years before the Fifth Assembly of the World Council of Churches meeting in Nairobi spoke of unity among the churches, a unity based on "a common understanding of the apostolic faith, by a common ministry, and a common eucharist."[8] The road from Nairobi to Lima ran through the ecumenical center in Bangalore. In 1978, the Faith and Order Commission met there to explore "a common profession of faith." Taking its cue from the Nairobi assembly, the commission agreed that, in order to reach visible unity, three fundamental requirements must be met. The churches must reach

> (a) consensus on the apostolic faith; (b) mutual recognition of baptism, the eucharist and the ministry; (c) structures making possible common teaching and decision-making.[9]

A Roman Catholic member of the Faith and Order Commission, the Canadian Dominican J. M. R. Tillard, delivered a paper at Bangalore in which he said,

> This world of ours puts radical questions to our faith, questions which go farther than those dealt with in the agreements so far drawn up or in process of being approved. They are concerned with God himself, with his relationship to human freedom, with the real nature of salvation, with the existence of the kingdom of God of which the sacraments are the sign and pledge. How are we in these circumstances to give an account *together* of our hope and of the faith on which it rests if we are not consciously agreed on at least the central points of this faith?[10]

The Bangalore meeting in effect challenged the oft-repeated nostrum of the ecumenical movement. "Doctrine divides, service unites" was a slogan popularized by the old Life and Work Conference, a group of Christians inspired by Nathan Soderblom, the Lutheran archbishop of Upsala (Sweden). Impatient of waiting for doctrinal differences to be resolved, they aimed to organize the churches in a united front for social causes. The churches, however, found that a political alliance merely for purposes of social action signaled, to use Tillard's phrase, "an appalling schizophrenia." Christians are simply unable to separate fidelity to Christ from love of neighbor. Thus in uniting in so far as possible for service, the churches found they could not avoid asking about the faith that brought them together. Faced with the same challenges of contemporary culture and sharing the common mission to preach the gospel, the churches have been led to focus more sharply on certain aspects of biblical teaching that in the past did not form part of the content of faith explicitly mentioned in the creeds. Today the confession of Christ as Lord and Savior must acknowledge the inseparable link between salvation in Christ and the cause of peace and justice in the world.

INTERPRETING THE CREED

Confronted with the allegation that the ancient Creed is no longer accessible to the modern believer, churches and theologians have responded in two ways. Many have attempted to compose new summaries of the Christian faith. As will be evident in examples cited in the closing chapter of this book, these attempts seek not only to find language "relevant" to the modern believer, but also to emphasize other beliefs that are part of the Christian heritage.

The second way of responding to the challenge of obsolescence is to restore meaning and relevance to the ancient Creed by interpreting it in the light of today's questions. The continuous flow of commentaries from patristic times to the present indicates that the church has recognized the need to interpret the Creed for each new audience. It is not a question of inventing new teachings, but of recovering old traditions and presenting them in a new context.

The Christian Creed stands like a giant arch spanning the centuries. One foot is planted deep in history, and the other is grounded firmly in present praxis. In order to appreciate why it has withstood the storms of controversy and the erosion of time it is necessary to examine both footings.

By situating the texts of the creeds in a historical context, we gain insight into why certain beliefs were given prominence. Emphasis on the phrases "only begotten" and "born of the Virgin Mary," for example, becomes clear in light of the anti-gnostic stance that the church took in the second century. Although the original intent of such affirmations as "light from light, true God from true God" is initially intelligible only in the context of the subordinationist controversies of the fourth century, Christians today who stand beneath the arch and look at these same beliefs from the vantage point of history, must ask what they mean. A doctrine as apparently marginal as Christ's descent into hell (or as we now say, "among the dead"), whose original meaning is buried in the sands of time, has paradoxically become a symbol of inclusiveness of salvation for all peoples.

In affirming God as creator of the "seen and unseen" the early church stressed the *seen*; the modern church stresses the *unseen*. At the beginning of the Christian era, many were more dubious about God's relationship to the material universe than about the divine origin of a world of unseen spirits. Today the situation is the reverse. Modern science accepts as a given the inherent goodness and usefulness of matter but is hesitant to affirm the existence of a spiritual dimension that is beyond the ken of microscopes and telescopes.

Just as Christians of the future will be in a better position to appreciate the significance of developments and controversies of our time, in many ways Christians of the twentieth century have a better understanding of the dynamics that operated in the ancient church than the Christians of the time did. Sometimes people are too close to a situation to understand it; distance often provides a better perspective. The generation that was active as participants and spectators in the Second Vatican Council brings new insights to the interpretation of the ecumenical councils of the first eight centuries. The specific issues were different, but the overriding concern to safeguard the apostolic faith was the same. Although it is too early to give a final assessment of the achievements of Vatican II, which now has a permanent place in the history of the church, its achievements can be properly measured only against the background of Nicea, Constantinople, Ephesus, and Chalcedon, not forgetting Nairobi and Bangalore.

All of this is to say that in looking at the ancient Creed in light of today's theology, this commentary also views today's theology in light of the Ecumenical and Apostles' Creeds. The comments on the Creed in the next chapter begin with a few reflections on the problem of religious language; they end in the last with some further remarks on the quest for a common profession of faith.

Notes

1. H. N. Bate, ed., *Faith and Order. Proceedings of the World Conference Lausanne, August 21–31, 1927* (New York: Geo. H. Doran Co., 1927), p. 162.

2. David M. Paton, ed. *Breaking Bread. Nairobi 1975: The Official Report of the Fifth Assembly of the World Council of Churches* (Grand Rapids: Wm. B. Eerdmans, 1976), p. 66.

3. *Origins*, July 18, 1985, p. 127.

4. E. A. Payne, *The Baptist Union: A Short History* (London, 1958), p. 27. Quoted by W. M. S. West, "Baptists and Statements of Faith," in *Expository Times* 91 (1979–80):233.

5. Wolfhart Pannenberg, "The Place of Creeds in Christianity Today," in *Expository Times* 91 (August 1980): 328–329.

6. Joseph Stephen O'Leary, "Has the Nicene Creed Become Inaccessible?" in *Irish Theological Quarterly* 49 (1981):240–255.

7. Roberta C. Bondi, "Some Issues Relevant to a Modern Interpretation of the Language of the Nicene Creed, With Special Reference to 'Sexist' Language," in *Union Seminary Quarterly Review* 40:3 (1986):21–30. See S. Mark Heim, "Gender and Creed: Confessing a Common Faith," in *The Christian Century*, April 17, 1985, pp. 379–381.

8. Paton, *Breaking Bread*, p. 61.

9. *Sharing in One Hope*, Reports and Documents from the Meeting of the Faith and Order Commission, Bangalore, 1978. Faith and Order Paper No. 92 (Geneva: World Council of Churches, 1978), p. 243.

10. J. M. R. Tillard, "Toward a Common Profession of Faith," in *Sharing in Hope*.

The First Article:

Father and Creator

We believe in one God,
the Father, the Almighty,
maker of heaven and earth,
of all that is seen and unseen.

1

God Talk
and the Limits of
Language

"We believe in one God, the Father, the Almighty"

Anyone now doing theology must sooner or later face the issue of sexist language. Anyone commenting on the Creed confronts the issue immediately in the first statement of belief: WE BELIEVE IN ONE GOD, THE FATHER, THE ALMIGHTY. The term sexist language is new, but the problem is not new in theology. Exasperated by the Arians' habit of pressing every epithet for the Godhead beyond the limits of language, St. Gregory of Nazianzus (c. 330–389) once exploded, "Probably you could be foolish enough to suppose our God male . . . because the word is?"[1] The problem of language is not a superficial issue. It goes to the heart of what theology is all about and ultimately to the basic issue about the essence of God's very being. In this chapter we first make some general comments on theological language; then we reflect on what it means—and doesn't mean—to confess our belief in God as Father. We look briefly at atheism and finally say a word about the God who at one and the same time attracts and inspires awe.

28

THEOLOGY AS "GOD TALK"

Theology is a form of discourse professing to speak about God. It is rooted in the Greek terms *theos* (god) and *logos* (word). Theology, then, is "god-talk."[2] Prayer is another kind of god-talk, and preaching is still a third. These various ways of speaking about and to God use much the same vocabulary, but theology uses words in a more reflective and systematic way. Theology is a special form of God-talk; when we do theology we use words in a different way than in ordinary speech. Whether pointing to actions, attitudes or qualities, in our everyday conversation verbs, nouns, and adjectives refer to concrete realities. But, at a more abstract level, as in philosophy, our language still relates directly to the world of substance and accidents and relationships of one kind or another. Theological terms, on the other hand, have more in common with figures of speech—allegories, metaphors, and similes—than with common nouns and adjectives.

Jesus used figures of speech to teach about the "kingdom of God," which, we shall see, is itself a figure of speech. He taught in parables that he used sometimes as allegories, sometimes as simple comparisons to get a point across (e.g., "The reign of God is like a buried treasure." Mt 13:44). St. Paul made the point that now we see as in a mirror, darkly (1 Cor 13:12), but in the time to come we shall see clearly. Mystics from Meister Eckhart in the fourteenth century to Teilhard de Chardin in the twentieth have had to coin words to describe their experience of the divine presence in the world.

In explaining the use of images in the Bible and theology, one of the more influential Catholic theologians of recent years, Yves Congar, O.P., says that "the crudest comparisons are often the best" because they employ figures of speech unlikely to be confused with the divine mystery. He states, however, that in his view

> the fact that God is revealed above all in images has a much deeper reason. It is this: the most material images are metaphors which do not in any sense claim to express being in itself, that is, the quiddity of what they are speaking about; they only express behaviour and what that represents for us. God is a rock, Christ is a lamb, the Spirit is living water. This does not mean that God is a mineral, Christ is an animal, or the Spirit is a liquid with a known chemical formula. It does, however, mean that God is, for us, firmness, Christ is a victim offered for us, and the Spirit is

a dynamic bearer of life. Revelation, in other words, by being expressed in images, is essentially an expression of what God is *for us*. It also, of course, discloses something of what God is in himself, but it only does this secondarily and imperfectly.[3]

THE PRINCIPLE OF ANALOGY

Theologians have always understood that human language is never adequate to represent revealed mystery. Even the doctrinal statements of the church councils, normative though they be, express only partial truths, which is not the same as saying they only are partially true. (For instance, it is entirely correct to say that Jesus is perfectly human, but it does not tell the whole truth; he is also divine.) When we describe God as a creative, good, and loving being, or when we say God acts in history, the words take on a different meaning from when they are applied to our fellow humans. The descriptions give us a glimpse into the divine reality, but our experience—even when empowered by revelation—is too limited, too conditioned by time and space to permit us to get more than a hint of what the eternal, infinite Godhead is *really* like.

In an effort to ground god-talk on a firm basis, St. Thomas Aquinas established the principle of analogy. He stated it in several ways, but in its simplest form the principle of analogy, as applied in theology, means that there exists a common denominator between certain human qualities and the divine attributes. We experience love in the relationship between husband and wife, between parents and children; so we say that God is love. We recognize goodness in the moral integrity of highly motivated individuals and in the generous service of social workers; so we say that God is good. We prize the intelligence of scientists capable of sending satellites into orbit; so we say that the Creator of the heavens is an intelligent being. The fact is, many of our figures of speech are based on a kind of analogy, as, for example, when I tell a friend her voice is "music" to my ears; when we say that the sun "rises"; that a person is a "lightweight"; or that the teacher is "deep" in thought.

All the great theologians in the Christian tradition have recognized in one way or another that there is an immense difference between saying that this is a good book and saying that God is good. Applying the principle of analogy, St. Thomas had an easy three-step rule of thumb to guide god-talk. 1) Every positive statement about God must at first be discounted. God is so different from the created universe that in the very act of affirming that God is good, we must deny that God is good in the sense that we know goodness from our own experience. 2) Only after this negation has been taken seriously are we in a position to make a statement based on the limited similarity between creation and Creator. Despite the enormous difference between God and us, it is true to say that God is good because there is a certain—though limited—common denominator underlying the goodness of creatures and the goodness of their Creator. 3) St. Thomas then calls on us to transcend the limitations of our human vocabulary and to extrapolate from our experience of the finite to affirm the goodness of God to the nth degree.

These steps are sometimes referred to as the *tres viae*—"three ways"—of speaking about divine attributes: the way of negation, the way of affirmation, and the way of eminence. This last step prescinds (in so far as possible) from the limitations of language and from conditions that restrict human discourse; in attributing perfections to God it affirms them in an absolute way that transcends the mode of existence in which they are found in creatures.

The principle of analogy must be kept in mind when we speak of three "persons" in one God. God is not person as we know persons. Unlike human persons, God is not defined by psychological traits and social relationships. In order to make it clear, however, that God is not simply a cosmic power, a creative force, "impersonal" and indifferent to the universe, it is proper to speak of God as a personal being. In this latter sense the analogy is based on our experience of humans at their best—as intelligent, loving beings, capable of understanding, fidelity, and compassion.

NAMING GOD

It is ironic that the Hebrew Scriptures, which sharply prohibit every attempt to picture God in any form (Ex 20:40), use an amazing variety of graphic, poetic images to describe God's activity in the world. Isaiah writes, "The Lord goes forth like a hero, like a warrior he stirs up his ardor." He has the Lord shout, "I cry out as a woman in labor, gasping and panting" (Is 42:13,14). The psalmist uses an electrical storm to describe the power, awesomeness, and majesty of God (Ps 29). Yet Elijah finds the Lord neither in the strong wind nor in the earthquake nor in fire, but in "a tiny whispering sound" (1 Kg 19:11-

12). The Lord speaks to Moses from a burning bush—a bush that was not consumed by the fire (Ex 3:2ff).

It is evident that the Bible uses many figures of speech to describe God. God is at once bridegroom of Israel, warrior, king, and nursing mother. Each figure gives some insight into the godhead and into divine activity in the universe. Few persons, if any, read them literally, however. Believers, while recognizing the limitations of this manner of speech, accept it as helpful to understanding something about God.

Keeping these limits in mind, we are now in a position to return to the issue of sexist language and specifically to the question of naming God "Father." "God" is a noun but not a name, just as "man" is a noun that tells something about my nature but is not my name. At the risk of over-simplification let us note that Israelites used both a noun and a name for God. The noun *El*, a common word for deity in the Semitic languages of the ancient Near East, suggests power, a cosmic force. The name *Yahweh* was first revealed to Moses on Mt. Horeb (Sinai).

> "But," said Moses to God, "when I go to the Israelites and say to them, 'The God of your fathers has sent me to you,' if they ask me, 'What is his name?' what am I to tell them?" God replied, "I am who am." Then he added, "This is what you shall tell the Israelites: I AM sent me to you. . . . This is my name forever; this is my title for all generations." (Ex 3:13-14,15b)

Today there is general agreement that *Yahweh* derives from an archaic form of the Hebrew verb "to be." (Some versions of the Bible render the Exodus text "He who is" rather than "I am who am.") Many modern scholars propose that it derives from the causative form of the verb and that Yahweh is only the first word of the entire name, "The One who brings into being whatever comes into being." Thus the name Yahweh designates God as Creator. It denotes the unique character of Yahweh and connotes God's relationship with Israel experienced in the Exodus and covenant.[4]

We customarily address a person *by name*. Individuals, however, are frequently known by more than one name. Public figures sometimes have professional names or "throne names" such as Pope John Paul II, who was born Karol Wojtyla. My father's name was Joseph, but I generally addressed him as "Dad." "Pope" and "Dad" are titles that designate particular roles and imply kinds of relationships. Nicknames, another kind of name, are generally more interesting than given names because often they describe some character trait or serve as terms of endearment.

In any case, names are not intended as definitions, if by definition we understand a determination of the nature of a thing as it is in itself. Thus for Christians to name God "Father" is not to define God but to acknowledge the special relationship that exists between the "Father" and Jesus Christ his "Son."

ONE GOD AND FATHER OF ALL

The Christian tradition is rooted in the religious heritage of Israel and of the Old Testament, which commonly refers to "the God of our fathers." Thus the association of God with the father image is shaped by the role the father played in Israelite family life. The social structure was the extended family of several generations, which looked to one of the elders—a patriarch—as the ultimate authority. The tradition, which took its inspiration from Moses, himself a patriarchal figure, spoke of "the God of your fathers" and thereby distinguished Yahweh from the gods of mythology and of fertility cults. The God of Israel was identified by means of historical associations and was never thought to be the "biological" parent as were the pagan deities of mythology.

The Old Testament names God "Father" in only eleven places and never uses the term as a form of direct address in prayer. This stands in stark contrast to the New Testament, which puts the word "Father" on the tongue of Jesus some 170 times.[5] "Father" was the common way Jesus addressed and spoke of God. The special relationship was revealed when, at Jesus' baptism, the voice from the heavens spoke, "You are my beloved Son" (Mk 1:11). In his final discourse at the Passover meal Jesus repeatedly spoke of his Father (Jn 14: *passim*), and in the garden of Gethsemani Jesus prayed, "My Father, if it be possible let this chalice pass from me" (Mt 26:39,42).

Jesus held up the paternal love and care of God as a model for his disciples (Mt 5:43-45; 6:26; 7:11; 10:29-31; 18:14. Lk 11:13). On several occasions he offered the Father as an example of forgiveness, most notably in the parable of the prodigal son (Mt 6:14; 18:35. Mk 11:25. Lk 15:11-32). The themes of loving care and forgiveness find exalted expression in the Lord's prayer, "Our Father in heaven, hallowed be your name. . . ." (Mt 6:5-15). It is no small thing to address God as Father and thereby claim for the relationship of creature to Creator the intimacy that exists between child and parent. Although Jesus did not introduce the fatherhood of God as an entirely new concept, the special relationship it implies was cause for boasting among Christians (1 Jn 3:1-3).

There is a difference, however, between the way Jesus spoke of his own relation to the Father and the way he spoke of the Father's relationship to the disciples. The difference is most evident when he thanks the Father for what he has hidden from the wise and clever and has revealed to the little ones. He then adds, "Everything has been given over to me by my Father. None knows the Son but the Father, and no one knows the Father but the Son—and anyone to whom the Son wishes to reveal him" (Mt 11:25-28). Most of the passages in which the distinction between "my Father" and "your Father" is explicit or implicit are concerned with the mission and authority of Jesus (Mt 15:13; 16:17; 18:10,19,35; 20:23; Lk 2:49; 22:29). The distinction is particularly strong in John's Gospel (3:35; 5:20; 10:17; 14:16; and *passim*).

We will have more to say about the relationship of God the Father and Jesus his Son later in connection with the second article of the Creed. For the moment, however, it must be emphasized that when we speak of God as Father we are using a figure of speech. Our experience of human fathers is always related to our relationship with males, but God is neither male nor female. Thus in applying St. Thomas' three steps we first deny that God is father in the sense in which humans experience fatherhood. Then we affirm the basis for calling God father, namely, those ideal qualities we associate with fatherhood: the giving of life, love, faithfulness, continued care and protection, and wisdom that guides and instructs. Finally, we attribute them to God, insofar as we are able, in an eminent way, without the imperfections that distort our view of fatherhood.

Other human relationships embody many of these same qualities. Obviously, mothers too are parents. They give life, bestow love, and remain faithful; they care for and instruct their children. The Bible relies on motherhood as a source for such figures of speech as the Lord nurturing Israel like a nursing mother (Num 11:12. Is 49:15) and like a loving mother, comforting Israel in time of affliction (Is 66:13).[6] In expressing our relationship to the Lord as father or mother, it is not as if we are making God one or the other parent and pitting the one against the other. Both fatherhood and motherhood give a particular insight into God's loving concern for human beings as individuals and as a group. The opposite of the parent-child relationship is indifference and non-involvement.

But father is not mother and mother is not father. Culture and society assign each parent certain roles and functions in family life that color our use of metaphors and models. In the period of the ancient patriarchs the social and familial organization, reinforced by legal and economic structures, made the male dominant and granted women only inferior status.[7] The rights and responsibilities of fathers and mothers were clearly defined by custom and law. But even at a more primitive level the bonding between mother and child and that between father and child are different. During the period of gestation and breast feeding, mother and infant experience an intimacy that a male can know only vicariously. A male can refuse to acknowledge his offspring (and males have done so). On the other hand, one thinks ahead to the New Testament and Joseph, whose trust in the angel caused him to accept Mary and her infant as his own even though he was not the father (Mt 1:18-25).

Later we shall have occasion to ascend to the rarified atmosphere of trinitarian theology (Chapter 4) where we shall see that any similarity to a male parent or patriarchial figure seems purely coincidental. St. Athanasius, the Capadoccians, and John of Damascus in the East and St. Augustine and the Scholastics in the West became concerned with the Father as "the absolute source of divinity," in the sense that the Father is the principle of the divinity and goodness we contemplate in the Son and Spirit.[8] In this context the Greek theologians referred to the Father as both "monarch" and "anarch": *Monarch* because God is the unique source of all being; *Anarch* because there is no source for God apart from God's own being. Medieval theologians in the West found the Father's uniqueness rooted as much in *innascibilitas* ("unbegottenness") as in *paternitas* ("fatherhood").

MONOTHEISM

The bond of fatherhood does not exist unless the male acknowledges his role as parent. In the Old Testament, Yahweh is called father of Israel; the term applies because God freely recognizes Israel as his people, acknowledges them as his children. The Israelites are the "chosen" among the people of the earth. God is not their ancestor in any way comparable to the way of Abraham or of any other patriarch. The fatherly concern God shows for the Jews is based more immediately on the notion of "election" than on that of begetting life.

The special relationship between God and the people of Israel is referred to as a "covenant." The foundation of the covenants (there were several; see Rom 9:4) was the call of Abraham (Gen 12:1-3). He was God's elect. The Bible gives no reason why he was chosen; he simply responded with faith and trust to God's commands and promises. God established a special bond with Abraham, promising to make his descendants a great people (Gen 12:2; 13:15; 15:1) and directing their destiny in the world (e.g., Gen 26:2; 46:3). The sign of the covenant was bodily circumcision (Gen 17: 1-14). Moses was the intermediary in a covenant that expanded the pact that God made with the early patriarchs so that Israel was Yahweh's chosen and Yahweh was their God. The Mosaic covenant was sealed in the context of a sacrificial meal (Ex 24:1-11). It was sanctioned by a decree of the Lord in which God, like a divine king, regulated the worship, the sacrifices, and the annual feasts of Israel (Ex 34:10-28). The Mosaic covenant was not an agreement based simply on blood ties but was a conditional pact in which the twelve tribes of Israel—a "mixed multitude"—committed themselves to observe the religious and moral demands made upon them by Yahweh. The Lord, on the other hand, pledged to sustain and safeguard the people and lead them to the promised land. Later when Israel proved unfaithful to the terms of the covenant, the prophets berated them for their ingratitude to a generous and loving Father (Deut 32:1-18; Is 63:16; 64:7; Jer 3:19).

The Mosaic covenant is presented as a contract based on the Decalogue—"the ten words" (Ex 20:1-17). Coming down from Mount Sinai, Moses repeats these "words" to the people, and they pledge themselves to observe the ordinances they contain. The first commandment imposes a rigorous monotheism on Israel: "I, the Lord, am your God, who brought you out of the land of Egypt, that place of slavery. You shall not have strange gods beside me" (Ex 20:1). Christians situate themselves squarely in this tradition of Mosaic monotheism when they say in the Nicene Creed, WE BELIEVE IN ONE GOD, THE FATHER, THE ALMIGHTY. It is noteworthy, at least from a historian's point of view, that the Apostles' Creed, like the other Western creeds, does not emphasize the *oneness* of God. On the other hand, the Eastern creeds (of which the Nicene-Constantinopolitan confession is the best known) "almost without exception" assert belief in ONE GOD THE FATHER, THE ALMIGHTY.[9]

In confessing the oneness and omnipotence of God, the Christian creeds follow the Jewish tradition. According to many commentators, the formula quoted by St. Paul in appealing to the Christians at Ephesus to maintain unity and peace in the community may be borrowed from non-Christian sources: "one God and Father of all, who is over all, and works through all, and is in all" (Eph 4:6). Whatever its origins, it seems to echo a creedal formula known in the primitive church.[10] Like Jews earlier and Moslems later, Christians in confessing "one God" do more than affirm a kind of philosophical monotheism. They proclaim that no other person, no other force, exercises such far-reaching dominion and sovereignty over nature and history, heaven and earth, the people of Israel and all the nations of the world, the public behavior and secret thoughts of all peoples. (For more on God's power and might, see the following chapter.)

In the earliest Christian creeds the confession "one God" is a protest on the one hand against the polytheism of the pagans, and on the other hand, a response to Jewish accusations of apostasy from service of the only true God (Deut 6:4-6). We worship the one God of Abraham, Moses, the prophets, and Jesus. Jews insist—and Christians concur—that Yahweh is not a national God of Israel in the way the that deities of other ancient peoples were their gods. Israel's God is the one God, the *only* God of every nation and of the whole universe—the *real* God. The unqualified, absolute oneness of God is a foundational doctrine of Christianity, grounded not simply on revelation but on reason as well. It represents a philosophical—a metaphysical—position, describing what *is*. St. Paul argued that whatever can be known about God is clear even to the irreligious and perverse: "Since the creation of the world, invisible realities, God's eternal power and divinity, have become visible, recognized through the things he has made" (Rom 1:20).

ATHEISM

Christians find it necessary to defend their belief against a sundry array of skeptics. Self-declared atheists deny outright the existence of God, some because they disallow the possibility of absolute truth, some because they reject all reality that cannot be verified by scientific testing. (One recalls the remark of the Soviet astronaut in his first venture into outer space: "I did not see God.") Others are more agnostic than atheistic in that they suspend judgment; their position is that any ultimate reality is unknown and probably unknowable.

In order to meet the objections of skeptics and agnostics, Protestants generally have recourse to the Scriptures, Catholics to proofs for the existence of God. In confessing God to be "maker of heaven and earth, of all things seen and unseen," Christians in effect identify the God of the Bible with the Primal Cause, the First Mover of the philosophers. The Second Vatican Council, slow to pass harsh judgment on sincere individuals, admitted that some "atheists" reject a caricature of God: "Some form for themselves such a fallacious idea of God that when they repudiate this figment they are by no means rejecting God of the gospel."[11]

In stating that atheism continues to be "among the serious problems of our age," Vatican II also recognized that "atheism is applied to phenomena which are distinct from one another."

For many the existence of God is not a metaphysical problem but an existential issue. Paradoxically, about the time that men and women began to explore outer space in the 1960s, the attention of philosophers and people in the street had turned inward. Moderns became less concerned with who made the universe than with trying to discern their place in it. When the question of meaning is raised, the point of reference is generally the individual, one's personal freedom and responsibility. Individuals question the meaning of their own existence. They look at themselves, as it were, in a mirror to find out who they are. Like St. Augustine, who tells his story in the *Confessions*, they plumb the depths of their souls seeking a sense of direction in their consciences, guidance for moral decisions in their feelings, and purpose in the inherent restlessness of their hearts.

Augustine searched for half a lifetime before discovering God's subtle ways of working in and around him. Today many have given up the quest. Like Vladamir and Estragon in Samuel Beckett's *Waiting for Godot*, they have all but despaired of God. They hesitate even to deny the existence of God, for they know that it is as impossible to demonstrate the non-existence of God as it is to prove that God exists. Moderns find Nietzsche's notion, "the death of God," an appropriate if ambiguous epitaph for the times. They do not mean that God has died in the ordinary sense, but suggest rather that God is no longer a living presence in human life. There is no evidence that God determines human history, and traditional religion no longer speaks to real human problems and experience. Not only God but the God question itself is dead for many people.[12]

THE GOD OF PHILOSOPHERS, GOD OF FAITH

Beginning with the Frenchman Blaise Pascal (1623-62), it has been fashionable for some theologians and believers to pit the God of revelation—"the God of Abraham, the God of Isaac, the God of Jacob"—against the God of the philosophers and scientists as if one must choose between two different kinds of deity. Pascal, a child prodigy, mathematical genius, and sometime apologist for Jansenism,[13] had a "vision" one fateful night that changed his life. He described the experience on a small sheet of parchment that he kept sewn in the lining of his coat; it was discovered by a servant at the time of his death. Paschal was careful to record the date and time: "The year of grace 1654. Monday, 23 November . . . from about half past ten in the evening until half past midnight." The note was intended as a constant reminder (it is called Pascal's *memorial* of the event). It begins with the word FEU ("fire") written in capital letters. The reference is quite clearly to Moses' vision of the burning bush where the voice speaks: "I am the God of your fathers . . . the God of Abraham, the God of Isaac, the God of Jacob" (Ex 3:6; Pascal also cites Mt 22:32). After quoting the text, the young visionary adds by way of contrast, "not of philosophers and scholars." He continues, "God of Jesus Christ. . . . He can only be found by the ways taught in the Gospel. . . ."[14]

Though a generation younger, Pascal was a contemporary of another mathematical genius, René Descartes (1596-1650), who is sometimes considered the progenitor of modern science. The background and interests of the two men were alike in many ways; but Pascal wrote, "I cannot forgive Descartes: in his whole philosophy he would like to do without God; but he could not help allowing him a flick of the fingers to set the world in motion; after that he had no more use for God."[15] Pascal found it unpardonable that Descartes was content with the abstract and remote God of philosophy, not bothering about the true God of the Bible.

Pascal's distinction is an artificial one based on the questionable assumption that the God of the philosophers is some kind of pure being or pure thought whose unchangeableness and endless duration exclude any relationship with the changeable and transitory world. From this perspective God is recognized as the first cause, the creator of the universe, but not as the caring and concerned Father revealed by Jesus. Christians recognize the God of the philosophers as their own while at the same time seeing this God as the one who "in times past spoke in fragmentary and varied ways to our fathers through the prophets; [and who] in this final age, . . . has spoken to us through his Son. . ." (Heb 1:1-2). Revelation tells us that the God of creation is a God to whom we can and must pray. Regardless of what Pascal thought, his God and the God of Descartes are the same God!

That the God of faith and the God of the philosophers are one and the same is expressed in the Creed by closely linking the title of Father with a second epithet, ALMIGHTY. It points back to the Old Testament, which speaks of "Lord Almighty" (= *Yahweh Sabaoth* in Hebrew, which literally translated is "God of hosts" or "God of powers"). In some biblical texts "the Almighty" stands alone as a noun; in these cases it translates the Hebrew *El Shaddai*, "God of the mountain." Although "almighty" appears rarely in the New Testament, early Christian writers frequently use it to describe God's majesty and transcendence.[16] It is clear that the original Greek term *Pantokrator* means "all-ruling," "all-sovereign." (The Latin translation is *omnipotens*, "all-powerful.") St. Theophilus of Antioch, writing about A.D. 180, explains, for example, that God is called almighty "because he rules and compasses all things. For the heights of the heavens and the depths of the abysses and the limits of the world are in His hand."[17]

Significantly, this juxtaposition of the two titles, "Father" and "Almighty," presents a tension in the Christian's belief about God. The first suggests a personal God, an accessibility to God and an intimacy between the divine and the human. The second points up the majesty and transcendence—the total otherness—of the Godhead. Rudolf Otto (1869-1937) spoke of this tension as the great mystery that is at once awesome in its grandeur and fascinating in its attractiveness—*mysterium tremendum fascinans*.[18] To confess WE BELIEVE IN GOD, THE FATHER, THE ALMIGHTY is to affirm in one breath the three realities that served as an outline for this chapter. 1) The *mysterium* refers to the divine presence that transcends human experience and defies our efforts to capture it in thought and speech. 2) The *tremendum*, like the epithet "Almighty," stresses the "otherness" of God that causes creatures to tremble and stutter in the divine presence. 3) The *fascinans*, on the other hand, points up the magnetic attraction of the divine presence which, like a parent's love, overcomes differences and builds faith and trust.

It is unlikely that the second- and third-century catechumens had clearly developed thoughts along these lines as they repeated the words of the Creed; but as their faith deepened they came to realize that no one name, no one epithet, is adequate to represent the divine. They named God as Father, knowing that he is both more and different; they confessed God to be almighty, aware that they could not imagine what it means to enjoy power without limits. Christianity, true to its Old Testament roots, insists that God transcends all images, visual and verbal, and that any pretense to define the divine essence is doomed to failure. As we shall emphasize in the following chapter, the Bible attributes all creation to God, the alpha and the omega, the first cause and ultimate destiny of all that is.

Notes

1. The fuller text runs, "Probably you could be foolish enough to suppose our God male . . . because the word is? Or the Spirit neuter because he neither begets nor bears? Or even that God cohabited with his own Will [grammatically feminine in Greek], according to the old myths, to beget the Son—which posits the androgynous God of [the gnostics] Marcus and Valentinus?" (*Orations* 31.7) Quoted by Robert W. Jenson, *The Triune Identity* (Philadelphia: Fortress Press, 1982) p.20. See S. Mark Heim, "Gender and the Creed: Confessing a Common Faith," *The Christian Century* April 17, 1985: 379–381.

2. John Macquarrie, *God-Talk: An Examination of the Language and Logic of Theology* (New York: Harper & Row, 1967), pp. 11–32.

3. Yves Congar, *I Believe in the Holy Spirit* Vol. III. (New York: Seabury Press, 1983), p.5. Henceforth, *I Believe.*

4. John L. McKenzie, *Dictionary of the Bible* (New York: Macmillan Publishing Co., 1965), pp. 315–318. Henceforth, *Dictionary.*

5. Robert Hamerton-Kelly, "God the Father in the Bible and in the Experience of Jesus: The State of the Question," in J-B. Metz and E. Schillebeeckx, eds. *God as Father?* Concilium 143 (New York: Seabury Press, 1981), pp. 96–98. See Elizabeth A. Johnson, "The Incomprehensibility of God and the Image of God Male and Female," *Theological Studies* 45:3 (1984):441–464.

6. Marianne Sawicki, *Faith and Sexism: Guidelines for Religious Educators* (New York: Seabury Press, 1979).

7. The substance of the feminist critique of the patriarchal tradition is that it extends the image of God as father to legitimate the masculine mindset—a particular world view, a whole way of ordering reality—that leaves little place for feminine outlook and needs. In the debate over sexist language, "It is therefore a mistake," writes Sallie McFague, "to focus on God the father as a limited model for talk about God; rather, it is patriarchalism—the expanded, intransigent model radical feminists take to be the root-metaphor of christianity—that is at issue." *Metaphorical theology* (Philadelphia: Fortress Press, 1982), pp. 147–148.

8. Congar, *I Believe* Vol. III, p. 133.

9. Kelly, *Creeds*, pp. 132, 195.

10. Although there are pre-Christian parallels for reference to "one God and Father of all," it is distinctly Christian in the way it is joined to the formulas praising the Spirit and Christ. The trinitarian structure is obvious, even though the sequence is in reverse order. See Markus Barth, *Ephesians: Translation and Commentary on chapters 4-6*, Anchor Bible 34 A, (Garden City, NY: Doubleday and Co., 1974.) pp. 462–464.

11. *Gaudium et Spes*, n. 19.

12. Walter Kasper, *An Introduction to Christian Faith*. (New York/ Ramsey: Paulist Press, 1980), pp. 135–136.

13. Jansenism takes its name from one Cornelius Jansen (d. 1638), author of *Augustinus*, a treatise on grace. It was a movement characterized by its peculiar notion regarding the irresistible operation of grace, moral rigorism and, later, its violent opposition to Jesuit influence in the church. See *Oxford Dictionary of the Christian Church*, s.v. "Jansen" and "Jansenism."

14. Hans Küng, *Does God Exist?* (Garden City, NY: Doubleday and Co., 1980), pp. 58–59.

15. Quoted in Küng, ibid.

16. Kelly, *Creeds*, p. 133.

17. Ibid., p. 137.

18. Otto's classic work was translated into English as *The Idea of the Holy* (New York: Oxford Univ. Press, 1958).

2

Creation:

More than a Beginning

"Maker of heaven and earth"

One can make the case that the most distinctive tenet of Christianity is its teaching about creation. It is alluded to in the first line of the Bible, "In the beginning, when God created the heavens and the earth. . . " (Gen 1:1). The Gospel according to John opens on the same note: "In the beginning was the Word. . . . Through him all things came into being, and apart from him nothing came to be" (Jn 1:1,3). The theme recurs time and again in the Psalms (e.g.,90, 104, 136, 139, 146, 147, 148), in "Second" Isaiah (see 40:28-31; 43:1-13; 44:24-26), in Wisdom literature such as Proverbs (8:22-31) and Job (38:1ff), and elsewhere, to the very end in the book of Revelation, which quotes a hymn:

> O Lord our God, you are worthy to receive glory and honor and power! For you have created all things; by your will they came to be and were made!

The primary importance of God's role as Creator is reaffirmed in the first article of the creed, MAKER OF HEAVEN AND EARTH, OF ALL THAT IS SEEN AND UNSEEN. This is the basic belief from which flows all else that

44

Christians say about God, about the universe they live in, about their history, destiny, and hope.[1] It answers the fundamental question, Who is this God in whom we put our trust?

In commenting on this tenet of the Creed we begin with a synopsis of the biblical accounts of creation by way of contrasting their style and content with the polytheistic cosmologies prevalent in the ancient Near East. We then turn to a consideration of gnosticism and Saint Irenaeus of Lyons. Gnosticism graphically illustrates how a group's theology of creation shapes its views on salvation and reflects basic assumptions it makes about revelation and the Scriptures. The lengthy excursus on gnosticism may seem an unwarranted digression, but as is evident from the writings of St. Irenaeus, its most articulate opponent, this second-century heresy forced the church to clarify its thinking on creation and a number of related issues and therefore is crucially important. In passing we consider briefly particular issues such as the classic theological question of *creatio ex nihilo* ("creation from nothing"), the contemporary debate between the proponents of evolution and creationism, and the singular position that human beings enjoy in the galaxy of created beings. Although we touch on a number of profound issues, our intention is not to outline a comprehensive theology of creation but to draw out some of the implications of what it means to acknowledge God as MAKER OF HEAVEN AND EARTH.

THE GENESIS ACCOUNTS

The Book of Genesis presents two accounts of creation. The first, the newer account, opens with "In the beginning when God created the heavens and the earth" and closes with the formula "Such is the story of the heavens and the earth at their creation" (Gen 1:1 - 2:4a). It adopts the literary framework of a seven-day week to describe the work of creation, which unfolds in stages: 1) light and darkness separated as day and night, 2) upper and lower waters separated by heaven, 3) earth and seas separated; and vegetation began to grow; 4) luminaries in the heavens (sun, moon, stars); 5) living creatures in the sea and the sky; 6) animal life on earth, and the human species made in the image and likeness of God; and 7) God's rest (according to the Torah, Jewish Law, the Sabbath rest is as integral to the cosmic order as is the divine creativity).[2] Creation is accomplished by fiat—"Let there be. . . ." or, as the psalmist puts it, "He spoke and it was made; he commanded and it stood forth" (33:9; see also v.6 and Ps 148:5).

After each successive stage of creation we read the repeated declaration "God saw how good it was," and after the creation of living things, "God looked at everything he had made, and he found it *very* good" (Gen 1:31). The description of God's pleasure with his own artistry may seem naive to modern readers, but the simplicity of the account cloaks a profound insight. The basic belief in the essential goodness of the created universe exerted a powerful influence on the Israelites and shaped their outlook on life and on the world in which they lived. God gave humans "dominion over the fish of the sea, the birds of the air, and all the living things that move on the earth" (Gen 1:28). Everything was ordered to their well-being: the fruit of the trees, plants and grains, birds and animals were given to them as food. The psalmist extols the glory and dignity that God has bestowed on human creatures:

> When I behold your heavens, the work of your fingers,
> the moon and the stars which you set in place—
> What is man that you should be mindful of him,
> or the son of man that you should care for him?
> You have made him little less than the angels,
> and crowned him with glory and honor.
> You have given him rule over the works of your hands,
> putting all things under his feet:
> All sheep and oxen, yes, and the beasts of the field,
> The birds of the air, the fishes of the sea,
> and whatever swims the paths of the seas. (Ps 8:4-9)

Humans are not creatures of blind cosmic forces, helpless and hopeless before the relentless rhythms and cycles of nature. On the contrary, they are endowed with dignity, purpose and power by their Creator.

The second account of creation, much older than the first,[3] begins with the phrase "At the time when the LORD God made the earth and the heavens" (2:4b) and focuses on the creation of man and his privileged place in the Garden of Eden. The narrative ends with God's recognition of the human need for companionship and the resultant creation of woman (2:24).

The biblical insights into creation stand in sharp contrast to the views in most myths of the ancient Near East, and nowhere are the differences more striking than in the accounts of the creation of man and woman. In the polytheistic mythologies, creation is always described in terms of procreation; the primal creative force is sex. The Babylonian epic *Enuma Elish*, one of the most famous myths emanating from the ancient world tells, for example, how Apsu and Tiamat, the male and female powers respectively, gave birth to the first generation of gods through "the commingling of their waters."[4] Thus the element of sex predates the cosmos, and the gods were themselves products of it. By way of contrast, Israel's God creates by fiat. The thought of God as a sexual being is utterly alien to the biblical accounts, and the Creator in Genesis, without gender, has neither a male counterpart nor a female consort. In making it clear that it was God who created sexual differentiation, Genesis presents an antithesis to the pagan notion of the creator god.

Genesis sets out purposefully to correct the accounts of creation of human beings common in the cosmologies of the Near East. In the *Enuma Elish* story, for example, the creation of man and woman is almost incidental: they are fashioned as an afterthought to be servants who provide for the physical needs of the gods. The Bible, by contrast, differentiates in subtle ways the creation of man and woman from that of other creatures so as to emphasize their unique position and their privileged relationship with God. Genesis prefaces the creation of humans by a formal declaration of divine intention and purpose: "Let us make man in our image, after our likeness" (Gen 1:27). And in turn God declares, "It is not good for the man to be alone. I will make a suitable partner for him" (Gen 2:18). Only in the case of man and woman is the material from which they are made explicitly mentioned. Adam alone has the breath of life blown into his nostrils by the Creator and thereby draws life directly from God. Both of the creation accounts in Genesis present the human species as the culmination of creation and focus the narratives on man and woman as the main characters in the story.

GNOSTIC DUALISM

The biblical accounts of creation, which challenged the polytheistic cosmologies of ancient Mesopotamia, were a stumbling block also for gnosticism. Gnostic sects, often in rivalry with one another, mixed ideas from the religions of Persia, the Near East, and Egypt and later included teachings borrowed from Judaism and Christianity. Though most Jewish and Christian gnostics paid lip service to Genesis, they in fact reinterpreted the stories so as to distort their meaning and present a caricature of the Creator God. For Christians gnosticism mounted the most formidable threat to the integrity of the gospel message that the church has ever had to face. Out of contempt for the flesh, gnostics denied the reality of the Incarnation, ridiculed the resurrection of the body, and disdained marriage. Unlike most other heretical movements, gnosticism was not confined to particular localities and regions. Adherents of this complex religious movement surfaced in all the principal centers of Christianity.[5]

Although Christian gnosticism took many forms, certain features were common to the movement as a whole. One feature highlighted by all gnostics was the claim to secret knowledge—privileged information, as it were—that surpassed the simple faith of ordinary Christians. The name, derived from the common Greek word for knowledge (*gnosis*), became a generic label for these sects that laid claim to special revelation known only to the insiders. Some gnostics claimed their secret *gnosis* was derived from an underground tradition traceable to one of the apostles or to an early disciple of Jesus; others claimed the source of their information was a direct revelation given to the founder of their particular sect.

Another common feature of gnostic teaching was the claim to special knowledge, again based on special revelation about the origin of the world, about how evil had come into existence, and about the secret of being delivered from its destructive power. Gnostics distinguished between the "creator god"—a demiurge or inferior deity—and the supreme Divine Being, who was remote and unknowable. The demiurge was usually said to have issued from the supreme deity through a series of emanations that became more flawed the further removed they were from the perfection of the Divine Being, much as a river becomes more polluted the more distant it is from its headwaters. The demiurge in turn was the immediate source of the created universe and was the ruler of the world. In most gnostic systems the material world came about through mischance or mischief at some pre-cosmic point in the series of emanations. Although creatures, and human beings in particular, embody a spark of the divine, the Supreme Deity never intended to create a universe of matter. It was an unwanted mistake, the fault of some lesser god, that needed to be undone.

Gnostics regarded the natural order of things as totally alien to the supreme God and to the principle of good. They compared and contrasted the teaching of the Old Testament with that of the New. The gnostics imagined an antithesis between the creator God, the God of justice, whom they associated with the axiom of an eye for an eye and a tooth for a tooth in the Hebrew Scriptures, and the loving Father proclaimed by Jesus in the Gospels and Epistles. In effect they exalted the value of the New Testament, especially the writings of St. Paul, at the expense of the Old Testament.

Gnostics succumbed to the dualist temptation that has been the downfall of many religious-minded people. They saw all reality divided into two categories: the world of light and spirit, the principle of good, and world of darkness and matter, the principle of evil. People fell into one of the two categories: they were either "spiritual" or "carnal." (Certain sects posited a third group, an intermediate class, who stood somewhere between the world of the flesh and the world of the spirit.) According to most Christian gnostics, Christ came into the world as the agent of the Supreme God, revealing the true *gnosis*: the way of escape from the world of matter and flesh. It goes without saying that gnostics had no place in their system for the resurrection of the body— Christ's or anyone else's. They interpreted Christian ritual and ascetical practices as a means of liberating the spiritual element in creation, purifying the principle of good from the evil dross of matter which imprisons it.

MARCION AND VALENTINUS

Commonly included among the gnostics is one Marcion of Pontus, said to be the most formidable adversary of the church in the second century.[6] Born in Sinope (near the site of modern Sinop on the Black Sea), Marcion was the son of a bishop who later excommunicated him. As a young man he had amassed great wealth from arms sales. He eventually made his way to Rome, where he presented himself as a faithful Christian and made a sizeable donation to the church there. In Rome, sometime about the year A.D. 144, Marcion compiled his only written work, *Antitheses*, edited his own version of the Bible, and established the first of many churches.

In line with basic gnostic tenets, Marcion held to the dualistic view that matter is evil, spirit is good. Thus he was prepared to divide the universe into two spheres, the invisible and visible. The invisible world is the work of the Supreme God, who resides there and is known only to those who have entry to the world of the spirit. The visible world is the work of the demiurge, who, knowing nothing of the sovereign God and the invisible world, thinks himself to be master of all things. According to Marcion the Old Testament is inspired by the demiurge, who, though not the god of evil, is the despot who made human beings and placed them in this miserable world of matter. Although the supreme deity—the "Stranger God"—owed nothing to the human race, he willed to save it. Christ Jesus, who is distinct from the Supreme God only in name, reveals the existence of the invisible world and the identity of its deity. Needless to say, in Marcion's system Jesus could not take on a material body; thus he had only the appearance of a corporeal being.

Thus Marcion's version of the Bible had no place for Old Testament writings, and of the New Testament he retained only the Gospel of Luke (omitting the infancy narratives and the story of Jesus' baptism) and ten Epistles of Saint Paul; he rejected the pastoral Epistles and the Epistle to the Hebrews. Marcion further excised anything in the Epistles that he regarded as favoring Judaism, which he attributed to false apostles. This strong anti-Jewish bias is even more evident in his *Antitheses*. It is essentially a compilation of texts from the Hebrew and Christian Scriptures that Marcion selected to illustrate the opposition between the two testaments and consequently between the Supreme God of the invisible universe and the demiurge, the creator of things visible. This anti-Jewish bias explains in part Marcion's popular appeal, for his theology was neither consistent nor profound. He made his influence felt chiefly through the extensive network of churches he organized in the major population centers of the Empire.

The most influential of the Christian gnostics was Valentinus, a native of Egypt. For about thirty years (c. A.D. 135-165) he lived in Rome, where he broke with the church. Later he took up residence in Cyprus. According to his disciples, Valentinus had been instructed in the Christian faith by Theodas, a pupil of St. Paul. Until recently the teachings of Valentinus were known to us only secondhand in the accounts of his opponents. In 1945, however, a discovery of major significance uncovered hitherto unknown gnostic documents in a cemetery near the Egyptian village of Nag Hammadi (about sixty miles down the Nile from ancient Luxor). The Nag Hammadi materials, while confirming the reports of Irenaeus, Tertullian, Clement of Alexandria, and other early Christian writers, have also thrown new light on gnostic sources and doctrine. The recently discovered documents include several attributed to Valentinus or one of his disciples.

The Valentinians, as his followers were called, described an elaborate doctrine of "aeons" that emanated from the Divine Being in a succession of pairs. Their ultimate offspring was the demiurge, the God of the Old Testament, who created the visible world. Salvation, however, came through another aeon, Christ, who appeared as a human in the person of Jesus and took up residence in his body at the time of his baptism. Christ revealed the true *gnosis*, but it was given only to the "spirituals," that is, the Valentinians. Not being privy to this true knowledge, ordinary Christians could not come to the fullness of salvation in Christ; lacking the authentic gnosis, they had to rely on faith and good works to arrive at even the intermediate realm of the Demiurge. The rest of humanity, "clods" engrossed in matter, were destined to eternal perdition.

Unlike Marcion, the Valentinians had no particular interest in deprecating the Old Testament. Some did, however, distinguish three levels of authority in the Old Testament texts: 1) the passages inspired by God; 2) the sections inserted by Moses by way of concession to the hardness of people's hearts; and 3) texts of an inferior quality added by the Jewish elders (these texts had no special authority). Along with their founder, the Valentinians traced the source of their teachings to Jesus, who, they said, had given a revelation to his disciples that they in turn handed down secretly by word of mouth. According to Valentinus this underground tradition coexisted with the public teaching of the church.

As in other systems based on a dualistic view of reality, gnostics' disdain for the material universe led them to regard physical acts with an indifferent eye. Moreover, they were fatalistic about the destiny of humans, maintaining that the world was in the control of planetary forces and despotic powers. Aloof from the mainstream of society and church, they took no responsibility for government, which they held in low esteem. Encouraged by St. Paul's teaching on freedom from the law, gnostics felt no constraints on their actions. Nonetheless Valentinus, like the majority of Christian gnostics, demanded an ascetic life of his followers. Strict rules governed the mortification of the flesh, and there was a special prohibition on marriage (or at least on procreation). The purpose was to turn the attention of the elect to higher things and to free the spirit from the bonds of matter, flesh, and bodily appetites. Some gnostic sects, however, drew the opposite conclusion from the same basic premises. Their indifference to physical activity—eating, drinking, sexual intercourse—contributed to the gnostics' reputation for amoral behavior. (The admonition in the Epistle of Jude against the sexual excesses of certain individuals was probably directed against a gnostic element that threatened the early Christian community.)

ST. IRENAEUS OF LYONS AND THE "RULE OF FAITH"

Until the gnostic manuscripts were discovered at Nag Hammadi in 1945, our principal source of information regarding Valentinus and the Valentinians was the writings of St. Irenaeus of Lyons. By far the most important theologian of the second century, Irenaeus was only a few generations removed from the apostles. As a youth he had listened to the sermons of St. Polycarp, bishop of Smyrna (d. 156), who was reputed to be the disciple of St. John the apostle. We do not know the circumstances that took Irenaeus from Asia Minor to Gaul, where he became a presbyter in the church of Lyons. While Irenaeus was on a mission to Rome in 177, the ninety-year-old bishop, Pothinus, was martyred. When Irenaeus returned to Lyons, he was named to head the see.

Irenaeus administered the diocese of Lyons, acted as a mediator in disputes among his brother bishops, and dedicated himself to the task of refuting heresy. Though he wrote it in Greek, his main work is best known by its Latin title, *Adversus Haereses*—"Against Heresies." An English translation of the original Greek title more clearly identifies Irenaeus's target: "The Detection and Overthrow of the Pretended False Gnosis." In all, *Adversus Haereses* consists of five books composed over a longish period of time and seemingly without a prearranged plan. Book I (the "detection"), a history of gnosticism, begins with a detailed description of the teachings of the Valentinians and then turns to earlier forms of the heresy. Book II (the "overthrow") presents the refutation. In Book IV Irenaeus, in reaction against Marcion, reaffirms the unity of the two Testaments, bound together in the divine plan of revelation and salvation. In dealing with the last things, particularly the resurrection, in Book V, Irenaeus shows that the flesh is not essentially an evil principle (as the gnostics maintained) and is capable of salvation.

Book III, however, is the core of the work. Not content simply with refuting heretics, Irenaeus accepted their challenge and appropriated whatever valid insights they offered, incorporating them into a systematic theology of creation and salvation more consonant with traditional church teaching. Scripture and tradition are the foundation on which his system rests.[7]

Irenaeus measured the teachings of the gnostics against something he called "the rule of faith," a brief summary of the principal revelatory and redemptive events described in the Scriptures; it reads like a paraphrase of the baptismal creed:

> The Church, although spread everywhere as far as the boundaries of the earth, has received from the apostles and their disciples faith in one single God, the Father Almighty, who has made heaven and earth and the seas and all that is in them; and in one Christ Jesus the Son of God, who was incarnate for our salvation; and in one Holy Spirit, who through the prophets announced the dispensation, the advent and virginal birth, and passion and resurrection from the dead, and bodily ascension into heaven of the well-beloved Christ Jesus our Lord, and his [second] coming, when He shall appear in heaven at the right hand of the Father to restore all things and raise up all flesh and all [humanity. . . .] (III, iv:2)[8]

The crux of the summary, for reasons of argument against the gnostics, lies in its emphasis on the *unity* of the Scriptures. The God of the Old Testament and the God of the New Testament are one. As Irenaeus presents it, creation and re-creation are a single theme that runs through both Testaments, giving the Bible a unity and coherence seldom found in anthologies of any kind.

The author of *Adversus Haereses* recognized that the appeal of gnosticism lay in the comprehensive vision it presented. Details differed from sect to sect, but the picture, at least among Christian gnostics, was basically the same. The gnostics had integrated their teaching into a mythology that gave a panoramic overview of cosmic history. Irenaeus sparred with them over specific issues and even parodied their writings, but his arguments from authority were defensive, and he seemed to realize that his apologia did not match the perennial appeal of the gnostic myth. His principal response was to counter the gnostic myth by presenting a cosmic vision based on traditional church teaching. He explained the diverse beliefs of the Christian faith in the context of a panoramic worldview and in effect created a Christian mythology to challenge that of the gnostics.[9] But Irenaeus recognized that it was not enough to unmask the novelty and misrepresentations of gnosticism. The church needed also to present the story of salvation as a coherent and comprehensive whole.

Irenaeus' theology of creation is grounded on the bedrock of the "rule of truth," which affirms the existence of "one God, the Father, the Almighty, maker of heaven and earth." In his mind there is no question of distinguishing the Supreme God or the God of Jesus from God the Creator. The Father "made all things by his Word, and fashioned and formed out of that which had no existence, all things that exist." Irenaeus reads the accounts of the creation of Adam and Eve in Genesis as evidence that it is the work of the Trinity:

> For with Him were always present the Word and Wisdom, the Son and Spirit, by whom and in whom, freely and spontaneously, He made all things, saying, "Let Us make man after Our image and likeness". . . . (III, xx: 1)[10]

Unlike the gnostic demiurge, God, the Almighty Father, creates freely and purposefully. Nothing in the universe nor in the divine essence compelled God to create. God made all things out of sheer goodness which is reflected in the created world. But Irenaeus saw "creation" as more than a beginning. It is a process of *becoming* which reaches its fulfillment through an orderly succession of events. Unlike the Supreme Deity of gnosticism, the God of the Bible is not remote from the world but shows care and directs the course of history.

In biblical religion, humanity is the centerpiece of God's handiwork, and in the same vein, Irenaeus says that humans were not made for the sake of the universe, but the universe for the sake of humans (V, xxix:1). Since human beings have an open, unfinished, temporal nature, the end of creation is not achieved until the final judgment. The bodies of all human beings, created as they are in the likeness of the Son, who was to become incarnate, are in the image of God. Adam, originally endowed with incorruptibility, lost it for himself and for his posterity. Only a totally gratuitous gesture on the part of God restores it. From the very outset, according to Irenaeus, Christ is key to the

story of creation and re-creation. More will be said about the christological focus in commenting on the second article of the Creed. For
now, it is sufficient to indicate that the author of *Adversus Haereses*
was not the first to call attention to Christ's role in begetting the world.
St. Paul quotes what seems to be an ancient formula that suggests that
the christological dimension was central to the church's belief from the
beginning: ". . . for us there is one God, the Father, from whom all
things come and for whom we live; and one Lord Jesus Christ,
through whom everything was made and through whom we live" (1
Cor. 8:6). The Pauline text has polemic overtones. St. Paul is intent on
affirming the cosmic roles of both Father and Son and "asserting the
unity of the Christians' God as contrasted with the 'many gods and
many lords' of paganism."[11]

CREATION AND SCIENCE

Neither the Bible nor the Creed teaches that God's creative action is a
thing of the past. The Nicene Creed simply declares that God is
MAKER. While translations of the Bible—Greek, Latin, English—use
tenses of the verb that seem to describe activity that took place at the
beginning of time, the Hebrew forms of the verb point beyond space
and time. The Bible does not say that the act of creation took place at
some instant in the distant past but rather suggests (as Irenaeus observed) that God is eternally engaged in a creative process.

The Greek term used in the Nicene Creed for MAKER is *poieten*—a
cognate of "poet," but closer in meaning to the English word "artist."
The artist shapes and forms and brings into being. For humans "to
create" means to organize given materials—wood, stone, metal, gestures, colors, or sound—into some kind of meaningful whole. The
creative act imposes design and gives order to formlessness. The creativity of the human artist gives us some insight into the creative work
of God: Genesis describes creation as bringing order out of chaos.
God separated light from darkness, land from water, and thus imposed
design and purpose on the "formless wasteland" of the primeval universe. Unlike the creative act of the human artist, however, who works
with marble or pigments or sound, God's creative act begins from
scratch.

According to all the biblical accounts, the creative power of God
resides in a divine fiat, "Let there be. . . ." and it was done. Unlike the

words of deities in much ancient mythology, God's word is not a magic formula that simply unleashes hidden forces and actualizes potential already there. Creation is an exercise of the divine will. The word of God is power in the strict sense. As recognized by the psalmist ("He spoke and it was so"), it has the inherent force to bring something into being out of nothing, to bring into being something that was not. Thus Christian theology says that God created *ex nihilo*—"out of nothing."

In the ancient world the belief that God created the "visible" world, the world of matter, was questioned. Mystery and magic were accepted as a matter of course; if the world was not the product of unseen powers and extraterrestial forces, it was thought to be at least governed by them. In the modern world, questions arise more frequently about things "unseen": the world of spirits, of angels, of the human soul. The empirical mentality that puts no credence in anything it cannot see, feel, smell, or hear questions the very existence of an "invisible" world. Science, it is claimed by some, unmasks mythology and destroys mystery. On the other hand, many moderns find that science and technology enlarge their vision. Just as they recognize truth in poetry, so they accept myth as a way of grappling with the deeper questions of existence and meaning. In this context, to call something a myth is not to suggest that it is untrue but that it defies the categories of ordinary language and discourse.

Today, as in Irenaeus' time, for example, some misconstrue the meaning and purpose of the Bible in an effort to maintain a particular doctrine of creation. "Creation-science" or "creationism" is pitted against the hypothesis of evolution. The advocates of creationism cite the Book of Genesis as their principal authority. Despite the fact that they interpret the biblical text literally, few today go as far as the Cambridge scholar John Lightfoot (1602-75), who calculated on the basis of numbers in the Pentateuch that the creation of Adam and Eve took place on Friday—"the sixth day"—October 23, 4004 B.C. at 9 a.m.[12] Whereas most biblical scholars accept the conclusion of geologists that the earth has been in existence for some 4.5 billion years, fundamentalists contend that according to the biblical chronology, God created it a mere 10,000 to 20,000 years ago—too short a time to allow for the evolution of all the diverse species of life on this planet.

The issue that splits "creationists" into various camps is not whether God created the universe and all that is in it, but how and when. Catholic teaching excludes the human soul from the evolutionary process, but the church does not officially take a stand as to whether lower forms evolved into higher forms of life. Many theologians subscribe to some form of the evolutionary hypothesis, pointing out that God is no less the Creator whether the divine fiat brought the universe into existence instanteously or gradually over billions of years. In fact, they say it is no less of an achievement—and is perhaps an even more dramatic testimony to divine wisdom and power—to have brought it about through the complex interaction of physical force, chemical catalysis, and nuclear power.

The proponents of creationism would make the Bible a sourcebook for science and history, despite the fact that students of the Bible from Augustine to Aquinas through Luther and Calvin to most modern exegetes see it chiefly as a witness to the experience of God's revelation. In speaking to the Pontifical Academy of Sciences a few years ago, Pope John Paul II warned that any attempt to base a scientific theory of creation of the world on the account in Genesis "is alien to the intention of the Bible." "The Bible," he said, "speaks to us of the origin of the universe and its make-up, not in order to provide us with a scientific treatise, but in order to state the correct relationship of man with God and with the universe." Paraphrasing the famous phrase of Galileo, the pope stated, "The Bible does not wish to teach us how heaven was made, but how to go to heaven."[13]

A CHRISTIAN VIEW OF CREATION

Contemporary scholars have made much of the close association in Genesis between the divine likeness in man and woman and their dominance over the rest of nature. Within lines of a single verse we read: "Let us make man in our image, after our likeness. Let them have dominion over the fish of the sea, the birds of the air, and the cattle, and over all the wild animals and all the creatures that crawl on the ground" (1:26). The biblical author strongly implies that in however many ways humans resemble God, one is the power over the created universe—including humans themselves—entrusted to them (see Ps 8:4-9, quoted above). Humans, who according to most Near Eastern myths were created to be the slaves and yoke-bearers of the gods, are according to Genesis the masters of all they survey.

"Dominion," writes Bruce Vawter in his commentary on Genesis, "is not a license to caprice and tyranny but, in the best sense, a challenge to responsibility and the duty to make right prevail."[14] It is not a dominion of exploitation but a responsibility modeled on God's own. Conservationists who believe that the earth and all living beings have been delivered into human hands as a sacred trust can find justification for their position in the biblical theology of creation. There are many allusions to events surrounding creation in biblical literature from the Pentateuch through the Psalms to the Wisdom books and the later prophets. All present an attitude toward nature greatly different from the animism of religions where God is understood as a life force, some form of spirit that is all but indistinguishable from the living beings in which it resides. The Bible, in effect, declares men and women free from the mystique that idolizes nature and makes humans fearful of blind fate and passive before impersonal forces beyond their control.

The Judaeo-Christian doctrine of creation implies a positive outlook on many aspects of reality that other religious systems regard negatively. Unlike the Hindu tradition, notably the Buddhist expression of it, Christian tradition puts a positive value on the physical world, the human body, the thirst for life, and human relationships in the world. Unlike some ancient Greek traditions, the Judaeo-Christian tradition sees change in terms of becoming and growth. But there is also a negative side to the biblical doctrine of creation in the sense that it rejects a dualistic interpretation of the universe. It denies polytheism ("many gods, many lords"; see 1 Cor 8:6). In sum, the Creed affirms: 1) there is no god but God, who is the creator and governor of all beings, seen and unseen; 2) there is purpose in God's creation, and humans are its organizing force; 3) God is distinct but not indifferent toward nor distant from the created universe; 4) all that God makes—the natural order of things, spirit and matter—is good.

There is a sense, moreover, in which creation is said to be "not a doctrine of Christianity, but a Christian doctrine."[15] As Irenaeus interpreted it, creation is inextricably entwined with salvation; and, as we shall see as we turn our attention to the second article of the Creed, together they spiral upward like the axes of a double helix converging in the person of Christ.

Notes

1. Langdon Gilkey, *Maker of Heaven and Earth* (Garden City, NY: Anchor Books, 1965, p. 4.

2. The linkage between the weekly sabbath and creation is made in the Ten Commandments: "Remember to keep holy the sabbath day. Six days you may labor and do all your work, but the seventh day is the sabbath of the LORD, your God. . . . In six days the LORD made the heavens and the earth, the sea and all that is in them; but on the seventh day he rested. That is why the LORD has blessed the sabbath day and made it holy" (Ex 20:8-10a,11).

3. Modern scholars identify different documents that the redactor of Genesis incorporated into the text. The first account (Gen 1:1-4a) is thought to be from the "priestly" tradition (the P source) because of its emphasis on the law and the ancient rituals of Israel; it is dated as late as the fifth century B.C. The second account belongs to the "Yahwehistic" tradition (the J source after the older spelling "Jahweh"), so called because it commonly employs the name of God revealed to Moses; it is dated as early as the ninth century B.C.

4. The *Enuma Elish* epic is particularly helpful in understanding many of the biblical references to battles between and among cosmic forces. It reflects the Near Eastern culture that surrounded ancient Israel. In the Babylonian epic, Apsu personified the primeval sweetwater ocean; Timat, represented as a ferocious monster, personified the primordial saltwater ocean. The commingling of the two waters begot the first generation of divine offspring, who in turn gave birth to a second generation of deities. The process was repeated successively until the time came when the noise and revelry of the younger gods disturbed the peace of Tiamat and Apsu. The latter set out to destroy the unruly young gods but were thwarted in their plan by the all-wise Ea, the earth-water god. (This summary and other references to the *Enuma Elish* epic are based on Nahum M. Sarna, *Understanding Genesis* (New York: Schocken, 1970), pp. 1–23.)

5. Jules Lebreton and Jacques Zeiller, *Heresy and Orthodoxy* (New York: Collier Books, 1962), pp. 23–48. See also Robert M. Grant,

Gnosticism and Early Christianity, revised edition. (New York: Harper & Row, 1966).

6. Lebreton and Zeiller, *Heresy and Orthodoxy*, pp. 49–61.

7. Ibid., pp. 74–77.

8. Quoted in Lebreton and Zeiller, pp. 78–79. Irenaeus has other paraphrases of the Creed in his works. One appears in the *Demonstration of Apostolic Preaching*, vi, which differs from the one quoted above from *Adversus Haereses* in that the latter includes the mysteries of the Christ's life in the third article, whereas in the *Demonstration* Irenaeus attaches them to the second article. See Lebreton and Zeiller, p. 112.

9. William P. Loewe, "Myth and Counter-Myth: Irenaeus' Story of Salvation," in *Interpreting Tradition*, ed. Jane Kopas (Chico, CA: Scholars Press, 1984), pp. 39–54.

10. Quoted by Loewe, pp. 43–44.

11. Kelly, *Creeds*, p. 19.

12. Another seventeenth century scholar, James Ussher (1581–1656), sometime archbishop of Armagh, compiled the scheme of world chronology that remained standard into the nineteenth century. His *Annales Veteris et Novi Testamenti* (1650–54) was the source of the dates that were regularly inserted in the margins of the King James Version of the Bible: creation, 4004 B.C.; the Flood, 2349; the Exodus, 1491; and so on. See Alan Richardson, *The Bible in the Age of Science* (Philadelphia: Fortress Press, 1961), pp. 41–42 and James Barr, "Why Was the World Created in 4004 B.C.: Archbishop Ussher and Biblical Archeology," *Bulletin of the John Rylands University Library of Manchester* 67:2(Spring 1985): 575–608.

13. *Origins* 11(Oct. 15, 1981):279.

14. Bruce Vawter, *On Genesis: A New Reading* (Garden City, NY: Doubleday, 1977), p. 57.

15. Robert Butterworth, *The Theology of Creation* (Notre Dame, IN: Fides Publishers, 1969), pp. 9, 22.

THE SECOND ARTICLE:
SON AND REDEEMER

We believe in one Lord, Jesus Christ,
* the only Son of God,*
* eternally begotten of the Father,*
* God from God, Light from Light,*
* true God from true God,*
* begotten, not made, one in Being with the Father.*
* Through him all things were made.*
* For us men and for our salvation*
*   he came down from heaven:*
* by the power of the Holy Spirit*
*   he was born of the Virgin Mary, and became man.*
* For our sake he was crucified under Pontius Pilate;*
*   he suffered, died, and was buried.*
*   On the third day he rose again*
*   in fulfillment of the Scriptures;*
*   he ascended into heaven*
*   and is seated at the right hand of the Father.*
* He will come again in glory to judge the living and the dead,*
*   and his kingdom will have no end.*

3

Names, Titles
and Relationships

"One Jesus Christ, the only Son of God"

The anonymous, the nameless, are persons without identity. They are at best marginal to society. It is as if no one knows them; they are not people who can "be called," addressed as persons. To be human is to have a name. The name of each one of us points to family ties, establishes social relationships, situates us in time and place, and is basic to conversation and dialogue. Thus the first clue to a person's identity, including that of Jesus of Nazareth, is one's name.

The second article of the Creed in both of its most common forms, the Apostles' Creed and the Ecumenical Creed of Constantinople, introduces the name of Jesus joined to a series of titles that further define his mission and ministry. WE BELIEVE IN ONE LORD, JESUS CHRIST, THE ONLY SON OF GOD. Each of the titles—Christ, Lord, only Son—points up a particular aspect of his work; taken together they present a composite of christologies.[1] Epithets or tag words, they function as convenient labels for the beliefs that Christians came to hold about Jesus. Those mentioned in the Creed, though the oldest and most important, are only a few of the honorific titles conferred on Jesus in

62

the New Testament. In this chapter we first consider the significance of Jesus' name and the titles Christ, Lord, and Son of God, with the insights they bring to our understanding of his person and his work. Then, we make some remarks on the uniqueness of Jesus in connection with the creedal affirmation THE *ONLY* SON OF GOD.

NAMES AND TITLES OF JESUS

"The Name"   "Jesus" is actually the Greek form of the Hebrew *Yeshua*, which in turn was a shortened form of *Joshua* (*Yᵉ hosu'a*). Yeshua, a common name at the beginning of the Christian era, means "Yahweh saves." To the Semitic mind, one's name revealed something of one's character and calling. The angel who appeared to Joseph in a dream told him Mary was "to have a son and you are to name him Jesus because he will save the people from their sins" (Mt 1:21). Thus in New Testament times the name of Jesus, regarded as almost inseparable from his person, becomes the object of meditation and theological reflection.

In the earliest days of the church "the Name" took on special significance. In speaking to the crowd gathered on Pentecost, Peter quoted the prophet Joel saying, "Then shall everyone be saved who calls on the name of the Lord" (Acts 2:21). When the Jewish leaders asked "by what power or in whose name" John and Peter had restored a cripple to health, Peter answered:

> . . . you and all the people of Israel must realize that it was done in the name of Jesus Christ the Nazorean whom you crucified and whom God raised from the dead. In the power of that name this man stands before you perfectly sound. (Acts 4:10)

Jewish and, later, Roman authorities persecuted the Christians because of "the Name," but the disciples were elated "that they had been judged worthy of ill-treatment for the sake of the Name" (Acts 5:21).

We have already noted how in the ancient world a name is the extension of the person. Reverence for one's name is reverence for the person. Thus it became the custom to bow one's head at the mention of Jesus' name in the liturgy. The origins of the practice are obscure, but it was fostered in the spirit of the ancient hymn in Philippians, ". . . at Jesus' name every knee must bend . . . and every tongue proclaim to the glory of God the Father: Jesus Christ is Lord!'" (More on the hymn below.) In the eleventh century St. Bernard of Clairvaux frequently discoursed on Jesus' name. His words have an intensity that is at once inspirational and poetic:

> The name of Jesus is not only light, it is also food. Are you not strengthened whenever you meditate on it? What else can so renew your fatigued spiritual powers, bolster virtue, make good and upright habits grow, foster pure affections? . . . "Jesus" is honey to the mouth, sweet song to the ear, joyful delight to the heart. But it is also a medicine. Is someone sad among us? Let "Jesus" come into his heart and from there leap to his lips. And behold, as the light of His name arises, all clouds pass, and cheerfulness returns. Has someone lapsed into sin? Worse, is despair pushing him headlong into a trap where death awaits his soul? Surely, if he invokes the name of Life, he will be revitalized at once.[2]

Very early on, Christians began to develop a kind of theology of the Name. For them it conjured up the person of the Savior and everything he stood for. They ascribed many offices and titles to him in order to explain what he did and how he appeared, but these "nicknames," as it were, were culturally conditioned in a way that the name Jesus, like any proper name, is not.

"The Anointed One"   In response to Jesus' question, "Who do people say that I am?" Peter answered, according to one account, "You are the Messiah!" (Mk 8:28-29). And in another account he added, "the Son of the Living God" (Mt 16:16). "Messiah" was translated into Greek as *christos*. It designates an "anointed one," a person singled out by God for a special mission. Peter's confession of faith seems to indicate that already during his earthly life Jesus was recognized as the "christ," that is, the "anointed." In the Acts of the Apostles Peter says, "I take it you know what has been reported all over Judea about Jesus of Nazareth, beginning in Galilee with the baptism John preached; of the way God anointed him with the Holy Spirit and power. He went about doing good works and healing all who were in the grip of the devil, and God was with him" (Acts 10:37-38).

It is worthy of note that this text that speaks of the anointing of Jesus also refers specifically to Jesus' baptism. The anointing, coming as it did at the beginning of his public ministry, evokes the Old Testament images of king, priest, and prophet, all three of whom were traditionally anointed as they were commissioned. The Hebrew Scriptures used "messiah"—"the anointed one"—to designate the kings of Israel. It carried with it political connotations associated with the endurance of the Davidic dynasty (see Pss 18:51; 89:39,52; 132:10,17). In the period after the destruction of Jerusalem when the dynasty was no more, the title came to be used for the high priest (Lev 4:3,5). Later, when the faithful remnant returned from the Babylonian exile to rebuild the city and the Temple, the national hopes of the Jewish people began to reshape their messianic expectations. They looked to the future for a messiah—one who was to come—a glorious figure like David who would reestablish the kingdom.

It is obvious that the followers of Jesus would have had difficulty in picturing Jesus as the messiah of these late Jewish expectations strongly flavored with nationalism. In human terms he did not have an aura of glory or victory, nor had he delivered Israel and reestablished the kingdom. In fact the Gospel accounts make it appear that Jesus felt it necessary to correct the grandiose expectations that his early disciples had for him. At Caesarea Philippi, when Peter acclaimed him as the Messiah, Jesus charged him and the other disciples to keep such thoughts to themselves. Furthermore, it was on that very occasion that he proceeded to make the first announcement of his passion, death, and resurrection. The popular image of the Messiah as a champion of Jewish nationalism had to undergo a major transformation before it could be applied to Jesus. He not only rejected all political aspirations, but he never made an explicit claim to be the Messiah. The closest Jesus came to applying the title to himself was when Pilate asked him point blank, "Are you the Messiah, the Son of the Blessed One?" Jesus answered: "I am; and you will see the Son of Man seated at the right hand of the Power and coming with the clouds of heaven" (Mk 14:61-62). "The Son of Man," the epithet that Jesus himself seems to have preferred, competes with the image of Messiah in the New Testament accounts. Both titles relate to the eschatological work of Jesus, and we shall have occasion to discuss "Son of Man" at greater length in connection with the *parousia* (Chapter 13).

After Jesus' death and resurrection his disciples began to develop a more spiritualized notion of the Messiah. The title was seen to refer not to the courtly splendor of an earthly monarch but to interior glory and moral power, to a savior who delivered Israel not from political bondage but from the bondage of sin. They began to understand what Jesus had said about suffering (see Lk 24:26,46) and realized that his own suffering and death were necessary steps on the way to establishing the messianic kingdom. The unique mission that Jesus claimed for himself in preaching the kingdom came to be identified with his role as Messiah. Later they recognized, as is evident in the infancy narratives (Mt 1:23; 2:6; Lk 1:31-33), that Jesus was Messiah from the moment of his Incarnation, and it was only a matter of time before they came to see that Jesus' messiahship was grounded in his divinity.

A reading of the New Testament makes it clear that "messiah" was the preferred title for Jesus. In its Greek form, *christos*, it came to be regarded almost as a surname. In the works of St. Paul, for example, the Greek form appears very frequently, but Paul seldom uses it in the sense that "messiah" was understood in Judaism (for an exception, see Rom 9:5).[3] While "Jesus Christ" commonly appears in Pauline writings as a proper name, "Christ Jesus" is frequent in Ephesians (e.g., 2:6; 3:6; 3:21) and the Pastoral Epistles.

"Christ Jesus" is the form found in the oldest examples of the Creed. In the baptismal rite described by St. Hippolytus in *The Apostolic Tradition*, the catechumen—before being immersed the second time—is asked, "Dost thou believe in Christ Jesus, the Son of God . . .?" Thus into the third century the term retained something of the original significance of a title, "the anointed." J. N. D. Kelly says "Christ Jesus" is the early form and indicates the primitive origins of the second article of the Creed.[4] The special appeal of "messiah" (Christ) for early Christians was that this title better than any other captured the rich diversity of Jesus' ministry. It clearly situated Jesus in the Davidic line; it spoke of his saving work; and it pointed to the present and future kingdom of God. In short, it "embraced the fullness of meaning found in the person of Jesus, his earthly activity and his fate."[5]

Even as the understanding of "messiah" evolved and changed in the Christian community, the church continued to underscore the idea of anointing because of its obvious connection with the baptismal ritual in which the anointing with oil—chrism (a cognate of *christos*)—has a prominent part.[6] The disciples came to be called Christians (Acts 11:26), not simply because they were followers of Jesus, whom they had come to regard as the Messiah, but because they themselves were anointed.

"Jesus Is Lord"   Throughout the New Testament the title *Christos* is frequently joined to another popular epithet, *Kyrios*—"Lord." Peter concluded his address on Pentecost with the cry, "Therefore let the whole house of Israel know beyond any doubt that God has made both Lord and Messiah this Jesus whom you crucified" (Acts 2:36). The phrase "Jesus is Lord," found repeatedly in Paul's writings (Phil 2:11; 1 Cor 8:6; 12:3; 2 Cor 4:5; Rom 10:9; Col 2:6), is thought to represent the oldest creedal formula in Christianity. John's Gospel narrates how Thomas, "one of the Twelve," after overcoming his skepticism about the resurrection, professed, "My Lord and my God!" (Jn 20:28). Judging from the Epistles of Saint Paul, the earliest written records we have, it was not long before "the Lord" became the customary designation for the Risen Christ.

"Jesus is Lord" recalls the ancient symbolism of kingship and enthronement. From the beginning, Christian preaching—the kerygma—identified Jesus with the Davidic king whom the psalmist had exalted: "The Lord said to my Lord, 'Sit at my right hand till I make your enemies your footstool' " (Ps 110:1). Of all the Old Testament passages quoted by New Testament writers, this opening verse of Psalm 110 is the most frequently cited. The glorified Jesus sits now at God's right hand (Acts 2:33; 5:31; 7:55; Rom 8:34). The concept of Lord, even more than "Son of God," expressed for the primitive Christian community the reality of his divine sonship and power. "Yours is princely power in the day of your birth, in holy splendor; before the daystar, like the dew, I have begotten you" (Ps 110:3).

Kyrios is the preferred title for Jesus in the Pauline writings. Paul, aware of the fact that the pagan religions of Asia Minor, Syria, and Egypt called their gods and goddesses *kyrios* and *kyria*, says that "for us" there is only one Lord, Jesus Christ (1 Cor 8:6). The Roman emperors were also called *kyrios* in recognition of their sovereignty and power, and while the title referred primarily to their political power, in much of the Mediterranean world it carried with it the suggestion of divinity. Among the Jews of Palestine the Aramaic equivalent of *kyrios* was *mar*. Texts in the Gospels indicate that in addressing Jesus the disciples at times used some form of *mar*—for example, *mar'i* and *mar'an*, "my Lord" and "our Lord" respectively. This usage caused him to say at one point, "None of those who cry out, 'Lord, Lord,' will enter the kingdom of God" (Mt 7:21; Lk 6:46).

The disciples in Jerusalem continued to address Jesus as "Lord" after his death and resurrection, but the title takes on a different meaning. The Aramaic expression *maranatha*—"Our Lord, come!"— seems to have been a liturgical formula. Its primitive character is indicated by the fact that St. Paul, though writing in Greek, quotes the Aramaic form at the end of his First Epistle to the Corinthians. It appears again in the Book of Revelation 22:20 and in the eucharistic text in the *Didache* (10, 6). The Risen Christ has become the object of worship and adoration. "Lord" has become a majestic title given to Christ in view of his resurrection and exaltation at the right hand of God. It clearly implies belief that Jesus is divine.

The imagery of royal enthronement expresses the conviction that Jesus uniquely mediates the authority of God (see below, Chapters 7 and 12). In coming to refer to him as "Lord," especially in the context of the liturgy, the early Christians had in effect bestowed on him a title that was used for Yahweh. Transcending ordinary limits of humanity, he represents God to men and women of all times and exercises sovereignty, the prerogative of the Lord God Almighty, over all creation. The ancient hymn quoted by St. Paul indicates that by the time Paul wrote the Epistle to the Philippians the church had already carried this belief a step—a giant step!—further. Jesus does not act merely as an agent of God's rule but is in fact the one of whom Isaiah, speaking of the Lord God, had said, "I am God; there is no other! . . . To me every knee shall bend. . . ." (Is 45:22,23). The Isaiahan text is clearly the source of the hymn's closing line:

> Though he was in the form of God,
>   he did not deem equality with God
>   something to be grasped at.
>
> Rather, he emptied himself
>   and took the form of a slave,
>   being born in the likeness of men.
>
> He was known to be of human estate,
>   and it was thus that he humbled himself,
>   obediently accepting even death,
>   death on a cross.
>
> Because of this,
>   God highly exalted him
>   and bestowed on him the name
>   above every other name,

So that at Jesus' name
  every knee must bend
  in the heavens, on the earth,
  and under the earth,
  and every tongue proclaim
  to the glory of God the Father:
JESUS CHRIST IS LORD! (Phil 2:6-11)

"Son of God"   The multiple meanings invested in the title "Lord" indicate how culture and the meanings of words change. Today, Christians are more likely to point to the title "Son of God" as evidence of their belief in Jesus' divinity. In the course of time, many theologians contrasted it with another biblical title, "Son of Man," and used the distinction to emphasize the two natures in Christ. It is noteworthy, however, that this important title, which is the basis for the expression in the Creed THE ONLY SON OF GOD, does not appear in the primitive kerygma. In oriental religions "son of god" commonly designated kings, who were thought to be begotten by gods, and the designation was extended to miracle workers and others who seemed to exercise divine power. The phrase was also common in Israel, but there it signified a special election or call from God rather than implying divine power. The Old Testament referred to the whole people of Israel as the "Son of God." The title was also applied to kings and people who had a special commission from God such as angels (and perhaps the Messiah). Thus in the ancient world and even in the Bible, "Son of God" carried connotations different from what it has today. As we shall see in the following chapters, the full implications of Jesus' divine sonship developed through a number of stages. Here we simply examine the title as a creedal statement that along with "Lord" and "Messiah" is among the most ancient faith formulas that have come down to us.

In Mark's Gospel the title, though infrequent, is prominent. The Gospel opens with "Here begins the gospel of Jesus Christ, the Son of God" and climaxes at his death when the Roman centurion who has observed the execution declared, "Clearly this man was the Son of God!" (15:39). While none of the examples of St. Peter's preaching in Acts makes reference to the Son of God, at Caesarea Philippi (according to Matthew) Peter confesses Jesus not only as Messiah but as "Son of the living God" (16:16). Jesus' resurrection confirmed the disciples in this knowledge that "no mere man can reveal" (Mt 16:17). Paul echoes an early profession of faith when he speaks in the introduction to the Epistle to the Romans of "the gospel concerning his Son, who was descended from David according to the flesh but was made Son of God in power according to the spirit of holiness, by his resurrection from the dead: Jesus Christ our Lord" (1:3-4).

Similarly the First Epistle of John quotes an ancient creed: "When anyone acknowledges that Jesus is the Son of God, God dwells in him and he in God" (4:15; see 2:23). Further evidence of the title in the earliest creeds is found in Hebrews, which speaks of "Jesus, the Son of God" and adds, "let us hold fast to our profession of faith" (4:15).

The great New Testament scholar Oscar Cullmann conjectures that this early creed "quite probably" had a place in the earliest baptismal liturgy.[7] A trace of this primitive formula of faith made its way into the account of the baptism of the Ethiopian eunuch in Acts (8:36-38). To his question "What is to keep me from being baptized?" Philip answers, "If you believe with all your heart, you may." And in turn the eunuch replies, "I believe that Jesus is the Son of God." Even if this exchange, which is not found in some ancient manuscripts and is omitted in most modern English translations, is an interpolation, it is a very early one. What more fitting occasion to confess Jesus as "Son of God" than baptism? It was at Jesus' own baptism that "a voice came from the heavens: "You are my beloved Son. On you my favor rests" (Mk 1:11).

By adding the title "savior" to the formula put into the mouth of the eunuch, the early Christians constructed a popular acrostic still seen in churches and even on automobile bumper stickers. They used the first letter of each of the Greek words for "Jesus Christ, Son of God, Savior": ('Iesous Christos Theou Yios Soter) and thus spelled the Greek word for "fish," (ICHTHYS). Tertullian, the first Christian Latin author of consequence, writing about the year A.D. 200, says that the baptized, "after the example of our ICHTHUS," are like little fishes (pisciculi) who are born in the water and cannot thrive apart from the water.[8] Already in the second century the fish appears as a common symbol of Christ in literature, inscriptions, and art. Because of its sacramental significance it is associated with the eucharist as well as with baptism. The fish is pictured as food in banquet scenes in the Roman catacombs, and other eucharistic associations are found in funeral inscriptions—Christ is the "fish of the living."[9]

"God's Only Son"   It was also in the second century, again in response to the the Valentinian gnostics, that the adjective ONLY was inserted into the Creed. The Greek for "only son" is *monogenes* (literally, "only begotten"); it appears several times in the writings of John (e.g., Jn 1:14,18; 3:16,18; 1 Jn 4:9) but nowhere else in the New Testament. The Valentinians read it as a proper name, the designation of their aeon Nous, whom they referred to as *Monogenes*. They boldly cited the author of the Johannine Gospel for support on the basis of the text, "We beheld his glory, glory as of an *only begotten [Mono-genes]*. . . .") (1:14). St. Irenaeus counterattacked by arguing that the true *Monogenes* is none other than the Word, who, in obedience to his father, became flesh as our Lord Jesus Christ, suffered for us, and rose again.[10] By all accounts it was about the same time that the title was introduced into the Creed as a rebuttal to Valentinus and his disciples.

The title "Son of God" is invested with a quite exact meaning in the Johannine writings. It occurs twenty-five times in John's Gospel and twenty-two times in his First Epistle. It is only in John's Gospel that we find Jesus appropriating the title to himself (10:36). John restricts it to Jesus and never applies it, as does Paul, to humans. (For the evangelist people are children (Greek = *tekna*) of God, but only Jesus is God's *son*.[11] It is because Jesus and he alone is Son of God in a divine sense that he can give believers the "power to become God's children" (Jn 1:12). Thus the designation *Monogenes* connotes "only" in the sense of "unique"—a relationship to God that differs from everyone else's.

Another connotation is suggested in Luke and Hebrews. Luke tells that Jesus raised the "only son" of the widow of Nain from the dead (7:12). Hebrews cites the typology of Abraham, who was prepared to sacrifice his "only son" Isaac (11:17; see Gen 22:1-9) and adds that Abraham "reasoned that God was able to raise from the dead, and so he received Isaac back as a symbol" (v. 19). The author sees in Isaac's deliverance a figure of the resurrection of Christ. (The Roman Canon, Eucharistic Prayer I, also alludes to the Abraham-Isaac typology but uses it to emphasize the idea of sacrifice.)

It is, however, the uniqueness of Jesus in the Johannine sense that attracts the attention of contemporary theologians. Every individual is by definition unique, one of a kind, even in his or her relationship to God. The New Testament, however, clearly distances the kind of relationship Jesus had with the Father from that of other humans. The Johannine Gospel makes a clear distinction in having Jesus say, "I am ascending to my Father and your Father, to my God and your God" (Jn 20:17). It is a distinction consistently maintained thoughout the Gospel accounts. Jesus, aware of his own unique relationship to God, is quoted only once as speaking of "our Father"—in teaching the Lord's prayer (Mt 6:13). The question is, Why is Jesus' relationship to God so special, different and definitive?

The reason why Jesus' name is above every other name is that it is joined with Yahweh's own title, "Lord." In calling Jesus "Lord" in an unqualified sense, Christians attributed to him dominion over the created universe, which is the prerogative solely of Yahweh, and the right to be adored by all creatures. Philippians 2:10 echoes Isaiah 45:23: "To me every knee shall bend; by me every tongue shall swear." It was the Christians' way of confessing their faith in the divinity of Christ. (Later the title will be used also for the third person of the Trinity in recognition of the Spirit's divinity.)

The full implications of Jesus' position as the *only* Son of God will become clear in the next chapter as we work out a fuller presentation of christology; but by way of conclusion to these reflections on the name and titles of Jesus it is important to emphasize that because of his unique vocation as Son of God we have in him the full and definitive revelation of God as Father. We can no longer think of the Godhead apart from Jesus Christ:

> Everything has been given over to me by my Father. No one knows the Son but the Father, and no one knows the Father but the Son—and anyone to whom the Son wishes to reveal him. (Mt 11:27; see Jn 14:6)

God, it is true, made and continues to make the divine presence known in many ways, but these manifestations, preliminary and provisional, are interpreted in the light of the revelation made known by and in Jesus. His message will not be superseded; it is the final word:

> In times past, God spoke in fragmentary and varied ways to our fathers through the prophets; in this, the final age, he has spoken to us through his Son, whom he has made heir of all things and through whom he first created the universe. This Son is the reflection of the Father's glory, the exact representation of the Father's being, and he sustains all things by his powerful word. (Heb 1:1-3)

It took centuries for the church to agree on language that properly delineated the relationship of the Father and the Son. The effort, painful and often divisive, is the story of the next chapter.

Notes

1. "Titles of Christ," in *Jerome Bible Commentary*, vol.2, pp. 769–777. Henceforth, *JBC*. Oscar Cullmann, *The Christology of the New Testament*. 2d ed. (London: SCM Press, 1963).

2. Sermon 15 on the Canticle of Canticles, quoted in Vincent Taylor, *The Names of Jesus* (London: Macmillian & Co., 1962), p.8.

3. *JBC*, vol.2, p. 774, #37.

4. *Creeds*, p. 139.

5. Wolfhart Pannenberg, *The Apostles' Creed* (Philadelphia: Westminster Press, 1972), p. 57.

6. Kelly, *Creeds*, p. 141.

7. *Christology*, p. 290.

8. Andre Hamman, ed., *Baptism: Ancient Liturgies and Patristic Texts* (Staten Island, NY: Alba House, 1967), p. 30.

9. *NCE* 5:943–946; 7:323–324.

10. Kelley, *Creeds*, p. 142, n. 7.

11. Joseph A. Fitzmyer, *JBC,* vol.2, p. 776.

4

The Son a Lesser God?
The Arian Controversy

"Eternally begotten, one in being with the Father"

The most obvious difference between the Apostles' Creed and the Nicene-Constantinopolitan Creed is length. The latter is substantially longer, principally because of the insertion of several lines that further explain the relationship of the Son to the Father:

> . . . eternally begotten of the Father, God from God, Light from Light, true God from true God, begotten, not made, one in Being with the Father. Through him all things were made.

The addition of these lines was intended to clarify Christian belief about the Godhead. They do not represent a change in church doctrine, but they do signal a new form and function of the Creed. In the Introduction we quoted the English scholar C. H. Turner, who said of the Nicene Creed, "The old creeds were creeds for catechumens, the new creed was a creed for bishops."[1] Because the transition took place in the cauldron of controversy, the change was neither conscious nor abrupt. The issues and circumstances surrounding this change and the first steps in the development of the so-called Nicene Creed are the subject of this chapter.

Early in the fourth century the fortunes of the church changed dramatically. Constantine had wrested control of the Roman Empire from his rivals. His mother, Helen, was a Christian, and he himself was well disposed toward the church, though Christians were only a small minority within the empire. In 312, he issued the Edict of Milan, which guaranteed the civil rights of Christians and restored church property confiscated by his predecessors. With the threat of persecution removed, Christianity was no longer an underground movement. Its bishops and leaders became public figures, and the Roman authorities, especially the emperors, took an interest in the internal affairs of the church. Thus when controversy broke out in the Christian community over sacramental practice (as it did in North Africa), over the organization of dioceses (as happened in Asia Minor), and over doctrine, the imperial authorities intervened both directly and indirectly.

COUNCILS AND CONTROVERSY

The public forum in which questions of organization, discipline, and doctrine were handled was the council, an assembly of church leaders. There was precedent for these open confrontations in the "Council of Jersualem" about A.D. 49, when Paul and Barnabas, representing the Antioch church, met with James, Peter, and John, the leaders of the Palestinian community, to work out a policy regarding the obligations of Gentile converts toward the Mosaic Law (see Gal 2:1-16). Throughout the period of persecutions, bishops of an area met in regional councils to deal with such issues as the date for Easter, the life-style of clerics, and questions of doctrine. By the third century the bishops in North Africa met in council twice a year. Councils also met regularly in Egypt and in Syria and Palestine. After the Edict of Milan, these regional councils continued to meet, but with the church's new status it was possible to hold ecumenical—worldwide—councils which brought together bishops of many provinces and regions.

Ecumenical councils were held at Nicea (the site of the present-day Turkish village of Iznik, about sixty miles from Istanbul) in 325 and 787. In between there were five others: three at Constantinopole (modern Istanbul), in 381, 553, and 680; one at Ephesus in 431; and one at

Chalcedon in 451. The sites were chosen for the convenience of travel: all were easily accessible by water or land from the imperial capital. There were other councils, but it is these seven that are recognized by Eastern and Western churches alike as truly "ecumenical." While it is the practice of most general histories of the church to focus (as we do here) on the theological issues discussed at these councils, it should be noted that they dealt with a broad range of topics covering many aspects of church life. The number of participants at these early assemblies, never more than a few hundred, was not nearly as great as at Vatican II, and the procedures were different, but the group dynamics were much the same. There were committees, factions, and compromises—the standpatters on the right and the progressives on the left, each pushing hard to sway the majority who made up the middle. But one important difference distinguishes these early councils from the Vatican II: the active interest that the civil authority, the emperor, took in the proceedings. The bishops looked to imperial authority to back their decisions—with force when necessary. The emperor came to see himself as the vicar of Christ on earth, responsible for the well-being of the church.

The underlying issue in the early councils, though often obscured by personal rivalries, political machinations, and abstract theological reasoning, continued to be Jesus' question: "Who do people say that I am?" The question continues to be asked today. It touches the very core of the Christian message. Despite the fact that the bishops and theologians seem at times to be dealing with matters far removed from everyday life, the more insightful leaders never lost sight of the pastoral implications of the arguments. In reviewing the events surrounding the early councils, this chapter concentrates on the christological question, always with an eye to the broader issues involved. Furthermore, in the years since Vatican II the christological question has once again emerged as the number-one topic of discussion in theological circles. The christological controversies of the fourth and fifth centuries continue in a variety of ways to shape the contemporary debate. Then as now it proved impossible to consider christology apart from the mystery of the Trinity.

For reasons of clarity and brevity we present the christological debate as if it were a three-act play, with Act II having a number of scenes.

ACT I: MONARCHIANISM

The first act predates the Peace of Constantine and sets the stage for the great councils. The place is Rome, where the debate over the relationship of the Father and Son preoccupied bishops, clergy, and lay leaders for the greater part of the third century.[2] At this time the focus was on the Trinity: How does one explain to the simple believer that the Father is divine, the Son is divine, and the Holy Spirit is divine (though this last did not figure prominently in the debate at this time), and at the same time insist that God is one?

Although the debate was not confined to Rome, it was in the Eternal City that three different approaches to the question dramatized the issues. The first, heavily dependent on the Fourth Gospel, is called *Logos christology*; in time it would prove dominant. Though the other two approaches started from very different premises, they are generally grouped under one label, *monarchianism*—modalistic monarchianism and dynamic monarchianism—because they were not willing to allow any differentiation whatsoever within the godhead. (It was Tertullian, the early African writer, who coined the term "monarchians" to describe anti-Trinitarian doctrines that held that God is one in *person* as well as in nature.) Of the two groups, the "modalistic monarchians" were the more numerous in Rome. They held that God appears now in one guise (*modus*), now in another: in creation as the Father, in the Incarnation as the Son, and at Pentecost as the Spirit. They are simply three names of the one God, manifested in different ways according to circumstances. They went so far as to say "that Christ was the Father himself, and that the Father himself was born and suffered and died."[3] (That was why St. Cyprian, another African writer of the third century, nicknamed them Father-sufferers, "patripassians.") The most noted leader of the modalist school in Rome was Sabellius, whose name became permanently linked with the doctrine so that modalism and Sabellianism are all but synonymous.

Modalism had a certain intellectual appeal in that it clearly repudiated the polytheism of the pagans and any hint of "tritheism" that some might read into the Christian doctrine of the Trinity.[4] Although modalism was rejected because of the rank nominalism implicit in the absolute identification of Father, Son, and Spirit (the only differences in the Trinity were the names), by the same token it maintained the equality of their roles. This latter point distinguished modalism from the other common form of monarchianism, *dynamic monarchianism*. Dynamic monarchians maintained that the spiritual power ("dynamism") enjoyed by the Son was not his by nature but was gift from the Father.

The dynamic monarchians held that Jesus was Son of God by adoption. They accounted for his "divinity" in several ways. Some saw him as a man of holy life, born of the the Virgin Mary, upon whom the divine Christ (or Holy Spirit) descended at his baptism. Others held he became divine at his resurrection. The godly quality in Jesus, they said, was the spiritual power of the Father. They reduced the relationship between Father and Son to human categories and thus made it easier to understand. As with all systems that take an adoptionist approach, dynamic monarchianism, even while exalting Jesus' power beyond that of mere mortals, portrayed him as less than the Father.

The third approach, the one that gradually came to be accepted as the church's official teaching, developed a position known as *Logos christology*. It relied heavily on the Fourth Gospel, especially the prologue:

> In the beginning was the Word; the Word was in God's presence, and the Word was God. He was present to God in the beginning. Through him all things came into being, and apart from him nothing came to be. (Jn 1: 1-3)

The Johannine prologue is fundamental to the Christian doctrine of the Trinity. It presents the Word of God as coeternal with the Godhead itself and as collaborator in the work of creation. As St. Irenaeus noted in his polemic against the gnostics, the Word was a partner in creation, not a product of it. Early on, St. Justin, philosopher and martyr (d. 156), as well as Irenaeus, emphasized that Jesus embodied the *Logos* (the "Word") of God. Because the Logos is the mirror image of God, the Father and Son are distinguishable but inseparable. Their nature is the same. The advocates of Logos christology insisted on the Son's preexistence—that is, that he coexisted with the Father even before the Incarnation. (It goes without saying that they rejected the notion of dynamic monarchianism that the Logos, regarded by them as an impersonal force, came to dwell in Jesus only at the time of his baptism or after the resurrection.)

While the bishops of Rome were prominent in opposing the various forms of monarchianism, Tertullian of Carthage must be credited with turning the tide in favor of Logos christology. Although Tertullian was a difficult character in many ways and ultimately broke with the church over sacramental discipline, his exposition of the doctrine of the Trinity (all the more noteworthy because it was one of the earlist theological works in Latin) laid the foundation for a sound christology. He formulated a description of the Trinity as three "persons" in one divine nature and clearly distinguished the divine from the human in Jesus.

ACT II: ENTER ARIUS

Scene I   With Act II the action shifts eastward: first to Alexandria and then to Nicea and Constantinople. In Scene 1 we see the beginnings of the Arian controversy that was to split the church into warring factions, pitting East against West and bishop against bishop. Arius, the man whose teaching ignited the bitter wrangling, was a highly regarded presbyter in the church at Alexandria who was charged with the pastoral care of one of the city's major boroughs, Baucalis. Many factors accounted for the popularity of his teaching, not the least of which was his Platonic view of the universe (neo-Platonism was the dominant philosophy of the day). Arius' christology was grounded on the Platonic premise that God's absolute transcendence situates the Godhead in such splendid isolation from the cosmos that no direct relationship with the created world is possible.[5]

For Arius, Christ was a mediator, a god of secondary order, not begotten in eternity but fashioned, like other creatures, out of "nothing." Created—made—by God's free will, he was a lesser god. Arius allowed that the Son was "the first born" of creatures and God's agent in making the world, but he denied that the Son could be coeternal or one in essence with the Father. "The Son," he said, "had a beginning, but God . . . is without beginning."[6] To Arius' way of thinking, Christ was neither truly God nor truly human. In the Incarnation the Logos, who Arius agreed preexisted, entered a human body without, however, appropriating the functions of the human intellect and will. Thus Christ was a *tertium quid*—something of a hybrid—a position that many, including the bishop of Alexandria, found unsatisfactory regarding both his divinity and his humanity.

Arius' teaching brought him into conflict with Alexander, the bishop of Alexandria. The controversy soon grew bitter. About the year 320 Alexander assembled a regional synod at which Arius and a number of his sympathizers were condemned. Arius appealed for help to a friend from his student days in Antioch, Eusebius of Nicomedia, then the eastern capital of the Roman empire. Aided by his influential friends in the episcopacy, Arius lined up support for his position. Alexander, for his part, wrote widely to his fellow bishops, explaining and defending the action he had taken against Arius. Soon the whole ecclesiastical establishment in the eastern half of the empire was in turmoil. Such was the situation in 324 when Constantine crushed his brother-in-law, Licinius, with whom he had shared the imperial power, and became master of the East as well as the West.

Scene 2: The Council of Nicea   Constantine was not the kind of administrator who tolerated any factionalism or quarreling that might threaten order and unity within his realm. He summoned all the bishops of the empire to Nicea for a council which assembled in June 325. Some 300, many accompanied by lower clergy, came at government expense to discuss a variety of topics (including a uniform date for the celebration of Easter), but the principal item on the agenda was to settle the Arian controversy once and for all. Eusebius of Caesarea, the great church historian, left an eyewitness account of the proceedings.[7] Although it is somewhat self-serving, his account is of real value because it recalls that many of the bishops who assembled in the great hall of the imperial palace showed scars of the tortures they had suffered in the persecutions under Constantine's predecessors: some were blind, some lame. They fell into three groups distinguished by their stand vis-a-vis Arius. A small, hard-core faction led by Eusebius of Nicomedia were thoroughgoing Arians; a slightly larger party led by Alexander of Alexandria were equally adamant in their opposition to Arius' teaching; and the third group, the large majority, as a whole were either not well versed in the issues or had not yet made up their minds. In addition Emperor Constantine was conspicuous in the assembly and, though not yet baptized, took an active part in the proceedings.

The popular account of the proceedings, still found in many church history texts, has it that while the bishops easily and quickly repudiated the creed compiled by Arius, they found it more difficult to agree on the best way to phrase a declaration of faith that expressed orthodox belief. The historian Eusebius of Caesarea offered the baptismal creed of his own church as a basis for agreement. It was a confession of faith in the traditional mode and was wholly indefinite as to the theological issues involved. The problem was to find a formula that Arius and his sympathizers could not twist to suit their own purpose, as they had managed to do with every biblical text brought forward to witness to the unity and equality of the Father and Son. The Caesarea creed, therefore, was amended to include a clear anti-Arian statement. The key word inserted, according to Eusebius, at Constantine's insistence, was *homoousios*—"consubstantial," or as modern translations of the Creed have it, ONE IN BEING WITH THE FATHER.

According to this popular account, based on a letter Eusebius sent to his flock in the church of Caesarea, the "Nicene Creed" is basically the baptismal creed of Caesarea with some anti-Arian additions. Eusebius' version of events at Nicea is somewhat suspect, however. Compromised in the eyes of his fellow bishops by his early support of Arius, Eusibius, feeling it necessary to vindicate himself, seems to have exaggerated his own role in the council. A more accurate if less dramatic account of the proceedings suggests that a drafting committee indeed took a local baptismal creed, probably of Syro-Palestinian origin, inserted a number of anti-Arian clauses into the body of the text, and, by way of conclusion, directed a number of unambiguous anathemas (solemn curses!) against Arius' teachings. The addition to that text of the creed made at Nicea is the series of phrases, in italics:

> And in one Lord Jesus Christ, the Son of God, begotten from the Father, only-begotten, *that is, from the substance of the Father, God from God, light from light, true God from true God, begotten not made, of one substance with the Father, through Whom all things came into being, things in heaven and things on earth.*[8]

The phrases inserted were intended as a deliberate rebuttal of the principal tenets of the Arians. Arius and his followers held first of all that the Son, created out of nothing, had nothing in common with the Father as regards his being. Thus the council fathers found it necessary to close every loophole that might mislead Christians to regard the Son's glory merely as a reflection of the Father's and his divinity as less than the Father's. The Nicene Creed ammended the text of the baptismal creed GOD FROM GOD, LIGHT FROM LIGHT, TRUE GOD FROM TRUE GOD, adding ONE IN BEING WITH THE FATHER to make it even clearer that far from being a creature in any sense of the term, the Son was generated from and shared the substance or being of the Father. Even though the

Arians were willing to speak of the Word as "God," they said he was God in name only but not "true" God (see Jn 17:3). Nicea insisted that splendor of the Word shines forth like light from the sun, not like the reflected light of the moon.

But ultimately it was the term *homoousios* that became the slogan of Nicea: The Son is ONE IN BEING WITH THE FATHER. The Arians could not explain it away by clever exegesis. It may have been, as some bishops claimed later, that the phrase had a Sabellian ring, but at the close of the council there was no doubt in anyone's mind, beginning with the Emperor Constantine, that it represented a clear repudiation of the Arian position.

ACT III: THE DEMISE OF ARIANISM

The Council of Nicea had dealt a fatal blow to Arianism, but the movement was a long time in dying. Led by Eusebius of Nicomedia (not to be confused with Eusebius the historian), the Arian party regrouped and set about rehabilitating Arius (in fact, he died in 336 on the day before his friends were formally to restore him to fellowship in the church). Their strategy was simple: by discrediting the leaders of the opposition they would undermine the decisions taken at the council. Their tactics were to enlist the support of the emperor (Constantine died in 337 and was succeeded by his sons, who divided the empire among them) and to make it seem that only the stubbornness of Athanasius and his allies stood in the way of an amicable solution to the controversy that threatened the unity of the church and peace of the empire.

While still a deacon, Athanasius had attended the Council of Nicea as Alexander's secretary. Upon Alexander's death in 328, Athanasius succeeded him as patriarch of Alexandria and as leader of the Nicene party—a group made up of the bishops who would tolerate no compromise with Arianism. Anthanasius spent many of his forty-five years as bishop in exile. Whenever the pro-Arian forces were able to get the ear of the emperor, they managed to banish Athanasius—five times in all—from his see. His fortunes fluctuated with the ebb and flow of the Nicene faith. Because of his charismatic leadership and commitment to the cause of orthodoxy, Athanasius captured the imagination of church historians early on. He was not, however, the intransigent sometimes pictured by friends and enemies alike.[9] Athanasius recognized that Arius' teaching represented in fact a denial of the Trinity as an eternal reality (see Chapter 15). But his decisive criticism of Arius was based on the practical theology of the redemption. For Athanasius the issue was one of salvation: if Christ is not true God, then our hope of redemption is built on sand. "God became man," he wrote, "that we might become gods." The term *homoousios* appears only occasionally in his writings, for he knew that the Nicene faith did not rest on a single term, and he collaborated with bishops who, while repudiating Arius' teaching, had honest objections to the use of *homoousios*.

The years following the Council of Nicea were a time of turmoil, intrigue, and a rolling series of regional synods and councils. For a brief period (353-361) when Constantine's sole surviving son, Constantius, reigned as sole emperor over East and West, imperial policy was decidedly anti-Athanasian. A pagan historian noted that during Constantius' reign the number of bishops traveling back and forth to church synods was such as to disrupt the efficiency of the imperial transport system! Many synods published formulas of faith that were circulated to displace the Creed of Nicea. Some were compromise documents, drafted with the best of intentions; a few attempted to camouflage their pro-Arian sympathy with vague phrases and generalities. Ultimately, however, the leadership of the Arian movement fell into the hands of an uncompromising group known as "Anomoeans"—radicals who, in the tradition of Eusebuis of Nicomedia and Arius himself, openly asserted that the Son is "unlike" (*anomios*) the Father.[10]

The extremism of the Anomoeans sharpened the theological issues and divided the ranks of the bishops who were suspicious of the term *homoousios*. Many bishops, whom history has mistakenly labeled "Semi-Arians," believed that to say the Son is "the same as" or "one in being" with the Father was open to a Sabellian, that is, modalist, interpretation. They favored instead the term *homoiousios*, that is, the Father and Son are of "like substance," and spoke of "three hypostases" in the Godhead. The Homoeousians, adamant in their hostility toward the Anomoeans, came gradually to join forces with Athanasius and his followers in opposition to the Arian position.

The Arian cause, which seemed destined to triumph in the early years of Constantius' reign, went into rapid decline after his death in 361. Another event contributing to the ultimate death of Arianism was a synod held in Alexandria in 362. Presided over by Athanasius, who had recently returned from his fourth exile, the synod helped clarify the issues by setting the groundwork for an agreement regarding terminology. It recognized that it is possible to speak of the Godhead in terms both of "one hypostasis" or "ousia" and of "three hypostases" provided that "one" is not understood in the modalist sense and "three" does not connote "alien in essence."[11]

In summary, two factors were important for the victory of the homoousian party: 1) the extreme Arians (the "Anomoeans") over-played their hand in once again asserting that the Son is "unlike" (*anomoios*) the Father, a position repugnant to most Semi-Arians; and 2) theologians clarified the distinction between substance or nature (*ousia*) and person (*hypostasis*). Once the slogan "one nature, three persons" caught on, the homoousians were able to rid themselves of the stigma of Sabellianism. Thus, in the course of time, the issues surrounding the Arian controversy were clarified and distinctions were made which enabled the Council of Constantinople to agree on a common creed—the Ecumenical Creed that is still in common use in the church today.

THE CREED OF CONSTANTINOPLE

Act III of the christological drama comes to a close in A.D. 381 with the Council of Constantinople. Although we shall have more to say about the council in connection with the third article of the Creed, its actions regarding Arianism were anti-climactic. Nicea had dealt Arianism the death blow; Constantinople nailed the coffin shut. The Creed of Constantinople, sometimes described as "a legitimate expansion" of the Nicene Creed,[12] is in fact not the Creed of Nicea. Like a number of fourth-century creeds, it was made to conform to the Nicene faith by careful editing. Originally the Creed of Constantinople seems to have been a local baptismal creed either of the Antioch or Jerusalem families into which the homoousian teaching of Nicea was incorporated. It is known in the ancient texts and to church historians as "the creed of the 150 Fathers," a reference to the number of bishops who attended the council of 381. In time the Creed of Constantinople became the most widely used formula of faith in Christendom. The cultural domination and political influence of Constantinople, together with the Creed's majestic style and balanced theological content, account for its prominent place in the liturgy. By the sixth century it had become the baptismal confession of almost all the churches in the East, and a Latin translation was used even in Rome for catechetical purposes and in the rite of baptism itself.[13] In the fifth century the Nicene-Constantinopolitan Creed began to be recited in the eucharistic liturgy, for reasons that will be explained below. In the Latin West it was introduced gradually, beginning in Visigothic Spain in the sixth century, where it was seen as a formal gesture repudiating the lingering vestiges of Arianism. The last holdout, Rome, bowing to pressure from the German emperors (who saw themselves as successors of Constantine) introduced it into the Mass in the eleventh century (see Chapter 16).

The reaction against Arianism had an impact on the liturgy of the church in other ways as well. The earliest examples of liturgical prayer were all addressed to the Father, whereas in the fourth century they began to be directed to the Son. The Georgian-Jacobite liturgy, said to have been composed by St. Athanasius, always addresses the Son. From Egypt the practice of praying to the Son spread to all the Eastern liturgies. Moreover, the doxology "Glory to the Father through the Son in the Holy Spirit" was altered because the Arians cited it to show that the Son is subordinate to the Father. Instead, Athanasius substituted the formula we use today: "Glory be to the Father and to the Son and to the Holy Spirit." The old formula was intended to emphasize the priestly mediation of Christ and was perfectly orthodox. The new wording, however, stressed more the equality of the persons in the triune God. (It should be noted, however, that the Roman liturgy did not adopt the practice of praying to the Son until later. Even now the Eucharistic Prayer I—the Roman Canon—invokes the Father, and other liturgical prayers are made in the name of Jesus or "through Christ our Lord.")[14]

The curtain had not come down on the Arian controversy when new aspects of the christological question began to unfold. The Councils of Nicea and Constantinople were concerned with christology only as it touched on the Trinity—namely, how the Son of God related to God in the framework of the three divine persons. Even before that issue was entirely resolved, people began asking about the relationship between the divine nature and the human nature in Jesus. The homoousian doctrine had clarified the position of the divine Logos within the Godhead, but now the question was how the divine Logos—the Word—relates to the human Jesus. It is not only a theological problem but an anthropological one as well. The classic christological controversies which dominated the fifth century as Arianism had dominated the fourth bring us to face the question of what it means to be human. This last question is the subject of the following chapters.

Notes

1. Kelly, *Creeds*, p. 205.

2. William G. Rusch, *The Trinitarian Controversy* (Philadelphia: Fortress Press, 1980), pp. 8–17. Jaroslav Pelikan, *The Emergence of the Catholic Tradition (100–600)* (Chicago: University of Chicago Pres, 1971), pp. 172–190.

3. W. Walker, *A History of the Christian Church*, rev. ed. (New York: Charles Scribner's Sons, 1959), p. 69. Henceforth *History*.

4. The Jehovah Witnesses charge traditional Christianity with "tritheism," for example, see *"The Word"—Who Is He? According to John* (Watch Tower and Tract Society of Pennsylvania, 1962), p. 7.

5. In recent years a number of important books have appeared which reexamine Arius and his teaching. These new studies investigate the sources and the methodology used in interpreting them; they attempt to reconstruct the political, social and theological milieux which formed the background for the Arian controversy. See Charles Kannengiesser, "Arius and the Arians," *Theological Studies* 44:3 (1983):456–475.

6. Walker, *History*, p. 107.

7. The text of Eusebius' letter can be found in Rusch, *Trinitarian Controversy*, pp. 57–60. See Timothy D. Barnes, *Constantine and Eusebius* (Cambridge, MA: Harvard University Press, 1981), pp. 212–219.

8. Kelly, *Creeds*, pp. 205–230.

9. The sixteenth centenary of Athanasius' death (A.D. 373) seems to have been the occasion for renewed interest in his life and works. Charles Kannengiesser, "The Athanasian Decade 1974–1984: A Bibliographical Report," *Theological Studies* 46:3 (1965):524–541.

10. Kelly, *Creeds*, pp. 283–284. Pelikan, *Catholic Tradition*, pp. 201–209.

11. Kelly, *Creeds*, p. 284. Walker, *History*, p. 115.

12. Kelly, *Creeds*, p. 332.

13. Kelly, *Creeds*, p. 347; Joseph A. Jungmann, *Missarum Solemnia. The Mass of the Roman Rite* (New York: Benziger, 1951–1955), vol. I, pp. 461–474.

14. K. Adam, *The Christ of Faith* (New York: Mentor-Omega Books, 1962), p. 42–43.

5

Salvation and Sin

"For us and for our salvation"

Cur Deus Homo? is the title of a work by St. Anselm of Canterbury (d. 1109). It asks a question that continues to bother the theologian in the classroom and the person in the pew: "Why did God become man?" Why the Incarnation? In the Creed we confess that FOR US AND FOR OUR SALVATION HE CAME DOWN FROM HEAVEN. But as the monk Boso said to Anselm, "It appears a neglect if, after we are established in the faith, we do not seek to understand what we believe."[1] Despite Anselm's reluctance to put his hand to such a lofty subject, Boso insists that he attempt to explain what caused the almighty God to assume "the littleness and weakness of human nature for sake of its renewal." We join Boso in seeking to understand. In this chapter and the next we ask, What does it mean to say FOR US AND FOR OUR SALVATION HE CAME DOWN FROM HEAVEN? What do we mean by "salvation"?[2]

Salvation is a theme central to all religions. It takes us to the heart of the mystery of Christianity. In the language of every day, the verb "save" is used in both the active and the passive voice. We *save for* something—for a vacation, for a down payment on a house, for college education for our children, for retirement. And we are *saved from* things—from small embarrassments to major disasters. In the lan-

88

guage of religion, it seems that salvation most often implies *being saved from* something. In fact, cultured detractors sometimes express disdain for religion, and Christianity in particular, as a hopeless "salvage operation." In the final analysis, salvation defies abstraction; it has little or no meaning apart from concrete situations and experience.

In the Hebrew Scriptures, Yahweh is seen as the salvation of the people of Israel. God delivers them from mortal danger time after time. The Psalms sing Yahweh's praise for freeing them from the blind forces of nature, from slavery in Egypt, defeat in battle, starvation, and the punishments their sins deserve. Individuals see the hand of God in being saved from illness, slander, costly lawsuits, and personal ruin. Implicit in these prayers of thanksgiving for God's deliverance is an awareness that Israel was also saved *for* something: that the People of God have a mission—a special purpose—in the world.

The fundamental Christian experience of salvation is described in the framework of the Hebrew Scriptures (i.e., the "Old Testament") as interpreted by Jesus and the apostolic church. New Testament writers borrowed a number of stories, historical episodes, models, and metaphors to give insight into Jesus' life and work. They adapted three themes in particular to explain salvation: the creation motif; the Exodus events; and the unfolding of revelation.

CREATION/RE-CREATION:
SALVATION FROM CHAOS AND THE FORCES OF EVIL

In the Bible, creation is presented as the overture to the first movement in the great symphony of salvation. As we saw in Chapter 2, the chief concern of the Book of Genesis is not to describe the origin and constitution of matter, but to make a statement about the absolute subordination of all creatures to their Creator. One of the distinguishing features of the Genesis account is the expression of God's pleasure after each completed act of creation. And finally, "God looked at everything he had made, and he found it very good" (Gen 1:31). The apparent naiveté of this self-satisfaction veils a profound insight that marks off the biblical cosmogony from that of the general run of Mesopotamian myths. Behind the visible and invisible world of creation there is a willful, beneficent Force who has endowed the cosmos with design and purpose.

God's work of creation goes forward in time. Order continues to be imposed on chaos. Distinction is made between the dry and the damp. Light overcomes darkness. Ecology balances the disappearance of some species with the emergence of others. Humans, themselves creatures, share responsibility for the created universe. Man and woman find themselves in a symbiotic relationship of mutual dependence. However hostile the environment, humans do not despair, because they put their faith in a Creator God who saves. Every notion of enmity and conflict between God and nature is foreign to the Hebrew Scriptures. The biblical fragments that refer to a cosmic battle use the language of myth and metaphor to symbolize the forces of evil and God's conquest of them. The wicked of the earth, the targets of divine wrath, are designated by the names of mythological monsters—Leviathan, "the coiled serpent" (Is 27:1); Rahab, the sea-monster, symbol of Egypt (Is 30:7; 51:9-10); Job 26:12-13)—who are restrained, overwhelmed, and destroyed by divine power. The conquest of the primeval forces of chaos and darkness inspires confidence that God's mighty power will continue to to save Israel from those who would despoil and plunder it (Is 51:9-10; Ps 74:12-18; Hab 3:8-16).

The texts of Second Isaiah are among the clearest expressions of the Israelite theology of creation. Faced with a situation that threatens the very existence of Israel, Second Isaiah sees salvation as a consequence of creation: *because* God created Israel, God can be counted on to deliver them:

> But now, thus says the LORD, who created you,
> O Jacob, and formed you O Israel:

> Fear not, for I have redeemed you;
> I have called you by name; you are mine.

> When you pass through the water, I will be with you;
> in the rivers you shall not drown.

> When you walk through fire, you shall not be burned;
> the flames shall not consume you. (Is 43:1-2; see 42:5-6; 54:5)

The theme of creation is also prominent in the Psalms. The Israelites sing praise because they see in the work of creation Yahweh's saving hand (see Pss. 74, 89, 93, 95, 135, 136). God created with a purpose. God saves us from chaos, confusion, and self-destruction, and for an end:

> Praised be the God and Father of our Lord Jesus Christ. . . .
> God chose us in him before the world began, to be holy and
> blameless in his sight, to be full of love; he likewise predestined
> us through Christ Jesus to be his adopted sons—such was his will
> and pleasure. . . . (Eph 1:3-5)

St. Paul speaks of a "new creation" in Christ (Gal 6:15; 2 Cor 5:17);
and, according to many commentators, creation is the principal framework for the Pauline understanding of salvation. Everything God created was good, well ordered, and life sustaining. The human
element—"Adam"—in its effort to short-circuit God's grand design
unleashed excess, imbalance and destruction. In defying God's will,
Adam introduced "sin" into the world. Instead of being secure in
justice, peace, and life, creation teetered on the brink—and in the view
of some continues close to the edge—of injustice, hatred, and annihilation. St. Paul contrasts the results of Adam's disobedience with the
effects of the obedience of Christ, the new Adam. Whereas the sin of
Adam brought slavery, despair, and death, Christ restored freedom,
hope, and life (Rom. 5:12-21).

It is easy enough for humans to know what we must be saved *from*,
but it is only in Christ, the Risen Lord, that we get some inkling what
we are being saved *for*. Everyone "in Christ" is a "new creation," says
Paul. "The old order has passed away; now all is new" (2 Cor 5:17). It
is through the advent of Christ that the ultimate purpose of creation is
for the first time fully understood (Rom 8).

When discussing faith in ONE GOD, MAKER OF HEAVEN AND EARTH, in
Chapter 2, we noted that internecine strife among the gods, rivalry of
the principalities and powers, and the capriciousness of the personified
forces of nature are characteristic of the polytheistic cosmogonies of
the ancient world. While the Hebrew Scriptures refer to this titantic
struggle only in passing (Gen 1:21; Ps 74:12-17), it is fundamental to
the way the New Testament pits Jesus against the demonic forces that
threaten the well-being of men and women (e.g., Mk 1:23-39; 3:20-27).
St. Paul warns Christians against "empty, seductive philosophy . . .
based on cosmic powers rather than Christ." The baptized share in the
fullness of Christ, who dominates "every principality and power."
Making all things new in Christ, God disarmed "the principalities and
powers. He made a public show of them and, leading them off captive,
triumphed in the person of Christ" (Col 2:15). In dying and rising in

baptism to life in Christ, Christians are created anew and saved from the power of demons and the paralyzing fear of cosmic forces.

St. Paul introduced the Adam-Christ dialectic that is basic to St. Irenaeus' vision of the recapitulation of all things in Christ. Paul contrasted the first Adam, in whose image we were born, with the last Adam (Christ), whose image we shall bear in the resurrection (1 Cor 15:45-59). Adam is "the type of the one who is to come" (Rom 5:14), and Christ overcomes the transgression of this primordial figure who failed creation and subjected it to futility and death. As the new Adam, Christ is the true image of God. He exercises dominion over the whole created world, freeing it from slavery to corruption and bringing it to share in the glorious freedom of the children of God (Rom 8:20-24).

THE EXODUS: SALVATION FROM SLAVERY AND OPPRESSION

As important as it is, the theme of creation is only an introduction to the Bible's main story line, the action of God in history. The Exodus is the central motif of both the Old and the New Testament. It is the archetype of Yahweh's saving action. Jews (including St. Paul) look back to the deliverance of the Hebrews from oppression in Egypt as the decisive moment that shaped their national identity and their destiny. It is the basis of Israel's faith in the will and power of Yahweh to save. Today liberation theologians cite the various events of the Exodus account to illustrate how God enters into human affairs to save us from those who enslave and destroy us—and even to save us from ourselves.

Exodus, the Latin version of the Greek word for departure (escape!), is the title of the second book of the Bible. The Book of Exodus describes the oppression of Israel's descendants in Egypt, the call of Moses, the ten plagues, the flight of the Hebrews, and their safe passage through the sea. It then traces the wanderings of the Hebrews through the desert to Mt. Sinai, where Moses receives the Law of the covenant (the "ten commandments"). It describes the ark of the covenant and tells the story of the golden calf. Thus "the Exodus" refers not only to the book by that name but to the events surrounding the Israelites' flight from oppression and slavery. The Exodus is prominent in the recitals of the saving acts of Yahweh heralded in the Psalms (see, Pss 78: 12ff; 105:23ff; 106:8ff; 114:1ff; 135:8ff; 136:10ff). Later, Second Isaiah uses images drawn from the Exodus and the wanderings in the desert to remind the people of Israel of God's saving action and to serve as surety for the coming of the kingdom promised by Yahweh (4:18; 42:16; 43:l9; 48:21; 49:10).

Familiarity with the events of the Exodus and with its significance in Israel's history is necessary to appreciate many parts of the New Testament. In Matthew's Gospel, Jesus is presented as the new Moses; the Sermon on the Mount is a parallel to the law given on Mt. Sinai. The synoptic accounts, especially Matthew and Luke, following the tradition that the Israelites wandered forty years in the desert, where they were tempted and tried, have Jesus begin his public career spending forty days in the desert, where he is tempted by Satan. The reference to Jesus as "the Lamb of God" in John's Gospel (1:29) and the entire account of the Lord's supper in all the Gospels recall Israel's last meal in Egypt and the saving blood of the lamb. St. Paul interpreted Israel's safe passage through the sea as a figure of Christian baptism.

The story of the Exodus will never lose its appeal as long as people are exploited and oppressed. Moses was a hero in the spirituals of the American slaves, who, like the ancient Hebrews before them and South African blacks after them, look to Yahweh for deliverance. The Exodus is our assurance that God acts in history. Liberation theologians hold it up as the paradigm of salvation from injustice and economic exploitation. They regard the emancipation of the Hebrews as a political action. It marks a break with slavery and the making of a people, a new society. God wants the loyalty of a free people, not the obeisance of slaves. Liberation theologians see the incident of the golden calf (Deut 9:7-21) as evidence that humans must be saved from themselves as well as from the oppression of others. Like the Hebrews of old we lose patience and look back, preferring the security of servitude to the risk of freedom (Ex 14:11-12; 16:3). Jesus is the new Moses, the new savior. His proclamation of the kingdom of God, like the promise of a land flowing with milk and honey, announced a new order of things. Because he presented a threat to the religious establishment of his time, he was tried and executed. The evidence is that his "crimes" were political, his preaching and ministry to the disenfranchised a threat to the power brokers. Christians have always interpreted Jesus' death/resurrection as a "passover" to new life, and the shedding of innocent blood as reminiscent of the paschal lamb that meant salvation for the Hebrews in Egypt.

REVELATION: SALVATION FROM IGNORANCE
AND MEANINGLESSNESS

If a modern editor were compiling the Bible today, he or she might well make the Epistle to the Hebrews the first book in the New Testament. It bridges the Hebrew and Christian Scriptures, interpreting events, figures, and themes of the Old Testament in light of the New. The opening verses describe the gradual revelation of God's saving plan:

> In times past, God spoke in fragmentary and varied ways to our fathers through the prophets; in this, the final age, he has spoken to us through his Son, whom he has made heir of all things and through whom he first created the universe. (Heb 1:1-2)

These few verses sweep from revelation universally present in creation and culture, through the Old Testament prophets, to the fullness of revelation in Christ Jesus. God leaves fingerprints everywhere. Every manifestation of divine power and wisdom, whether in nature (the created universe) or in "signs of the times" (historical events), reveals the being of the Creator for anyone who has eyes to see. But God reveals in another sense as well: God speaks, and those who have ears to hear understand.[3] The spoken word provides the closest analogy to God's self-manifestation: the speaker becomes known in the act of speaking. The fullness of revelation is identified with the Godhead— the very Word of God.

A popular misconception assumes that the context of revelation consists of a body of ready-made statements that provide information beyond the reach of ordinary ways of knowing. The fact is, as Jesus' preaching made abundantly clear, revelation is the communication of being and life and truth. It is grace in the sense that it is a gift of God that seizes one's whole being. Though humans find it useful, even necessary, to express revelation in words, verbal formulations are at best feeble attempts to capture transcendent mystery in finite language. For Langdon Gilkey the content of revelation is summed up under three headings.

> Revelation means the self-manifestation of the divine power and meaning on which all depends and in and through which all is fulfilled, that is to say, in our tradition, "God." At its most fundamental level, therefore, revelation means the communication of the divine *power* (being, life, health, and eternal life), of

the divine *truth* (order, illumination, insight, and meaning), and of the divine *love* (mercy, forgiveness, and renewing, reuniting love).[4]

While revelation cannot be reduced to propositions, it does in fact point especially to the cognitive dimension in the human experience of divine power, truth, and love. "The Law and the prophets," a common phrase in the Bible, explains how God revealed the plan of salvation and at the same time is bringing it to fruition. In New Testament usage "the Law" designates precepts and moral norms, the Pentateuch as a whole or a particular law found in it, the Decalogue, and even the entire Old Testament.[5] The basis for the Law, understood in the broad sense, is the original covenant revealed to Moses by Yahweh, who is the author, custodian, and expositor of the moral order. Like all law, the Mosaic Law had a dual purpose: besides regulating behavior it had a pedagogical function. Specific precepts of the Law both instructed the Israelites as to God's will and guided their feet on the path of righteousness.

Yahweh revealed the divine presence in appearances in the burning bush and on Mt. Sinai. In other epiphanies, particularly during the monarchy and in the time of exile, God revealed the divine will to the Israelites through prophets. Charged with proclaiming God's word, the prophets put events in motion and interpreted every sort of happening in the light of revelation. They explained how God acted in cataclysms (storms, drought, prosperity), events of history (victories, defeats, the rise and fall of empires), and personal tragedy (sin, obstinacy, death).

In the Hebrew Scriptures the Law is associated with the idea of light and life. The Law illumined the way so that individuals and nations could proceed without stumbling. The Law was a force in the struggle against the powers of darkness which threatened their existence. In the Gospel according to John, Jesus—like the Law—is the light of the world who keeps people from faltering along the path to salvation. He is quoted as saying, "I am the light of the world. No follower of mine shall ever walk in darkness; no, he shall possess the light of life" (Jn 8:12). Jesus is the "true" light in contrast to the deception and illusion of sin. The revelation of God in Jesus is for the enlightenment of the world. Through him, "the light shines on in darkness" (Jn 1:5). Light is truth; darkness, error. The dialectic of truth/error is in the moral sphere of human behavior. Nicodemus, who came to Jesus in the darkness of night, heard him say,

"The judgment of condemnation is this: the light came into the
world, but men loved darkness rather than light because their
deeds were wicked. Everyone who practices evil hates the light;
he does not come near it for fear his deeds will be exposed. But
he who acts in truth comes into the light, to make clear that his
deeds are done in God." (Jn 3:19-21)

The reference to rebirth, "water and the spirit," earlier in the passage (vv.4-5) makes it evident that John is thinking of Christian baptism. The reference to light should be read in the same context. The
final stage of preparation for baptism has traditionally been called the
period of "enlightenment" or "illumination." St. Augustine links the
illumination with the light that is the first day in the Book of Genesis.
St. Gregory of Nazianzus quotes the psalmist who says the Lord "is
my light and my salvation." Baptismal illumination, he continues, is a
light that "expels the devil who is darkness and a counterfeit of the
light."[6]

Although the Law was God's gift through Moses, the fullness of
revelation has come only through Jesus (Jn 1:17; 6:31-38). Revelation
is not merely a matter of doctrine; as the manifestation of the divine
presence in the world it is existential truth. God acts in history, unveil-
ing the plan of salvation for all to see, and making it a reality in the
person of Jesus Christ.

SIN AND SINS

Each of the three models of salvation—creation, Exodus, revelation—
takes the fact of sin as a given: if the world were not rescued, it would
self-destruct. The models, however, describe the effects of sin rather
than the nature of sin itself. Nonetheless it is clear that the Bible
presents a twofold aspect of sin: sin is a failure in personal relationships among groups and between individuals in their relationships with
God; and sin is a force, a power in the world greater than the sum of
the individual sins of human beings.

Sin is a failure in human relationships. The Bible's vocabulary of sin
is determined to a large extent by the notion of covenant. Covenants
were contractual arrangements of various kinds, but in the religious
world of the Old Testament they were more. They had a sacred dimension based on fidelity to one's word. Covenants covered all kinds of
human relationships: treaties among nations, agreements among individuals, marriage contracts, business dealings.[7]

The theology of both the Old and the New Testament is based on the notion of covenant. God takes the initiative: God creates, God chooses Israel. God's saving acts elicit a response. As God's elect, the Israelites agree to reflect the mercy and kindness that Yahweh has shown them in their dealings among themselves and with others, especially with the most disadvantaged (*anawim*). The covenant spells out the obligations that Israel takes upon itself as God's chosen people. The arrangement is built on the foundation of God's *hesed* (mercy, love, kindness), which is absolute and unshakeable. To breach the covenant is to sin. Sin is basically a refusal to respond appropriately to God's love and mercy. Thus, to speak of sin in purely legal terms—as the breaking of a law—is to ignore an important ingredient in the biblical understanding of sin. Sin is "relational": it represents a lack of fidelity, a failure to respond to God's love. In fact the Bible commonly compares sin to the breakup of a marriage because of the unfaithfulness of one of the spouses. It is a rupture in the covenant relationship.

God made a covenant with Adam and Eve. In their failure to respond to God's love, a failure symbolized in the eating of the forbidden fruit, they breached the covenant and suffered the consequences. The episode of the golden calf (Deut 9:16ff) is another example. When Moses on coming down from the mountain witnessed the Israelites worshiping an idol, in disgust and anger he broke the stone tablets to symbolize the breaking of the covenant relationship, the personal bond of which the Ten Commandments were the concrete expression. In John's Gospel those who prefer darkness to light, blindness to sight, deafness to hearing symbolize those who sin because they close their eyes to the person of Jesus and shut their ears to his words.

The second aspect of sin prominent in biblical theology is sin as a force in the world. It presents a conundrum that is as unanswerable as the question, "Which comes first: the chicken or the egg?" Which is first: the fact of sin or the act of sin? Are we sinners because we sin, or do we sin because we are sinners? The crimes and passions of individuals and communities first ignite and then fuel the power of sin. The rupturing of the covenant is like the breaking open of Pandora's box which, according to Greek mythology, unleashed all the Spites which plague mortals—Old Age, Work, Sickness, Insanity, Vice, Passion. Humans, left to their own resources, can never get the Spites back into the box; they lack the capacity to master the force of evil in the world.[8] In an autobiographical passage which almost every adult can make his or her own, St. Paul recognizes the power of sin in his life.

> I am weak flesh sold into the slavery of sin. I cannot even understand my own actions. I do not do what I want to do but what I hate. When I act against my own will, by that very fact I agree that the law is good. This indicates that it is not I who do it but sin which resides in me. I know that no good dwells in me, that is, in my flesh; the desire to do right is there but not the power. What happens is that I do, not the good I will to do, but the evil I do not intend. But if I do what is against my will, it is not I who do it, but sin which dwells in me. (Rom 7:14-20)

Paul attributes a semi-autonomous existence to sin. Elsewhere biblical writers speak of it as "the power of darkness" and "sin of the world." In so far as sin "resides" in every mortal from the moment of conception, prior to any personal lapse, it is called *original sin*. Looked at from the outside, original sin names the human condition—the broken covenant, the universal estrangement, the ambiguous predicament— that is the lot of every individual born into a world where sin reigns. (To speak of it as a "stain" or a "mark on the soul" is to disregard the cosmic proportions of evil and to trivialize the real significance of original sin.)

The classic scriptural texts that reveal the doctrine of original sin (though the phrase itself never appears in the Bible) are found in the Epistles of St. Paul.[9] In the text from Romans just quoted, Paul makes it clear that we are sinners before we sin! In another text in the same Epistle, Paul accounts for the sin of the world by describing "the fall" of the first Adam. Sin and death entered the world because of the offense of one man (Rom 5:12-21). Yet we cannot put all the blame for our plight on Adam because de facto all of us sin on our own "and are deprived of the glory of God" (Rom 3:23). We become, as it were, accomplices after the fact.

St. Paul finds in the fall of Adam deeper theological significance than is evident in the Genesis account. The authors of the first eleven chapters of Genesis were concerned to explain the presence of evil in the world and to make it clear that it should not be attributed to God the Creator. Stories and folk tales of murder, vengeance, pride, and natural calamities told of evils in the world from the beginning. Unlike some other accounts, Israelite tradition attributed the source of these evils to the personal sin of human beings. The Israelites knew that Yahweh, who had saved them from slavery, made a covenant with them, and led them to the promised land, could not be responsible for evil. It was left to St. Paul and the New Testament writers to explain how Christ, the Savior who would bring the ultimate victory over sin, is the new Adam.

THE INEVITABILITY OF THE INCARNATION

In the Middle Ages people interpreted the Bible more literally than either the ancients or we moderns do. Medieval theologians asked, "Would God have become man had Adam not sinned?" St. Anselm answered for most (including St. Thomas) in arguing that the reason HE CAME DOWN FROM HEAVEN was original sin. They followed in the spirit of St. Augustine, who expressed a very ambivalent attitude in the *Exsultet,* his great Easter hymn, which contains the often quoted phrase, *"O felix culpa":*

> O happy fault, O necessary sin of Adam,
> which gained for us so great a Redeemer.

Some medieval theologians (the great Oxford divine, Duns Scotus, among them), however, took the position that the Incarnation was integral to the divine plan of creation from the beginning. In the person of the Logos, God would have assumed human nature even if Adam had not sinned. (Whether or not Jesus would have suffered a violent death were it not for sin is another question; it will be discussed in Chapter 8.) According to many modern scholars this latter position is closer to the theology of St. Paul. Even in the classic passages in the Epistle to the Romans that are the basis for the church's teaching on original sin, Paul's principal emphasis is on the saving power of Christ. We cannot fully appreciate the universal significance of Christ's death and resurrection for all of creation unless we are aware of the power of sin that is at the root of all evil in the world.

It is sometimes asked whether Paul came to an awareness of the power of sin through reflection on the saving work of Jesus Christ, or whether reflection on the former brought him to his understanding of the latter. In answer, the late Eugene Maly wrote:

> The question is legitimate inasmuch as modern catechists might ask whether to emphasize the positive aspect of what Christ brought us, namely life, or the negative aspect of what Christ

saved us from, namely sin and death. Some theologians so stress the first seven chapters of the letter to the Romans that they continually present man as a sinner, while others so stress the following chapters of Romans (where the more positive aspect is developed) that for them man is the one redeemed in Christ. The first might more fittingly exclaim, "We are sinners, and *Miserere* is our song." The observation of the latter might be, "We are a paschal people, and *Alleluia* is our song."[10]

The question is another like the one about the chicken and the egg. Although we may never know all the steps St. Paul took in arriving at his theology of salvation, he has told enough about his own conversion to lead us to believe that he experienced that conversion before he truly understood the enormity of sin in the world. He had a vision of what he was being saved *for* before he fully appreciated what he was being saved *from*. As difficult as the questions about salvation are, not to seek to understand what we believe is, in the word of Boso the monk, negligence.

Implicit in each of the three models developed at the beginning of this chapter is a notion of human powerlessness before cosmic powers, socio-political forces, and the search for meaning. Theoretically it may be true that we human beings, entrusted by our Creator with dominion over all the earth, once had the power to control the environment and our inner drives, but the fact is that we messed up. Our forebears sinned. We sin. We lost control, the reins slipped from our grasp, and the horses ran away. Without outside help we can no more regain mastery over our being and our destiny than we could get the Spites back into Pandora's box. We needed a savior to come and right the situation. The person and nature of that savior is the subject of the next chapter.

Notes

1. Chapter 2. Monk and later abbot of Bec (1124–36), Boso spent several years with Anselm at Canterbury. In *Cur Deus Homo?* he is cast as Anselm's interrogator.

2. Gutierrez complains that theologians presume that everyone knows what salvation means but that few take the time to discuss it. An exception is E. Schillebeeckx for whom salvation is *the* theme of the Christian message. See *Christ*, pp. 724ff.

3. R. Schnackenberg distinguishes extra-biblical revelation, which he says is attained through "seeing," from biblical revelation, which is essentially "hearing." In the latter sense revelation is more than the natural disclosure of God through visible creation as in Rom 1:19ff. "Biblical View of Revelation," *Theology Digest* 13 (Summer 1965):120–134.

4. *Message and Existence* (Minneapolis: Seabury Press, 1979), pp. 43–44.

5. J. L. McKenzie, *Dictionary*, p. 500.

6. A. Hamman, ed., *Baptism: Ancient Liturgies and Patristic Texts* (Staten Island: Alba House, 1967), pp. 18–19. The symbol of light has a prominent place in the religions of the world. Buddhism, for example, implies that "enlightenment" is of the essence of religion. Although Buddhists do not speak of salvation as we have here, a "Buddha" is simply one who has become enlightened.

7. E. Maly, *Sin: Biblical Perspectives* (Dayton: Pflaum, 1973), pp. 9–15, 43–46. John Macquarrie writes, " 'Sin' is a religious term, and it has connotations that differentiate it from notions like 'guilt' or 'wrongdoing,' though presumably 'sin' includes these notions." *Principles of Christian Theology*, 2cd ed. (New York: Charles Scribner's Sons, 1977), p. 71.

8. "Delusive Hope," another of the Spites freed when Pandora opened the box, uses lies to discourage mortals from mass suicide. See R. Graves, *The Greek Myths* I, (Baltimore: Penguin Books, 1955), p. 145.

9. See Maly, *Sin*, pp. 69–75.

10. Ibid., pp. 44–45.

6

Christology:
Two Approaches

"He came down from heaven"

Theologians have come to distinguish between christology and soteriology. The first designates the systematic reflection upon the one whom Christians confess as Lord and Savior; the latter is the systematic study of the doctrine of salvation. The two are closely linked, even inseparable, in that we know the identity of Jesus, whom we call the Christ, only through his saving works.

The significance of Jesus' words and works (not overly impressive when compared with those of Old Testament figures such as David and Isaiah or with those of such Greeks as Aristotle and Alexander the Great) lies in who he is rather than what he did. In 451 the Council of Chalcedon boldly stated the Christian belief that Jesus "is perfect in Godhead and perfect in humanity, true God and true Man." The bishops gathered at Chalcedon saw themselves only making explicit what had already been acclaimed in the "creed of the 150 fathers" endorsed at the Council of Constantinople seventy years earlier. The journey, however, from Constantinople to Chalcedon—only a few kilometers distant from each other across the Sea of Marmara—was long and tortuous. Some bishops traveled by way of Alexandria in Egypt, some by way of Antioch in Syria. In most cases the journey was ideological as well as geographical. Their approaches to christology, very different in their points of departure, finally converged at Chalcedon.

The participants in the christological controversies of the fifth century were animated from first to last by soteriological interests. However theoretical and abstract their arguments may seem at times, the bishops and theologians saw the issues as practical, shaping the way people thought about God, the way they prayed, and the way they understood what it means to be human. In an effort to explain what it means to confess HE CAME DOWN FROM HEAVEN, we review the main features of "descending" and "ascending" christology and highlight the events leading up to Chalcedon. Finally we look at some of the practical implications of this phrase for our devotion and spirituality.

"FROM ABOVE": DESCENDING CHRISTOLOGY

Over the centuries there have been two general approaches to christology. The one that enjoys greater popularity today is described as christology "from below," or "ascending christology," because it begins from the premise that humans can grasp God and his word only in the context of their experience. This approach asserts that we can come to know the invisible reality of the Godhead only in the visible reality of Jesus' humanity. We shall have more to say about this approach below (no pun intended). The other approach—implicit in HE CAME DOWN FROM HEAVEN—is the one that St. Anselm and a majority of theologians after St. Athanasius through St. Thomas Aquinas to Calvin and many contemporary writers follow; it is called christology "from above," or "descending" christology. Theologians of this school emphasize that humanity's movement toward God (from below) is possible only because of God's prior reaching out to humanity (from above).[1]

In the early church, christology from above is generally associated with the great metropolis of Alexandria. Alexandria, founded by Alexander the Great near the mouth of the Nile, was the most cultured city in the Roman empire, and it was there that the greatest champions of high christology—Origen, St. Athanasius and St. Cyril—did their work. In general the theologians of the Alexandrian school favored a "contemplative" view of God and the universe; their thinking was more speculative than concrete, more abstract than historical. Their point of departure was always the Godhead: the divine Logos—the Word of God—who *assumed* human nature. They had an axiom, "Only that which is assumed is healed," which they cited to emphasize that if humans are to be redeemed in their whole being, God had to take to himself human nature in its entirety, body and soul, heart and mind.

Despite the axiom, however, the position of the Alexandrian theologians is described as *logos-sarx*—"word-flesh"—christology. The fact that they were generally content to sum up the Incarnation with the biblical phrase "and the Word was made flesh" illustrates the shortcoming of their approach. Even the great Athanasius, whose orthodoxy is unquestioned, laid little stress on Jesus' humanity and had little to say about his human intellect and will. A lesser theologian such as Apollinaris of Laodicea, however, said that Jesus had no need of a human mind because as Logos he relied on his divine will and knowledge. It was the person of the Logos who animated and energized Jesus' physical body—"the flesh."

Apollinaris' position was condemned in a series of synods and by the Council of Constantinople in 381. Nonetheless he had planted seeds that in the next century would blossom into monophysitism, a heresy that would not die even after it was condemned by the Council of Chalcedon in 451. The monophysites argued that by reason of the Incarnation there existed a unique, permanent union that was neither brought about by nor dependent on the free will of human nature. In Jesus the union of the two natures meant that the divine Logos appropriated human nature to himself, so overwhelming it with divine characteristics that the divine and human can be distinguished only theoretically. In reality, according to the monophysites, there is only one nature in Jesus (a literal translation of *mono-physis* would be "one nature"), the divine, which entirely absorbed the human. Monophysitism is also known as Eutychianism after Eutyches, archimandrite of a monastery near Constantinople, who championed the cause. Eutyches advanced the view that the Incarnation brought about a fusion of the divine and the human in Christ. Eutyches was was hardly a world-class theologian. His influence was due to his political connections and his ability to explain his teaching with homey examples: just as a few drops of water cannot be tasted when mixed with strong wine, so Jesus' humanity is absorbed into and overwhelmed by his divinity. Despite support from the Alexandrian school, his position was eventually condemned at the Council of Chalcedon in 451 because it compromised the human identity of Jesus.

"FROM BELOW": ASCENDING CHRISTOLOGY

Before describing the action of the Council of Chalcedon in detail, we must briefly consider the other approach, christology from below. It takes the *human* figure of Jesus as its point of departure. Beginning with the Jesus of history and the world of experience, it ascends from the visible to the "invisible." This approach, fashionable among contemporary theologians and biblical scholars, has antecedents in ancient times in the christology associated with the school of Antioch. Where theologians of the Alexandrian school favored a metaphysical and contemplative view of God and the world, theologians of the Antiochene school tended to stress the empirical and the historical. Where the former were intent on defending the true divinity of Christ, the latter were concerned to safeguard his human identity.

Christology from below, in both its ancient and modern versions, stresses Jesus' self-consciousness as a human being. Does this mean that Jesus had a human "self" as well as a divine "self"? An affirmative answer to this question then leads to the further question regarding the union of divinity and humanity in Christ. The Antiochene theologians in their emphasis on the integrity of Jesus' humanity—"true man"—tended to regard it as a "moral" union, that is, a union arising out of the reciprocal love of the human self for the divine self of the Logos. The relationship bonded their wills through a continual exchange of love.

As well thought out as it was, the Antiochene position had its weaknesses. In explaining how Jesus' divine and human selves cooperated, many Antiochenes compared it to the union of husband and wife in marriage, citing the text from Ephesians "and the two shall be made into one" (5:31). The example illustrates the difficulty of this kind of christology from below: the union between divinity and humanity is an accidental, external union; theoretically at least, the two selves could come to resist each other and, like some marriages, break down because love is no longer mutual.

The great achievement of the Antiochene theologians was that they exposed the errors of Apollinarianism. In fact it was in the controversy with that heresy that the Antiochenes began to develop a basic *dyophysite* (i.e., "two natures") christology that was ultimately endorsed by the Council of Chalcedon. First, however, dyophysitism needed to be refined and its own weaknesses exposed. This occurred in the Nestorian controversy, which brought the school of Antioch into open conflict with theologians of the Alexandrian school.

NESTORIUS CONDEMNED: THE COUNCIL OF EPHESUS

The monk Nestorius, renowned in Antioch for his eloquence, was named patriarch of Constantinople in 428 and took possession of his see in April of the following year. With the zeal of the "true believer," Nestorius set out to rid the capital of heretics and error. His own troubles began when the priest Anastasius, who had accompanied him from Antioch, said in a sermon, "Let no one call Mary *Theotokos* [literally "God bearer"; generally translated "Mother of God"], for Mary was but a woman; and it is impossible that God should be born of a woman."[2] Anastasius' words stirred a hornet's nest; he had challenged both popular piety and a phrase commonly used by Alexandrian theologians. Nestorius preached a series of sermons in defense of his chaplain. In the first he said in part:

> Hath God a mother? Then we may excuse paganism for giving mothers to its divinities. Then was Paul a liar when he testified concerning Christ that He was "without father, without mother, without descent"? No: Mary was not the mother of God. For "that which is born of flesh is flesh: and that which is born of Spirit is spirit." A creature brought not forth Him who is uncreated; the Father begat not of the Virgin an Infant God, the Word; for "in the beginning was the Word," as John saith: a creature bore not the Creator, but rather a man who was the organ of Deity. For the Holy Ghost created not God the Son: and "that which is conceived of her is of the Holy Ghost"; but He fabricated of the Virgin a Temple wherein God the Word should dwell. God was incarnate, but never died; yea, rather, elevated him in whom He was incarnate; He descended to raise that which had fallen, but He fell not Himself. On account of the Employer, then, I venerate the vestment which He employed; on account of that which is concealed, I adore that which appears.[3]

In defending the integrity of Christ's humanity, Nestorius pushed the principles of the Antiochene position beyond acceptable limits. In more abstract and theological terms, he posited two "sons" of God, the one natural (i.e., divine) and the other adopted (i.e., human). The reciprocal love of the Logos and Jesus' human self in effect elevates the latter to divine sonship, he said. Mary bore the adopted son, Jesus. While she can be called "mother of Christ," she cannot be properly called "mother of God," because Mary cannot be mother of him who is of a nature different from her own.

Battle lines began to form. Nestorius had the support of the imperial court, but the clergy and monks of Constantinople opposed him. One of the priests, Proclus, the future patriarch, preached a sermon in the presence of Nestorius in which he openly contradicted the bishop:

> If Christ be one, and the Word another, then we have no longer a Trinity, but a Quaternity. The Lord came to save: but in so doing, to suffer. A mere man could not save: a mere God could not die. So God became man. That which was, saved: and that which was made, suffered. The Self-same was in the Father's bosom and the womb of His mother. He lay in a mother's arms, while He walked upon the wings of the wind. He was adored by angels, while He sat at meat with publicans. The Cherubim durst not behold Him, while Pilate condemned Him. The servant smote Him, and creation shuddered. He hung upon the Cross, but He was not absent from the throne of glory; and while he lay in the tomb, He was spreading out the heavens like a curtain. Oh! what mystery! I see the miracles, and I proclaim the Godhead: I behold the sufferings, and I deny not the manhood. What clearer proof could I want that Mary is Mother of God indeed.[4]

Proclus' words echoed Alexandrian theology, and it was not long before the bishop of Alexandria, Cyril, was drawn into the controversy. Cyril had succeeded to the see on the death of his uncle in 412; he was the equal of Nestorius as a theologian and a better political strategist. Appealing to the pope, to the emperor in the East, and to everyone else of any influence, Cyril represented Nestorius' teaching as destroying every basis of salvation. Nestorius too wrote Pope Celestine, but the pope sided with Cyril. The Eastern emperor, Theodosius II, acting in concert with his brother emperor in the West, summoned a general council to meet in Ephesus in June 431. Cyril, never one to leave things to chance, arrived early with an entourage that included some fifty bishops and an assortment of lower clergy, strong monks, and burly seamen. He enlisted the support of Memnon, the bishop of Ephesus, who had on hand a hundred or more of his suffragan bishops and a group of sturdy peasants in case of trouble. Nestorius too had his bodyguards, but his principal defender among the bishops, John of Antioch, was very slow in arriving, as were the papal representatives. After delaying the opening of the council for two weeks, Cyril and Memnon decided to proceed without the bishop of Antioch and his suffragans (about thirty in number). Moving with deliberate haste, Cyril managed to have Nestorius condemned and deposed in a single day's session.

TOWARD A SOLUTION: THE COUNCIL OF CHALCEDON

Although the Council of Ephesus banished Nestorius, it ended some months later in dissension without resolving the doctrinal issues. Antioch's criticism of Alexandrian christology, especially as it was formulated by Cyril, continued to divide the church. Many felt that Cyril's favorite slogan (derived from Apollinaris), "The nature of the Incarnate Word is one," was misleading if not downright heretical. Finally in 433 a truce of sorts was patched together through an exchange of letters between Cyril and John of Antioch. Cyril subscribed to a confession of faith drawn up by John that is known variously as the Creed of Antioch, the *Symbolum Ephesinum,* and the Symbol of Union. Cyril could sign it in good conscience because he saw it not as something new or different from what he always believed but as a clarification of the Nicene faith.

> We confess, therefore, our Lord Jesus Christ, the only begotten Son of God, perfect God and perfect Man, consisting of a rational soul and a body begotten of the Father before the ages as touching his Godhead, the same, in the last days, for us and for our salvation, born of the Virgin Mary, as touching his Manhood; the same of one substance with the Father as touching his Godhead, and of one substance with us as touching his Manhood. For of two natures a union has been made. For this cause we confess one Christ, one Son, one Lord.
>
> In accordance with this sense of the unconfused union, we confess the holy Virgin to be *Theotokos,* because God the Word became incarnate and was made man, and from the very conception united to himself the temple taken from her. And as to the

> expressions concerning the Lord in the Gospels and Epistles, we are aware that theologians understand some as common, as relating to one Person, and others they distinguish, as relating to two natures, explaining those that befit the divine nature according to the Godhead of Christ, and those of a humble sort according to his manhood.[5]

It was an uneasy truce kept in place by pressure from the emperor. Despite the confession of faith agreed upon by Cyril and John, the monophysites continued to argue their case. They justified their position by citing the phrases "For of two natures a union has been made. For this cause we confess one Christ, one Son, one Lord." Eutyches, the monophysite spokesman, stated, "I confess that our Lord was of two natures before the union [i.e. the Incarnation], but after the union one nature."

After the death of Cyril in 444 the smoldering embers flamed again into a raging fire. It continued to be fueled by petty rivalries between factions and cities, especially by the Alexandrians, who saw themselves losing out as the upstart, Constantinople, grew more powerful in ecclesiastical affairs. A concerted effort by the imperial authorities, notably the empress Pulcheria, and the bishop of Rome brought the fire under control at the Council of Chalcedon in 451. It was a clear victory for the dyophysites, and if Nestorius had still been alive he might have read the statement of Chalcedon and been heard to murmur from his exile in the wilds of the Egyptian desert, *That is what I was trying to say all the time.*[6]

Incorporating the ideas and much of the wording of the letter of John of Antioch into its own creed, the Council of Chalcedon sharpened the distinction between "nature" (*physis*) and "person" (*hypostasis*). It used the term *homoousios*, introduced at Nicea, to reaffirm the integrity of both Jesus' divinity and his humanity, saying that he is "one in being with the Father regarding his Godhead" and "one in being with us regarding his humanity." Chalcedon described the union between the two natures as a "hypostatic," that is, a "personal," union, which is to say that it was neither the *moral* union described by the Antiochenes nor the *physical* union taught by the Alexandrians. While the divine and human natures coexist in Jesus, they cannot be divided or separated as Nestorius seemed to imply they could. On the other hand, the council clearly repudiated Eutyches and every form of monophysitism by adding that the natures are neither so changed nor fused so as to lose their identity. Thus Christ is not a divinized human, but God enfleshed, God in a human being.

While it may not have been a clear-cut victory for the Antiochene school, the Chalcedonian formula is definitely "dyophysite." People who were convinced that the only orthodox approach to christology is from above found it difficult to accept. Theologians sympathetic to monophysitism tried for centuries first to discredit Chalcedon and then to undermine it. In the sixth century, for example, some were teaching that while Jesus had two wills, one divine and the other human, it was only the divine will that made the decisions. The human will, overwhelmed by the Godhead in Jesus, was inoperative. This teaching, known as monothelitism ("one will"), was condemned at the Third Council of Constantinople in 681.

The significance of the Council of Chalcedon was not that it resolved all the christological issues but that it set the boundaries of future discussion. Its final statement repudiates every hint of schizothymia, which would attribute to Jesus a double identity—two autonomous selves. He is one person, the divine Logos, incarnate. In Jesus, humanity is so closely and permanently joined to the Logos that all his actions, even those that are purely human such as eating and drinking, are at the same time actions of the Logos. Every deliberate thought and action of Christ originates in the Logos-self. While his human nature has its existence in the Logos, it is not subsumed by it. Chalcedon reaffirmed the integrity of both the divine and the human nature in Jesus: while distinguishable, they cannot be separated; while joined, they are not changed. The council left many issues unresolved, but it did sharpen the questions.[7]

Although sometimes lost in the heat of the debate (and modern authors writing the history of the christological controversy seldom allude to it), the underlying issue remained "Why did God become man?" While the Alexandrians and Antiochenes took different approaches to the Incarnation, they agreed on the basic principle *Quod non est assumptum non est sanatum*: Only if human nature is raised up in its entirety can it be restored in its entirety (literally, "What is not raised up cannot be healed"). St. Anselm subscribed to the same principle, but modern authors think he compromised it, especially regarding Jesus' human mind. The author of *Cur Deus Homo?* approached christology from above; he felt it would have been counterproductive for God to "assume" ignorance when becoming human. Anselm asks, How will people believe in the God-man "if they find him ignorant"?[8]

Modern theologians who approach christology from below see the problem in existential terms: What does it mean to be human? If the God-man did not know anxiety and uncertainty, even the felt need of redemption, which are part and parcel of human experience, can he said to be truly human? They find a justification for their approach in the Gospel accounts where Jesus cries over the loss of friends, is frustrated and angry at the hucksters in the Temple precincts who have no regard for the sacred, and is anxious in the face of death. Medieval theologians following Anselm allowed that Jesus had to learn such mundane skills as fastening his sandals and learning Aramaic grammar; but, given that he was also blessed with divine omniscience, they taught that he had the answers to all the essential questions. Not only was he the prince in pauper's clothing; he was conscious of being the prince. For modern as for fifth-century theologians, it is difficult to safeguard the human experience of Jesus when one approaches christology from above.

SPIRITUALITY AND DEVOTIONS

Chalcedon traced a narrow path between Scylla and Charybdis, between the destructive boulder of Nestorianism on the left and the dangerous whirlpool of monophysitism on the right. But it was not merely a matter of condemning formal heresies. The Chalcedonian formula also represents a warning against more subtle forms of these errors. Good Christians often display attitudes and behaviors in their prayer and devotional practices that are symptomatic of monophysite and Nestorian tendencies. The latter is evident in "social Christianity," which tends to picture Christ only as "the leader" or "the militant." It is observed in the kind of egalitarian ideology that, confessing Christ as "our brother," restricts his uniqueness to his superior moral qualities. The Christmas crib serves as a dramatic reminder of the Incarnation and all it implies from gestation to birth to nursing and everything associated with the beginnings of human life. There are times, however, when devotions surrounding the infant Jesus degenerate into sentimentality that borders on poor taste if not downright lack of reverence.[9]

On the other hand, the monophysite tendency surfaces whenever the humanity of Jesus is not taken seriously. Many believers, consciously or not, think it is God who acts directly (*formaliter*, in theological terms) in Jesus. God does everything. This tendency is most evident in some expressions of "sacramental spirituality." For example, some explanations of the "real presence" in the eucharist emphasize the divine presence, forgetting that the consecrated bread is more properly the sacrament of the body and blood of Jesus—his glorified humanity—united to the Word. It is true that God acts in the eucharist and all the sacraments, but it is also true that the means and the ground of our relationship and union with the Godhead is Christ's human nature.

We turn to the subject of mariology in the next chapter, but here in discussing Christ's role as mediator we should note how the monophysite tendency sometimes distorts Marian piety. There is a school of Catholic spirituality that so exaggerates human lowliness that even faithful Christians think themselves unworthy to approach the Son of God. Because they do not take the human qualities of Jesus seriously they posit the need for a "purely human" intermediary, Mary, who stands between the God-man and the rest of humanity. In effect this view denigrates the mediatorial role of the Logos who FOR US AND FOR OUR SALVATION CAME DOWN FROM HEAVEN.

In concluding this overview of the christological controversies we must emphasize once more that Athanasius, Cyril, and the church fathers who were active in the councils of the fourth and fifth centuries (and probably Nestorius as well) were concerned not with philosophical abstractions but with the question of salvation. For them the fundamental principle of soteriology is that the significance of Jesus' redemptive work rests first and foremost on *who he is* and only secondairly on what he did. He is mediator between Creator and creatures not only by reason of his mission and deeds, but by the very fact that he is God incarnate.

A balanced soteriology needs to keep christology from above and christology from below in a creative tension. The former must take into account all aspects of what it means to be human, including the very human uncertainty about existential issues—meaning and purpose and self-identity. On the other hand, christology from below, for all its emphasis on the human, must recognize that it is in the person of Jesus that we encounter God. Karl Barth compared christology from on high to a waterfall cascading straight down from a height of 3000 meters.

He describes soteriology based on christology from below that does not acknowledge the need for help from a superhuman power as a "desperate attempt to raise water from a stagnant pond to the same height by using a hand-pump."[10]

In a later chapter we shall see how St. Anselm's way of answering the question "Why did God become man?"—though he affirmed the teaching of the ancient councils—led to a certain tension between the "theology of the Incarnation" and the "theology of the cross." The former became dominant in Catholic tradition, especially in the East, while the latter, emphasizing certain passages in St. Paul, received fuller development in the West during the late Middle Ages and the period of the Reformation.[11] As will be evident below when we turn to the phrase CRUCIFIED, DIED AND WAS BURIED, both the theology of the Incarnation and of the cross have exercised decisive influence on spirituality, that is, on the attitudes, rituals, structures, values, and priorities of Christian life.   But first we must reflect on Jesus' conception and birth.

Notes

1. W. Kasper, "Orientations in Current Christology," in *Theology Digest* 31:2 (Summer 1984):107–111.

2. Socrates, *Ecclesiastical History*, Bk. VII, Ch. 32. NPNF, 2nd Ser, II, p. 170.

3. Quoted in B. J. Kidd, *A History of the Church to A.D. 461* (Oxford: The Clarendon Press, 1922), vol. III, p. 201.

4. Quoted in Kidd, *History*, vol. III, pp. 203–204.

5. J. Stevenson, ed., *Creeds, Councils, and Controversies* (London: SPCK, 1973), p. 291.

6. About 450, shortly before the Council of Chalcedon, Nestorius composed a work in which he severely criticized the decisions of

Pope Leo and Patriarch Flavian of Constantinople. Because he had been banished and silenced, Nestorius was forced to publish under a pseudonym, and therefore the work is known as "The Bazaar of Heraclides of Damascus." The only known copy, a Syriac translation, was discovered in 1895. See Johannes Quasten, *Patrology*, vol. III, (Westminster, MD: Newman Press, 1960), p. 516. See J. F. Bethune-Baker, *Nestorius and His Teaching. A Fresh Examination of the Evidence* (Cambridge University Press, 1908), pp. 189–196.

7. For a brief but informed evaluation of the council's work, see J. Macquarrie, "The Chalcedonian Definition," in *Expository Times*, 91 (Dec. 1979):68–72.

8. Bk II, ch. 13. St. Anselm, *Basic Writings*, trans. S. N. Deane, 2d ed. (La Salle, IL: Open Court Publishing Co., 1982), p. 260.

9. These reflections on the way christology is expressed in devotional practices are based on an article by Canon Charles Moeller, sometime official at the Congregation of the Holy Office, "Jesus Christ in the Mind of Moderns," *Lumen Vitae*, 7 (1952):509–527.

10. Quoted by Kasper, "Orientations," p. 108.

11. Joseph Ratzinger, *Introduction to Christianity* (New York: Herder and Herder, 1970), p. 170.

7

From the Infancy Narratives
to Mariology

*"By the power of the Holy Spirit
he was born of the Virgin Mary"*

A spin-off of the on-going Lutheran-Catholic Dialogue is a study on Mary in the New Testament.[1] The participants in the Dialogue recognized that mariology, albeit controversial, is a subject of great importance and interest to Christians of all stripes. Believers aside, art students and tourists cannot page through a picture book of Byzantine icons or visit a medieval cathedral without confronting evidence of the Marian cult that has been so much a part of Catholic culture. Even though attitudes toward Mary in the post-Reformation West are sharply divergent, scholars agree that her name is prominent in the Gospel accounts and that it appeared in baptismal creeds already in the second century.

It is impossible in the short space of a few pages even to outline all aspects of mariology and Marian devotions. We shall return to the subject again in discussing the third article of the Creed, but here we must be content with explaining some fundamentals. We concentrate first on the role assigned to Mary in the New Testament, with special emphasis on the infancy narratives, and then we present an overview of Marian devotions, with a final word on the dogmas of the Immaculate Conception and Assumption. In the course of this presentation it will be evident that mariology and christology do not exist as separate themes but form a single, organic whole.[2]

MARY IN THE NEW TESTAMENT

The letters of St. Paul, the earliest books in the Christian canon, do not mention Mary by name. Paul does, however, refer in several places to the birth of Jesus. At the beginning of the Epistle to the Romans, he witnesses to "Jesus Christ our Lord," God's son "who was born of the seed of David" (1:3-4). In the Letter to the Galatians, where Paul is concerned to relate salvation to the Incarnation—that is, the moment when Jesus became a member of the human race and the Jewish people—he writes, "But when the designated time had come, God sent forth his Son born of a woman, born under the Law" (4:3-4). "Born of a woman," a frequently used Semitic idiom implying the human condition, is an oblique reference to Mary in her maternal role.

One other passage in Galatians that relates to Mary's maternal role (again without mentioning her name) provides some background for the Creed's CONCEIVED BY THE HOLY SPIRIT. It occurs in a text where Paul interprets the story of Hagar and Sarah as an allegory. He introduces an element not found in the original Genesis account (see Gen 16:15; 21:1-14): the birth of Isaac "according to the Spirit" (Gal 4:29). Although this passage is intended as a theological reflection on what it means to be "children of promise" (v. 28), it has been read as a stage in the development that links the miraculous birth of Isaac with the Spirit's initiative in the conception of Jesus.

THE INFANCY NARRATIVES

In the synoptic Gospels we distinguish two kinds of texts in which the name Mary of appears. First there are those which deal with Jesus' public life and ministry. Mary is mentioned in a number of passages dealing with the family background of Jesus and her faith in him. Then there are the so-called infancy narratives, the description in the Gospels of Matthew and Luke of the events surrounding Jesus' birth.[3] Mary figures prominently in these accounts, which are told with an eye on the Old Testament in order to emphasize that they are the fulfillment of Israel's hope and to situate them in the context of the covenant. Although the infancy narratives seem to have been composed later than the Gospel accounts of Jesus' public ministry, we treat them first because they are key in understanding the theologies of Matthew and Luke and because of their importance in the development of mariology.

Matthew begins with a long genealogy—"a family record of Jesus Christ, son of David, son of Abraham" (1:1). Even though Joseph has the leading role in the dramatic events surrounding Jesus' birth, Mary's part is of more interest to us here. At the very end of the genealogy Matthew breaks the monotonous pattern of paternity—A was the father of B, B was the father of C, C was the father of D, etc.—to report that "Jacob was the father of Joseph the husband of Mary. It was of her that Jesus who is called the Messiah was born" (1:16). The explanation for this rather unexpected change of rhythm is found in verses 18-25 (which Krister Stendahl says should be read as "an enlarged footnote" to verse 16). They provide details about the peculiar circumstances surrounding Jesus' conception and birth.

The narrative presupposes some knowledge about the Jewish marriage customs of the time. There was first a "betrothal," a formal exchange of consent before witnesses that in effect constituted a legal marriage giving the husband rights over the woman, though she continued to live with her own family. When the husband was able to assume the wife's support there occurred what might today be called the wedding. If in the meantime, however, the wife had sexual relations with anyone else, the act would be regarded as adultery. This is the background for Matthew's account. Mary was betrothed to Joseph, but "before they lived together" she was found to be with child. Since Joseph knew he was not the father, Mary's pregnancy suggested adulterous behavior, which, in Jewish law, was cause for divorce. Although Matthew has already informed his readers that Mary was with child "through the power of the Holy Spirit" (1:18), he describes how Joseph learned of it in a dream (1:20-24). Thus the evangelist clarifies verse 16, where he establishes Jesus' Davidic ancestry while at the same time being careful not to say that Joseph sired the child.

In the dream an angel assures Joseph it is by the Holy Spirit that Mary has conceived and that he should take her into his home as his wife.[4] Matthew further explains the significance of the angel's message, citing Isaiah's prophecy about a virgin conceiving and giving birth to a son (Is 7:14). The Gospel writer reports that Joseph carried out the angel's command so scrupulously that, in the words of the Lutheran-Catholic study, "Mary, who had conceived as a virgin, remained a virgin till she bore Jesus."

For most of the drama (see also Mt 2:13-15, 19-23) Joseph is at center stage, while the extraordinary role played by Mary is alluded to only indirectly. Matthew calls attention to her special position not only by listing her name in the family tree of Jesus, but by mentioning it along with the names of four other extraordinary women: Tamar, Rahab, Ruth and "the wife of Uriah." (It is unusual to find the name of one woman in a genealogy, let alone five!) We have already noted the peculiar circumstances in the marriage of Joseph and Mary. The marriages of Tamar, Rahab, Ruth, and Bathsheba were also irregular and the cause of gossip. Nonetheless, God used them to accomplish his messianic purpose, and now in an even more extraordinary way, God has Mary conceive the Messiah by divine intervention.

In the Matthean account of Jesus' conception and birth, Mary appears as an instrument in God's plan of salvation, and her personal reaction to the motherhood is never mentioned. The picture in Luke's Gospel is quite different. There she takes center stage, with her words and even feelings being reported.

Luke prefaces his description of the birth of Jesus with an account of the birth of John the Baptist. In fact, the Lucan narrative moves from the annunication of John's birth (1:5-25) to the annunication of Jesus' birth (1:26-38), back to the actual births, first of John (1:57-58), then of Jesus (2:1-20), and then to the circumcision of the one and then the other(1:59-66; 2:21). Chapter 1 ends saying of John, "The child grew up and matured in spirit. He lived in the desert until the day when he made his public appearance in Israel" (v. 80). A similar passage in Chapter 2 brings the account of Jesus' infancy to a close: "The child grew in size and strength, filled with wisdom, and the grace of God was upon him" (v. 40). The evidence is that the author drew these parallels to compare and contrast the roles of the two men. He clearly presents Jesus as the superior of the two (1:41-44). Mary is prominent in the account, especially in the visitation scene, where she encounters Elizabeth, John's mother, and recites the Magnificat (1:39-56).

Although the annuniciation scene is said to be the occasion for more reflection and literature than any other Marian text in the New Testament, Luke's primary emphasis is christological. He follows a standard biblical pattern in which an angel reveals the future greatness and destiny of a prophet (see also 1:8-17), and he thereby accomplishes two things: he focuses on Jesus' vocation as Messiah and Savior, and he places Jesus squarely in the prophetic tradition of the Old Testament.

> . . . the angel Gabriel was sent from God to a town of Galilee named Nazareth, to a virgin betrothed to a man named Joseph, of the house of David. The virgin's name was Mary. Upon arriving, the angel said to her: "Rejoice, O highly favored daughter! The Lord is with you. Blessed are you among women." She was deeply troubled by these words, and wondered what his greeting meant. The angel went on to say to her: "Do not fear, Mary. You have found favor with God. You shall conceive and bear a son and give him the name Jesus. Great will be his dignity and he will be called Son of the Most High. The Lord God will give him the throne of David his father. He will rule over the house of Jacob forever and his reign will be without end."

> Mary said to the angel, "How can this be since I do not know man?" The angel answered her: "The Holy Spirit will come upon you and the power of the Most High will overshadow you: hence the offspring to be born will be called Son of God. . . .

> Mary said: "I am the servant of the Lord. Let it be done to me as you say." With that the angel left her. (1:26-38)

The passage echoes certain key themes and phrases that we heard in the opening verses of Paul's Epistle to the Romans (1:3-4): Jesus' Davidic descent, Son of God, power and Spirit of Holiness (i.e., Holy Spirit). What is different about the Lucan text is that it links the divine sonship to the conception of Jesus *by a virgin*. Luke is more indirect and subtle than Matthew in making the point because he is also concerned to exalt Jesus over John the Baptist. The argument runs that if the conception of John is marked by a special divine intervention, then God's intervention with regard to Jesus can be expected to be even more noteworthy. In John's case the power of God intervened to overcome the natural obstacle of his parent's sterility, made more hopeless by their age; in Jesus' case God's power is even more manifest because it dispenses with human initiative altogether. Luke attests to the virginal conception again later when he gives the genealogy of Jesus and says he was the son of Joseph, "so it was supposed" (3:23)—a remark that makes little sense if he had been begotten by Joseph.

THE FAMILY OF JESUS

In the Gospel of Mark, Mary appears in only one scene:

> His mother and his brothers arrived, and as they stood outside
> they sent word to him to come out. The crowd seated around him
> told him, "Your mother and your brothers and sisters are outside
> asking for you." He said in reply, "Who are my mother and my
> brothers?" And gazing around him at those seated in the circle
> he continued, "These are my mother and my brothers. Whoever
> does the will of God is brother and sister and mother to me."
> (3:31-34)

The final verse in the passage (v. 35) is thought to be one of those
"sayings" of Jesus that came to have an existence all their own and,
much like some biblical texts today, were quoted in more than one
context (see Lk 11:28). Considered in itself the verse tells us who in the
eyes of the believing community really make up Jesus' family. Jesus'
"eschatological family," called into being by the proclamation of the
kingdom of God, is constituted of those who hear the word of God
and do the will of God. Mark clearly distinguishes the "eschatological
family" from Jesus's natural family. The "outside"-vs.-"inside" stag-
ing dramatizes that the reality that really matters in the kingdom is not
blood ties but obedience to the will of God. Matthew's account is
much the same, but he softens the contrast between the natural and the
eschatological families of Jesus (12:46-50). Whereas Mark says that
Jesus looked on the listeners "seated in the circle" about him as
mother and brothers to him, Matthew says he pointed to "his disciples" as his true family (v. 49). The parallel account in Luke does not
contrast the physical and eschatological families and, in fact, seems to
include Mary and his "brothers" among the disciples (8:19-21).

The discussion of these passages is of interest for two reasons. The
first is, the mention of Jesus' "brothers" suggests that he had siblings
and that, according to some authors, Mary was their mother. Second,
the eschatological family and the notion of discipleship provide the
theological foundation for mariology.

The issue of Jesus' "brothers" would not in itself be important if it
were not for the fact that in the Catholic tradition (including the
Byzantine) Mary has been honored as "ever virgin" (*semper virgo*)—
that is, she remained a virgin even after the birth of Jesus. On the other
hand, Protestants, even those who tenaciously hold for the virgin

birth, do not put the same emphasis on the continued virginity of Mary. The New Testament is silent on the matter, and it is only because of the development of mariology and Marian devotions that attention has focused on the exact relationship between Jesus and these "brothers" and "sisters."

Sometime about 300, written documents begin to speak of the blessed Mary "ever virgin." It became a stock phrase in medieval works and continued to be used in Protestant writings in the sixteenth century. In the course of time, "ever virgin" was interpreted to mean that Mary was virgin "before, during and after" the birth of her one and only child, Jesus. The essential notion attested to by the New Testament and echoed in the Creed is Mary's viriginity before birth (*ante partum*); that is, she conceived miraculously by the power of the Holy Spirit. The Gospel accounts in Matthew and Luke describe extraordinary events that coincided with the actual birth of Jesus, but apocryphal writings of questionable authority go further. They recount colorful vignettes surrounding the birth of Jesus that become the basis for the belief that Mary remained virgin *in partu*—that is, that Mary did not suffer the normal pangs of childbirth and that she remained physically unaffected. Others, however, reacting to the danger of docetism (a heresy which held that Jesus only "appeared" to be human), insisted that Jesus was born in the normal way. The second-century writer Tertullian was one of those who reacted strongly against docetism; for him it was enough of a sign that Jesus was conceived miraculously.

The tradition of Mary's perpetual virginity is a corollary of the virgin birth. It implies that she remained virgin even after the birth of Jesus (*post partum*). The image of Mary as "ever virgin" is clearly connected with exaltation of the virgin as a prototype of holiness, of the one who is single-minded and steadfast in commitment to the things of the Lord. In Christian circles this image was reinforced by St. Paul. For him virginity had an eschatological connotation: with the resurrection in the final days (which Paul thought were imminent) marriage would pass away (see also Mk 12:25; Mt 22:30). Thus virginity already anticipates the life of the resurrection and in that sense represents an ideal state (1 Cor 7:1-40).

The virginity of Mary typifies in another way the Christian call to holiness. A text in the prologue to John's Gospel once thought to be a reference to the virgin birth describes the disciples who accepted Jesus and in turn were empowered to "become children of God. These are they who believe in his name—who were begotten not by blood, nor by carnal desire, nor by man's willing it, but by God" (1:12-13). According to Luke, Mary is the model of Christian discipleship. Throughout the infancy narrative her response is one of humble openness, acceptance, and obedience to God's call (see Lk 1:38; 2:19). Although she addressed Mary with "Blest are you among women and blest is the fruit of your womb," Elizabeth made it clear that the basis for her praise is not purely the physical motherhood. Elizabeth adds, "Blest is she who trusted that the Lord's words to her would be fulfilled" (Lk 1:42,45).[5] Simeon tells Mary she will know the test of discipleship in suffering: ". . . you yourself shall be pierced with a sword—so that the thoughts of many hearts may be laid bare" (Lk 2:35). And though it would take time for Mary to understand everything that was happening to her, she, like her son Jesus, puts obedience to the heavenly Father above family ties:

> . . . a woman in the crowd called out, "Blest is the womb that bore you and the breasts that nursed you!" "Rather," he replied, "blest are they who hear the word of God and keep it." (Lk 11:27-28)

Mary appears in two dramatic scenes in John's Gospel, one at the beginning of his public ministry, the other at the end: the wedding feast at Cana (2:1-11), and on Calvary, where she stands at the foot of the cross. In these accounts Mary's particular claim on Jesus rests not so much on her status as physical mother as on her relationship with the disciples of Jesus.

> Near the cross of Jesus there stood his mother, his mother's sister, Mary the wife of Clopas, and Mary Magdalene. Seeing his mother there with the disciple whom he loved, Jeus said to his mother, "Woman, there is your son." In turn he said to the disciple, "There is your mother." From that hour onward, the disciple took her into his care. (19:25-27)

The scene at the foot of the cross brings together two idealized figures for whom John never gives personal names—"the mother of Jesus" and "the disciple whom he loved." Their ties with Jesus during his lifetime become the grounds for a new familial relationship in terms of discipleship. Mary is entrusted with a spiritual role as mother of the disciple, and the disciple assumes the role of her son.

This incident climaxes Jesus' earthly ministry; he realizes "Everything was now finished" (v. 28). He dies leaving behind, and symbolically gathered at the foot of the cross, a small community of believing disciples. In other New Testament writings it is the eschatological community that takes shape in the post-resurrection and Pentecost period. For John, however, the lifting up of Jesus on the cross marks his exaltation at the right hand of the Father, and symbolic references to the Spirit anticipate Pentecost (see Jn 19:30,34). At this point Mary's role no longer pertains to Jesus' earthly ministry but to the history of the church.

BLESSED AMONG WOMEN

Mary sings out in the Magnificat, "All ages shall call me blessed" (Lk 1:48). The New Testament witnesses that she enjoyed a preeminent place from the beginning, and the development of popular Marian devotions in both East and West makes her words prophetic. Historically the cult of Mary includes three elements: 1) veneration; that is, Mary receives special honor in recognition of her unique role as Mother of God; 2) imitation, because as virgin and as disciple par excellence (in the sense explained above) she is the model of holiness; and 3) invocation, which acknowledges Mary's power of intercession (a notion that will be explained later in discussing the "communion of saints").

About the time baptismal creeds were taking shape in the second century, the cult of Mary focused on her as a "new Eve." It appears as a corollary of the Pauline typology which pictures Christ as a new Adam (Rom 5:12-21). St. Irenaeus elaborates on the theme: he contrasts Adam, born of the virgin earth, with Christ, born of the Virgin Mary. Eve, who cooperated with the devil in bringing death into the world, is contrasted with Mary, whose obedience undid Eve's disobedience and set the stage for redemption and salvation in Christ.[6]

In the fourth century, influential writers such as St. Athanasius in the East and St. Ambrose in the West proposed Mary as a model of holiness for dedicated virgins. By the next century popular devotion to Mary was so widespread that when Nestorius, the patriarch of Constantinople, refused to call Mary *Theotokos* (usually translated in English as "Mother of God," but literally meaning "Godbearer"), he caused a schism in the church. The Council of Ephesus (431) condemned Nestorius and declared authoritatively that "the holy Virgin is Mother of God [*theotokos*]." After Ephesus, Marian feasts begin to appear in the liturgical calendar in increasing numbers.[7] The cult of Mary at this time was inextricably tied to christology; it focused on her holiness and her role as Mother of God.

MARIAN DEVOTIONS AND DOGMAS

The medieval period, especially in the Latin church, concentrated on Mary's power of intercession. The cult of Mary grew apace with devotions to the saints, with "St. Mary" exalted above all others. Marian devotions took on a variety of expressions. Cathedrals and abbeys dedicated to her became centers of pilgrimage. In Carolingian times Saturday began to be observed as "Mary's day," paralleling the observance of Sunday as the Lord's day, with special prayers in the liturgy of the hours and eucharistic celebratiions. The literature of the period is filled with prayers, poetry, and sermons honoring Mary. Great theologian-preachers such as St. Bernard of Clairvaux (whose devotion to Mary is immortalized in Dante's *Paradiso*), St. Bonaventure, St. Thomas, Duns Scotus, Jean Gerson, and St. Bernardine of Siena (to mention only a few) were all exuberant in praise of her.

The words of the infancy narratives, already in use as antiphons in the liturgy, become the prayers of popular piety. About the twelfth century the Hail Mary begins to take shape; it uses the greetings of the Angel Gabriel and Elizabeth, to which is later added (in the fifteenth century) the petition asking Mary's intercession for mercy on our sins and for a happy death.[8] Another medieval custom that has endured is the practice of reciting three Hail Marys at daybreak, noon, and sundown to recall the mystery of the Incarnation. Each Hail Mary is prefaced with an antiphon that paraphrases a Scripture text. The first such antiphon begins "The Angel [*angelus*] of the Lord declared unto Mary" (see Lk 1:25), and thus the prayer is known as the Angelus.

The Hail Mary is recited almost as a mantra in the rosary, a meditation on the mysteries of Jesus' life. The mysteries, usually fifteen in number, form three groups of five: the "joyful mysteries," which focus attention on the infancy narratives; the "sorrowful mysteries," which recall the passion and death of Jesus; and the "glorious mysteries," which include the resurrection and exaltation of the Lord at the right hand of the Father. Taken together these fifteen mysteries are a compendium of Christ's saving work. Ten Hail Marys—"the decades of the rosary"—are recited while one reflects on each of the mysteries. From another perspective the rosary is called "a poor person's psalter" because it consists of 150 Hail Marys, corresponding to the 150 Psalms. In the Middle Ages people would pray the mysteries of the rosary while working, traveling, etc., much as the monks prayed the liturgy of the hours.

The rosary illustrates a common trait that distinguished medieval devotion to Mary: its emphasis on the human nature of Jesus (not to mention the human needs of the petitioners), especially his passion and death. Mary's compassion with the sufferings of her son became a favorite theme, as can be seen in poetry and hymns such as the Stabat Mater. Devotion to specific "sorrows" in the life of Our Lady (e.g., Simeon's prophecy, the crucifixion) gave rise to liturgical feasts commemorating them. Another trait of medieval mariology can be seen in Dante's literary masterpiece, the *Divine Comedy*, which attributes to Mary intercessory power throughout the entire universe—earth, purgatory, heaven, and even hell.

The cult of Mary became the object of criticism during the Reformation. The early Reformers for the most part did not attack Marian devotions as such; their criticisms came indirectly as corollaries to their doctrinal position regarding the intercession of the saints and their denunciation of excesses in popular piety. The Protestant confessions of the sixteenth century regarded the invocation of Mary under such titles as "Spiritual Mother" and "Queen of Heaven" as detracting from Christ's unique role as mediator.

The Catholic defense of the cult of the saints in general and of Mary in particular led to developments in mariology that have evoked criticism from even Catholic theologians. Already in the eighteenth century the great scholar L. A. Muratori (with the blessing of Pope Benedict XIV) reacted against piety that exaggerated Mary's role; for example, he repudiated the notion that Mary could give orders in heaven. In general, theologians have been critical of all tendencies in practice and theory that give mariology an identity independent from christology.

In most ways (including the exuberance and sometimes the exaggeration), Marian devotions in the last two centuries have been in continuity with the spirit and practices of the Middle Ages. This is true of devotions honoring the immaculate conception and the assumption of Mary, two great Christian mysteries celebrated for centuries which have received official expression as dogmas only in the modern period. Christians who have not been brought up in the Catholic tradition debate them for a number of reasons. Principally they question the immaculate conception and the assumption because 1) they do not see how these dogmas are supported in Scripture; and 2) they question the manner in which they were declared doctrines of the church. We shall wait to consider the latter point in connection with the papacy, but the former issue belongs properly in any discussion of mariology.

Before addressing the question whether the dogmas of the Immaculate Conception and the Assumption of Mary are supported by Scripture it is necessary to clarify their intent and meaning. In the spirit of ecumenism Protestant theologian John Macquarrie writes,

> I believe that these two dogmas, when purged of mythological elements, can be interpreted as implications of more central Christian teaching. Theologically, of course, their significance does not lie in anything they say about the private biography of Mary but as pointing to moments in the life of the community of faith, for here again there is an intimate parallel between Mary and the Church.[9]

It is presumed that Mary was conceived like every other human being, and therefore the "immaculate conception" speaks not of the manner in which she was begotten but of the fact that from the first moment of her existence she was "graced." Macquarrie puts in nicely: "Immaculate conception, in spite of the negative adjective, is, like the sinlessness of Jesus, a thoroughly affirmative idea."[10] There is indeed a negative side: that Mary was preserved from original sin. But it is the positive side that better explains the dogma's significance. It is the symbol par excellence of "free grace": Mary was justified from the first instant of her existence independently of anything she desired or did (*ante praevisa merita*). The dogma of the Immaculate Conception implicitly affirms that God predestined Mary to be the mother of God and for that reason immunized her, as it were, against all sin.

The dogma represents a development and clarification of the church's understanding of Mary's holiness. Early in the history of the church, sermons, especially in the East, eulogized the sanctity and purity of the Mother of God, affirming without any special emphasis that she was sinless throughout her life. Theologians in the medieval West, however, preoccupied as they were with the universality of

R 11/31/86

This review copy comes to you with the compliments of

TWENTY-THIRD PUBLICATIONS

Please let us know if you like this book enough to recommend it to others.

We will appreciate hearing from you.

Title: The Creed

Author: Berard Marthaler

Publication date: 1-7-87   Price: $14.95

XXIII

P.O. BOX 180 ● MYSTIC, CT 06355 ● 1-203-536-2611

ISBN 0-89622 –320–5

Christ's redemptive work, found it difficult to reconcile the immaculate conception with their understanding of original sin. It was St. Thomas who formulated the crucial objection against the immaculate conception:

> If the soul of the Blessed Virgin had never been stained with the contagion of original sin, this would have detracted from Christ's dignity as the savior of all men.[11]

When the Franciscan theologian Duns Scotus (d. 1308) resolved Thomas' difficulty, acceptance of the immaculate conception became general. Scotus argued that Mary, far from not needing Christ's redemptive work, was its greatest beneficiary. Whereas everyone else knows the saving work of Christ as a cure for sin, Mary experienced its preventative effects.

Sometime about 1480 Rome authorized the liturgical feast of the Immaculate Conception (now celebrated on December 8), but it was only in 1854 that Pope Pius IX, after consulting with bishops throughout the world, declared it a doctrine of the church. Almost a hundred years later (1950), Pope Pius XII took similar action regarding in the assumption of Mary into heaven. Belief that Mary "when the course of her earthly life was finished" (as Pius XII so carefully phrased it) was taken body and spirit into heavenly glory in the presence of the Risen Lord can be traced at least to the fifth century.

The two dogmas nicely complement each other. Just as the immaculate conception exemplifies God's initiative in extending love—grace—toward creatures more in terms of what they are called to be than because of anything they have done, so the assumption exemplifies the destiny that awaits the members of Jesus' eschatological family. As "the first fruit of the redemption," Mary typifies, in a way that Jesus (who did not need redemption) could not, what it means to be redeemed in Christ. While neither the immaculate conception nor the assumption is mentioned in Scripture, they nonetheless reaffirm truths which are clearly implied in the mystery of grace and election. They illustrate once again how church doctrine affirms more about human nature and needs than about the Godhead—an axiom that seems especially true of the Marian dogmas.

The present wording of the creed, CONCEIVED BY THE POWER OF THE HOLY SPIRIT, HE WAS BORN OF THE VIRGIN MARY, dates from the fourth century. It more clearly distinguishes the conception by the Holy Spirit and the birth from the Virgin Mary than did earlier versions. St. Augustine whose creed apparently lacked the distinction between CONCEIVED and BORN, found it necessary to explain that Jesus is not *literally* born from the Holy Spirit.[12] We shall have more to say about the work of the Spirit in Article Three; in this chapter our focus has been on the birth of Jesus of a woman, an affirmation of his human condition and of his Jewish lineage. We take up the Jesus of history again in the next chapter but from a different point of view.

Notes

1. R. E. Brown, K. P. Donfried, J. A. Fitzmyer, J. Reumann, eds., *Mary in the New Testament: A Collaborative Assessment by Protestant and Roman Catholic Scholars* (Philadelphia: Fortress Press and New York: Paulist Press, 1978).

2. E. Schillebeeckx, *Mary the Mother of the Redemption* (New York: Sheed & Ward, 1964), p. 1.

3. Raymond E. Brown, *The Birth of the Messiah* (Garden City, NY: Doubleday, 1977).

4. Re "according to the Spirit," see Brown et al., pp. 45–48. Like the other evangelists, Matthew was influenced by the concerns and questions of his own community in writing his Gospel. The internal evidence (e.g., the sayings in Chapter 23) suggests a polemic against the scribes and Pharisees, and the presence of an increasing number of Gentile converts (21:43,46). Matthew had to develop a christology that would be convincing to diverse points of view. On the one side, he amassed biblical citations that explained to non-Christian Jews the role of Jesus in God's plan of salvation. On the other side, he justified the presence of the Gentiles in the community by showing that God had from the beginning included them in the plan of salvation (3:7–10).

5. Elizabeth says in praise of her, "Blest is she who trusted that the Lord's words to her would be fulfilled" (1:46). It is fitting that the first of these "marcarisms" (from the Greek *makarios*, for "blessed" or "happy") in Luke's Gospel is declared of Mary because they are

characteristic of the way Jesus describes his disciples in Luke's Gospel, "Blest [*makarios*] are you poor," "Blest are you who hunger" etc. (Lk 6:20ff).

6. *Mary in the New Testament*, pp. 252–257. See Hilda Graef, *Mary: A History of Doctrine and Devotion*, 2 vols. (New York: Sheed & Ward, 1963).

7. The oldest Marian feast is the "Remembrance of Mary," corresponding to the *dies natalis* of the martyrs. See *NCE* 9:365.

8. "The oldest prescription relative to the recitation of the Hail Mary is found at the end of the 12th century. Bishop Odo of Siliac in the Synod of 1198 required the clergy to see that the faithful recited not only the Our Father and the Creed but also the Hail Mary . . . Shortly after, the councils of many other nations made similar prescriptions. . ." *NCE* 6:899.

9. J. Macquarrie, *Principles*, p. 397.

10. Ibid., p. 398.

11. *Summa Theologiae* (Henceforth *ST*) 3a, 27.2 ad 2 (quoted in *NCE* 7:380).

12. Kelly, *Creeds*, pp. 376–377.

8

In Quest
of the Historical Jesus

"Suffered under Pontius Pilate"

In reciting the Creed, more often than not the phrases fall off our lips like names in a roll call. A break in the cadence, however, causes us to hesitate, to pause and look again at the text. "Pontius Pilate"? The Creed mentions only two names other than that of Jesus Christ himself: Mary and Pilate. The first, one expects; the second comes as a surprise; and yet both appear in the primitive versions of the creeds dated the second century. They pass over Peter and the apostles, Mary Magdalene, and the faithful women who were early disciples, to enshrine the name of the Roman bureaucrat who authorized the execution of Jesus.

Christians probably learned of Pilate when they heard the gospel message proclaimed for the first time. He is named in the Acts of the Apostles (3:13; 4:27; 13:28) and in the early creeds. Paraphrasing one of the most primitive forms of the creed that has come down to us, St. Justine Martyr stated "Our Teacher of these things is Jesus Christ, who was crucified under Pontius Pilate, procurator of Judea, in the reign of Tiberius Caesar."[1] Two reasons why second-century Christians

130

"busied themselves," as J. N. D. Kelly puts it, "to an astonishing degree with the figure of Pilate" are these. First, they desired to fix the time in which Jesus died and thus, as we would say today, establish the fact that he was not a fictional hero but a figure of history. Second, they cited Pilate's witness to Jesus' innocence to exonerate Jesus (and by implication the Christian community) of charges that Jesus presented a threat to Rome's political power.[2] These two points are developed in this chapter. In connection with the first we look at the methods of source, form, and redaction criticism and at the value of the Gospel accounts as historical documents; in connection with the second we discuss the perennial issue about who was really responsible for Jesus' execution: the Romans or the Jews. But first we must say a word about Pilate's own niche in history.

The Roman historian Tacitus, one of the few non-Christian authors to corroborate a fact described in the Gospels, reported that Christ "suffered the extreme penalty during the reign of Tiberius at the hands of one of our procurators, Pontius Pilate."[3] A Roman noble of inferior rank, Pilate governed the province of Judea for a period of about ten years (c. 26-36). The ancient Jewish writers, Josephus and Philo, picture him as violent, cruel, insensitive to Jewish customs, and guilty of executing individuals without due legal process. The New Testament writers present a less harsh picture and, according to some modern scholars, one which may be closer to the truth.[4]

THE GOSPELS AS HISTORY

Shortly after the turn of the century, Albert Schweitzer wrote a provocative book which, translated into English as *The Quest of the Historical Jesus*, received a good deal of notoriety.[5] People who know only the English title (and have not read the book) sometimes think that Schweitzer had doubts about whether Jesus existed. Schweitzer doubted many things, but he took for granted (as all professional scholars do) the historical evidence that almost two thousand years ago there lived a Jew named Jesus who was crucified during the time when Pontius Pilate was Roman procurator in Palestine (c. A.D. 26-36). The subtitle, *A Critical Study of Its Progress from Reimarus to Wrede*, is closer to the original German title and better describes Schweitzer's intent to take a careful look at nineteenth-century attempts to write biographies of Jesus.

Greatly influenced by the English deists, Herman Samuel Reimarus (1694-1768), professor of Oriental languages in Hamburg, was skeptical about the value of the Gospels as historical accounts. He denied the possibility of miracles (the only miracle he admitted was creation itself!) and maintained that Jesus had messianic illusions. According to Reimarus, Jesus preached straightforward, practical morality in preparation for the imminent establishment of the kingdom of God. Reimarus distinguished Jesus' understanding of his mission from the way that mission was interpreted by the disciples after his death on the cross. It was only after Reimarus' own death, however, when the poet and man of letters G.E. Lessing published excerpts from his writings, that these views became widely known.[6]

The skepticism in Reimarus' writings reflected the mood of the Enlightenment. Despite their reservations about "revelation," the leading intellectuals of the period put unlimited trust in reason (and thus in England the era is called "the Age of Reason"). The rationalists, in Germany at least, studied the Scriptures in a new spirit. They pointed out differences between the Old and the New Testaments, and discrepancies within each. They asked whether it was John's Gospel or the Synoptics, that preserved the more accurate picture of Jesus. Did he talk in long, allegorical discourses as in John, or in parables as in the Synoptics? Did his public ministry last one year, as the Synoptics suggest, or three, as John indicates? When did he purge the Temple of hucksters and money changers: early in his ministry (Jn 2:13-17), or in Holy Week at the very end of his life (Mt 21:1-14; Mk 11:1-11,15-17)? These and other questions caused a new generation of scholars to investigate the sources and to ask questions about the ways the evangelists compiled their material.[7]

It was evident to scholars at the beginning of the nineteenth century that the Gospels were not biographies of Jesus, but they believed that the life of Jesus "as he really was" could be reconstructed if only modern biographers were critical in using the sources. The publication of Reimarus' writings marked the beginning of the "quest for the historical Jesus" and laid the foundation for "source criticism," which was to be charactristic of New Testament studies for the next hundred years and into the twentieth century. By using the methods of literary criticism and "scientific" historical investigation, biblical scholars sought to get to the story behind the story.

Thus Reimarus set the stage for a long series of "lives" of Jesus. The *Life of Christ* by D. F. Strauss, published in 1835, was a watershed in New Testament studies. Up to then, such works had either followed the orthodox interpretation of Jesus as the embodiment of the divine in human history or, following the radical approach of Reimarus and the Enlightenment, had discounted the miraculous in the Gospels and explained Jesus in purely rational terms. Strauss, however, charted a third course: "the mythological interpretation," which says that there is a historical basis for the Gospel accounts but that the actual events have been transformed and embellished by the faith of the church. Nonetheless he concluded that any attempt (his own included) to write a biography of Jesus is doomed to failure because of the nature of the sources.

Another celebrated work of the period was the *Vie de Jésus* (1863) by the French scholar Ernest Renan, whose influence was due in large part to an attractive literary style. Renan's romantic view of Jesus as an "incomparable man" was enshrined in the Harvard Classics, which incorporated an English translation of his work.

Although nineteenth-century biblical criticism is faulted for its rationalism and skepticism, it had a positive side. Its distinction between the Jesus of history and the Christ of faith—the different ways a mere observer and a true believer viewed events in the life of Jesus—provided an important starting point in interpreting the Gospel message for modern readers. For the most part scholars were concerned lest the figure of Jesus dissolve into a vague spirit or "idea." On the broader issue of New Testament studies they worked hard to develop the historical method. They compiled convincing arguments for the "two-source theory," which indicates that the Gospel of Mark and another primitive source known as "Q" (from the German word for source, *Quelle*), stood very close to the original apostolic tradition and were used by the other evangelists in writing their Gospels. The two-source theory gave many reason to believe that with some refinements the historico-critical method would indeed prove Strauss wrong and provide a way to get at the historical Jesus, whose real identity is veiled by dogmatic trappings.

Schweitzer's work exposed the fatal flaw in source criticism. He cited the research of Wilhelm Wrede, who, using the same literary and historical methods as other source critics, demonstrated the fundamental inconsistency of many studies in their attempts to reconstruct a picture of the historical Jesus based on Mark's Gospel. Wrede showed that Mark's account was as much an interpretation of Jesus based on belief in his divinity as were the other Gospels. In short, nineteeth-century scholars pushed source criticism as far as it would go in their efforts to reconstruct the Jesus of history, only to become more skeptical than ever about the value of the Gospels as historical sources.

FORM CRITICISM

Source criticism as it was generally understood in the nineteenth century had a built-in limitation in that it restricted itself to a study of the documents at hand. It concentrated chiefly on the written text in its various versions and manuscript traditions. Before the quest could begin again it was necessary to find a new method that could get beneath the written documents.[8] Shortly after World War I, New Testament scholars were heartened by the success of the distinguished Old Testament scholar Herman Gunkel (1862-1932), who was able to reconstruct the oral traditions underlying many of the written accounts of events told in Genesis and the Psalms. It was his contention that the Bible was the end product of a long process that incorporated sayings, stories, and myths that had been kept alive from generation to generation by word of mouth. For Gunkel the most important part of his research was to reconstruct the *Sitz im Leben* (the "situation in life") that gave rise to the oral tradition in the first place.

Among the first to adapt Gunkel's approach to New Testament study were the German scholars K. L. Schmidt and Martin Dibelius; later came Rudolf Bultmann (1884-1976), perhaps the most formidable New Testament scholar of the twentieth century. They are the founders of the school of "form criticism," so called because of the importance they attribute to literary form (or genre). Although these pioneers and others who advocate the methods of form criticism differ among themselves on some points, they tend to agree on basic principles. Thanks to their work, it is now commonly accepted that a generation or so separated the events of Jesus' public life and the writing of Mark, the first canonical Gospel (dated about A.D. 65). In the intervening period the gospel message was proclaimed orally—the "kerygma" (= proclamation)—and various Christian communities began to collect the sayings of Jesus and anecdotes about him. Handed on at first by word of mouth, they were soon written down and circulated as separate units. (It is likely that each church in the larger cities had its own collection, though many of the stories were common to several collections.)

Many of the sayings and stories had a practical value in that they embodied Jesus' teachings or showed by way of example how he dealt with religious issues and challenges to his mission. These pericopes, i.e., the individual stories and sayings that make up the Gospels, were like a random collection of precious gems, waiting for a jeweler to string them into a necklace. As the early form critics saw it, the evangelists were the jewelers, each of whom gave the necklace a different design according to his own taste. Using the methods of literary criticism, scholars distinguish in the four canonical Gospels traces of these various collections and classify them according to their literary form. In the end, however, the form critics—like the source critics before them—agree that the Gospels are not so much biographies of Jesus as they are reflections of the faith and life of the primitive church.[9]

Form critics are like archeologists in that they begin at the top and dig downward; they examine the surface remains that are there for all to see; then they unearth the foundations; and finally they get down to bedrock. Thus form critics distinguish three layers: 1) the Gospel accounts as we know them in the canon; 2) the local, ecclesial contexts in which the stories and sayings were first recalled—namely, the needs and interests of particular primitive Christian communities; and 3) the circumstances that surrounded an individual story or saying in the actual life of Jesus and the meaning of that story or saying. These three stages in the formation of the Gospel material are commonly referred to by German phrases: 1) *Sitz im Evangelium*; 2) *Sitz im Leben der Kirche*; and 3) *Sitz im Leben Jesu* or *Sitz im Historie*.[10]

PONTIUS PILATE AND FORM CRITICISM

Since this chapter is concerned with the Roman procurator Pontius Pilate, it might be helpful to illustrate the method of form criticism by saying something about the attitude of the early Christians toward the Roman Empire that Pilate represented. One recalls in the synoptic Gospels how some Pharisees and Herodians ask Jesus, "Is it lawful to pay the tax to the emperor or not?" Jesus, realizing that they were trying to trap him, gave his celebrated response, "Give to Caesar what is Caesar's, but give to God what is God's" (Mk 12:13-17; see also Mt 22:15-33 and Lk 20:20-39). Mark's account presents the *Sitz im Evangelium*, which in this case is probably close to the way the incident actually happened in the life of Jesus—the *Sitz im Leben Jesu*. It is a good story, but why was this incident remembered and others forgotten? According to the form critics one must look to the problems besetting the early Christian community for an answer—the purpose the story served in the life of the church, its *Sitz im Leben der Kirche*. In the first century, in Palestine, Antioch, Alexandria, and elsewhere, Christians had to ask themselves the political question about obedience to the Roman authorities. They remembered the anecdote about Jesus, and his answer guided their own attitudes and behavior just as it affirms for many modern Christians the policy of separation of church and state.

The prominence of Pontius Pilate in the New Testament might be explained in much the same way. All four of the Gospel writers dramatize his role in the passion and death of Jesus. They further relate how he delivered the body to Joseph of Arimathea for burial, and Matthew tells how Pilate permitted the Jewish leaders to set a guard at Jesus' tomb (27:65). The New Testament writers are much less harsh in their judgment of Pilate than are the ancient Jewish sources of about the same period that describe him as violent, cruel, and insensitive to Jewish legal procedures. The Gospel accounts have Pilate testify to Jesus' innocence, and they make it seem that he pronounced the death sentence only under pressure. There is reason to believe (as will be discussed below) that the narratives describing Jesus' passion and death report the events fairly accurately.

Before the Gospels were written, moreover, Pilate was prominent in the early examples of the kerygma—the oral proclamation of the "good news." Peter chides his fellow Israelites for handing over "the Holy and Just One" and disowning him "in Pilate's presence when Pilate was ready to release him" (Acts 3:13). And Paul in a similar discourse says, "Even though they found no charge against him which deserved death, they begged Pilate to have him executed" (Acts 13:28). As we noted at the outset of this chapter the Christian community cited Pilate's witness to Jesus' innocence to make it clear that he was not a political revolutionary and, by implication, that his followers were innocent of such charges too.

Although Pilate's prominence in the Creed does not have a parallel in the primitive kerygma, he is named in the First Epistle to Timothy:

> Fight the good fight of faith. Take firm hold on the everlasting life to which you were called when, in the presence of many witnesses, you made your noble profession of faith. Before God, who gives life to all, and before Christ Jesus, who in bearing witness made his noble profession before Pontius Pilate, I charge you to keep God's command without blame or reproach until our Lord Jesus Christ shall appear. (1 Tim 6:12-13)

This passage reflects a second strand in the oral tradition. It suggests that the confession of faith made by Christians at baptism is similar to Jesus' own profession before Pilate.

THE NEW QUEST FOR THE HISTORICAL JESUS

Although form critic Rudolf Bultmann was skeptical about the quest for the historical Jesus (and for theological reasons thought it an *illegitimate* inquiry), he admitted as "fact" the existence of a man, Jesus of Nazareth, who, during the time when Pontius Pilate was Roman procurator, suffered death by crucifixion. This much is confirmed by the Roman historian Tacitus. Other biblical scholars, however, have greater confidence in historico-critical methods, including form criticism. Furthermore, they see the question of the historical Jesus as important if the claims of Christianity are to be taken as more than fantasy and projections of illusory hope. To ignore the earthly Jesus represents a failure to take seriously the concern of the first Christians to identify the Risen Lord exalted at the right hand of the Father with the Suffering Servant, humiliated and executed by enemies of the kingdom. To negate the significance of Jesus' historical existence is to rob him of his full humanity and to lapse into a modern form of docetism.

It is ironic (and also somewhat inaccurate) that the "new quest for the historical Jesus" is said to have its beginnings among former students of Bultmann. They had come to see (as many English and American scholars and some Germans such as Joachim Jeremias had insisted all along) that there are pieces in the synoptic tradition that historians have to acknowledge as authentic if they are to claim to be historians at all. All agree that the picture of Jesus that emerges from the New Testament is seen through the eyes of faith. They concur that the disciples and first Christians, more concerned with the events themselves than with their sequence, do not provide enough data to establish a chronology for Jesus' public ministry. While the sayings of Jesus are more like paraphrases than exact quotes, they do capture his spirit and reflect his impact on listeners. Prominent New Testament scholar Reginald H. Fuller has used the form-critical methods to examine the miracle stories and concludes that analysis of the sources confirms the picture of Jesus as a miracle worker. All the early sources contain references to Jesus' healings, and unfriendly sources affirm that Jesus was charged with sorcery—an apparent confirmation of the claim that he performed exorcisms. The great English scholar C. H. Dodd reconstructed the context in which many of Jesus' parables were told by applying the methods of form criticism. His efforts to get behind the parables as they are reported in the Synoptics—the *Sitz im Evangelium*—to the form in which they were originally spoken by Jesus—the *Sitz im Leben Jesu*—have been widely accepted. Dodd's methods were further refined by Jeremias, whose study of the use of the parables made by the early church—the *Sitz im Leben der Kirche*—anchors the tradition in the teachings of Jesus.

Significant differences in attitude and belief notwithstanding, the early form critics were the children of the nineteenth-century source critics and the protagonists of the "new quest" are their grandchildren. Because the new quest has been more modest in its expectations, it has claimed certainty for relatively few facts and has been content with a generalized picture of the Jesus of history, enough to ground the faith and preaching of the New Testament church on a firm foundation: Jesus, a Jew from Nazareth in Galilee, was thought to be the son of Joseph the carpenter. He was baptized by John and began to preach in towns along the Lake of Galilee. He told parables that announced the imminent reign of God and insisted on the need for repentance. Going about healing and doing good works, he met opposition from the Pharisees. Finally he was crucified in Jerusalem under Pontius Pilate. More important, however, than the facts themselves was the eschatological significance of his preaching: in announcing that the kingdom of God is at hand he called men and women to discipleship, that is, to make an existential decision about how they will live their lives and how they see their relationship to God and to their fellow humans.

THE PASSION NARRATIVES

As minimal as the foregoing facts might seem to be, it should be noted that they affirm much more than is suggested by the Creeds. Both the Apostles' Creed and the Ecumenical Creed of Constantinople jump from the birth of Jesus to his passion and death without a word about his ministry of preaching and healing! Even though the passion narratives are heavily laden with theological interpretation (a subject we return to in the next chapter), they describe the most fully attested historical "facts" in the life of Jesus—his suffering and death under Pontius Pilate. The passion narrative forms the longest single section in all the Gospels. All four Gospels, moreover, are in substantial agreement about how Jesus was betrayed, arrested, tried, tortured, and given over to the executioners.

From the standpoint of chronology the most notable difference in the passion narratives is the date of the Last Supper. According to Mark and the other two Synoptics, Jesus ate a *Passover* meal with his disciples on the night before he died, and the crucifixion took place on the feast of the Passover itself (Mk 14:12-17). The lunar calendar in use at the time marked the beginning of a new day at sunset, so that in the synoptic accounts, all the events from the Last Supper through the burial took place on the feast of the Passover, the fifteenth day of the month of Nisan.

John tells a different story. In his account the meal took place "before the Passover" (13:1; 18:28), and Jesus was already dead and buried when the feast of the Passover began (19:31). According to the Johannine account the crucifixion took place on Passover eve—"the Preparation Day for Passover" (19:14), the fourteenth day of Nisan. Nisan corresponds roughly to the month of April in the Gregorian calendar. Modern astronomers calculate the date of Jesus' death to have been April 7, A.D. 30. Mark and John do agree, however, that the day of the week was Thursday evening/Friday—that is, the day of the week that preceded the Sabbath (Mk 15:42; Jn 19:31). From another standpoint, moreover, the uncertainty regarding the date, a matter of twenty-four hours, is not important. Even in the Johannine account the meal that Jesus ate with his disciples had features of a Passover celebration. (One thinks of Christmas parties and Thanksgiving dinners that anticipate the feasts themselves.)

This one notable difference nothwithstanding, the evangelists' general agreement even with regard to details seems to justify the speculation that the primitive church produced a coherent account of the passion soon after the events. Several factors contributed to the early development of the passion narratives. First there was the natural curiosity on the part of the disciples about Jesus' last hours, and then there was the celebration of the eucharistic liturgy. In what is the earliest recorded reference to the betrayal and crucifixion, St. Paul says the eucharist proclaims "the death of the Lord until he comes!" (1 Cor 11:26). Liturgical celebration, which requires a solemnity and fixed ritual, probably explains a certain stylizing of language that runs through the various accounts. And finally, when rumors that distorted the facts about his death began to circulate (Mt 28:11-15), it was necessary to set the record straight.

REDACTION CRITICISM

Many of the differences that do exist in the accounts and give each its particular character are explained by redaction criticism to be the result of sophisticated literary techniques and refined theological interpretation. Redaction criticism is concerned with the Gospels as finished products. It investigates how the various units—individuals sayings and stories as well as pre-canonical collections of the same—came to be incorporated and interpreted as they are in the canonical Gospels. Although it is an outgrowth of form criticism, redaction criticism represents a reaction against the early critics who regarded the evangelists as mere (and not always skillful) compilers. Redaction criticism sees them as creative authors who, taking the oral and written traditions known in a particular Christian community, shaped them into a tightly woven narrative. Like the makers of mosaics, the evangelists use the same "tiles" but in the end present highly individualized portraits of Jesus.[11]

The redaction critic, for example, finds that a comparison of the descriptions of the agony in the garden in the Synoptics reveals a contrast in style and tone. Mark's account is overshadowed by gloom and a sense of fear. Jesus had reached a point where death seemed like welcome relief. Prostrate on the ground, he put his destiny into the hands of his Father. Here, as in so many passages, Matthew closely follows Mark, but Luke reports the incident from a different perspec-

tive. In the Lucan account Jesus does not come to the disciples pleading with them to keep watch with him; rather he exhorts them to
remain steadfast during their long period of trial. In John's Gospel the
scene takes place earlier. In the Johannine account Jesus resists the
temptation to ask the Father to save him from the hour of destiny,
rejoicing rather at the opportunity it presents for glorifying the Father
(Jn 12:27-28). Although John does not describe the agony in the garden of Gethsemane, elements scattered throughout his Gospel are reminiscent of the accounts in the Synoptics.

Mark's Gospel begins by proclaiming, "Jesus Christ, the Son of
God" and climaxes at his death with the confession of the centurion,
"Clearly this man was the Son of God!" (Mk 16:39). The Marcan
description of the agony in Gethsemane is consistent with Mark's
premise that everything Jesus did was in fulfillment of the Father's will.
One of Matthew's favored techniques is to interpret events in the light
of Old Testament texts. Although this approach is not evident in his
description of the agony, it does run through his version of the passion
narrative (as it was also evident, as we saw in the previous chapter, in
the infancy narratives). Luke too has favorite themes that shape his
handling of the material in the passion narratives. Despite Jesus' own
distress, he is pictured telling people to weep not for him but for
themselves because of what awaits them (Lk 23:18). In the agony in the
garden Luke has Jesus urge the disciples (and by implication the
church) to pray for strength during the trials that lie ahead.

THE TRIAL

Given the unique structure of John's Gospel, it is even more striking
that his account of the passion is so similar to that of the Synoptics.
Despite some differences in detail, all four evangelists leave the impression that it was the Jewish leaders who conspired to have Jesus executed because of his religious claims. When Jesus was in the docket
before Pilate, members of the Sanhedrin acted as prosecutors. They
charged, "We found this man subverting our nation, opposing the
payment of taxes to Caesar, and calling himself the Messiah, a king"
(Lk 23:2). In effect they alleged that Jesus was a revolutionary with
monarchical pretensions. Although they accused him of political sub-
version, Pilate was not convinced: "I do not find a case against this
man" (Lk 23:2,4).

The tendency to magnify the reponsibility of the Jews and to minimize the role of the Roman authorities, principally Pilate, predates the written Gospels. The sermons attributed to Peter in Acts charge his Jewish listeners with handing Jesus over to die (3:14-15; 4:10; 5:30; see 13:27-28). The earliest Christian writing, St. Paul's Epistle to the church in Thessalonika (A.D. 51), speaks of the Jews "who killed the Lord Jesus and the prophets, and persecuted us" (1 Thess 2:14-15). On the other hand, the efforts to exculpate Pilate grow stronger with each succeeding Gospel. In Mark's account Pilate attempts to release Jesus but does not push the issue (Mk 15:6-15). Matthew reports the dream of Pilate's wife Procla, who tells him that Jesus is innocent, and has Pilate himself state, "I am innocent of the blood of this just man" (Mt 27:19,24-25). In Luke, Pilate solemnly declares three times that he finds Jesus not guilty (Lk 23:4,14, 22). John reports that Pilate made a determined effort to have Jesus pardoned and goes so far as to have Jesus flogged and presented to the people in an attempt to win their sympathy (Jn 18:28-19:16).

It was in the church's interest not to blame the Roman authorities for the death of Jesus. Christians living in the empire wanted the imperial government to look on them with benign tolerance, and it would have worked to their disadvantange if it was thought that their Lord had planned a political revolution. A closer reading of the text indicates that the Romans were more implicated than sometimes thought. John reports that the temple guards had the assistance of the Roman military in arresting Jesus (Jn 18:3,12). By all accounts he was sentenced to death, however reluctantly, by the Roman procurator on the political charge that he claimed to be "the king of the Jews." And Roman soldiers carried out the execution. The evidence points to a conspiracy forged by an unholy alliance of power brokers who saw their authority undermined and threatened by Jesus (see Acts 4:27).[12]

Judicial proceedings are never simple, and when they are married to political intrigue, as in the case of Jesus, one can only guess at motives and speculate about circumstances that brought about his death. According to Dutch scholar Edward Schillebeeckx, the legal grounds in Jewish law for having Jesus put to death were found in Deuteronomy: "Any man who has the insolence to refuse to listen to the priest who officiates there in the ministry of the Lord, your God, or to the judge, shall die" (17:12). Jesus' behavior before the high priest was interpreted as insolence. His silence before the Sanhedrin (Mk 14:60-61) was regarded as contempt of court—defiance of Israel's highest authority. His refusal to submit to their jurisdiction angered the Jewish leaders and in the minds of some provided the juridical grounds for them to move against him.[13]

The Sanhedrin, the supreme governing council of the Jews, was made up of representatives of three classes (influential clans, the four high priestly families, and scribes—the latter, the lawyers who belonged mostly to the sect of the Pharisees), which were in turn divided into various factions. Schillebeeckx believes that despite pressure exerted by the Sadducee and Herodian factions, the Sanhedrin—as a whole a fair-minded group—found no adequate juridical grounds for condemning Jesus to death. A majority of the council did agree, however, for political reasons, to hand over Jesus to the Romans. Even if the Sanhedrin could have agreed to execute Jesus, the sentence would have had to be referred to the Roman authorities for confirmation, because the Sanhedrin's jurisdiction in capital cases was severely restricted (see Jn 18:31).

There is reason to believe that political motives were factors in causing the Sanhedrin to work with the Romans in apprehending Jesus. The Jewish leaders noted Jesus' popularity with the masses and feared that a populist movement might prompt the Roman authorities to intervene. Apparently Jesus was aware that he was being arrested as a revolutionary. He protested that none of his activities warranted treatment as a "guerrilla bandit" (Brown's translation of *lestes* in Mk 14:48 and parallels). During his trial the question arose about Jesus' threat to destroy the Temple—an act of sabotage as well as sacrilege (Mk 15:58; Mt 26:61). Christians reading the Gospels today presuppose that Jesus was speaking in a figurative way, but given the political climate at the time of the Roman occupation, his words had a different ring for many. The New Testament implies that it took Jesus' own followers some time before even they realized that his messianic kingdom was non-political.

RIVALRY BETWEEN CHURCH AND SYNAGOGUE

Similarly the anti-Jewish bias that runs through the New Testament must be read in the context of the polemics, theological controversy, and religious rivalries of the time. The polemical stance of Christians toward Jews is most evident in the Fourth Gospel.   John refers to "the Jews" seventy times (as compared with the five or six in each of the Synoptics), often in a derogatory way. In many passages "the Jews" are synonymous with the chief priest and the Pharisees (see Jn 8:13,18ff; 18:3,12). In other passages "Jew" has simply a religio-ethnic meaning (e.g., 4:22; 18:33,35; 2:6,13; 7:2), but generally the Johannine Gospel uses "the Jews" in a technical sense for "the religious authorities, particularly those in Jerusalem, who are hostile to Jesus."[14] According to John it was "the Jews" who brought Jesus before Pilate (18:28-31), whereas in Mark it was the Sanhedrin (15:1).

Given the rivalry—yes, even hatred—that developed between church and synagogue before the end of the first century, one cannot use New Testament generalizations about the Jews to justify anti-Semitism. In the sight of the Jewish establishment, Christianity appeared to be an aberration, a "heresy" distorting the mission of Israel. Most Jews opposed the spread of the gospel message; but on the other hand, most of those who did heed the message of Pentecost were Jews. Vatican II reminds the world that the church has its roots deep in Judaism.[15] Without the Hebrew Scriptures the mission of the church, like that of Christ, is unintelligible. St. Paul, even when berating the Jews for not accepting Jesus, asks: "Has God rejected his people? Of course not! I myself am an Israelite. . ." (Rom 11:1). And Jesus was a Jew. His mother and his early disciples were all Jews. Christians romanticized the figure of Pontius Pilate, but history shows it was the Romans, not the Jews, who persecuted the church.

Mythic figures do not generate polemics and controversy the way Jesus did and still does. Underlying the apologetic, theological, and literary considerations that shaped the telling of the passion story were the real-life events of the betrayal, arrest, trial, and crucifixon of Jesus attested to by non-Christian sources. The circumstances of Jesus' tragic end, however, left his disciples with many questions. Even after they had experienced the resurrection, they still had to ask the meaning of his passion and death. Their answers are the subject of the following chapter.

Notes

1. *Apology* I, ch. 13. *Writings of Saint Justin Martyr*, Fathers of the Church (New York: Christian Heritage, Inc., 1948), p. 46. See Kelly, *Creeds*, p. 72.

2. *Creeds*, pp. 149–150.

3. *Annals*, XV, 44. Quoted in J. Stevenson, ed., *A New Eusebius: Doucments Illustrative of the History of the Church to A.D. 337* (London: SPCK, 1963), p. 2.

4. In 1961 an inscription bearing Pilate's name was discovered at Caesarea, which refers to him, not as procurator, but as "prefect." For this and other references to Pilate in ancient sources and modern writings, see Raymond E. Brown, *The Gospel According to John XIII–XXI,* Anchor Bible, 29A (Garden City, NY: Doubleday and Co., 1970), pp. 794–795, 846–847.

5. Albert Schweitzer, *The Quest of the Historical Jesus.* Reprint (New York: Macmillan Company, 1964).

6. Joachim Jeremias, *The Problem of the Historical Jesus* (Philadelphia: Fortress Press, 1964).

7. John S. Kselman, "Modern New Testament Criticism," in *JBC*, vol. 2, pp. 7–20.

8. James M. Robinson, *A New Quest of the Historical Jesus* (London: SCM Press, 1981), pp. 32–47, 73–76.

9. Edgar V. McKnight, *What Is Form Criticism?* (Philadelphia: Fortress Press, 1969).

10. In 1964 the Biblical Commission in Rome issued a qualified endorsement of the "form-critical method," while noting that interpreters should be cautious in using it "because quite inadmissible philosophical principles have often come to be mixed with this method" (Par V). An English translation of the Instructions can be

found in the Appendix to Joseph A. Fitzmyer, *a Christological Catechism: New Testament Answers* (New York/Ramsey: Paulist Press, 1982), pp. 131–140. Fitzmyer introduces the Instruction with a scholarly commentary, pp. 97–103.

11. Norman Perrin, *What Is Redaction Criticism?* (Philadelphia: Fortress Press, 1969).

12. Fitzmyer, "Who Is Responsible for the Death of Jesus?" *A Christological Catechism*, pp. 58–62.

13. *Jesus: An Experiment in Christology* (New York: Crossroad, 1981), pp. 312–318.

14. Brown, *John*, p. 849. See also Anchor Bible 29, pp. LXXI–LXXII.

15. The Vatican II Declaration on the Relationship of the Church to Non-Christian Religious contains an important section on "the spiritual patrimony common to Christians and Jews" which deplores "anti-Semitism directed against the Jews at any time and from any source." It states, moreover, that Jesus' death "cannot be blamed upon all Jews then living, without distinction, nor upon the Jews of today" (*Nostra Aetate*, n. 4).

Subsequently the Vatican Commission for the relations with the Jews issued "Guidelines and Suggestions for Implementing the Conciliar Declaration *Nostra Aetate*" (1974) and, on the twentieth anniversary of Vatican II, "Notes on Jews and Judaism in Preaching and Catechesis" (1985). For the text of these statements see *The Living Light* 12 (Spring 1975):143–149; 22 (Jan. 1986):113–123.

9

The Sacrifice of the Cross
and Senseless Suffering

"He was crucified . . . suffered, died, and was buried"

In discussing the formation of the Gospels in the previous chapter we noted that the events of Jesus' passion and death were the first to be shaped into a coherent and systematic account. The story of Jesus' last hours, told in some detail by each of the four evangelists, is preserved in the Creed. The Apostles' Creed in particular is careful to list successive stages of Jesus' passion: SUFFERED . . . CRUCIFIED, DIED, AND WAS BURIED. Given the relative brevity of both the Gospels and the Creeds, the amount of attention focused on these last days of Jesus' life seems disproportionate and needs to be explained.

This chapter focuses on the redemptive significance of Jesus' death, first as it was remembered and celebrated in the liturgy, and then as it was seen to fulfill Old Testament prophecies. The latter interpretation relies heavily on the Epistle to the Hebrews in which the death of Jesus on the cross is typified in figures and rituals of the Hebrew Scriptures and Jewish liturgy. The theology of the cross pervades the New Testament, but it was above all the apostle Paul who exalted the cross as the means of salvation so that it became a center of Christian devotion

147

down through the ages. To round out the chapter, St. Anselm's classic explanation as well as more modern interpretations of Jesus' redemptive suffering are summarized.

ANAMNESIS: "DO THIS AS A REMEMBRANCE OF ME"

One explanation of why the account of Jesus' passion and death took shape early is its place in the liturgy. The eucharistic celebration, as is especially evident in the Roman Canon (Eucharistic Prayer I), is first and foremost a memorial of Christ's passion and death, resurrection, and glorification. In the language of theology this memorial is referred to as *anamnesis*, a Greek word found in the New Testament (1 Cor 11:24; Lk 22:19) that means "calling to mind." *Anamnesis* says more than mere pageantry or a mental recollection of times past; it implies a ceremonial re-presentation of a historical event of lasting significance. Ritual and symbolism are used to reenact the event and somehow make it present and powerful again and again to successive generations of believers.

The Last Supper as described in the synoptic Gospels was itself the yearly *anamnesis* of the epic events of the Exodus. According to Mark and Matthew, Jesus had brought the Twelve together for the traditional seder meal, a memorial of the original Passover in Egypt. There they recalled the circumstances of God's covenant with the people of Israel: how the blood of the lamb saved them from the angel of death; their liberation from slavery in Egypt; the crossing of the Red Sea; the manna that sustained them in the desert. The sequence of events reached a climax at Mt. Sinai with the formalizing of the covenant: the Israelites declared their fidelity to Yahweh, and Moses sprinkled them with blood of the sacrificial bulls, saying, "This is the blood of the covenant which the Lord has made with you" (Ex 24:8). Their entrance into the promised land followed in due course.

Jesus gave new meaning to the Passover ritual. In his hands it becomes the basis for a new covenant. He identifies himself as the true paschal lamb. In John's Gospel Jesus is condemned to death at noon on Passover eve (Jn 19:14), the very hour at which the temple priests began to slaughter the paschal lambs for the feast. Luke's account refers explicitly to the New Covenant:

> Then, taking bread and giving thanks, he broke it and gave it to
> them, saying: "This is my body to be given for you. Do this as a

remembrance of me." He did the same with the cup after eating, saying as he did so: "This cup is the new covenanat in my blood, which will be shed for you." (22:19-20)

The breaking of the bread symbolized his death. The obvious identification with the paschal victim lies behind St. Paul's words: "Christ our Passover has been sacrificed" (1 Cor 5:7; see Jn 19:20). His exodus from this world to the Father carried with it liberation from human slavery to sin and the inauguration of the kingdom.

As noted in the previous chapter, Mark's account of Jesus' passion and death is straightforward. Mark's only attempt to explain the meaning of the events is the rather subtle description of the Last Supper, filled with symbolism and discreet references to the Passover and Exodus. Matthew's description is less subtle; he expands on Mark's account, incorporating a "fulfillment" interpretation of Old Testament texts (reminiscent of his style in the infancy narratives). Although Luke's references to the Passover are less explicit, he has the Risen Lord appeal to "all that the prophets have announced," and "beginning, then, with Moses and all the prophets, he interpreted for them every passage of Scripture which referred to him" (24:25,27). Thus the early church, led to search the Hebrew Scriptures for clues to unlock the mystery of Jesus' passion and death, discovered that the "new" covenant is not an abrogration of the old but an extension of it to the Gentiles.

THAT THE SCRIPTURE BE FULFILLED

Like Matthew, John explains several happenings by saying "that the scripture may be fulfilled" (see Jn 13:18; 19:24,28).[1] The Christian community found reassurance in knowing that Jesus stood in that line of Israel's prophets whose message was rejected and who were put to death (Mt 5:12; 23:29-39. Lk 6:23; 11:47-51; 13:31-35). The songs of the Suffering Servant in Second Isaiah join the notion of the persecuted prophet to the oppression and martyrdom of the innocent (Is 40-55). "The righteous one who must suffer" becomes a fixed phrase in the Psalms, and the Gospel writers are led to interpret the events of Golgotha through the lens of Psalms 22, 31, and 69 (see Mt 27:34; Lk 23:46).[2] The fourth of the songs of the Suffering Servant (Is 52:13-53:12) develops the theme that the righteous one has taken upon himself the guilt of others; his suffering atones for the sins of his people.

References to the Old Testament are found throughout the Gospels and Epistles, but, as one might expect from the title, it is the Epistle to the Hebrews that draws most extensively on the rituals and cultic theology of the Jewish feast of the Atonement to interpret the death of Jesus on the cross.[3] The humiliated Son "when he had cleansed us from our sins . . . took his seat at the right of the Majesty in heaven" and is exalted above the angels (Heb 1:3-4). The redemptive work of Christ takes on cosmic proportions.

The main argument of the Epistle can be summarized more or less as follows. Jesus, offering sacrifice for our sins, plays the double role of faithful high priest and sacrificial victim. He was a priest "according to the order of Melchizedek" (Heb 7:11), a figure of mysterious origins and lasting power. Like the priesthood of Melchizedek but unlike that of the priests in the line of Aaron, Jesus' priesthood is limited neither by term of office nor by death itself; it endures forever. He is the one authentic priest in the world; his sacrifice is once and for all time. Up to the time of Jesus' death all attempts to conciliate God were inadequate because of the infidelity of those offering sacrifice and because God does not seek burnt offerings and the blood of bulls. Like the prophets of old, Jesus exposes the worthlessness of external worship divorced from interior dispositions and moral living. The sacrifices of the Old Covenant, based on the idea of substitution and representation, were, like the clay models of a sculptor, rough drafts of the masterpiece to come. Because he offered himself—his own blood—Jesus rendered the perfect sacrifice, not in the hidden precincts of the Temple but on the cross for all to see. He now appears in glory "before God on our behalf" (Heb 9:24). In his abasement, he is exalted and glorified. All of this is perceived by faith.

According to a rabbinical adage, "There is no expiation without shedding blood." Blood sustains life, and the Bible all but identifies blood and life (see Lev 17:11,14; Gen 9:4-6). The pouring out of blood symbolizes the giving of one's life, and thus there is no pardon unless people invest something of themselves in reconciliation. The blood rite, central to the Passover and the covenant—the two sacrifices that the New Testament explicitly links to the death of Christ—served also as a rite of purification and consecration (Lev 16:1-19). In the first Passover the blood of the lamb (referred to explicitly in Rev 7:14 and

12:11) marked the Israelite households and thus spared them from the angel of death. Stanislaus Lyonnet, for many years a leading light at Rome's Biblical Institute, interprets it as "a rite of consecration, separating Israel from the pagan world, making of them a people apart."[4] It was like the X that "the man in white" marked on the foreheads of the faithful Israelites (see Ez 9:3-6), and the seal that marked the one hundred and forty-four thousand (Rev 7:2-8) who carried on their foreheads the name of the Lamb and the name of his Father (Rev 14:1). In the Book of Revelation the seal is an obvious reference to baptism.

The blood rite involved the Israelites in the covenant sacrifice so that it became their own. Moses poured the blood of the young bulls first on the altar of sacrifice; then when the assembly of the twelve tribes agreed to observe the precepts of the covenant he splashed the remaining blood on the people (Ex 24:3-8; see Heb 9:19). The words of Jesus at the Last Supper, repeated in the eucharist, must be read in this context: "This is my blood, the blood of the covenant, to be poured out on behalf of many" (Mk 14:24); these words cast him in the dual role of priest and victim. Christians who attend the eucharist reaffirm their commitment to the New Covenant and all it demands.

St. Paul too is explicit in saying, "Christ our Passover has been sacrificed"; therefore we are to purge ourselves of the old yeast of corruption and wickedness and celebrate the feast "with the unleavened bread of sincerety and truth" (1 Cor 5:7-8). It is more common, however, for Paul to describe the work of Christ as a "purchase" (Greek *lutron*), as a slave in ancient times would purchase his freedom: "You have been purchased, and at a price" (1 Cor 6:20). By his sin Adam had in effect indentured himself and his descendants to a life of slavery to sin and the law, but Christ redeemed us, that is, bought back our freedom (Gal 3:13; 4:5). We are now indentured to the Lord, not as slaves but as freedmen (1 Cor 7:23). And even in the context of "repurchasing," Paul alludes to the Passover and the sealing of the covenant at Mt. Sinai, the two great events that are the archetypes of deliverance and consecration. In one of the rare passages in which he speaks of Christ Jesus as "Savior," Paul writes, "It was he who sacrificed himself for us, to redeem us from all unrighteousness and to cleanse for himself a people of his own, eager to do what is right" (Titus 2:13-14).

ST. ANSELM'S THEORY OF SATISFACTION

Like any metaphor, Paul's example of the manumission (that is, the formal liberation of a slave) must not be pushed too far. Preachers and some early medieval theologians carried it to the point of working out an elaborate scheme in which the devil was said to have "rights" over the created universe. They pictured Adam as selling himself and his posterity to Satan, so that in ransoming us from slavery Christ had to pay a ransom to the devil! It was the achievement of St. Anselm of Canterbury (d. 1109) to have discredited this so-called rights of the devil theory as belittling the power of God and exaggerating the dominance of Satan. His *Cur Deus Homo?*, mentioned at the beginning of Chapter 5, is the first work taken up totally with the question of the atonement. Anselm evolved a theology of redemption known variously as "satisfaction theory" and "theory of penal expiation." The former refers to the fact that humans had to make reparation for their wrongdoing; the latter emphasizes the punishment due sin. It shaped catechesis and theology, Catholic and Protestant, and went almost unchallenged into the last century.[5]

Anselm wanted to prove "by necessary reasons," that is, without appealing to revelation, that God had to become human and die the way he did if we are to be saved from sin and death. In order to follow Anselm's logic one needs to recall that feudal society in his time was a web of rights and duties woven of customs, laws, and contractual arrangements. Liberty and equality were neither realities nor even ideals. Social status determined one's responsibilities and manners. Serfs did not speak to their liege lords unless spoken to. Although the knights and nobles were as much slaves of the system as the lower classes were, privileges and honors made their condition somewhat easier to bear. In the feudal scheme of things the seriousness of a crime was measured in proportion to the dignity of the person offended. Thus an offense against one's liege lord would be more severely punished than a similar injury done a peer or a beggar. Also there was little room for mercy in the system. A simple apology would not do. Nor was simple restitution enough. Even when a lord forgave an offense, he had also to exact some satisfaction by way of payment for the slight to his honor and name. Further, it was all but impossible for a vassal, because of his inferior status, adequately to repair dishonor done to his lord without the patronage and intercession of an equally powerful noble.

This medieval mindset is evident in every page of Anselm's *Cur Deus Homo?* Adam's disobedience offended God and in fact made him and his posterity outlaws. Humans could not repair the injustice because their inferior status was now worsened by their sins. It would not be fitting for God in his mercy simply to forgive the offense, for that would allow sin to go unpunished. This, says Anselm, is unseemly, for it would put the sinner and the innocent person on an equal footing before God. Further, God "owes" it to himself to see that proper reparations are made to his honor; otherwise justice is not served.

Thus Anselm builds the case for the Incarnation: on the one hand, because sinners are humans, a human must make satisfaction; on the other, because God is offended, no one less than God can make adequate amends. Thus justice is served and God's love is manifest in sending his only Son to earth to suffer and die as a human on behalf of—"for"—sinners. Jesus' death was significantly different from that of the rest of humanity in that he freely embraced it. In Anselm's scheme, death is a punishment for sin; since Jesus was totally innocent of sin, death for him was *supererogatory*—that is, over and above anything required of him. His willingness to carry the Incarnation to the extreme, even to death itself, in order to establish solidarity with the human condition went beyond the reparation demanded by strict justice and in the end made satisfaction for the sins of Adam and of all Adam's descendants. It was out of love for his fellow human beings that Jesus willingly suffered the consequences of sin. Anselm was careful to emphasize that the crucifixion was not punishment exacted by God.

The logic and ingenuity of Anselm's reasoning accounts for the enduring popularity of his work. It takes as its premise that it "was for us and for our salvation" that the Son of God came down from heaven and "was crucified" for us. But even though his theory seems to accord with the presentation of Jesus' passion and death in the New Testament, it has been faulted on many counts. Anselm was in fact selective in the Scripture texts he used to bolster his position. He has Jesus' death alone, apart from his life, constituting the essence of "satisfaction." Nor did Anselm take Jesus' resurrection into consideration. Furthermore, God appears merciless and relentless in pursuit of justice and honor—or if not merciless, helpless in that God appears fenced in by laws of his own making.[6]

THE "HYPER" FORMULA

For some, Anselm's explanation does not go far enough. Why did the suffering and death of one man have such universal significance? One school of thought developed a notion of "penal satisfaction," which in its more extreme form is known as "substitutionary punishment." According to this explanation someone needed to appease God's wrath. It argues that Jesus became the scapegoat, the object of God's anger, and was punished by the Father not simply on our behalf but in our stead. Karl Barth (1886-1968), one of the great theologians of this century, showed himself an intellectual heir of John Calvin (1509-64) when he wrote that Jesus "stands before the Father at Golgotha burdened with all the actual sin and guilt of man and of each individual man, and is treated in accordance with the deserts of man as the transgressor of the divine command."[7] But the passages in the New Testament that are cited in support of this theory (Rom 5:6. 2 Cor 5:14) can be better interpreted in other ways. God's wrath is directed against sin, not against the sinner, and least of all against the Christ.

A text in St. Paul that echoes the ancient kerygma and predates the accounts of Jesus' passion and death in the Gospels, says "Christ died for our sins in accordance with the Scriptures" (1 Cor 15:3). It uses the so-called *hyper* formula (from the Greek word meaning "for" or "on behalf of"), which also appears in the creedal statement, FOR OUR SAKE HE WAS CRUCIFIED UNDER PONTIUS PILATE. This and similar texts leave no doubt that we are the beneficiaries of Jesus' heroic action, but they in no way suggest that the benefit we receive is the softening of the Father's anger. (It is a vindictive people who expect its God to be vindictive.) *Hyper* captures the essence of love, of being for another; it is the antithesis of vindictiveness. In the discourse that is tantamount to a last will and testament Jesus says, "There is no greater love than this: to lay down one's life for one's friends" (Jn 15:13). The same theme is sounded in Jesus' prophetic words at the Last Supper: "This is my blood, the blood of the covenant, to be poured out on behalf of many" (Mk 14:24). J. A. T. Robinson, in a memorable phrase, names Jesus "the man for others." Josef Ratzinger calls "for" the "decisive principle of human existence."[8]

Theologians speak of a "subjective" and an "objective" dimension of salvation. In the messianic kingdom, salvation comes through *metanoia*—repentance and change of attitude (the subjective dimension)—effected not by human initiative but through the victory of Christ Jesus over sin and the forces of evil (the objective dimension).

The New Testament makes it clear that the suffering and death of Jesus has an objective value independent of what people think of him (if they think of him at all!). This does not mean, however, that salvation is something done to us or for us as when doctors pump the stomach of a person who has taken a poison in attempting suicide. To put such excessive emphasis on the objective value of Jesus' self-sacrifice risks making it impersonal and distant from its beneficiaries. Thus the subjective interpretation approaches the issue from the standpoint of the people—the subjects—who are saved. In life Jesus preached love of neighbor and concern for the world, especially for the underprivileged, and in death he gave the supreme example of the extremes he was willing to suffer for the sake of others. By word and example he teaches us what it means to be human, and he sparks in his disciples a response to God's call to love.

Although the subjective approach is a needed corrective to the objective interpretation of Jesus' suffering and death, it too risks distortion when it reduces Jesus' ministry to the guidance of a spiritual guru or a moral philosopher. The New Testament affirms both an objective and a subjective dimension to the redemption in asserting on the one hand that Jesus suffered and died "for our sake"; and on the other, that we must repent and live according to his teaching if we are to be saved.

Whatever its shortcomings, each of these explanations offers some insight into the meaning of the passion and death of Jesus. Even though many agree with John Macquarrie in judging the theory of subsitutionary punishment to be "sub-Christian,"[9] it has the redeeming merit of confronting us with the gravity of sin and the viciousness of evil. It is to Anselm's lasting credit that he recognized the need to reinterpret redemption in language that the "Bosos" of his time could understand. Like Paul before him and many lesser theologians and catechists after him, Anselm knew he had to use concrete examples and figures of speech familiar to his contemporaries if they were to find any meaning in the passion and death of Jesus. He was not interested in reconstructing the history of a bygone tragedy but in showing how it altered the human condition for all time, how it was as much a saving event for medieval Europeans as it was for ancient Palestinians. In faith's continuing quest for understanding, each succeeding generation of Christians has had to confront the meaning of the cross—the passion and death of Christ.

THE CROSS: SCANDAL AND ABSURDITY

The loathsome practice of scribbling graffiti in public places is probably as old as writing itself. The fact is that the graffiti of ancient Rome give us some of the most valuable information we have about early Christianity. One example, probably from the third century, depicts the head of an ass mounted on a cross, crudely drawn, with the sarcastic inscription "Alexamenos worships his God." The sketch is "the oldest crucifix in existence!" The cartoon, not meant to be flattering to either Jesus or Christian beliefs, was in poor taste; but in fact it contained more truth than humor. The crucifixion itself has been called a "bad joke."[10] St Paul said it was "a stumbling block to Jews, and an absurdity to Gentiles" (1 Cor 1:23). In the eyes of Romans, it was sheer disgrace. (In a culture where the cross has become a religious symbol Paul's point has lost some of its edge. Can we think of the guillotine or the electric chair becoming a religious symbol and having a place of honor in places of worship? D. T. Suzuki, a prominent Zen Buddhist of our time, is quoted as saying, "Whenever I see a crucified figure of Christ I cannot help thinking of the gap that lies deep between Christianity and Buddhism.")

Paul must have recognized the irony in the statement—written in his own "large handwriting!"—"May I never boast of anything but the cross of our Lord Jesus Christ! Through it, the world has been crucified to me and I to the world" (Gal 6: 11, 14). The cross challenges human values. It questions the world's criteria for success. Even as one recoils at the violence and extends sympathy for the victim, deep down none can ever be sure where he or she would have stood on that fateful Good Friday. The cross exposes the cracks in one's self-confidence, even while holding out hope.

It was natural that in time the "instrument of our salvation" should become an object of special respect and veneration among Christians. During the age of persecution the cross was not displayed openly, though the *Sign of the Cross* had become a devotional practice already in the second century. With the peace of Constantine, however, a dramatic change occurred. Christianity came into the open and with it the cross. Constantine claimed to have seen the cross in the heavens on the eve of battle as he set out to gain control of the Empire. He regarded it as an omen and had it blazoned on the shields of his soldiers. A short time later, according to legend, the Empress Mother, St. Helena, discovered the cross on which Jesus had been executed when she was having the site of Calvary excavated in preparation for the construction of a church. The feast of the Exaltation of the Cross (still celebrated on September 14) began in connection with the dedication of the churches she had constructed on the sites of the Holy Sepulchre and Calvary in 325.[11]

The emphasis in this period, it should be noted, was on the cross, not on the crucifix. Constantine interpreted the cross as a sign of victory—"*in hoc signo vincis.*" He had picked up the boast of Christians that the cross is the trophy of Christ's victory over the forces of evil, even death. The *crucifixion* scene did not become a common theme in Christian art before the end of the sixth century. The first examples were highly stylized, depicting a living Jesus with arms outstretched in the prayer—the classic pose of the *orans*. By the eighth century it had become a very popular way of portraying Christ and, consequently, became the object of a particularly vehement attack by the iconoclasts (see Chapter 16). The crucifixion scene embodied the things that most irritated the opponents of icons: it represented Christ in human form, and it was the object of veneration by the faithful. In reaction the iconodules, led by the monks, painted crucifixion scenes everywhere. The monks made it a favorite theme in the psalters and other illuminated manuscripts.

Generally in Byzantine art as in the Byzantine liturgy, the passion and death of Jesus are presented as an important event in the work of redemption, but it never attained the preeminence that it gained in the West in the late Middle Ages where it became the center of popular spirituality without reference to the resurrection.[12]

The practice of tracing a cross on one's forehead with the thumb or index finger came into widespread use in the liturgy also in the fourth century. It is used in conjunction with the baptismal anointings and for many centuries it was common in the Western (as it still is in the Eastern) liturgy to make the sign of the cross over the oblation in the eucharist. The "large" sign of the cross made by touching the forehead, breast and shoulders, developed later. Used first in private devotions, it seems to have been introduced into the liturgy in medieval monasteries. The sign of the cross as the symbol of God's salvific work has a trinitarian significance as well. In the West it is accompanied by the formula reminiscent of baptism, "In the name of the Father, and of the Son, and of the Holy Spirit"; in the East, the sign is made with the thumb and two fingers.

Christians revere the cross, not in itself, but as a talisman against evil; it is a sign and symbol of redemption—victory over sin and death. The cross causes one's mind to wander from Calvary to Moriah where Abraham witnesses to his fidelity to the covenant even though it might have meant the sacrifice of his beloved son, Isaac (Gen 22: 1-19). The cross reminds the baptized of Paul's words:

> I have been crucified with Christ, and the life I live now is not my own; Christ is living in me. I still live my human life, but it is a life of faith in the Son of God, who loved me and gave himself for me. (Gal 2: 19-20)

The cross represents the very essence of grace and love. God does not judge people according to human standards; God's love is unconditioned and total. Saint Irenaeus emphasized the significance of the cross for all peoples—Jew and Gentile—when he wrote:

> By the wood of the Cross the work of the Word of God was made manifest to all: his hands are stretched out to gather everyone together. Two hands outstretched, for there are two peoples scattered over the whole earth. One sole head in the midst for there is but one God over all, among all and in all.[13]

A MODERN APPROACH

The church has never tried to formulate the doctrine of redemption in the same detail in which it has defined the person of Christ. It does not attempt to resolve all the anomolies in the New Testament, recognizing that the authors themselves took different approaches. The Johannine Gospel, for example, emphasizes that salvation comes via enlightenment through the person of Christ; the Pauline Epistles emphasize his work: salvation comes through Jesus' sacrifice and his paying the price of his own blood. Despite their different theologies, however, the New Testament authors agree on several truths. 1) Salvation is not possible apart from Jesus Christ. 2) By his suffering and death the innocent Jesus unilaterally made amends to God on behalf of others. 3) Obedience to the will of the Father and love for humanity led him freely to make reparations for sinners. 4) The objective value of Jesus' work in no way exempts men and women from the need to repent, seek forgiveness, and enter into a new relationship with God.

In one way or another, orthodox explanations of the atonement seek to safeguard these truths. Underlying all orthodox explanations, moreover, are two basic principles abstracted from Scripture: 1) the fidelity and steadfastness of God's love toward all human beings, even though they sin; and 2) God's *compassion*—sympathy in the literal sense of solidarity in human suffering—a solidarity grounded in the Incarnation. God weeps with us when we are in pain!

Many modern theologians take as their point of departure the premise that suffering and death are constitutive of human existence. Thus the story of Jesus' passion and death is the strongest possible affirmation of his humanity. But it should be noted that Jesus repudiates the idea that suffering is in all cases linked to sin. In speaking of the man born blind, the disciples ask Jesus, "Rabbi, was it his sin or that of his parents that caused him to be born blind?" To which Jesus replied, "Neither. . . . It was no sin either of this man or of his parents. Rather, it was to let God's works show forth in him" (Jn 9:2-3).

Although the Scripture affirms that sin is one cause of suffering, not all suffering is the result of sin. Suffering is a conflict situation between what is and what should be, between sickness and health, between failure and achievement, between competitiveness and collaboration, rivalry and love. At one level suffering simply describes the tensions that torture nerve ends in people's efforts to be whole. At the level of sin, suffering is aggravated by the conflict that arises from self-centeredness, estrangement, and compromise of ideals. In neither case is suffering a value in itself. It is one thing to say, as in the passage of John quoted above, that suffering reveals the work of God; it is quite another to assert that it has redemptive power.

In any case the New Testament makes it clear that it is God's intention to exterminate suffering. On the one hand men and women are called upon to repent of their sins and be saved from suffering. On the other, God sent his only Son into the world to lay the foundations for a new kingdom, and "he shall wipe every tear from their eyes, and there shall be no more death or mourning, crying out or pain, for the former world has passed away" (Rev 21:4). In the presence of God, evil and suffering have to give way.

Dutch theologian Edward Schillebeeckx is in the mainstream of Catholic thought when he writes, "Even for Christians, suffering remains impenetrable and incomprehensible, and provokes rebellion. Nor will the Christian blasphemously claim that God himself required the death of Jesus as compensation for what we make of our history."[14] It is one thing to say that suffering is constitutive of human existence; it is quite another to assert that it is inherent in the grand design that God has for the universe. Given the image of God as creator and faithful shepherd revealed in the Hebrew Scriptures, and given the divine presence in the world made known in the person of the Incarnate Word, suffering of the innocent is simply unfathomable.

Even in their denials skeptics sometimes show a greater appreciation for the Christian notion of God than do believers. They take seriously the radical contradiction between the Christian notion of a loving, caring deity and the reality of evil in the world.[15] On the other hand, theologians in their efforts to construct a comprehensive theory of redemption do not always face up to the unbridgeable gulf between the coexistence of evil and an all-powerful God who opposes it. Schillebeeckx says that reason fails before suffering and evil. All attempts to explain and interpret their existence, even in the context of Jesus' saving work, seem to treat evil on the same level as good, as if it had some right to exist. According to Schillebeeckx the only meaningful reaction to the suffering and evil is "to offer resistance, to act in a way meant to turn history to good effect."[16] The Gospel does not offer an explanation of suffering and evil, but calls on Christians to resist it in all its forms and eradicate its causes.

Just as it is impossible to reconcile human suffering and the existence of evil with God's goodness and love, so it is equally beyond human comprehension to understand the divine reason—purpose—for the passion and death of Jesus. It is in this context that Schillebeeckx says, "We have to say that we are not redeemed *thanks to* the death of Jesus but *despite* it." The parable of the prodigal son, or as some prefer to name it, of the loving father, gives a better insight into God's saving action in Jesus than do the most elaborate theologies of redemption. Even though it must have been against his better judgment, the father in the story gave the younger son the means to seek his own way in the world. All the while the son was dissipating his goods and hell-bent on destroying himself, the father remained hopeful. When finally the son came to his senses, admitted his sin, and returned home, he found his father waiting. The father came out to meet the prodigal and welcomed him with open arms. He did not need to be appeased. Jesus used the parable to illustrate the mercy and love of the heavenly Father. It was the jealousy and resentment of the older brother, the human reaction, that needed to be soothed and satisfied.

The deeper significance of the suffering and death of Jesus, cruel and senseless in human terms, appears only in the events that followed Good Friday. His suffering is not romanticized nor explained away. His death, the work of sinful humans, remains an evil but not the absolute evil that is separation from God. By his passion and death Jesus witnesses to the fact that in the depths of mental anguish and loneliness, fatigue and physical pain, at the breaking point of one's endurance and hope, one still can encounter the divine presence. Even though Jesus seems to have felt abandoned by God, it was in the very act of dying—the moment he gave himself totally for others—that he was glorified by the Father. We return to this aspect of Christ's death in Chapter 11 after we discuss in the next chapter two nettlesome phrases in the Creed, WAS BURIED and DESCENDED AD INFEROS.

Notes

1. Raymond E. Brown, *The Gospel According to John XIII-XXI*, The Anchor Series, 29A (Garden City, NY: Doubleday & Co., 1966), p. 554.

2. Edward Schillebeeckx, *Jesus: An Experiment in Christology* (New York: Crossroad, 1981), p. 284-290.

3. These themes are developed in great detail by Schillebeeckx, *Christ: The Experience of Jesus as Lord* (New York: Seabury Press, 1980), pp. 237–293.

4. "The Pauline Conception of Redemption," in John R. Sheets, ed., *The Theology of the Atonement: Readings in Soteriology* (Englewood Cliffs, NJ: Prentice-Hall, Inc., 1967), p. 179.

5. There is some difference of opinion among modern interpreters as to the success of St. Anselm's effort. Without denying Anselm's important contribution, Josef Ratzinger says of his theory, "Even in its classical form it is not devoid of one-sidedness." Ratzinger is even more critical of the "vulgarized form" of the theory, which he says, "looks cruelly mechanical and less and less feasible." Joseph Ratzinger, *Introduction to Christianity* (New York: Herder and Herder, 1970) p. 172.

6. "True, this is not the exact significance which Anselm gave to his theory of atonement, but that was the way in which in fact it lived on in many spiritual books." Edward Schillebeeckx, *Christ*. p. 700.

7. Quoted in Gerald O'Collins, *The Calvary Christ* (Philadelphia: Westminster Press, 1977), p. 95.

8. John A. T. Robinson, *Honest To God* (Philadelphia: Westminster Press, 1963), p. 64–83. Ratzinger, *Introduction*, p. 191.

9. *Principles*, p. 315.

10. H. Küng, *On Being a Christian* (Garden City, NY: Doubleday & Co. 1976), p. 396. A photograph of the drawing can be seen in the *NCE* 4:474.

11. For a good summary of the various accounts of the finding of the cross, see *NCE* 4:479–482.

12. It is noteworthy that the Good Friday liturgy, in its present form, celebrates Christ's victory by focusing on the cross of glory, not the crucifix. See Jaroslav Pelikan, *Jesus Through the Centuries* (New Haven: Yale University Press, 1985), pp. 95–108.

13. Quoted in Henri de Lubac, *Catholicism: A Study of Dogma in Relation to the Corporate Destiny of Mankind* (New York: New American Library, 1964), p. 210.

14. *Christ*, p. 728.

15. Schillebeeckx, *Christ*, p. 725 quotes Ivan in Dostoievsky's *The Brothers Karamazov* to this effect; see Küng, *On Being Christian*, p. 431.

16. *Christ*, p. 726.

10

The Nether World

"He was buried. He descended to the dead"

The Apostles' Creed contains two phrases that puzzle commentators. The one, found also in the Constantinopolitan Creed, mentions Jesus' burial; the other says HE DESCENDED *AD INFEROS*. Commentators are puzzled as to why the first is included in the Creeds at all. The puzzlement over the second is illustrated by the problem of translation. The Book of Common Prayer authorized by the Episcopal Church, for example, calls for the recitation of the Apostles' Creed as part of evening prayer. In the newly revised edition there are two rites for this service and two translations of the Creed. In the first we read, HE DESCENDED INTO HELL; in the second, we find, HE DESCENDED AMONG THE DEAD. Similarly Roman Catholics of an older generation spoke of a descent "into hell," whereas the authorized translation for the newly revised rite of baptism refers to a descent "to the dead." But as will be seen below, the change in the English translation reflects a change in the Latin text as well from *ad inferna* to *ad inferos*.[1] This chapter reviews what scholars have had to say about these phrases but it does not pretend to resolve longstanding issues.

ENTOMBMENT

WAS BURIED is a phrase found in the apostolic kerygma. St. Paul recognized it to be of particular importance, citing it as one of the fundamental points in the catechetical instruction he had received (1 Cor 15:4).[2] Preaching in the synagogue in Pisidia, he made special mention of the fact that "they took him down from the tree and *laid him in a tomb*" (Acts 13:30). All four Gospel accounts dramatize the burial of Jesus, telling how Joseph of Arimathea asked Pilate's permission to remove Jesus' body and how he hurried to bury it because it was the eve of the Jewish sabbath (Jn 19:38-42; Mt 27:57-60; Mk 15:42-46; Lk 23:50-54).[3]

The question is, *Why* the emphasis on Jesus' burial—in the kerygma, the Gospels, and finally in the Creed? It is a question that has puzzled church writers from ancient to modern times. J. N. D. Kelly denies that the emphasis on WAS BURIED can be explained in terms of the later polemic against docetism. He says, "We may be certain that the reason for admitting the clause to the catechetical tradition had nothing to do with its guaranteeing the reality of the Lord's death." Furthermore, Kelly rejects the idea that the phrase was treasured because it was a fulfillment of an Old Testament prophecy. He attributes its prominence in kerygma, Gospel, and Creed to the fact that it was "the necessary prelude to His resurrection."[4]

Karl Barth calls it the "humblest part of our symbol [of faith]." Although he does not link it to the docetic controversy, he does argue that "it is another reminder of the true *humanity* of Christ." In discussing the meaning of SEPULTUS—"was buried"—Barth makes a passing reference to baptism that seems to be the key to unlocking the enigma. In the baptismal rite, Christians experience both the death of Christ symbolized by his burial, and new life in the resurrection. St. Paul writes to the faithful at Colossae, "In baptism you were not only buried with him but also raised to life with him because you believed in the power of God who raised him from the dead" (Col 2:12). In the ancient church the imagery was very vivid because catechumens were baptized by immersion: they went down into the baptismal font as if into a tomb, only to come out again "raised from the dead," purified, and committed to leading a sinless life.

It is enlightening to note how Cyril of Jerusalem (c. 315-386) handles this phrase. In accord with the practice of the time, Cyril explained the meaning of the "mysteries"—that is, the sacraments—to a catechumen only after the person had been baptized and fully initiated into the body of Christ. Thus in the pre-baptismal catechesis based on the text of the Creed he discusses Jesus' burial in the most prosaic terms: the location of the tomb, what it was made of, how was it constructed, etc. But in the mystagogical catechesis addressed to the newly baptized—the reflection on the sacraments of initiation—he expounds the text from Romans where St. Paul speaks of baptism as dying and rising to new life in Christ (Rom 6:3-14). He debriefs the newly baptized, helping them to understand the mysteries they had celebrated a few days before.

> . . . ye were led to the holy pool of Divine Baptism, as Christ was carried from the Cross to the Sepulchre which is before our eyes. And each of you was asked, whether he believed in the name of the Father, and of the Son, and of the Holy Ghost, and ye made that saving confession, and descended three times into the water, and ascended again; here also hinting by a symbol at the three days burial of Christ. For as our Savior passed three days and three nights in the heart of the earth, so you also in your first ascent out of the water, represented the first day of Christ in the earth, and by your descent the night. . . .And at the self-same moment ye were both dying and being born; and that Water of salvation was at once your grave and your mother. . .there was a time to die and a time to be born; and one and the same time effected both of these, and your birth went hand in hand with your death.[5]

The meaning of WAS BURIED is to be sought in the baptismal rite itself. Individuals who had participated in the rites of initiation knew firsthand what it meant to die and be buried with Christ in baptism. To them WAS BURIED was not a doctrinal statement but an expression rooted in an experience that was a necessary prelude to participation in the paschal mysteries. Writers, even church fathers, who view the Creed more as a statement of doctrine than as a confession of faith find themselves at a loss to explain the purpose of this reference to entombment. All admit, however, that reference to the entombment was part of the primitive kerygma.

AD INFEROS

DESCENDED INTO HELL is a phrase of another kind. Not part of the preached kerygma, it was introduced into the Creed relatively late, during the height of the Arian controversy. It first appeared in the Fourth Formula of Sirmium in 359, then gradually found a place in some Spanish creeds of the sixth century, and later was introduced into Gallican creeds of the seventh and eighth centuries.[6] Rufinus reports that the phrase was not found in the creed of the Roman church nor in the creeds of the Eastern churches. He says the meaning of DESCENDED INTO HELL "appears to be precisely the same as that contained in the affirmation BURIED, and he implies that the former was inserted to elucidate the latter."[7] On the other hand, the Catechism of the Council of Trent, in denying that DESCENDED INTO HELL is synonymous with WAS BURIED, states "There was no reason why the Apostles, in delivering an Article of Faith, should repeat the same thing in other and more obscure terms."[8] J. N. D. Kelly speaks of it as a modification "which really adds something of substance to the second article of the creed, and which involves exegetical difficulties of no mean order."[9] Most modern commentators agree that it is not to be taken literally, and many cite it as an example of how the church has resorted to the language of myth to express the ineffable mystery of salvation.[10]

The Fourth Formula of Sirmium affirmed that the Son "died, and descended to the underworld, and regulated things there, Whom the gatekeepers of hell saw and shuddered." What (where?) was this "underworld" to which the Son descended? Over the course of time, ideas on the subject changed. Originally "underworld" referred quite simply to the realm of the dead. Even the Latin texts do not agree in the wording; some say HE DESCENDED *"ad inferna,"* some *"ad inferos."*[11] The English "hell" (which, like the German *Holle,* stems from the Old Norse *hel* = *hehlen,* "cover" or "conceal") translates the Hebrew word *Sheol* (which literally means "no place") and the Greek "Hades," the underworld, the home of the dead. Used in this way, it was not thought of as a place of torment or punishment. As Christian thought became more refined, and especially among medieval scholastics, distinctions were made. The realm of the dead included the "blessed" in the heavens *above,* and the "damned" in hell *below.* Thus "hell" was also used to translate the Hebrew *Gehenna,* the place of torment where Jesus said there would weeping and gnashing of teeth

(Mt 5:29; 10:28; 18:8ff). In addition, a place called "limbo" (from the Latin *limbus; in limbo* means "on the border," "in between") was postulated—a kind of no-man's land between heaven and hell where the blessed who died before the coming of Christ resided.

Long before DESCENDED INTO HELL became a stock phrase in the Creed, writers such as St. Ignatius of Antioch (d. 107), St. Polycarp (d. 156), St. Irenaeus, and Tertullian explicitly mentioned the descent. They took it as a logical corollary of Jesus' death because in the tradition of the Hebrew Scriptures, to say that someone died and was buried was equivalent to saying that he or she had passed to Sheol. Belief in Jesus' descent into Sheol, accepted by Jewish Christians from apostolic times, said more than mere entombment; that is, it put the stamp of authenticity on his death and marked the final step in his *kenosis*—self-emptying. This is the mindset that prompted Tertullian to write:

> Christ our God, Who because He was man died according to the Scriptures, and was buried according to the same Scriptures, satisfied this law also by undergoing the form of human death in the underworld, and did not ascend aloft to heaven until He had gone down to the regions beneath the earth.[12]

In other words, Christ experienced the common lot of sinful humanity in coming to know what it really means to die. This appears to be the essence of the belief before it became the object of theological reflection.

Once theologians began to delve into the question of deeper meaning, various interpretations surfaced. Alexandrian theologians, for example, saw in the Descent a kerygmatic significance. Under the influence of Clement and Origen they linked the Descent to 1 Peter 3:19: "It was in the spirit also that he [Christ] went to preach to the spirits in prison." According to this tradition the "spirits" referred to are the souls of Noah's contemporaries dwelling in the nether world. Christ's soul proclaimed the good news of salvation among the dead during the three days between Good Friday and Easter and through his preaching brought about the conversion of Noah's unbelieving contemporaries.

It was common for other Greek writers, however, to assign a "soteriological" purpose to the Descent. Christ descended to Sheol to release the righteous—patriarchs, prophets, and all who had lived justly—waiting in hope for his coming. They noted how at Jesus' death "the earth quaked, boulders split, tombs opened. [And] many bodies of the saints who had fallen asleep were raised" (Mt 27:52-53). Earlier authors did not use the term "limbo of the fathers" (*limbus patrum*), but it is clear that they understood it was to this limbo— Hades ("hell" in the neutral sense)—that Christ descended upon passing from the world of the living. Although the Descent is not mentioned in his creed, Cyril of Jerusalem explained it in the course of pointing to Jonah as a type of the Risen Lord. Christ, he said,

> descended into hell alone, but ascended thence with a great company; for He went down to death, and many bodies of the saints which slept arose through Him. Death was struck with dismay on beholding a new visitant descend into Hades, not bound by the chains of that place. . . . The holy prophets ran unto Him, and Moses the Lawgiver, and Abraham, and Isaac, and Jacob; David also, and Samuel, and Esaias (Isaiah), and John the Baptist. . . . All the Just were ransomed, whom death had swallowed; for it behoved the King whom they had proclaimed, to become the redeemer of His noble heralds.[13]

In explaining the Descent, Rufinus of Aquileia closely follows Cyril and therefore is credited with popularizing the "soteriological" interpretation in the West.[14]

Although the African creeds did not mention the Descent, St. Augustine knew the tradition. He wrote in one of his letters, "It is established beyond question that the Lord, after He had been put to death in the flesh, 'descended into hell,' " and he asks, "Who, except an infidel, will deny that Christ was in hell?" Augustine explains that Jesus loosed those detained there from the pains of hell without himself being chained by them, much as a hunter releases prey from the trap that holds it.[15] While he speaks of the "pains of hell," Augustine denies that the just were subjected to punishment. The "bosom of Abraham" to which Jesus descended was a middle state between the hell of the damned and the paradise of the blessed. Augustine's position on this, as in so many other matters, was the one generally adopted by medieval scholastics.

Medieval theologians took the Descent as a point of departure for further reflection and speculations that went beyond the meaning assigned it by Augustine and other church fathers. In his *Summa Theologiae*, St. Thomas Aquinas, for example, devoted eight articles to the

Descent; in them he summarized the major issues as they had come to be discussed in the universities. Thomas examined the propriety of Jesus' descent into hell (art. 1); the reasons he descended only to the part of hell where the just were detained (art. 2); the manner in which the whole Christ was at the same time in heaven, on earth, and in hell (art. 3); and the length of his sojourn in hell, namely, until he arose in his body from the tomb (art. 4). Thomas quotes St. Augustine to the effect that all the just, detained because of original sin, were liberated by Jesus' descent into hell (art. 5); but he rejects the theory of universal salvation in denying that the Descent extended the fruits of the passion to those bereft of faith and charity as in the case of the unrepentant (art. 6) and of unbaptized infants (art. 7); nor did Jesus in his visit to the underworld declare an amnesty, for the souls in purgatory still had to be purified (art. 8).[16] Later, a year before his death in 1274, St. Thomas popularized many of these same ideas in a series of lenten sermons based on the Apostles' Creed.[17]

There were some differences among the scholastics on minor points, but they generally agreed, as did Luther and other early Reformers, that Jesus descended into "hell" to deliver the just who had lived in expectation of the coming of the Messiah. Some Reformers, however, returned to the position of Rufinus, finding in the phrase no more than a reaffirmation that Jesus really died. The Tridentine catechism insisted that it meant something more. John Calvin agreed that the burial and Descent were not the same, but he regarded the Augustinian notion that the souls of the dead were confined in a kind of prison as childish. To Calvin's mind the Descent into hell does not describe something Jesus experienced after death but describes the pain and agony of dying when he felt totally abandoned by God. He interpreted Jesus' dying words, "My God, my God, why have you forsaken me?" (Mk 15:34) to mean that he momentarily experienced the punishment of the damned—total estrangement from God—in order to save us from eternal hell.

In modern theology the most significant development with regard to the Descent has been the return to the text of 1 Peter 3:19. It is the only text in the New Testament that explicitly mentions Christ's activity in the world of the dead. Clement of Alexandria interpreted it in connection with the descent into hell, but Western authors, under the influence of St. Augustine, explained the Descent without reference to the Petrine text. Since the time of the Reformation, however, it has become the principal biblical text for the Descent. For the past hundred years or so, Protestant exegetes have tended to interpret it (together with 1 Peter 4:6) as did Clement and Origen: as presenting the dead with an opportunity for conversion. In the late sixteenth century St. Robert Bellarmine advanced a theory followed until recently by many Catholic scholars. He surmised that the Petrine texts (1 Peter 3:19 and 4:6) imply a "last minute conversion" on the part of sinners who perished in the flood. According to Bellarmine, the soul of Christ descended among the dead to proclaim to these repentant sinners the good news of their redemption.[18]

A NEW RELEVANCE FOR THE DESCENT

Despite (or is it because of?) the obscurity surrounding the Descent, contemporary theologians are finding a new relevance in this "forgotten and almost discarded article."[19] The lonely and despairing find their own frustration and suffering expressed in the death cry of Jesus, "My God, my God, why have you forsaken me?" (Mk 15:34). It is a prayer from hell. It is a prayer for today. Over the centuries theologians have attempted to explain the significance of the Descent for christology and soteriology and to draw out its significance in the struggle of men and women for salvation. In the twentieth century, existential considerations have prompted theologians to focus on an aspect of the mystery that has remained latent and largely undeveloped: suffering.

It is true that St. Thomas held that Christ experienced the trauma that all human beings undergo in their own descent into Sheol, and John Calvin had Jesus suffering not the sorrow of Sheol but the agony of Gehenna. But for the most part theologians overlooked the element of suffering in the descent AD INFEROS. Contemporary preoccupation with the spiritual hells of the human psyche—the hell of humanity's inhumanity as evidenced in the Holocaust, the hell of fear compounded by the threat of a nuclear winter, the hell of meaninglessness stemming from a lack of purpose—has led people to wonder if there might be more to the Descent than first appears. The Swiss writer Hans Urs von Balthasar, one of the pioneers in the "new theology," for example, argues that the Christian imagery of hell has proven indispensable to moderns in their attempt to articulate their experience of hopelessness and of the demons within.[20]

Von Balthasar reflects on the symbolism implicit in Jesus' agony on the cross and descent into hell. The Father was silent when the Son cried out in anguish. Jesus, crushed by suffering, unable to lift his eyes to heaven, saw only the earth. His body was buried, sealed in the tomb, and the Word ceased to sound in the world. His soul descended into hell so that, "on Holy Saturday, Nietzsche is right for just one day and God is dead."[21] For many, however, Holy Saturday—the death of God— symbolizes not just a momentary eclipse of the divine presence but the enduring reality. God is dead. Humans suffer the punishment of the damned—the pain of loss—not because of anything they have done, but because the Word of God is not heard. God is mute because God is not.

Joseph Ratzinger, who echoes many of Balthasar's ideas, writes:

> Thus the article about the Lord's descent into hell reminds us that not only God's speech but also his silence is part of the Christian revelation. God is not only the comprehensible word that comes to us; he is also the silent, inaccessible, uncomprehended and incomprehensible ground that eludes us.[22]

The image of the Descent is also echoed in the writings of the Christian mystics who describe their own "dark nights," when there is only void and loneliness. These experiences of nothingness are the black holes of human existence, where there is only spiritual emptiness alleviated by neither sight nor sound. Although the mystics describe their dark nights in much the same way as the death-of-God theologians describe their experience, there is one essential difference. Though their faith is tried and their hope tested, each mystic continues—with Jesus—to cry out to the living God: "My God, my God, why have you forsaken me?"

Von Balthasar interprets HE DESCENDED INTO HELL to mean that Jesus opened communications with those who, unable to raise their eyes to the heavens and incapable of seeing God, experience the sufferings of the damned. The Word is a silent whisper in the void of intellectual and psychic hell even when it is not heard. Where there is isolation and loneliness, Jesus stretches out his hand in the darkness to offer "fellowship." Von Balthasar concludes his reflection on the relevancy of the Descent in today's world by lauding Christian writers such as Claudel, Peguy, Gertrud von le Fort, and Bernanos for their sensitivity to the thoughts and feelings of the Godless. In presenting hell as a spiritual condition rather than as a place beyond human experience, such writers have infused new meaning into the creedal affirmation. These authors, according to Balthasar, are able to communicate with those who feel themselves lost, even "damned," because these writers can affirm that Christ goes into the innermost recesses of the mind and heart to proclaim the good news of salvation to those imprisoned in the nether world of their own loneliness and despair.

Another twentieth-century theologian who sought to invest the Descent with fresh meaning was the late Karl Rahner. In several of his early writings he noted that the Descent was a neglected topic that deserves more attention. In particular he felt that the positive aspect of the mystery needed to be emphasized.[23] To support his particular understanding of death, Rahner speculated on Christ's Descent into the underworld. To be specific: Jesus' dying not only changed the world but transformed the significance of death itself. Before Calvary, death, though a natural phenomenon, was a continual revelation of the reality of sin in the world. In Christ, death is seen in the context of new creation and eternal life. Rahner says, "What had been the manifestation of sin, thus becomes, without its darkness being lifted, the contradiction of sin, the manifestation of 'yes' to the will of the Father."[24]

Rahner argued that we are not merely passive victims before the reality of death; rather, we are actively engaged in the process of dying at the very time we live. The process of dying climaxes in the final instant of life; death is, in Rahner's view, the first act of the human spirit that is completely personal and fully free in that it is unencumbered with this-worldly considerations. The creedal affirmation of the descent *ad inferos* following immediately on the statement of Jesus' death indicates that dying extends beyond "empirical knowledge of the historical event." For Christians, as for Christ, death makes it possible to renew their human potential to be totally present to the cosmos and to be active agents in determining its well-being. Rahner speculates that Jesus, in his descent into the nether world, touched the very marrow of the created universe—"the most intrinsic, unified, ultimate and deepest level of the world"—and transformed it. The world as a whole and as the ground for personal action becomes very different from what it might have been had Jesus not died. By freely submitting to death, Jesus accomplished two things: first, he paid his dues as a human being and ratified the reality of grace which, in turn, revealed the power of his Lordship as a factor that shapes the whole of creation.

Rahner's position on this issue is summarized in the following sentence, characteristic of its author's complex style:

> The descent into hell is Christ's dying, insofar as he obediently accepts and realizes death which reduces man to impotence, and "in death" is exposed to (voluntary) total helplessness—wholly at God's disposal; but by this means his redemptive obedience wins him power over the universe and history, because his relationship with the whole of creation does not cease in death but rather becomes manifest as existing "at the heart of the world."[25]

By now it is obvious that HE DESCENDED *AD INFEROS* is another of the phrases in the Creed that need not be taken literally. The few texts in the New Testament that seem to say anything about the matter (notably 1 Peter 3:19 and 4:6) are so difficult to understand as to allow for a variety of interpretations. Even the wording of the article is problematic: should it be *ad inferna* or *ad inferos*?—he descended "into hell" or "among the the dead"? The attempts of contemporary theologians to find some existential meaning in the phrase can be justified to the extent that their interpretions of the phrase are grounded in the broad context of salvation history and christology. Ultimately the significance of Jesus' Descent is to be found not in his death or burial, but in his resurrection and exaltation at the right hand of the Father. These are the topics of the following chapters.

Notes

1. The translation which appears in the revised baptismal rites is the "official" translation of the Apostles' Creed for use by Roman Catholics in the English speaking world. Prior to the Second Vatican

Council, Roman Catholics had no authorized translation of the liturgical texts. Once Vatican II sanctioned the use of the vernacular, however, episcopal conferences in countries where English is the common tongue established the International Commission on English in the Liturgy (1964). ICEL, whose members include liturgists, language specialists, biblical and patristic scholars, and musicians, is charged with providing standardized liturgical texts for all English speaking Roman Catholics.

ICEL works closely with the International Consultatio on English Texts which is an ecumenical group. Formed in 1969, the task of ICET is to promote an English version of liturgical texts with a view toward their ecumenical possibilities. The texts recommended by ICET have been published in *Prayers We Have in Common* rev. ed. (Philadelphia: Fortress Press, 1975). For the most part ICEL simply adopted the ICET translations of the ancient Creeds. See *NCE* 17:294–296.

2. Kelly notes the grammatical structure using *oti*, "that," to set off "was buried" as "an independent article of faith." *Creeds*, p. 150.

3. One might further note how both John and Mark interpret the anointing of Jesus by Mary of Bethany as preparation for his burial (Jn 12:7, Mk 14:8). See Raymond E. Brown, *The Gospel According to John I–XII* The Anchor Bible Series, 29. (Garden City, NY: Doubleday & Co., 1966), p. 454.

4. Kelly, *Creeds*, pp. 150–151.

5. *Catechetical Lectures* 20, 4; *NPNF*, 2d ser., VII, pp. 147–148. It should be recalled that this catechesis took place in the church of the Holy Sepulchre in Jerusalem. See note 3 in *NPNF*, 2nd ser., VII, p. 148.

6. Kelly, *Creeds*, p. 289, 378–379.

7. *Commentary*, 18, *ACW*, p. 52.

8. Art. 5, (Bradley & Kevane), p. 65.

9. *Creeds*, p. 378.

10. Hans Küng, *Eternal Life*? (Garden City, NY: Doubleday & Co., 1984), pp. 124–129.

11. See *DS* 29, 30.

12. *De anima*, 55 (quoted in Kelly, *Creeds*, p. 380).

13. Catechetical Lecture 14, 18–19 (*NPNF*, 2nd ser. VII, 99); Rufinus, 29 (*ACW*, p. 62).

14. Par. 29 (*ACW*, p. 61).

15. Letter 164, "To Evodius," ch. 2, 3; ch. 3, 8 (*NPNF* 1st ser., I, 515–516, 517).

16. III, q. 52, art. 1–8.

17. Joseph B. Collins, ed. and trans., *The Catechetical Instructions of St. Thomas Aquinas* (New York: Joseph F. Wagner, 1939), pp. 29–34.

18. See W. J. Dalton, *Christ's Proclamation to the Spirits: A Study of Peter 3:18 - 4:6* (Rome: Pontifical Biblical Institute, 1965), p. 20. Dalton writes, "It can hardly be denied that the controversy between Catholics and Protestants over Purgatory entered at least indirectly into the choice of an interpretation on both sides." Catholics and Protestant exegetes do agree, however, that these verses in 1 Peter are among the most obscure in the New Testament (Dalton, p. 15).

19. Ratzinger, *Introduction*, p. 226. Karl Rahner, "Remarks on the Theology of Indulgences," in *Theological Investigations*, II (Baltimore: Helicon Press, 1963), p. 175.

20. *Science, Religion and Christianity* (Westminster, MD: Newman Press, 1958). Von Balthasar surveys the theme of hell in literary works from Milton to such twentieth-century authors as Sartre and Dostoievsky (pp. 120–129).

21. Ibid. p. 117.

22. *Introduction*, p. 225.

23. See "Current Problems in Christology," in *Theological Investigations*, I (Baltimore: Helicon Press, 1961), pp. 195, 218. *On the Theology of Death* (New York: Herder and Herder, 1965), p. 72.

24. *Theology of Death*, p. 70.

25. Karl Rahner and Herbert Vorgrimler, *Theological Dictionary* (New York: Herder and Herder, 1965), p. 124.

11

Life Is Changed,
Not Taken Away

"On the third day he rose again"

Much has been written in criticism of Rudolf Bultmann (1884-1976), the most influential New Testament scholar in the twentieth century. Whatever one thinks of his approach, he deserves a great deal of credit for bringing modern biblical scholars and theologians to focus once more on the *meaning* of the resurrection. By all accounts the resurrection of Jesus from the dead is the central mystery of Christianity. In the eyes of the apostolic witnesses and for succeeding generations it is the decisive moment in the order of salvation. Christians are by definition an "Easter people"; their faith rests on the reality expressed in the creedal statement ON THE THIRD DAY HE ROSE AGAIN IN FULFILLMENT OF THE SCRIPTURES.

A man of deep faith, Bultmann became disenchanted with the timidity and naivete of liberal theology. He felt that its preoccupation with the quest for the Jesus of history at the expense of faith and conversion was for many a failure of nerve or at the very least a distraction from facing up to the existential implications and moral imperatives of the gospel message. Even the standard textbooks used in

Catholic seminaries largely ignored the theological dimensions of Jesus' resurrection. The resurrection was rather the focal point of *apologetics*, which sought to establish its historicity and thereby to demonstrate the divinity of Jesus and legitimize his message. But once the seminary texts had defended the historical character of the resurrection they said little more about it. The resurrection did not figure in their treatises on soteriology despite the fact that St. Paul did not hesitate to declare that "if Jesus was not raised . . . you are still in yours sins" (1 Cor 15:16). It took biblical scholars such as Bultmann and, among Roman Catholics, Ferdinand Prat to show that the resurrection marked a turning point in the lives both of individuals and of the nascent Christian community. In the New Testament Jesus' resurrection is not offered as a proof of the gospel message, it *is* the gospel message.

Scripture scholars who struggled to have the church focus on a fuller meaning of the resurrection found a receptive audience and zealous allies in the ranks of the modern liturgical movement. Liturgists reminded the church that the paschal mystery—Jesus' death *and resurrection*, his descent among the dead, and his ascension to the right hand of the Father—is the reality celebrated in the sacraments of baptism and eucharist.

NEW TESTAMENT ACCOUNTS

Before looking more closely at the meaning of the resurrection as a key to understanding ON THE THIRD DAY HE ROSE AGAIN IN FULFILLMENT OF THE SCRIPTURES it will be helpful to review the New Testament accounts. It is generally admitted that the creedal formula in St. Paul's First Epistle to the Corinthians is the oldest witness we have to Easter:

> I handed on to you first of all what I myself received, that Christ died for our sins in accordance with the Scriptures; that he was buried and, in accordance with the Scriptures, rose on the third day. (15:3-4)

The formula reported by Paul probably originated in the Christian community in Jerusalem (see 1 Cor 15:1-2,6-11). The evidence suggests that the resurrection was the core of the kerygma from the beginning, but it took some time for the Gospel accounts of Easter to evolve into their present form.

The Gospels give us six different resurrection narratives:[1]

1. Mark 16:1-8 records how the women set out at sunrise on the first day of the week to anoint Jesus' body. Instead they found a young man dressed in a white robe who tells them not to be afraid and proclaims the message of Easter: "He is raised up; he is not here" (v. 6). This passage describes the bewilderment and fear of the women but neither the resurrection itself nor any appearances of the risen Jesus.[2] It says only that Peter and the disciples will see him in Galilee. In some of the better manuscripts this account concludes the Gospel according to Mark.

2. Matthew 28:1-20 likewise reports the discovery of the empty tomb and the Easter proclamation: "He is not here, for he has been raised exactly as he promised" (v. 6). It tells of a mighty earthquake as the angel of the Lord descended to roll back the stone (v. 2), an appearance of the Risen Christ to the women in Jerusalem, his promise to see the brothers in Galilee (vv. 9-10), and the report of the guard set to watch the tomb and the bribe offered the soldiers by the chief priests and elders (vv. 11-15). Matthew concludes the account and with it his Gospel by describing how Jesus commissioned the disciples to make other disciples by baptizing them and teaching them all that they had been taught (vv. 18-20).

3. Luke 24:1-53 also describes the bewilderment and fear of the women at going to the tomb at dawn on the first day of the week but not finding the body, and at hearing the words of two men in dazzling garments: "Why do you search for the Living One among the dead? He is not here; he has been raised up" (vv. 1-7). Luke tells how two of the disciples recognized the risen Lord in the breaking of the bread at Emmaus (vv. 13-35) and reports the appearance to the Eleven in Jerusalem (vv. 36-43). Finally the disciples are commissioned to give witness (v. 48), and he is taken up to heaven (v. 51).

4. John 20:1-29 tells how after Mary Magdalene found the tomb empty Jesus appeared to her and she mistook him for the gardener (vv. 11-18). Later, still on the first day of the week, Jesus appears to the disciples in Jerusalem when Thomas, one of the Twelve, is absent (vv. 19-23); he appears again a week later when Thomas is present (vv. 24-29).

5. John 21:1-23, regarded by most biblical scholars as an appendix, incorporates material from another tradition. It tells of another appearance—the third—this one to seven disciples fishing offshore on the

sea of Tiberias in Galilee (vv. 1-14). (The rest of the chapter contrasts the role of Simon Peter and that of the beloved disciple.)

6. Mark 16:9-20, "the longer ending," found only in some Greek manuscripts, reports three appearances of Jesus in and about Jerusalem on Easter Sunday and his being "taken up into heaven" on that same day.

"IN ANOTHER FORM"

Biblical scholars refer to the last eleven verses in Mark's Gospel as a "coda." Musicians describe a concluding passage that brings a composition to a proper close as a coda, and it is in this sense that scholars apply the term to the Marcan text. The evidence is that some ancient scribe, unhappy with the abrupt ending in verse 8, composed a more graceful conclusion.[3] A resume of the appearances of the Risen Jesus based on the material in the other traditions, particularly Luke 24 and John 20, it has been cleverly edited into a single, coherent whole in the spirit of the Marcan Gospel. Despite its brevity, moreover, the coda manages to incorporate the principal themes that are constants in the resurrection stories as told by the other evangelists. It emphasizes that 1) Jesus rose early on the first day of the week; 2) he first appeared to Mary Magdalene, who announced the good news 3) to the disciples still grieving over the loss. 4) Jesus' appearance was significantly changed and 5) the disciples were slow to believe. 6) Jesus sent them forth to proclaim the good news to all creation, to baptize and call others to believe. And finally, 7) though the Lord Jesus was taken up into heaven, he continues to make his presence felt in the world.

The change in Jesus' appearance is the key to understanding the resurrection or, to be more precise (because the mystery eludes understanding), the New Testament accounts of the resurrection. The disciples simply do not recognize him, nor are they overcome immediately by his presence. Mary Magdalene thought he was the gardener. Likewise the disciples who had sat at table with him a few days earlier were unaware that the one they saw frying fish on the shore of Lake Tiberias was Jesus. Though he walked the way to Emmaus with Cleopas and his companion, their eyes were opened only with the breaking of the bread. As the Marcan coda expressed it, he appeared "in another form."

If Jesus' appearance was so radically transformed, what was his risen body like? Although St. Paul says it is a "nonsensical question" (1 Cor 15:36), he was realist enough to know that it would continue to be asked. The apostle, therefore, attempts to answer it as best he can. He accepts the premise that there is some kind of real, though indefinable, continuity between our bodily mode of existence in our present state and the mode of existence of the risen body. But there is also discontinuity. Paul finds an analogy in the relationship between the seed that is sown and the plant that sprouts from it. His point is that the grain standing in the farmer's field is not the same as the seed that was buried in the ground.

> The seed you sow does not germinate unless it dies. When you sow, you do not sow the full-blown plant, but a kernel of wheat or some other grain. God gives body to it as he pleases—to each seed its own fruition. Not all bodily nature is the same. Men have one kind of body, animals another. Birds are of their kind, fish are of theirs. There are heavenly bodies and there are earthly bodies. The splendor of the heavenly bodies is one thing, that of the earthly another. The sun has a splendor of its own, so has the moon, and the stars have theirs. Even among the stars, one differs from another in brightness. So is it with the resurrection of the dead. What is sown in the earth is subject to decay, what rises is incorruptible. What is sown is ignoble, what rises is glorious. Weakness is sown, strength rises up. A natural body is put down and a spiritual body comes up. (1 Cor 15:36-44)

Paul makes explicit what is implied in the resurrection stories of the Gospels. The Risen Christ is not a revived corpse like Lazarus. As extraordinary as the raising of Lazarus was, he simply returned from the grave to resume his earthly life with his sisters Martha and Mary (Jn 11:1-44) and to await death again. The resurrection of Jesus is pictured for us as something quite different. His body is no longer subject to the earthly laws of biochemistry and physics: he disappears as suddenly as he appears; distance and locked rooms are not barriers to his moving about. The resurrection means that Jesus rose to "glory"; that is, he entered into a higher mode of life and is at the same time the source of new life for the world. He is "the first-born of the dead" (Col 1:18), who "will give a new form to this lowly body of ours and remake it according to the pattern of his glorified body, by his power to subject everything to himself" (Phil 3:21).

BEYOND DOUBT

The name of Thomas the Apostle is almost synonymous with skepticism: "I will never believe it without probing the nailprints in his hands, without putting my finger in the nailmarks and my hand into his side" (Jn 20:25). And the Marcan coda indicates that there were others who shared Thomas' skepticism (Mk 16:11,13,14,16). Doubt is a recurring theme in the resurrection stories.[4] The disciples seem to have had two questions. In Luke and John their doubt had to do with whether the one who appears is indeed Jesus of Nazareth who was crucified. At first they thought they were seeing a ghost, and even after he reassured them, "It is really I," they remained "incredulous for sheer joy and wonder" (Lk 24:37-41). Despite the transformation in Jesus' appearance, the New Testament is clear that the Risen One and the crucified Jesus are the same: even the skeptical Thomas, seeing the marks of the nails and his pierced side, became a believer.

The Gospels tell also of a second kind of doubt. Even after the disciples accepted the appearances of the crucified Jesus, there was still the question whether they would acknowledge him as the Christ. From an intellectual point of view it was the *christological* issue, from the existential point of view, it was a matter of *conversion*, of a change of heart as well as of mind. Matthew recounts how the Eleven made their way to the mountain in Galilee "to which Jesus had summoned them. At the sight of him, those who had entertained doubts fell down in homage" (Mt 28:17). The scene recalls Thomas' confession after he overcame his doubts: "My Lord and my God" (Jn 20:28). The Marcan coda succinctly summarizes the relationship between resurrection and conversion:

> Go into the whole world and proclaim the good news to all
> creation. The man who believes in it and accepts baptism will be
> saved; the man who refuses to believe in it will be condemned.
> (Mk 16:15-16)

The stress on the disciples' unbelief emphasizes that faith is a gift. Without special revelation humans are simply unable to understand the Jesus mystery. To recognize him as the Messiah is a grace; to confess him as Lord and God is the work of the Spirit.

Despite the fact that in some cases the transition from non-belief to belief seemed to have been instantaneous, on the whole the Gospels suggest that the disciples were slow to believe because they did not understand "all that the prophets [had] announced." On the way to Emmaus Jesus asked Cleopas and his companion,

> "Did not the Messiah have to undergo all this so as to enter into his glory?" Beginning, then, with Moses and all the prophets, he interpreted for them every passage of Scripture which referred to him. (Lk 24:25-28; see v. 44)

In other words, to appreciate fully the christological issue the disciples had first to understand the Scriptures—the Hebrew Bible.

As we saw in Chapter 9, the passion narratives are laced through with Old Testament citations. The resurrection accounts are briefer, of a different character, and speak of the fulfillment of Scripture in a more general way. Most often the examples we have of apostolic preaching present the death and resurrection of Jesus as two aspects of the same mystery. Peter in his famous Pentecost discourse tells his listeners how Jesus the Nazorean "was delivered up by the set purpose and plan of God; you even made use of pagans to crucify and kill him. God freed him from death's bitter pangs, however, and raised him up again, for it was impossible that death should keep its hold on him" (Acts 2:23-24). Peter cites Psalm 16:10, "Nor will you suffer your faithful one to undergo corruption," to show that God proclaimed "beforehand the resurrection of the Messiah. This is the Jesus God has raised up, and we are his witnesses" (Acts 2:31-32; see 5:30-31).

Paul follows much the same line of reasoning as Peter, even to the point of citing the same text from the Psalm 16 when preaching in the synagogue in Antioch (see Acts 13:23-37).[5] The primitive Christian community found the key to understanding Jesus' death and resurrection in the books of the Old Testament. In the classic creedal statement of 1 Corinthians 15:2-3 St. Paul insists that the church's belief is grounded in Scripture. As if to underscore this point, the phrase "in accordance with the Scriptures" occurs twice within a few lines in this short statement of beliefs. As we would say today, it was "a term of art"—a phrase that had acquired a special meaning of its own. The phrase was intended to affirm that the death and resurrection of the Lord Jesus marks the fulfillment of the promises found in the Old Testament. The proclamation of the Gospel and Christian faith is based on an event that happened "according to Scripture." As if they were checking this claim, the members of the Jewish synagogue at

Beroea, who "welcomed the message with great enthusiasm," are said to have studied the Scriptures each day "to see whether these things were so" (Acts 17:11).

The context clearly indicates that Paul returned to this earliest confession of faith to repudiate deviations from accepted teaching that were apparently rife in the church at Corinth. He intended to show that fidelity to accepted teaching rested in turn on faithfulness to Holy Scriptures. The claim of the Creed of Constantinople to present the authentic faith rests on the same principle IN FULFILLMENT OF THE SCRIPTURES.[6]

"THE THIRD DAY"

Similarly, Paul's testimony makes it abundantly clear that ON THE THIRD DAY HE ROSE AGAIN IN FULFILLMENT OF THE SCRIPTURES, as in the case of other phrases of the Creed, simply echoes the kerygma. It is a mistake, however, to read THE THIRD DAY as a simple reference to earthly time as if one were dating the resurrection event seventy-two hours after Good Friday. The phrase is charged with deeper meaning. It is an eschatological expression linked to the saving action of God in the person of the crucified Jesus. To the Jews' way of thinking "the third day" or "after three days" had a special significance even in their everyday manner of speech. It represented D-day, the decisive day, a turning point in the course of human events. In no less than thirty places the Hebrew Scriptures employ the phrase to indicate a critical moment when one thing is definitively concluded and a new thing begins. In some cases "the third day" signals calamity (e.g., 2 Sam 1:2; 1 Kgs 12:12), but more often it marks deliverance and promise of better things to come. The Lord instructed Moses to have the people "sanctify themselves today and tomorrow . . . and be ready for the third day; for on the third day the LORD will come down on Mount Sinai" to seal a covenant with Israel (Ex 19:10–11; see vv. 15–16). "On the third day" Esther begins her noble task of delivering Israel (Est 5:1), and "on the third day" Israel expects Yahweh to raise the people up "to live in his presence" (Hos 6:2-3). That is, the third day signals a speedy turnaround in Israel's fortunes and a new beginning, such as is promised in Hosea:

> He will revive us after two days; on the third day he will raise us
> up, to live in his presence. (6:2)

That Jesus rises from the dead on the third day marks a focal point in salvation, not in time. Apart from the two places in the New Testament that explicitly affirm the resurrection on the third day (1 Cor 15:4 and Acts 10:40), there are other texts that are less direct. There are, for example, Jesus' predictions of his passion; he indicated "to his disciples that he must go to Jerusalem and suffer greatly there at the hands of the elders, the chief priests, and the scribes, and to be put to death, and raised up on the third day" (Mt 16:21; see Lk 9:22; 18:33). When some of the scribes and Pharisees asked for a sign, he invoked the sign of Jonah: "Just as Jonah spent three days and three nights in the belly of a whale, so will the Son of Man spend three days and three nights in the bowels of the earth" (Mt 12:40; 16:4). On another occasion, he responded to the demand for a sign:

> "Destroy this temple," was Jesus' answer, "and in three days I will raise it up." . . . Actually he was talking about the temple of his body. Only after Jesus had been raised from the dead did his disciples recall that he had said this, and come to believe the Scripture and the word he had spoken. (Jn 2:19-22; see Mt 26:61)[7]

Although the third-day motif found its way into the kerygma and the Creed, it is totally absent from the Easter narratives in the Gospels. Instead the Gospels date the happenings "on the first day of the week" or "eight days later," which would have been again the first day of another week. The Gospel accounts thus fix the Easter events on the day after the Jewish sabbath (the last day of the week)—that is, on Sunday.

SUNDAY, "THE EIGHTH DAY": EUCHARIST AND REST

In all probability Christians observed a weekly commemoration of Jesus' death and resurrection on Sundays for some time before they celebrated Holy Week and Easter as annual feasts. On the occasion of Paul's visit to the church at Troas, Acts reports, "On the first day of the week when we gathered for the breaking of the bread. . ." (20:7). The eucharist was also the occasion when contributions were collected "for the saints." Paul writes to the church at Corinth, "On the first day of the week everyone should put aside whatever he has been able to save . . ." (1 Cor. 16:2). The observance of Sunday as a holy day is uniquely Christian in inspiration and meaning.

Although it is improper to describe it as the "Christian sabbath," Sunday did come to have a significance for Christians similar to that of the sabbath for the Jews. Sunday brings together and transcends the two great motifs of the Jewish sabbath: creation (Ex 20:8-11) and covenant (Ex 31:13). Sometime about A.D. 100, Christian writers began referring to Sunday as "the eighth day." The Epistle of Barnabas, for example, gives it a meaning that is suggestive of "the third day."

> Not the Sabbaths of the present era are acceptable to me, but [only that Sabbath] which I have appointed to mark the end of the world and to usher in the eighth day, that is, the dawn of another world. This, by the way, is the reason why we joyfully celebrate the eighth day—the same day on which Jesus rose from the dead; after which He manifested Himself and went up to heaven.[8]

This explanation of "the eighth day" is suggestive of "the third day" in that it marks the close of one era and the beginning of another. "The eighth day," however, adds an eschatological dimension in that it is a period beyond human chronology, an affirmation of the timelessness of the new day. For Christians the observance of Sunday as Sabbath is a weekly reminder both of the Last Adam and the creation in which everything is made anew, and of the New Covenant sealed in the blood of Jesus.

In Christian circles the first day of the week came to be known as "the Lord's day" (Rev 1:10), a tradition preserved in the romance languages (*domingo, domenica, dimanche*). Early in the second century St. Ignatius of Antioch wrote, "Christians no longer observe the Sabbath but live in the observance of the Lord's day on which our life rose again."[9] Early writers found a rich symbolism also in the pagan name *dies solis*, "day of the sun" and thus, "Sunday" in English and *Sonntag* in German. They drew out the obvious parallel between light and darkness. Justin Martyr, describing the Sunday eucharist, states, "We come together on the day of the *sun* on which God, changing darkness and matter, created the world, and on which Jesus Christ our Savior arose from the dead."[10] Eusebius of Caesarea wrote in the same vein, "It was on this day that at the time of creation when God said, 'Let there be light,' there was light; and on this day also the Sun of Justice arose in our souls."[11]

Sunday and eucharist, both symbolic of the Lord's resurrection, were closely linked from the beginning. It was simply taken for granted that Christians would assemble "on the Lord's own day" to break bread and offer thanks in common.[12] Christians felt obliged, not by precept but by faith and love and hope, to gather on Sunday for the eucharist. It was only in the sixth century (Council of Agde, 506) when individuals were being baptized before they were catechized that the church felt the need to legislate Sunday observance in an effort to bring the people to understand the significance of the day.

The tradition of Sunday eucharist is rooted in the New Testament; the origins of Sunday rest are not so clear. In Roman times Sunday was a workday. Christians worshiped in the night and in the early morning hours. It was only in A.D. 321 that Constantine decreed the "venerable day of the sun" a weekly holiday except for farmers whose work could not be interrupted.[13] The first recorded church law regarding Sunday rest dates from towards the end of the fourth century. The Synod of Laodicea (c. 380) was content to prescribe that on the Lord's day the faithful were to abstain from work as far as possible. The general law of the church dating from the thirteenth century forbade legal proceedings, business transactions, and "servile work," that is, most forms of manual labor. Many church fathers also spoke of servile work, which they understood in a figurative sense to signify sin. Thus Sunday rest was before all else a cessation of sinful activities. Origen stated,

> On Sunday none of the actions of the world should be done. If, then, you abstain from all the works of this world and keep yourself free for spiritual things, go to church, listen to the readings and divine homilies, meditate on heavenly things.[14]

Given the fact that the resurrection is cause for rejoicing, the church has regarded forms of penance such as kneeling and fasting as improper on Sunday.[15] Sunday observance that emphasizes what one cannot or should not do misses Sunday's unique significance. The Second Vatican Council summed up the spirit of the day as follows:

> By a tradition handed down from the apostles and having its origin from the very day of Christ's resurrection, the Church celebrates the paschal mystery every eighth day, which, with good reason, bears the name of the Lord's day or Sunday. For on this day Christ's faithful must gather together so that, by hearing the word of God and taking part in the eucharist, they may call

to mind the passion, the resurrection, and the glorification of the
Lord Jesus and may thank God who "has begotten them again
unto a living hope through the resurrection of Christ from the
dead" (1 Pet 1:3). Hence the Lord's Day is the first holy day of
all and should be proposed to the devotion of the faithful and
taught to them in such a way that it may become in fact a day of
joy and of freedom from work. Other celebrations, unless they
be truly of the greatest importance, shall not have precedence
over the Sunday, which is the foundation and core of the whole
liturgical year.[16]

One does not have to endorse Rudolf Bultmann's historical skepticism to appreciate his insistence that Jesus' death and resurrection is
not a detective story to be solved but a mystery to be lived. The
experience of the Risen One, as the disciples journeying to Emmaus
discovered, is something other than a merely human encounter. The
disciples were slow to believe that ON THE THIRD DAY HE ROSE AGAIN and
slower still to realize all its implications. They had to learn the meaning of the Scriptures before their eyes were opened. In the end the
resurrection became the foundation of Christian faith and the essential
element in the proclamation of the good news. From the beginning,
Christians recalled the mystery of a new creation and a new covenant in
the Sunday eucharist. As they began to understand the mystery better,
they saw that besides being lifted up on the cross and being raised to
new life in the resurrection, Jesus also ascended to glory at the right
hand of the Father—the subject of the next chapter.

Notes

1. Exegetes and biblical scholars have investigated the resurrection
stories from every conceivable angle. Two works that outline the basic
issues and give references to further reading are: R. E. Brown, *The
Virginal Conception and Bodily Resurrection of Jesus* (New York:
Paulist, 1973), pp. 69–129 and R. H. Fuller, *The Formation of the
Resurrection Narratives* (New York: Macmillan Co., 1971). For a
brief summary, see the excellent presentation by Jos. A. Fitzmyer, *A

Christological Catechism (New York: Paulist Pres, 1982), pp. 73–79. Also J. Feiner and L. Vischer, eds., *A Common Catechism* (New York: Seabury, 1975), pp. 162–185.

2. Though it may be implicit in the account, E. Schillebeeckx notes, "Nowhere in Mark do we read that the women themselves found the tomb empty." *Jesus: An Experiment in Christology* (New York: Crossroad, 1981), p. 333.

3. *The New American Bible* and other modern translations note two other endings found in some Greek manuscripts. One explanation for the abrupt ending is that the last page of a folio was lost; another is that the evangelist himself left the manuscript incomplete because for Christians the Gospel has no ending! See *The Interpreter's Bible*, vol. 7, pp. 916–917.

4. See E. Schillebeeckx, *Jesus*, pp. 358–360.

5. In both Acts 2 and Acts 13 the fulfillment of the Old Testament is seen in the permanent establishment, through the resurrection of Jesus, of the dominion of the house of David. In the Petrine discourse the resurrection is synonymous with the exaltation of Jesus at the right hand of the Father, a theme we return to in the next chapter. See C. F. Evans, *Resurrection and the New Testament*, Studies in Biblical Theology. Second Series—12 (Naperville, IL: Alec R. Allenson, 1970), pp. 12–14.

6. Heinz-Joachim Held, "According to the Scriptures," *The Ecumenical Review*, 37:2 (April 1985):190–191. The 1984 statement of the Pontifical Biblical Commission explains "the fulfillment of Scripture presupposes a certain *amplification of meaning*, whether it is a question of a meaning that the biblical texts originally bore, or a meaning that Jews, rereading these texts, were attributing to them in the time of Jesus. Indeed, such an amplification of meaning would scarcely be attributed to secondary theological *speculation*; it has its origin in the *person* of Jesus himself, whose own characteristics it sets in a better light" (1.1.11.2b). Joseph A. Fitzmyer, *Scripture and Christology: A Statement of the Biblical Commission with a Commentary* (Mahwah, N.J.: Paulist Press, 1986), p. 18.

7. E. Schillebeeckx, *Jesus*, pp. 526–532.

8. 15:8–9. *ACW*, no. 6, pp. 60–61.

9. *Ep ad Magnes.* 9, *NCE* 13:800.

10. *First Apology.* 67:7. Emphasis added.

11. *Comm. in psalmos* 91; quoted in *NCE* 13:797.

12. *Didache* 14:1. *ACW*, no. 6, p. 23.

13. St. Jerome repudiated the notion that Sunday observance was based on the Old Testament, an idea also condemned by the Council of Orleans in 538. The identification (and confusion) of the Sabbath and Sunday rest was popularized by a decree of Charlemagne (789) which forbad all work on Sunday as a violation of the Third (Fourth) Commandment. The excessive strictness in the observance of Sunday rest known as *Sabbatarianism* dates from the time of the Reformation. In its more extreme form it advocated cessation of activities along Old Testament lines and prohibited any kind of recreation on the Lord's day, even listening to music and reading books that were not strictly religious. This extreme rigorism, unknown on the Continent, was a development of the English and Scottish Reformation that bequeathed this heritage to the American colonies. See, *NCE* 12:777–778; 13:800; F. L. Cross, ed., *The Oxford Dictionary of the Christian Church*, s.v. "Sabbatarianism," 1196.

14. Hom. 23 on Numbers, 4; *NCE* 13:798.

15. *NCE* 13:798.

16. Constitution on the Liturgy, par. 106. In Mary Ann Simcoe, *The Liturgy Documents: A Parish Resource*, Revised edition (Chicago: Liturgy Training Publications, 1985), p. 28.

12

"If I Be Lifted Up . . ."

*"He ascended into heaven
and is seated at the right hand of the Father"*

A question often asked by people desirous of improving the quality of catechesis is: How was it that the church taught so effectively in the early days when it didn't have schools and structured programs? The question is a sweeping one touching on many complex factors. Any answer, however, would have to point to the liturgical year as the keystone in catechesis of the ancient and medieval church. Liturgy—public worship—stood at the crown of the arch that supported the edifice of Christian life. The public observance of religious feasts is not unique to Christianity: the festive days, even in pagan antiquity, were all religious in origin, and many holy days that the Jews still celebrate were adopted and given new meaning by the church. If indeed catechesis is less effective today than it was in former times, a principal reason is that the liturgical cycle is not taken seriously. Holy days, when observed at all, are seen as occasions for pomp and ritual which speak to churchgoers but do not affect the Christian community's self-understanding or influence society at large.

The point of this chapter is not to diagnose the reasons why the liturgical year no longer enjoys the esteem it once had in the life of

191

individuals and the community, but to show how the early church relied on it as a vehicle to both celebrate and proclaim the meaning of Jesus' death and resurrection. For example, the liturgy provides a key for unlocking the meaning of HE ASCENDED INTO HEAVEN AND IS SEATED AT THE RIGHT HAND OF THE FATHER. And the reverse is also true: an appreciation of the paschal mystery is central to understanding the liturgical cycle. The exaltation of Jesus in glory and power is the culmination of the paschal mystery; everything that follows is anticlimatic (which is not to say insignificant).

"FORTY DAYS"

In the beginning the church's liturgical calendar was simple. Jerusalem Christians prayed daily in the Temple and continued to celebrate the Jewish holy days, though the feasts began to take on different significance in light of Jesus' death and resurrection. They observed the sabbath and in addition met on the first day of the week for the breaking of the bread. For Christians the Sunday after Passover— Easter Sunday—climaxed the Passover celebration and gave it new meaning. Christ Jesus was the lamb who was slain; his passage to the Father marked the end of the Exodus and the beginning of a new day. Easter represented the fullness of the *paschal mystery*; in liturgical terms Easter embodied Good Friday, the Ascension, and Pentecost. Beginning in the second century the various facets of the paschal mystery were singled out and given a commemoration of their own, but the early church never lost sight of the fact that they were different aspects of one and the same mystery of salvation. In time, however, the separation of various feasts led to the dissociation of Jesus' death from his resurrection and of the resurrection from the ascension.

Already in the apostolic period the celebration of Christ's resurrection was prolonged for fifty days—the period from Easter to Pentecost (in Greek, Pentecost means "the fiftieth day"). It coincided with the Jewish "Feast of Weeks"—the seven-week period between "Sabbath of the Unleavened Bread" and "the feast of the first fruits" (Lv 23:11,15-16; Ex 34:22; Nm 28:26; Dt 16:10). The latter originated as a harvest feast, customary among agricultural peoples, but by the beginning of the Christian era the Feast of Weeks had come to commemorate the sealing of the covenant at Mt. Sinai. (Because of its association with the Sinai covenant the Qumran community celebrated Pentecost, as its principal feast.) By fixing the outpouring of the Holy Spirit on Pentecost the Acts of the Apostles subtly suggests that the event marks the advent of a new covenant.

New Testament writers who refer to the ascension do not describe it or fix it in time or place (e.g., Eph 4:8-10). The evangelist Luke, however, is an exception; in fact, he gives two accounts. Luke concludes his Gospel narrative by stating that Jesus led the disciples "out near Bethany, and with hands up raised, blessed them. As he blessed, he left them, and was taken up to heaven" (Lk 24:50-51). According to this account the ascension occurred on Easter Sunday. Some years later Luke introduced the Acts with the description of the ascension that has become the traditional mode for representing the event:

> In my first account, Theophilus, I dealt with all that Jesus did and taught until the day he was taken up to heaven, having first instructed the apostles he had chosen through the Holy Spirit. In the time after his suffering he showed them in many convincing ways that he was alive, appearing to them over the course of forty days and speaking to them about the reign of God. On one occasion when he met with them, he told them not to leave Jerusalem: "Wait, rather, for the fulfillment of my Father's promise, of which you have heard me speak. John baptized with water, but within a few days you will be baptized with the Holy Spirit. . . . You will receive power when the Holy Spirit comes down on you; then you are to be my witnesses in Jerusalem, throughout Judea and Samaria, yes, even to the ends of the earth." No sooner had he said this than he was lifted up before their eyes in a cloud which took him from their sight. They were still gazing up into the heavens when two men dressed in white stood beside them. "Men of Galilee," they said, "why do you stand here looking up at the skies? This Jesus who has been taken from you will return, just as you saw him go up into the heavens." (Acts 1:1-5,8-11)

No other passage in the New Testament fixes a date for the ascension. Elsewhere in Acts, Luke quotes St. Paul as saying, "God raised him from the dead, and for many days thereafter Jesus appeared to those who had come up with him from Galilee to Jerusalem" (13:30-31). And the Marcan coda, probably following Luke's Gospel account, suggests that the ascension took place on the day of the resurrection itself.

It is the account in the opening chapter of the Acts of Apostles that provided the time frame for celebrating the feast of the ascension forty days after Easter and then, ten days later, the feast of Pentecost. In the Bible forty is a "round number" ("forty years" is roughly a generation). It is not to be taken literally, and frequently it marks an indeterminate period of preparation. The *Jerome Biblical Commentary* says, "The intent of the 40 days is not to date the *ascension*. . . . but to imitate the rabbinic use of 40 as a norm for the disciples' learning and repetition of their masters' teaching." The *JBC* adds, "One should not rule out the intent to match the periods of Jesus' preparation (Lk 4:1-2) and that of the apostles', since the subject of their instruction (the Kingdom of God) is also that of Jesus' own preaching."[1]

CRUCIFIXION, RESURRECTION, AND ASCENSION

If the opening chapter of Acts provides the framework for the liturgical commemoration of Easter, the Ascension, and Pentecost, the Johannine tradition supports the more primitive practice of conflating all facets of the paschal mystery to a single feast. The subtle genius of the fourth evangelist manages to evoke the memory of the crucifixion, resurrection, and ascension all at once in recalling Jesus' words, "Just as Moses lifted up the serpent in the desert, so must the Son of Man be lifted up, that all who believe may have eternal life in him" (Jn 3:14-15). The reference to Moses recalls the incident in the desert when the Israelite camp was infested by saraph serpents "which bit the people so that many of them died." Moses, under instruction from the Lord, mounted a bronze image of the saraph on a pole, "and whenever anyone who had been bitten by a serpent looked at the bronze serpent, he recovered" (Num 21:6,9; see Wis 16:5-7). The mounting of the bronze serpent on the pole brings to mind the image of Jesus being hoisted on the cross, but the context of the Johannine passage makes it clear that it refers also to the ascension.

The context for Jesus' allusion to being "lifted up" is his exchange with Nicodemus. Jesus seizes Nicodemus' greeting as an invitation to discourse about the kingdom of God, and, in line with the Johannine style, Jesus moves the topic to a higher level. His response is meant to show that he has not come from God in the sense that Nicodemus thought, simply as one approved by God, but in the deeper sense of having descended from God's presence to raise people to God. Jesus tells him that entrance into God's kingdom is something that humans cannot accomplish on their own; individuals cannot enter the kingdom unless they are begotten from above of water and the Spirit. Nicodemus then inquires further about the action of God from above and through the Spirit.

Jesus teaches that he is the only one who can mediate the Spirit, since no one else has ever gone up into heaven. He claims the privilege of having seen God in a unique way (see Jn 1:18; 5:37; 6:46; 14:7-9) and explains that begetting through the Holy Spirit comes about only as a result of his being lifted up. Verse 14 is the first of three texts in John which speak of Jesus' being "lifted up." The second text is again a response to his listeners' failure to understand his unique relationship with the Father:

> When you lift up the Son of Man, you will come to realize that I AM and that I do nothing by myself. I say only what the Father has taught me. (Jn 8:28)

Jesus says that only his return to the Father will reveal his true origins, namely, that God is the one who sent him; that he bears the divine name ("I AM"); and that his works are the works of God.

"To be lifted up" conjures up the crucifixion scene on Calvary, where Jesus is suspended from the the cross. The third Johannine passage in which the phrase occurs ("and I—once I am lifted up from earth—will draw all men to myself") is followed by an editorial comment, "This statement indicated the sort of death he had to die" (Jn 12:32,33). The crucifixion, however, does not exhaust the image of being lifted up. In John's Gospel the phrase refers to one continuous ascent—crucifixion, resurrection, and ascension. In his rather detailed commentary on the phrase Raymond Brown writes,

> Jesus begins his return to his Father as he approaches death (xiii 1) and completes it only with his ascension (xx 17). It is the upward swing of the great pendulum of the Incarnation corresponding to the descent of the Word which became flesh. The first step in the ascent is when Jesus is lifted up on the cross; the second step is when he is raised up from death; the final step is when he is lifted up to heaven. This wider understanding of "being lifted up" explains a statement like viii 28: "When you lift up the Son of Man, you will realize that I AM."[2]

Brown finds other New Testament texts to support his interpretation that "to be lifted up" includes more than the crucifixion. Making allowance for the peculiar wording of the fourth evangelist, Brown sees the three Johannine passages to be equivalent to the three predictions of the passion, death, and resurrection found in each of the synoptic Gospels (Mk 8:31; 9:31; 10:33-34, and parallels). They are linked together by the reference to the "Son of Man," which is common to both the Johannine and the synoptic texts, as well as by the imperative of the divine will in John 3:14 and Mark 8:31: "So *must* the Son of Man be lifted up"; and "The Son of Man *must* suffer many things . . . be killed, and after three days rise again." Further support is found in the use of the Greek verb *hypsoun* ("to be lifted up") in the Acts of the Apostles where it describes the ascension of Jesus (2:33; 5:30). According to Brown the Johannine sayings were inspired by the theme of the Suffering Servant. Their emphasis on the fact that the Son of Man *must* be lifted up seems to be grounded on the prediction in Second Isaiah (especially chapters 52 and 53) that it was part of the divine plan: "My servant shall prosper, he shall be raised high (*hypsoun*) and greatly exalted" (Is 52:13).

Modern commentators divide John's Gospel into two parts: the "Book of Signs" and the "Book of Glory." The first describes Jesus' public ministry and its effect on the people. It reaches a climax in chapter 12 with Jesus' third reference to being lifted up and concludes with an evaluation of Jesus' public ministry, which acknowledges that not everyone believed in him (12:37-50). The Book of Glory begins with the first verses of chapter 13 which shifts the focus "to his own." It tells of the events from Jesus' Last Supper with his disciples on Thursday evening to his appearance after the resurrection. The theme of the Book of Glory is Jesus' return to the Father (13:1; 14:2,28; 15:26; 16:7,28; 17:5,11; 20:17), which entails his glorification (13:31; 16:14; 17:1,5,24) and the disciples' recognition of him as Lord and God. This second part of John's Gospel reveals the fullness of Jesus' glory, which was anticipated by the signs described in the first part and proclaimed already in the Prologue: "We have seen his glory: the glory of an only Son coming from the Father" (Jn 1:14). Fully glorified, he sends the Spirit of life.

Although it is implicit throughout the New Testament accounts of Jesus' saving action, the Johannine Gospel shows most clearly why the ascension is an integral part of the paschal mystery. In his last discourse Jesus explains that his departure and return to the Father is a condition for the sending of the Spirit:

> "It is much better for you if I go. If I fail to go, the Paraclete will never come to you, whereas if I go, I will send him to you." (Jn 16:7)

Only when Jesus was lifted up in glory would the communication of the Spirit constitute a continuing source of life for those who put their faith in him (see Jn 7:37-39). This is also the meaning of Jesus' words to Nicodemus; eternal life is given only to those begotten from above— life begotten "of water and the Spirit."

The fourth evangelist takes the Incarnation—"the Word became flesh"—as his point of departure, and John, like the other evangelists, never loses sight of the Jesus of history. For St. Paul, on the other hand, the beginning of the story is the resurrection. He never knew Jesus in the flesh and is not concerned to record the words and deeds of Jesus as handed down by tradition. For him, Christ transcended history. Paul's mission was to proclaim the Risen Lord as the alpha and omega—the source and goal—of salvation. In the first of his discourses recorded in Acts, Paul finds the fulfillment of the divine plan of salvation in God's "raising up Jesus" (13:32; see also Acts 26:23).

Paul presents an even more finely tuned theology of the resurrection in his Epistles. In an oft-quoted text in his Letter to the Romans he sees the resurrection as a principal element in justification—making things right:

> Our faith will be credited to us also if we believe in him who raised Jesus our Lord from the dead, the Jesus who was handed over to death for our sins and raised up for our justification. (4:24-25)

Even more fundamental is an idea in the opening lines of the same Epistle where Paul states that Jesus Christ our Lord "was made Son of God in power according to the spirit of holiness, by his resurrection from the dead" (1:4). Paul expresses in different language and from another point of view than John the significance of the exaltation of Jesus at the right hand of God.

In his Epistle to the church at Philippi in Greece, Paul quotes an early hymn which holds up the self-effacement of Jesus as the model for Christian service. The hymn recalls that, paradoxically, Jesus' divinity was concealed throughout his mortal life. Divesting himself of his divine prerogatives, Jesus presented himself in the role of a servant. Having fully assumed the human condition, he lived with the consequences, "obediently accepting even death, death on a cross." In turn, Jesus' true identity was revealed. God responded by exalting him on high and endowing him with his own name, "the name above every other name" (see Phil 2:6-11). The Greek verb *hypsoun*, here translated as "exalted" (as discussed above), implies resurrection and ascension as well as glorification.

Scholars have studied the many verb forms that the New Testament uses in speaking of Jesus' resurrection and exaltation. Reginald Fuller says the term "raising" or "being raised" is the language of Jewish apocalyptic literature. It derives from the everyday experience of waking from sleep, but in the apocalyptic writings it indicates a transition from one mode of existence (existence in this age) to another (existence in the age to come). Fuller stresses this last point in commenting on 1 Corinthians 15:4b; St. Paul makes it clear that resurrection does not mean a return to the former mode of existence, but a transformation and a transition to a new mode of existence.[3]

In Paul's theology it is God who intervenes to raise up Jesus from the dead; even when Paul uses a passive verb, it always has the sense of "raised by God."[4] It is by divine initiative that salvation is accomplished in Christ Jesus.

> God makes all things work together for the good of those who have been called. . . . Those whom he foreknew he predestined to share the image of his Son, that the Son might be the first-born of many brothers. Those he predestined he likewise called; those he called he also justified; and those he justified he in turn glorified. (Rom 8:28-29)

God has overcome every obstacle to salvation. The power of God's grace and glory manifested itself in "Christ Jesus, who died or rather was raised up, who is at the right hand of God and who intercedes for us" (Rom 8:34). The "right hand" is obviously the place of highest honor and greatest influence.

The exaltation of Jesus must also be read as a vindication of everything he claimed to be. At the trial when the high priest asked Jesus a second time, "Are you the Messiah, the Son of the Blessed One?" Jesus answered, "I am; and you will see the Son of Man seated at the right hand of the Power and coming with the clouds of heaven"

(Mk 14:61,62). Jesus' response, taken by the high priest as blasphemy, sealed his fate. The implication of his answer was not lost on the spectators; it evoked recollections of both Psalm 110 and Daniel 7:13 (which, as will be seen in the next chapter, refers to the "Son of Man"). Psalm 110:1 promises that God's servant will triumph over his enemies. In telling his prosecutors that they will see the Son of Man seated at the throne of Power, Jesus was clearly claiming that God would vindicate him by such an act of crowning deliverance.[5]

Passages that affirm the exaltation of Christ to the "right hand of God" echo Psalm 110, the psalm most quoted in the New Testament.[6] Biblical scholars maintain that it was composed for a particular occasion when a new king of Juda was enthroned (ninth or eighth century B.C.?). The psalmist anticipated great things in the era of the new monarch. The language and symbolism of his composition, however, seemed to look beyond the immediate circumstances of the coronation, and thus Psalm 110 was given a messianic interpretation. The church found in it, as in Isaiah 53 and other Old Testament texts, a forecast of the ministry and exaltation of Jesus.

The Pauline texts clearly establish that the paschal mystery—crucifixion, resurrection, and glorification—is the work of the Triune God acting in concert. It is the Father who lifts up—raises and exalts—the Son. Acting as one, Father and Son send forth the Spirit to give life and renew the face of the earth. In the chapters that follow, more will be said about the advent of a new age and the sending of the Spirit. In concluding these reflections on HE ASCENDED INTO HEAVEN AND IS SEATED AT THE RIGHT HAND OF THE FATHER, however, we return briefly to the remarks about the liturgical calendar that began this section.

LITURGICAL TIME

It has become commonplace to speak of "sacred" time. Mircea Eliade, for example, contends that the religious person lives in two time zones. There is ordinary time, "the historical present," and there is sacred time, which conjures up a kind of eternal present,[7] an event constantly repeating itself in ritual and in celebration of sacred festivals. Sacred time represents mystery and a break in the sequence of ordinary time. For the nonreligous person who acknowledges only the historical present, time has a beginning and an end; for the religious person, past and future are *now*.

For liturgical purposes the Christian calendar subdivides sacred time into "cycles." As we noted above in Chapter 11, each Sunday is a weekly celebration of the paschal mystery, but the Sundays are generally grouped into three cycles that make up the liturgical calendar: the Christmas cycle, the Easter cycle, and "ordinary time," which does not fall into one of the other two cycles. Thus each year the church rehearses the principal scenes in the drama of salvation as enacted in the person of Christ Jesus.

For Christians, as Eliade notes, "Time begins anew with the birth of Christ." The Christmas cycle runs from the first Sunday of Advent to Candelmas (February 2) and includes several feasts related to the epiphany of God in Jesus. Although the birth of Jesus was not celebrated until late in the third century, almost from the beginning Christians recognized the Incarnation as a watershed in human history, and sometime about the year A.D. 500 the Roman monk Dionysius "the Little" initiated the custom of dating everything in relationship to the birth of Christ—"in the year of the Lord" (= *Anno Domini*).[8] Advent, which now marks the beginning of the liturgical year, was at one time synonymous with Christmas and the Epiphany; all three terms referred to the Incarnation, God's coming into the world to dwell among us. The four Sundays of Advent exemplify how sacred time simultaneously looks backward and forward; they recall the long centuries of waiting for the coming of the Messiah and remind Christians that they now live in the day of the Lord while still awaiting his coming.

As is evident from the prominence given Christ's passion, death, and resurrection, first in Scripture and subsequently in the Creed, the focus of the liturgical year is Easter, the principal celebration of the paschal mystery. The Easter cycle runs from Ash Wednesday at the beginning of Lent through the fifty days after Easter to Pentecost. Originally the seven weeks of Lent were the time of final preparation for those who were to be baptized into Christ's death and thereby rise with him to new life on Easter Sunday. After the catechumenate fell into disuse about 600, Lent became more and more a season of penance focusing on conversion of life and the reconciliation of Christians who had admitted to serious sin. There is no fixed date for Easter; following the Jewish Passover, it is celebrated on the Sunday following the first full moon of spring.[9]

Sundays of the year that do not fall into the Christmas or Easter cycle are said to be in "ordinary time" and are designated by number— e.g., the Fourth Sunday in Ordinary Time. (Other Christian churches reckon the Sundays in ordinary time in relation to Pentecost and Trinity Sunday, the Sunday after Pentecost—e.g. the Third Sunday after Trinity.) The readings for the Sundays in ordinary time are something of a miscellany, without clearly identifiable themes such as characterize the Christmas and Easter cycles. In recent years a number of churches—the Roman, Anglican, Lutheran, Methodist, and others— have adopted more or less common readings for use in Sunday worship. The rule of thumb guiding the common lectionary is that the synoptic Gospels are read successively over a three-year period, with John's Gospel being the primary source for readings on the Sundays between Easter and Pentecost.

The Christian celebration of the principal events in salvation history is a way of making them eternally present to all who believe. Eliade points up the distinctive character of sacred time that sees the Incarnation as the great divide in human history. Perhaps the Advent cycle best illustrates how the Christian liturgy, unfolding in historical time, brings the presence of Christ, past and future, into the now. The present celebration of Advent merges two liturgical traditions, the Roman and the Gallican. The Roman emphasizes the coming of Christ in the Incarnation and focuses on Christmas; the Gallican introduces the theme of the Second Coming, which focuses on the future. Thus Advent reminds us that Christ has come once, and that he will come again and, indeed, has never left. We turn to the Second Coming in the next chapter as we consider the phrase HE WILL COME AGAIN IN GLORY TO JUDGE. . . .

Notes

1. *JBC*, vol. 2 p. 168.

2. Raymond Brown, *The Gospel According to John I–XII* The An-

chor Bible, 29 (Garden City, NY: Doubleday & Co., 1966), p. 146.

3. Reginald H. Fuller, *The Formation of the Resurrection Narratives* (New York: Macmillan Co., 1971), p. 17.

4. C. F. Evans, *Resurrection and the New Testament* (Naperville, IL: Alec R. Allenson Inc., 1970), p. 21.

5. Oscar Cullmann, *The Christology of the New Testament* (London: SCM Press, 1963), p. 160; J.A.T. Robinson notes that Jesus used Ps 110 to some effect against the Pharisees (Mk 12:36). *Jesus and His Coming* (London: SCM Press, 1957), p. 44.

6. *Interpreter's Bible*, 4:588. Psalm 110 resembles psalms of another group known as "enthronement psalms" (47, 93, 96–99). According to many scholars they were sung at New Year when, in solemn ceremony, Yahweh was heralded as king over the earth and its peoples. The enthronement psalms all contain the phrase "Yahweh is king." Ibid., pp. 502–503. See *JBC*, vol. 1, p. 572.

7. Eliade explains that in ritual and liturgical celebration "it is no longer today's historical time that is present—the time that is experienced in the adjacent streets—but the time in which the historical existence of Jesus Christ occurred, the time sanctified by his preaching, by his passion, death, and resurrection. But we must add that this example does not reveal all the difference between sacred and profane time; Christianity radically changed the experience and the concept of liturgical time, and this is due to the fact that Christianity affirms the historicity of the person of Christ. The Christian liturgy unfolds in *a historical time sanctified by the incarnation of the Son of God*. The sacred time periodically reactualized in pre-Christian religions (especially the archaic religions) is a *mythical time*, that is, a primordial time, not to be found in the historical past, an *original time,* in the sense that it came into existence all at once, that it was not preceded by another time. . ." Mircea Eliade, *The Sacred and Profane* (New York: Harper Torchbooks, 1961), p. 72; see pp. 110–113.

8. It is now widely recognized that Dionysius miscalculated the date of Jesus' birth by 4 to 7 years. The observance of Christmas on December 25 was probably adopted because that was the date (in the old Julian calendar) of the winter solstice (January 6 in the old Egyptian calendar). The practice of dating events which occurred before the Christian era, "Before Christ," was initiated much later. The *Annales Veteris et Novi Testamenti* of James Ussher (1581–1656) are said to be the source of the dates later inserted in the Authorized Version (1701 onward) of the Bible; see Chapter 2, note 12.

9. From the second to the eighth century there were repeated disagreements over the proper date for Easter. The controversies were generally caused by differences born of local custom and the fact that there was no universal calendar. See *NCE* 5:8-9.

13

The Second Coming and Judgment

"He will come again in glory
to judge the living and the dead"

No statement in the Creed has evoked richer imagery, more fanciful speculation, or greater distortion than HE WILL COME AGAIN IN GLORY TO JUDGE THE LIVING AND THE DEAD. The "Second Coming" has preoccupied Christians from the beginning. In his first Epistles—the earliest writings in the New Testament—Paul testifies to the longing he shared with the Christians in Thessalonika for Christ's return. Christians in the first century prayed *maran'atha*—"May the Lord come"—and Pope Paul VI in the years after Vatican II restored to the eucharistic liturgy the refrain "Christ has died, Christ is risen, *Christ will come again*" (emphasis added). The Second Coming has been an obsession with groups such as the Montanists in the second century and the Seventh Day Adventists and the Jehovah's Witnesses today.

The Second Coming is opaque enough in itself, and when linked, as it is in the Creed, with divine judgment, its meaning becomes even more complex. Although early Christians prayed that the Lord would not delay his return, popular preaching and literature came to depict the Second Coming and the day of judgment as *dies irae*—"the day of wrath." The sequence *Dies Irae,* of the old Requiem Mass, especially when accompanied by the music of Mozart, Verdi, or more recently Webber, presents judgment as unrelieved tragedy.[1] Like Jonathan Edwards' classic sermon "The Sinner in the Hands of an Angry God," the *Dies Irae* evokes remorse by striking fear in the heart. Popular presentations further distort the picture of judgment by emphasizing the judgment of individuals at the expense of the main theme of Scripture and the Creed: the judgment of the world.

And then there is the question "When?" The Scriptures emphasize the need for constant vigilance because the Son of Man will come without warning (Lk 12:39). Matthew insists, "As for the exact day or hour, no one knows it, neither the angels in heaven nor the Son, but the Father only" (24:36; Mk 13:32). Nonetheless there were those in the primitive church who thought the Second Coming was imminent, just as there are people today who are convinced that the apocalyptic signs described in the synoptic Gospels (Mt 24; Mk 13; Lk 21) are happening before our very eyes.

Some thirty years ago biblical scholar and future bishop of Woolwich, J. A. T. Robinson, remarked, "For some time the Cinderella of the Creedal doctrines, the doctrine of the Second Coming of Christ has now returned to the forefront of theological discussion."[2] Whatever the circumstances that prompted Robinson to make that statement, interest in the Second Coming has continued. Scholars see the Second Coming as central to the broader issue of eschatology—the topic of this chapter and the next—while the subject continues to fascinate the popular imagination with stories of Armaggedon and the end of the world. Since the turn of the century when Johannes Weisse, Alfred Loisy, and Albert Schweitzer argued that the expectation of the imminent parousia and the end of the present world were essential elements in the primitive kerygma and even in the preaching of Jesus himself (see above, Chapter 8), the study of the Last Things has taken a new turn. Until recently death, judgment, heaven, and hell got more attention from preachers and catechists than they did from systematic theologians. Today these themes are studied in a broader context of eschatology grounded on biblical exegesis and theological anthropology; in fact, eschatology raises questions that reach into christology, ecclesiology, and all major areas of theology.[3] Consequently HE WILL COME AGAIN IN GLORY TO JUDGE THE LIVING AND THE DEAD can hardly be discussed apart from other issues in eschatology.

THE PAROUSIA

The Second Coming is but one theme in a network of ideas that make up the hope of the church. The term most often used in theological discussion to evoke this cluster of ideas (including the Second Coming) associated with eschatology is *parousia*; the term appears in St. Paul's two Epistles to the Thessalonians, in Chapter 24 of Matthew, and in only four other passages in the New Testament (1 Cor 15:23; Jms 5:7ff; 2 Pet 3:4; 1 Jn 2:28).[4] In secular usage *parousia*, a Greek word meaning "presence" or "coming," referred to the ceremonial visit of a ruler to a city or country. Religious imagination associates the parousia with a broad range of eschatological themes, e.g., "the day of the Lord," the resurrection of the dead (the topic of a later chapter), the gathering of the elect, the end of world, and the last judgment; but more precisely it refers to the coming of Christ in glory. These ideas are woven together so tightly that the individual strands are not easily isolated.

The imagery and perception of the parousia in the New Testament derives mainly from Jewish eschatology, which believed that at the end of time Yahweh would come in a final, glorious theophany. Chapter 7 in the Book of Daniel presents the classic description of the event. (We have already noted in Chapter 12 that Jesus alluded to this text when the high priest asked him whether he was the Messiah.) The Book of Daniel is a prime example of the apocalyptic genre (*apokalypsis* = revelation), which flourished during the Hellenistic period. Literature of this kind had several identifying charactristics. First of all, the author wrote under a pseudonym, usually adopting the name of some personage from the past (in this case, Daniel) which both ensures anonymity and adds prestige to the work. Apocalyptic literature purported to be a revelation of the future, whereas in actuality it was most often a commentary on the times in which it was composed. The medium of the revelation, as in Daniel, was generally a dream or a vision. The language was further characterized by allegory and complicated symbolism that veiled direct references to contemporary events but that can be explained when the historical circumstances are sufficiently known. Apocalyptic literature projected a picture of the final period of world history, when judgment will be passed on the forces of evil and they will be routed after dreadful and bloody combat. (The

Book of Revelation 16:16 situates the climactic battle at Armageddon, probably a reference to Megiddo, the most celebrated battlefield of ancient Palestine.)

Apocalyptic literature developed in Judaism in the post-exilic period when prophets gave way to seers. In addition to the Book of Daniel, other examples of this kind of writing are found among the apocryphal works, e.g., the Parables of Enoch and the Second Book of Esdras. Although these latter works are not regarded as part of the biblical canon, they are important sources that contribute to an understanding of Jewish thought in the time of Jesus. The most obvious example of apocalyptic writing in the New Testament is the Book of Revelation (called in the old Douay-Rheims translation the Apocalypse), but apocalyptic passages are scattered through the synoptic Gospels (e.g., Mt 24; Mk 13; Lk 17 and 21).

The Book of Daniel was composed about 175 B.C. during the persecution of the Jews by Antiochus Epiphanes. In line with the main purpose of apocalyptic literature, it offered encouragement to the persecuted by foretelling the downfall of Antiochus. Chapter 7 recounts a dream of Daniel in which he saw four monstrous beasts come one after another out of the sea; they represented four great empires of the ancient world (the Babylonians, the Medes, the Persians, and the Greeks). As Daniel watched, "The Ancient One took his throne" (v. 9) and proceeded to pass sentence on the beasts. Wanting to be sure about the fourth beast, which differed "from all the others, terrifying, horrible, and of extraordinary strength,"[5] he continued to watch as the Ancient One pronounced judgment "in favor of the holy ones of the Most High, and the time came when the holy ones possessed the kingdom" (v. 22). Meanwhile he saw

> . . . One like a son of man coming, on the clouds of heaven;
> when he reached the Ancient One and was presented before him,
> he received dominion, glory and kingship; nations and peoples
> of every language serve him. His dominion is an everlasting
> dominion that shall not be taken away, his kingship shall not be
> destroyed. (vv. 13-14)

The image of "the Ancient One" depicts God's majesty and eternal existence: Yahweh wears clothing bright as snow and "the hair on his head [is] as white as wool." The vision uses imagery common in the Old Testament, as, for example, when Daniel reports "the court was convened and the books were opened" (v. 10); it is probably a reference to the "record book" (Mal 3:16) in which the good deeds (Neh 5:19; 13:14) and bad deeds (Is 65:6; Pss 51:3; 109:14) of individuals are written.[6] The description of the tribunal that passes judgment on the nations corresponds to notions long held in ancient Israel:

> I saw the LORD seated on his throne, with the whole host of heaven standing by to his right and left. (1 Kgs 22:19)

In his vision Daniel witnessed a mortal battle between "the horn" and "the holy ones." The horn was winning until the Ancient One arrived to pass sentence and dictate the annihilation of the kingdoms of this world.

The other figure in the vision, "the son of man," is more enigmatic. The Aramaic term *bar 'enasha* literally means "a son of mankind"— that is, a member of the human race. Thus the kingdom that "the holy ones of the Most High" are to receive is represented by a human being, in deliberate contrast to the worldly kingdoms represented by monstrous beasts. The human figure also stands in contrast to the Ancient One. In Daniel's vision "the son of man" personifies the saints of Israel; he is given

> dominion, glory, and kingship; nations of every language serve him. His dominion is an everlasting dominion that shall not be taken away, his kingship shall not be destroyed. (vv. 13-14)

In the New Testament, Jesus identifies himself as *bar 'enasha*—Son of Man—and the use of the title is unique in that only Jesus applies this designation to himself. (The one notable exception is Stephen in Acts 7:56, which is cited below.) On the basis of Daniel alone it is difficult to interpret "son of man" as anything more than a generic reference to Jesus' human estate. If the title had any messianic overtones in Daniel they were of the general kind associated with God's plan for the salvation of the chosen people. Later, however, in some of the apocryphal writings, specifically the Parables of Enoch and II Esdras, "son of man" refers not merely to a personification but to a person—the Messiah. Despite the disagreement about the significance of the title, it is generally agreed that the expression harkens back to Daniel 7:13.[7]

The Gospels present the theology of the Son of Man in two distinct stages. The first stage corresponds to his earthly career; some texts use the expression to describe his lowliness, some his identification with the Suffering Servant of God. In the second stage the Son of Man appears in the parousia, exalted and judge of the world.[8] Broadly speaking, the New Testament reflects the image of the parousia popular in late Judaism, with the striking adjustment that makes Jesus the central figure. He heralds the Day of the Lord and at the same time appears on that day as the Son of Man decked in glory and cast as judge over the living and the dead (Acts 7:55-56; 10:42; 1 Pet 4:5; 2 Tim 4:1).

JUDGMENT

The judgment represents the triumph of God's divine plan over its adversaries (Mt 8:29; Lk 4:34) and the vindication of Jesus' work. In the Gospels the judge who passes sentence is sometimes the Father in heaven (Mt 6:4; 10:32-33) but most often Jesus himself in the guise of the Son of Man. St. Paul preaches judgment of the world as an idea that could be understood by the Athenians. God, he said, "has set the day on which he is going to 'judge the world with justice' through a man he has appointed—one whom he has endorsed in the sight of all by raising him from the dead" (Acts 17:31). And elsewhere he writes that God "will pass judgment on the secrets of men through Christ Jesus" (Rom 2:16). The notion of judgment is a principal theme in Johannine theology, as is evident from the legal terminology—judge, witness, testimony, accuse, convict, advocate, etc.—that is laced throughout the Fourth Gospel.

The theme that nations and individuals are accountable before the judgment seat of God runs through the Old Testament. In the more primitive tradition little attention was paid to their fate after death; divine judgment was presented rather as recompensing human effort already in this life. Judgment meant that justice was done, that the righteous were given their reward and the wicked punished. The sentence was lived out in the sight of one's neighbors. Later on, the prophets proclaimed a day of reckoning for all. Using images from Israelite history and the allegorical language of Near Eastern cosmology, they announced that the time was imminent when the wicked (usually Israel's enemies) would be destroyed and the righteous rewarded. In various contexts the judgment was linked, as we have seen, to the day of the Lord, the messianic kingdom. Judgment represents the triumph of God's plan, victory over evil forces and over the enemies of Israel.[9] Although the Old Testament does not teach that individuals are judged separately, the notion of "particular judgment" seems to be implied if each person is to be held accountable for his or her actions.

The classic account of judgment in the New Testament is the description in Matthew 25:31-46.[10] As it stands, it is a conflation of several of Jesus' discourses into a whole. Be that as it may, the parable highlights the christological aspect of judgment alluded to above. The account leans heavily on the apocalyptic imagery of late Judaic writings, with the important difference that Jesus himself—alternately the "king" and the "Son of Man"—is cast in the role of judge of the individual's fate. And not only is he the arbiter of the fate of those who appear before the tribunal; their attitude toward him is the criterion by which they are measured. Elsewhere Jesus makes people's destiny hinge on their faith in his mission and on their witness to him and to fraternal love. In the Matthean account, however, charity toward the needy is interpreted as love for Jesus himself. While the phraseology suggests that originally the text referred to the members of the Christian community, the context extends it to all peoples of the world.

Matthew 25 is central to the notion of the "anonymous Christians," that is, those who, never having heard the gospel message, nonetheless struggle to live out its ideals in their dealings with others. Furthermore, the passage helps elucidate the central place of Christ in the universal economy of salvation, not simply among Christians. Already in this life committed Christians recognize that to serve others is to serve Christ. People of good will who do not know themselves as Christians will discover in death—at the moment of particular judgment—that whatever they did for someone in need they did for Christ. "Come. You have my Father's blessing! Inherit the kingdom prepared for you from the creation of the world" (Mt 25:34). People who denied someone in need denied Christ: "Out of my sight, you condemned, into that everlasting fire prepared for the devil and his angels!" (25:41).

PUNISHMENT AND REWARD

The earliest traditions in the Old Testament have nothing analogous to the everlasting punishment associated with hell. In the Old Testament, the *nephesh*—that is, the spirit—of both the good and bad inhabits the nether world of Sheol, which was feared, not because of torments but because of the pallid, shadowy existence it represented. That there would be punishment for Israel's enemies was an old idea, but that there would be retribution for all the wicked in the afterlife developed relatively late in Jewish history. It seems to have appeared along with the realization that individuals would be held accountable for their actions. Some historians maintain it appeared about the time when, under the influence of Hellenism, the idea of personal immortality was accepted.

It was also in the Hellenistic period that the image of everlasting fire began to be used to describe the punishment of the wicked. "Woe to the nations that rise against my people! the LORD Almighty will requite them; in the day of judgment he will punish them: He will send fire and worms into their flesh, and they shall burn and suffer forever" (Jdt 16:17). Here as elsewhere the New Testament adopted Old Testament notions and imagery. Jesus himself cited this passage from Judith in saying that the unrepentant will be thrown into Gehenna—a valley to the south of Jerusalem used as a dump, where fire burned continuously (Mk 9:47-48; see Mt 5:22). The Book of Revelation describes the Last Judgment in graphic language reminiscent of the Book of Daniel; it speaks of a "pool of burning sulphur" and says, "Anyone whose name was not found inscribed in the book of the living was hurled into this pool of fire" (Rev 20:10,15). Building on this, St. Justin Martyr argued already in the second century that hell fire is eternal; otherwise there would be no sanction regulating life.[11]

Less than a century later, Origen (d. A.D.253), one of the greatest minds in the history of Christian thought, argued the opposite point of view. He denied the eternity of hell for the most serious reasons: everlasting punishment would frustrate God's plan of universal salvation, and the very notion is repugnant to a God of love. The central point in Origen's system is "the restoration of all things" (apokatastasis panton) in Christ. At death the souls of sinners enter a purifying fire, but gradually all, even the devils, are ultimately cleansed and restored to the good state they were in before entering the material world. Although Origen taught that when final restoration occurred it would be the result of the sinner's conversion, the notion of apokatastasis was repeatedly condemned.[12]

For centuries Origen's "universalism" (that is, the view that all will be saved) was at best a minority opinion; at worst, it was regarded as heresy. Many church fathers in East and West, medieval scholastics, Catholic and Protestant theologians from the Reformation to the present held that the greater part of the human race is condemned—*major pars hominum damnatur*.[13] Theologians in the West were greatly influenced by St. Augustine's teaching that original sin has made humanity a *massa damnata*. They further supported their position with references to the faithful "remnant" of Israel and with New Testament texts such as "The invited are many, the elect few" (Mt 22:14) and "Many . . . will try to enter and will be unable" (Lk 13:24). Catholic authors were largely content to repeat the position of Gregory the Great (d. 604): hell, a punishment for serious sin, is eternal separation from God (*poena damni*) in a place of torment and suffering where the fire is "real" (*poena sensus*).

Modern theologians, however, are more loath to have anyone sentenced to eternal damnation. Some present an updated version of *apokatastasis*; others, who defend the possibility of an eternal hell, suspend judgment when it is a question of whether *in fact* anyone is condemned to everlasting punishment. J. A. T. Robinson, who defends a universalist point of view, acknowledges that judgment is absolutely necessary but says its only possible function is to manifest God's infinite mercy, which in effect renders judgment superfluous. The idea that human self-will could resist divine love so as to frustrate God's saving will is unthinkable to Robinson. Even to admit the possibility that some persons may be lost is for Robinson an inadmissible concession of a power outside God.[14]

Although John Hick favors universalism, he acknowledges that for many it seems impossible to reconcile that position with human freedom.[15] Most Catholic theologians, for example, argue that human freedom implies the *possibility* of hell as an eternal separation from God. Were God to override decisions freely made by creatures, human freedom becomes a sham. If there is some connection, however tenuous, between what we endeavor to accomplish in this world and our fate in the next, we must be allowed the possibility of making a wrong choice even in something so definitive as our destiny. Karl Rahner speaks for the common Catholic position when he says that the time comes when a person can no longer change his or her mind. In death each person either ratifies or reverses the fundamental choice lived throughout life, and accepts the consequences.

In discussing Jesus' descent into hell (Chapter 10), we made the point that hell is not a place. Whatever the "torments" of hell (Karl Rahner says "fire" is a metaphor), they are not tortures imposed by a vindictive judge. God does not pass judgment: those who believe in Christ are not judged, and those who do not believe are already judged (see Jn 16:8-10). Modern psychology is more helpful than medieval penology in understanding the suffering of the damned. Hell is a projection of the person, not a punishment imposed for sins that are now (perhaps) bitterly and belatedly regretted. Hell is an extreme narcissism that turns the sinner in on self and causes unending turmoil and frustration. Hell is estrangement from God and alienation from the created universe. The suffering of hell is compounded, according to St. Augustine, because God continues to love the sinner, who is not able to return the love.

Although contemporary theologians disagree on the *possibility* of an eternal hell, they are in general agreement that God *wills* to save all people. This represents a significant departure from the Augustinian tradition that salvation is for only the few. At the Last Supper Jesus told his disciples to drink of the cup, "for this is my blood, the blood of the covenant, to be poured out in behalf *of many* for the forgiveness of sins" (Mt 26:28; see Mk 10:45).[16] The reference to the "many" must be interpreted in the broader context of St. Paul's classic witness to God's universal salvific will:

> First of all, I urge that petitions, prayers, intercessions, and thankgiving be offered for all men . . . Prayer of this kind is good, and God our savior is pleased with it, for he wants all men to be saved and come to know the truth. And the truth is this:
> "God is one.
> One also is the mediator between God and men,
> the man Christ Jesus,
> who gave himself as a ransom for all." (1 Tim 2:1,3-6)

Would the coming of the Son of Man represent a triumph over evil and the forces of darkness in any meaningingful way if a majority of the human race is lost?

The gospel announces the "good news" of salvation, not a grim message of damnation and despair. Although heaven can no more than hell be described as a place, statements about the two are simply not on the same level. "Heaven" evokes the salvation accomplished in Christ Jesus, but it is even more difficult to find language adequate to the full implications of final salvation than it is to describe what eternal punishment might mean. The biblical accounts, expressed in parable, allegory, and symbol, assure the just of a reward. Stephen, faced with death, describes a vision that evokes the dream of Daniel:

> Stephen meanwhile, filled with the Holy Spirit, looked to the sky above and saw the glory of God, and Jesus standing at God's right hand. "Look!" he exclaimed, "I see an opening in the sky, and the Son of Man standing at God's right hand." (Acts 7:55-56)[17]

Ultimately, however, it is as St. Paul wrote: "No eye has seen, nor ear heard, nor the heart of man conceived what God has prepared for those who love him" (1 Cor 2:9).

PURGATORY

Given the church's teaching on Christ's victory over death, on individual judgment and personal salvation, the nature of sin and the need to make amends for it, and final glory, its position on purgatory follows logically. Probably no major tenet of Catholicism is more a consequence of theological development; or, to put it another way, there is little hard, incontrovertible data in revelation to substantiate the existence of purgatory.[18]

There are germs of the idea in the early church fathers. The martyrs were universally thought to attain the vision of God's glory at the moment of death. St. Augustine argued that all who die in the Lord enter immediately into God's presence if they have been entirely purified from sin. He interpreted, with some hesitation, the text in 1 Corinthians 3:12-15 as reference to a purgatory that the imperfect must endure:

> No one can lay a foundation other than the one that has been laid, namely Jesus Christ. If different ones build on this foundation with gold, silver, precious stones, wood, hay or straw, the work of each will be made clear. The Day will disclose it. That day will make its appearance with fire, and fire will test the quality of each man's work. If the building a man has raised on this foundation still stands, he will receive his recompense; if a man's building burns, he will suffer loss. He himself will be saved, but only as one fleeing through fire.

The effect of Augustine's interpretation was to focus on purgatory as a period of purification and suffering—"fleeing through fire." But it was the authority of Pope Gregory the Great more than of anyone that popularized the penal and expiatory character of purgatory. Gregory was also responsible for some of the more picturesque (not to say bizarre) images associated with the sufferings of the souls in purgatory.[19]

In the medieval discussions between Greek and Latin Christians over the differences that divided them, purgatory was one of the issues. The Greeks accepted, with reservations, the idea of a particular judgment immediately after death, and the notion of penal suffering, but not the existence of purgatorial fire.[20] They admitted only one fire, that of the final judgment. Later, Protestant Reformers questioned the doctrine of purgatory for other reasons. Reacting against some of the more materialistic representations of purgatory as a *place* of torment, and questioning the value of prayers for the dead, the Continental Reformers rejected the whole idea of purgatory as an intermediate state between hell and heaven.[21] The Council of Trent in response distinguished between "guilt" (*reatus culpae*) and "punishment" (*reatus poenae*): one is liable to punishment even after one has acknowledged guilt and is forgiven. Trent stated, "Purgatory exists, and the souls detained there are helped by the prayers of the faithful."[22]

The standard presentation of purgatory popularized in the theological manuals and catechetical texts took final shape in the seventeenth century in the writings of Robert Bellarmine and Francisco de Suarez, two great Jesuit theologians who left a lasting mark on post-Reformation Catholic theology. Official church teaching, however, says nothing about the place, the nature of the suffering, or the duration of purgatory. Ladislaus Boros sums up the Catholic position as follows:

> The only thing about purgatory that is absolutely certain theologically is the doctrine that every sin a man commits entails a debt of punishment (*reatus poenae*) which cannot simply be paid each time by turning away from the crime committed and nothing else. From this follows that the essential thing in the process of purification consists in paying this debt of punishment through the pains of satisfaction.[23]

The issue of purgatory is not now as divisive as it was for a long time between Protestants and Catholics. Paul Tillich (1886-1965), a leading Protestant theologian, seemed to recognize the possibility of some development after death, a kind of final purging in which one is cleansed from the distorting elements of temporal existence. He complains, however, that in the Catholic doctrine of purgatory "mere suffering does the purging." The fact is, most Catholics would agree with Tillich's statement that "it is a theological mistake to derive transformation from pain alone instead of from grace which gives blessedness within pain."[24] Another Protestant theologian, John Macquarrie, better captures the notion when he says:

> The kind of "suffering" envisaged in purgatory is not an external penalty that has to be paid, but is our suffering with Christ, our being crucified with him as we are conformed to him, the painful surrender of the ego-centered self that the God-centered self of love may take its place.[25]

Purgatory is not an experience that lies entirely in the future. It has its beginnings now in the process of sanctification. Growth to Christian maturity is a process of purification that climaxes in the final encounter with Christ in judgment. From our present vantage point purgatory is a lifelong process, but from the vantage point of eternity it is instantaneous. Every lover knows that the moment of joy that comes with the generous giving of self can also be a moment of shame for past infidelities. There is elation, but there is suffering that comes from a sense of failure, of not having done more. Love cauterizes those last vestiges of sinful attachment that are the only remaining obstacles to total forgiveness, the fullness of love, and vision of glory.

It is evident from the foregoing that even professional theologians find it difficult to sort out the essentials of faith from the metaphorical and allegorical language in which it is expressed. The biblical descriptions of judgment, heaven, and hell, and the final destiny of the world, expressed for the most part in apocalyptic language, were shaped by a cosmogony alien to the mindset of the twentieth century. Science and technology have shaped our language so as to leave little room for poetry, let alone the baroque imagery of the Book of Daniel. Even if we should succeed in arranging a seance with the dead, they could appear only as we are, not as they are.[26] Nor should the fate of the individual, our own included, so completely absorb attention as to distract us from the destiny of humanity and of the world as a whole. Since the paschal mystery has already initiated the final stage in salvation history, the "last things" are not just abstract ideas of theologians but are already realities in the present world. But more on this in the next chapter, on "the present and future kingdom."

Notes

1. The *Dies Irae*, of medieval origin, consists of seventeen three-line verses to which four others were added later. It consists of two parts greatly different from each other in tone and content. The first (verses 1–7) is a majestic and awesome description of the Last Judgment; the second is a passionate appeal to Christ's mercy. The text weaves together references to both the Old and New Testaments with allusions to classic literature (Vergil's *Georgics*) and medieval apocalyptic literature. See *NCE* 4:863–864.

2. *Jesus and His Coming* (London: SCM Press, 1957), p. 9. Henceforth *Coming*.

3. *JBC*, vol. 1, pp. 777–778.

4. J. A. T. Robinson, *Coming*, pp. 17, 106–111. *JBC*, vol. 2, par. 80, p. 780.

5. The empire of Alexander the Great was notably different from the other three in that it originated in the West. The period described by Daniel corresponds to the time of the Maccabees, and the measures taken against the Jews by Antiochus Epiphanes are summarized in 1 Mc 1: 41–63 and 2 Mc 6:1–10. In Daniel's dream the Seleucid dynasty (Alexander's successors in Syria) is represented by the ten horns.

6. Alexander A. DiLella, *The Book of Daniel*. The Anchor Bible, 23 (Garden City: Doubleday, 1978), p. 218.

7. Much debate surrounds the title "Son of Man" in the New Testament. Although many biblical scholars do not agree with his conclusion, Oscar Cullmann gives a useful survey of the works that first raised questions about its provenance and meaning: *The Christology of the New Testament*, 2nd ed. (London: SCM Press, 1963), pp. 136–192. *JBC*, vol. 2, p. 773. Joseph Fitzmyer, *A Christological Catechism: New Testament Answers* (New York/Ramsey: Paulist Press, 1982), pp. 88–89. DiLella discusses its use in Daniel, pp. 85–102.

8. *JBC*, vol. 2, par. 84, p. 781. See Raymond E. Brown, *The Gospel According to John I-XII* The Anchor Bible, 29. (Garden City, NY: Doubleday and Co., 1966), pp. 88–91.

9. Augustin George, "The Judgment of God," in E. Schillebeeckx and B. Willems, eds. *The Problem of Eschatology*. Concilium, vol. 41 (New York/Glen Park: Paulist Press, 1969), pp. 9–23.

10. J.A.T. Robinson, "The Parable of the Sheep and the Goats," *New Testament Studies*, 2 (1956):225–237.

11. *Second Apology*, ch. 9.

12. Wilhelm Breuning, "*Apokatastasis*: Restoring All Things," *Theology Digest* 31:1 (Spring 1984):47–50. J. P. Burns, "Economy of Salvation: Patristic Traditions," *Theological Studies* 37 (Dec. 1976):598–619.

13. E. J. Fortman, *Everlasting Life after Death* (New York: Alba House, 1977), pp. 176–177.

14. *In the End God* (New York: Harper & Row, 1968) p. 117. John Macquarrie, another who argues for a universalist position, calls the doctrine of an eternal hell "barbarous," *Principles*, p. 322.

15. *Death and Eternal Life* (New York: Harper & Row, 1976) p. 242. Quoted by Zachary Hayes, *What Are They Saying About the End of the World*? (New York/Ramsey: Paulist Press, 1983), p. 56.

16. The change is reflected in the Roman Missal. Whereas the Tridentine Mass had "for many," the text of the post-Vatican II missal reads, "This is the cup of my blood. . . . it will be shed for you and for all."

17. In effect Stephen asserts to the Sanhedrin that Jesus' words (Mk 14:62) before the same body have been fulfilled, an assertion that cost Stephen his life.

18. *Sacramentum Mundi* 5:166, 168. Piet Franzen, "The Doctrine of Purgatory," *The Eastern Churches Quarterly*, 13 (1959):99–112. Ladislaus Boros, *The Mystery of Death* (New York: Herder & Herder, 1965), pp. 129–141.

19. E.g., the belief that a sequence of Masses said for thirty days running frees a soul from purgatory is based on a story in Gregory's *Dialogues with the Italian Fathers* (and thus named, "Gregorian Masses"). St. Gregory the Great's *Dialogues*, Bk. 4, ch. 57, Fathers of the Church, vol. 36 (New York: Fathers of the Church, 1959), pp. 269–270.

20. *DS* 1305–6; 856; 1304.

21. Protestants are also influenced by the fact that the doctrine of purgatory does not seem well grounded in the Bible, and their understanding of justification, which also figures in the discussion, generally differs from the Catholic position.

22. *DS* 1820; 1867.

23. *Mystery of Death*, p. 129.

24. *Systematic Theology* III (New York: Harper & Row, 1963), p. 417.

25. *Principles*, p. 323.

26. "There is no place in Catholic Christianity for intercourse with the dead as individuals, such as spiritualism aims at." Karl Rahner, "The Life of the Dead," *Theological Investigations IV* (Baltimore: Helicon Press, 1966), p. 353.

14

The Present and Future Kingdom

"And his kingdom will have no end"

"If ever you hear anyone saying that there is an end to the kingship of Christ, hate the heresy. It is another head of the dragon which has sprouted lately in the region of Galatia." These words of St. Cyril of Jerusalem were directed against Marcellus of Ancyra (d. 374) and his followers, who flourished in and around the region of modern Ankara (Turkey).[1] The Marcellians, among the heretics condemned by the Council of Constantinople, caused the bishops to insert at the end of the second article AND HIS KINGDOM SHALL HAVE NO END. The phrase, taken verbatim from the angel's words to Mary in Luke's Gospel (1:33), reaffirmed the church's belief that Christ's reign is eternal.[2]

Although the phrase was a late addition to the creeds (and it does not appear in the Apostles' Creed) the kingdom was central to Jesus' message and ministry. Jesus' frequent references to the kingdom in the synoptic Gospels are all the more striking because they are uncommon in the other New Testament writings. Scripture scholars, often at odds with one another, agree that the kingdom of God was the focal point of most of his preaching and miracles. They also agree that the English word "kingdom" does not properly capture the spirit of the Greek term *basileia* or of its Semitic equivalents.³ *Basileia* suggests more the state of *being* king and thus denotes dignity and power. The *Jerome Biblical Commentary* suggests that "rule" or "kingship" would be a better translation than kingdom, and the *New American Bible* generally translates it "reign."

Jesus focused his ministry on the establishment of the kingdom of God and the concomitant destruction of Satan's power in the world. His weapons were twofold: mighty acts of power—miracles—directed against evil and its effects, and a distinctive style of preaching that relied on parables to expound the nature and destiny of the kingdom. In this chapter we take a brief look at miracles and parables as they functioned to institute the kingdom and reveal its nature; and then at greater length we examine Jesus' ethical teaching in the five Matthean discourses that describe the historical realization of the kingdom.

MIRACLES

Jesus cited his miracles as evidence that the kingdom of God was at hand. When John the Baptist sent his disciples to Jesus to ask him, "Are you 'He who is to come' or do we look for another?" Jesus replied,

> "Go back and report to John what you hear and see: the blind recover their sight, cripples walk, lepers are cured, the deaf hear, dead men are raised to life, and the poor have the good news preached to them." (Mt 11:3-5)

There is no doubt that this saying of Jesus was intended to affirm that the messianic age foretold by Isaiah had arrived (see Is 61:1; also 35:5ff).

The miracle stories dramatized Jesus' confrontation with evil in the world. The cures of the sick and the restoration of the dead to life illustrated his power over sin and its effects. The New Testament places the ministry of healing side by side with preaching in the church's proclamation of the kingdom. When Jesus sent the Twelve out on mission he instructed them, "As you go, make this announcement: 'The reign of God is at hand!' Cure the sick, raise the dead, heal the leprous, expel demons" (Mt 10:7-8; see Lk 10:9).

The expulsion of demons, exorcism, a common example of Jesus' miraculous power, pits the kingdom of God directly against the kingdom of Satan. The Beelzebul controversy, recorded in all three synoptic Gospels, clearly illustrates the point (Mk 3:22-30; Mt 12:25-37; Lk 11:17-33). When the notoriety of Jesus' healings began to attract large crowds, the scribes asserted that Jesus himself was possessed and that it was by the power of Beelzebul, "the prince of demons," that he cast out demons. Answering the charge, Jesus said that even the power of evil cannot be divided against itself, since every kingdom so divided must inevitably collapse. And he added, "If it is by the Spirit of God that I expel demons, then the reign of God has overtaken you" (Mt 12:28). Jesus made it clear that the kingdom of God had arrived. The forces of evil were already being undone. In Mark's account, Jesus' example of a strong man's house being plundered clearly implies that Jesus claimed to have greater power than Satan.[4]

The biblical significance of the expulsion of demons, and of Jesus' healings and similar manifestations of power is somewhat obscured by the fact that we group all of them under the heading of "miracles." There is no doubt that Jesus' cures of the blind and deaf and lame evoked awe and wonder, but more importantly, his prodigious actions revealed something about himself and about the kingdom he proclaimed. The word "miracle" (from the Latin *miraculum*—"something that causes wonder") does not appear in the New Testament. In the synoptic Gospels the common Greek term used to describe the cures and exorcisms is *dynameis*—"acts of power," manifestations of God's might. Jesus' miraculous deeds are attributed to the divine *dynamis* that is in him (Mk 6:14), just as it was said that "the power of the Lord made him heal" (Lk 5:17). Thus it is clear, as Alan Richardson says, that "any interpretation of the miracles of Jesus as the casual acts of a wonderworker of the Hellenistic type is entirely false to the theological standpoint of the New Testament, which sees in the miracles of the Lord a revelation of the power and saving purpose of God."[5]

The miracles were as much a vehicle for Jesus' message as were his words. Although the synoptic writers did not emphasize the point, they were aware that Jesus' miracles are symbols—prophetic actions—that both reveal the nature of the kingdom and bring it into existence. The cures are outward signs of another kind of healing. Jesus cured deafness, but his real concern was that men and women would hear the word of God. He opened people's eyes to the light of day and to a vision of the kingdom. He cured paralytics so that they could do the works of God. In the Semitic mind there is no separation of body and soul; just as sickness affects the whole person, so Jesus' healing brought salvation to the whole person. The ultimate sign of the kingdom, however, is Jesus' triumph over the power of death: "Dead men are raised to life" (Mt 11:4)—a new life in the Spirit (see Jn 5:20-21).

Although the Johannine Gospel uses different terminology and shifts the emphasis, it too describes Jesus' miraculous deeds as an essential element of Jesus ministry. The Fourth Gospel records few miracles (only seven in detail) and does not overtly stress their role in establishing the kingdom by overcoming Satan (there are no exorcisms). On the other hand, it has Jesus refer to his miracles as *erga* "works" (5:36, e.g.), thus presenting them as a continuation of the "works" of God in the Old Testament, like creation (Gen 2:2) and the Exodus (Ex 34:10; Ps 66:5). The miracles are an integral part of the work given to Jesus by the Father (5:17; 14:10). Both the evangelist, however, and third parties he quotes refer to Jesus' miracles as *semeia*, "signs," and thus shift attention to their religious significance and the insight they give into the person and mission of Jesus. The symbolism of the miracles, only a secondary element in the synoptic accounts, becomes primary in John. For example, Jesus' dialogue with the man to whom he had given sight centers on spiritual, not physical, blindness (Jn 9:35-41).

PARABLES

If miracles represented a frontal assault against the power of Satan, parables were the subversive element in the war. A parable is a literary form calculated to tease the mind into different patterns of thought. In the synoptic Gospels the parable is a common vehicle of Jesus' teaching about the kingdom and about the manner of life of the disciples (this literary form is not found in John). In most cases Jesus' parables take the form of stories that, though fictitious, are true to life, but they are stories with an unexpected twist—novel endings intended to provoke further thought and reflection. Because they are stories, they cannot be read as metaphysical treatises, even though they may express timeless truths.

A parable is a kind of extended simile that makes its point by way of comparison: "The kingdom of God is like . . ." introduces ten parables in Matthew's Gospel alone. The kingdom is like a man who sowed good seed in his field only to find that an enemy infested it with weeds (Mt. 13:24); a mustard seed (13:31); yeast (13:33); buried treasure (13:44); a merchant's search for fine pearls (13:45); a dragnet (13:47); a king who decided to settle accounts (18:23). It is like the owner of an estate who hired workmen for his vineyard (20:1); a king who gave a wedding banquet for his son (22:2); ten bridesmaids who await the arrival of the groom (25:1). Most of the New Testament parables are about the kingdom and are generally thought to embody the authentic teaching of Jesus, if not his exact words.[6]

Parables are intended to jolt the listener. Jesus, master storyteller that he was, used them to confront the establishment. He used them to expose sham and to challenge accepted values and priorities. Jesus told the story of two men who went up to the Temple to pray: the one a Pharisee—a religious man who scrupulously observed the Law, the other a tax collector, who in our modern idiom would be regarded as a corrupt politician. And as Jesus told it, it was the sinner who went away justified (Lk 18:9-14). He evoked sympathy for the prodigal son and disdain for the elder brother who was dependable and seemingly had acted responsibly (Lk 15:11-32). Jesus' story of the good Samaritan cast the priest and Levite—pillars of society—in a bad light. The heroes of Jesus' parables are the *anawim*—outcasts and the underprivileged: Lazarus the beggar who rests on Abraham's bosom (Lk 16:19-31); the widow whose persistence broke through the shell of the corrupt judge "who respected neither God nor man" (Lk 18:1-8). But then when we begin to think that the parables seem to fall into a predictable pattern, always making the *anawim* the heroes, Jesus tells the story about the nobleman who entrusted his servants with large sums of money, telling them to invest them wisely. The servants who invested boldly were amply rewarded; the servant who out of fear played it safe saw what little he had taken from him and given to the others. "The moral," Jesus said, "is: whoever has will be given more, but the one who has not will lose the little he has" (Lk 19:11-27). Jesus' parables, always provocative, were not simply anecdotes to entertain or even to reform society. They were integral to his message, calculated to expose hypocrisy and undermine entrenched injustice. Jesus used them to teach the real meaning of the kingdom of God and what is expected of its denizens.

The parables highlight the social character of the kingdom. Some evoke the picture of a group of persons bonded together by common concerns (the wedding banquet, the workers in the vineyard); others emphasize its organic nature and growth (the leaven, the mustard seed). Jesus never presents the kingdom as a private affair between God and an individual. Rather it is an active force in the world, a reconciling presence creating a sense of solidarity among people.

The presence of the kingdom, however, does alter the situation of the individual, as is evident from the parables of the hidden treasure and the pearl of great price. The discovery of the buried treasure led the man to change his life even before he had the treasure in hand: he sold all his possessions in order to purchase the field where the treasure was hidden. Similarly the merchant who found "one really valuable pearl" put up for sale everything he had to buy it. John D. Crossan says these parables provide a key to understanding all of Jesus' parables. According to Crossan they move through three modes of behavior—finds, sells, buys—that are characteristic of the way humans experience the kingdom: advent, reversal, action.[7] Jesus announces the good news of salvation: "The reign of God is already in your midst" (Lk 17:21), and people's lives begin to change. The advent of the kingdom means that people reverse their values and look at reality in a different way—they undergo "conversion." Those who heed the message, who repent and begin to do the word of God, find that the kingdom has an immediate effect on their behavior. Captives know freedom, the blind see, the deaf hear, and the oppressed hear the good news.

The parables of growth bring out the connection between the present and the future. The stories of the sower, of the weeds sown by an enemy, of the mustard seed, of the seed growing quietly by night (Mk 4:26-29) all indicate an indefinite period of development before the kingdom, already present in germ, comes to fulfillment. The experience of salvation, grounded on faith, looks beyond the present to the time when the kingdom will emerge in all its splendor. Meanwhile the weeds grow side by side with the grain, and the dragnet dredges up rubbish together with valuables, until the day of reckoning when the worthless goods will be sorted out from those worth saving (Mt

13:30,50). Until then we must stand ready for the coming of the groom and not be like the foolish bridesmaids who missed his arrival.

THE ETHICS OF THE KINGDOM

More than the others, Matthew is the evangelist of the kingdom. He incorporates the miracle stories and the parables into his account in a way that is characteristic of his style and purpose. Two features in particular distinguish his treatment of the kingdom from that of the Mark and Luke. 1) Matthew speaks of the kingdom of the Father and the kingdom of the Son of Man as two related but different realities. The kingdom of the Son of Man, inspired by the vision of Daniel (where, as we have seen it represents the community of redeemed Israel), in Matthew refers to the church. The relationship of the kingdom to the church is a topic that we shall return to later in Article Three of the Creed. 2) A feature that is more striking, because more obvious, is that Matthew prefers the wording "kingdom of *heaven*" to "kingdom of *God*." Matthew's reluctance to speak of the kingdom of God accords with the Jewish awe and reverence for the divine name. Furthermore, "the kingdom of the heavens," a phrase that appears in rabbinical writings from the time of the early Christian era, gives greater emphasis to the eschatological reality of the kingdom, which transcends its earthly (and partial) appearance in the Christian community.[8]

Matthew structured the first part of his Gospel around five carefully composed discourses. Each describes aspects of the kingdom as it comes to be realized in the world. The best known of these discourses, the Sermon on the Mount, grounds the kingdom in the finest religious traditions of the Old Testament and thus outlines the basic principles on which it is built (chs. 5-7). It is followed by the discourse on the apostolic mission (ch. 10), the discourse on how the kingdom comes (the parables in ch. 13), the instruction on church discipline (ch. 18), and finally, the eschatological discourse that contains Jesus' teaching about the fall of Jerusalem and the coming of the Son of Man in glory (chs. 24-25). Taken together, these discourses provide a manual of instruction for life in the Christian community.

The First Discourse   The Sermon on the Mount might well be subtitled "foundations of the kingdom." Beginning with the Beatitudes, it deals with the rewards and ethical demands of discipleship.

The Beatitudes hold out the promise of happiness to people suffering and in need, and they praise persons who manifest the dispositions expected of disciples: justice, mercy, simplicity, and peacemaking (Mt 5:3-12). Of the poor in spirit and those who are persecuted for the cause of justice, it is said explicitly that the kingdom of God is theirs (vv.3,10). Whatever is to be said of the charge that Matthew "spiritualized" the Beatitudes, he does not reduce them to mere internal dispositions. The verses that follow make it clear that Jesus' disciples are expected to embrace the values of the Beatitudes and to witness to them in their lives: "You are the salt of the *earth*. . . . You are the light of the *world*. . ." (vv. 13-16).

The style of life and the ethical demands of the kingdom refine the best in the Jewish religious tradition. (It is characteristic of Matthew to present Jesus as a scribe who, "learned in the reign of God, is like the head of a household who can bring from his storeroom both the new and the old" Mt 13:52). In the Sermon on the Mount Jesus makes it clear that "I have not come to abolish the law and the prophets . . . but to fulfill them" (5:17). The spirit of the law requires the disciples to do more than avoid committing murder and doing bodily harm to others; Jesus calls on them to shun anger and abusive language (vv. 21-22). Members of the community are instructed to take the initiative in settling differences with their neighbors (vv. 23-26). It is not enough for the disciples to refrain from sexual exploitation of others—and here the words are addressed directly to males; they are to avoid even fantasizing about illicit sex (vv. 27-30). Jesus urges the high ideal of marriage without divorce (vv. 31-32), at which even the *disciples* balked (Mt 19:10). Not only is perjury out of the question, but Jesus says it should not be necessary to take oaths at all. A person's word is his or her surety (vv. 33-37). The disciples are not to seek vengeance, but to continue to help people who have wronged them (vv. 38-42). They are to be satisfied with nothing less than perfection. Jesus calls on the disciples to emulate their heavenly Father in showing love for all: friends and enemies, the just and unjust alike (vv. 43-48).

The three religious duties—almsgiving, prayer, and fasting—insisted upon by the Old Testament prophets are presumed, but Jesus warns his disciples against concern for what people might think (6:1-3). His main emphasis, however, falls upon the prayer for the kingdom (vv. 9-13). In Matthew the form of the Lord's prayer (found also in the *Didache*, 8) is that which the community made its own: "Our Father in heaven . . . your kingdom come. . . ."[9] In praying that the kingdom become a reality, the church asks for a society built on the values of the Beatitudes. As is evident from what had gone before (ch. 5), the way to justice, mercy, simplicity, and peace is forgiveness. "If you forgive the faults of others, your heavenly Father will forgive you yours" (6:14). Lessons on forgiveness recur in the discourse on community discipline (18:21-35). Wherever the disciples gather in Jesus' name and reconcile their differences, the kingdom is present.

Although the heavenly Father is aware of the needs of his people (6:32), Jesus instructs the disciples to pray "give us today our daily bread" and to persevere in that prayer (7:7-11).[10] Poor in spirit and single-minded in pursuit of the kingdom of God, the disciples are called upon to put their values in proper order. They should not permit even legitimate cares to divert their attention from the kingdom. Your treasure is where your heart is. To set wealth as a goal is as unwise as it is unworthy of the disciples, for earthly goods are perishable and do not satisfy one's inner cravings for vision and knowledge. Jesus asks, Is life not more valuable than fine food, and health more important than clothes? Then why all the anxiety? Seek first God's kingship over you, emulate the divine way of holiness, and everything else will fall into place. As in the parables there is a paradoxical twist to Jesus' instructions to the disciples (6:19-34).

In concluding the Sermon on the Mount, Matthew inserts a collection of Jesus' sayings that have no unifying theme other than that they are further directives governing life in the Christian community. The disciples are to be lenient toward one another, more harsh in self-criticism than in judging others (7:1-5). "Do not give what is holy to dogs or toss your pearls before swine" seems to be a caution against exposing the gospel message to ridicule, wasting time with people who are not open to the word (v. 6). The Golden Rule is another example of how Matthew has Jesus bring out of his storehouse nuggets of ancient wisdom. "Treat others the way you would have them treat you" (v. 12) has parallels in Jewish literature. Jesus does not beguile his listeners with promises that entry into the kingdom is easy. The gate that leads to life is narrow, the road rough, and few the travelers who persevere through it all (vv. 13-14). Beware of wolves in sheep's clothing, teachers whose actions do not match their words. Judge them by performance (vv. 15-20).

The evangelist seems to have situated these particular sayings here because they addressed concerns of the primitive church.[11] Apparently there were some who claimed extraordinary gifts—prophecy, exorcism, miracles—that they exercised in Jesus' name. The sayings of Jesus, however, make it clear that the invocation of his name does not of itself guarantee that one is a genuine disciple. (St. Paul also says these gifts are vain without love; see 1 Cor 13:2.) The real criterion for discipleship is whether one does the will of the Father (7:21-23). The words of Jesus are a challenge to action. The person who hears them and does nothing in response is like the man who built his house on sandy ground. The rains came, the winds blew, and the house collapsed for want of a firm foundation. Lip service and intellectual assent to Jesus' teaching are not enough. One's response to the gospel must be firmly grounded on doing the word, not merely on hearing it (7:24-27).

The Sermon on the Mount does not provide guidelines for every aspect of life in the Christian community. The other discourses give further directives to the disciples, but even taken cumulatively they do not provide a complete code of conduct.

The Second Discourse   This discourse, the "missionary sermon" (9:35—10:42), commissions the Twelve to proclaim the imminence of the kingdom of heaven just as John the Baptist and Jesus have done (10:7). Matthew appends other sayings on discipleship that seem especially appropriate to the missionary context; the missionary sermon proper ends at 10:16.

The Third Discourse   This discourse (13:1-52) contains the parables of the kingdom that we have already discussed.

The Fourth Discourse   This "community discourse" (18:1-35) is occasioned by the disciples' question, "Who is of greatest importance in the kingdom of God?" Here as elsewhere Jesus stood the conventional wisdom of earthly power and prestige on its head by making the lowly the greatest. In answer to the disciples' question he pointed to a small child and said, "I assure you, unless you change and become like little children, you will not enter the kingdom of God" (v. 3). Like children, people of simple faith can easily be misled, and Jesus recognized that it is inevitable that scandal occur. However, those who cause the "little ones" to go astray can expect that the fire of Gehenna will be their fate (18:6-9). The simple folk are not to be despised. They have powerful friends, "their angels in heaven" (the belief that angels watch over the just is an idea found in the Old Testament).[12] And when they go astray they are not to be written off without an effort to bring them back. Does not the shepherd leave the flock in search of one stray sheep? And is there not rejoicing when it is found (vv. 10-14)?

In one of the two texts that explicitly mention "church" (Greek = *ekklesia*), Matthew sketches some of the steps the community should take to regain the stray. First an individual goes privately to the offending "brother" so as not to humiliate him; then a delegation "of two or three witnesses" goes; and finally if he continues recalcitrant, the process should be referred to the church. If the offender does not accept the decision of the church, that person must be expelled from membership. It is on the authority of Jesus that the church claims the power to condemn and acquit. "Whatever you declare bound on earth shall be held bound in heaven, and whatever you declare loosed on earth shall be held loosed in heaven" (18:15-18). The harshness of this saying, uncharacteristic of Jesus, who is generally presented as a friend of sinners and tax-collectors, is softened by Jesus' teaching on forgiveness that seems to know no bounds. How often is a person to be forgiven? Seven times? No, Jesus replied, "seventy times seven times" (18:21-22). It is in this context that Matthew recounts the parable of the unmerciful servant (18:23-35). An example of typical passive-aggressive behavior pictures this middle-management official groveling before the king to whom he owed money. The king forgave him the debt, only to have the same official have a fellow servant thrown into debtors' prison for non-payment of "a mere fraction of what he himself owed." When the master heard of his callousness, he handed the merciless official over "to the torturers until he paid back all he owed." And then Jesus draws out the moral of the story: "My heavenly Father will treat you in exactly the same way unless each of you forgives his brother from his heart."

The Fifth Discourse   Although the theme of the last days and final judgment is close to the surface in all five Matthean discourses, it emerges as the principal topic in the last, "the eschatological sermon" (24:1—25:46). This discourse describes the signs that will accompany the coming of the Son of Man—the parousia—and concludes on a note of urgency and with an admonition to be vigilant, "for you know not the day or the hour" (25:13). The final scene, the story of the Last

Judgment when the Son of Man comes to separate the sheep from the goats (discussed in Chapter 13), presents a surprisingly different picture of the saved: it indicates that in the final reckoning the ones who will inherit the kingdom "prepared from the foundation of the world" (25:34) are people who *do* the word of God even though they may never have *heard* it.

The New Testament symbol of the kingdom thus makes a collage of Old Testament images. From the story of creation in Genesis through the covenant and Law given at Mt. Sinai through the mottled history of Israel's kings, through the vision in the later prophets of a new covenant, a new people and a messianic age, God called humans to acknowledge divine dominion in the world and in their lives. The call culminated in Jesus' proclamation that the reign of God was (is) at hand. Jesus identified the kingdom on earth with the community of disciples and summarized the divine rule under the headings of two commandments—unconditioned love of God and unrestricted love of neighbor.

"WITHOUT END"

In the ancient world, Marcellus of Ancyra and his followers taught that the kingdom was transitory; once the forces of evil had been overcome, it would serve no more purpose and would end. In modern times Albert Schweitzer, the person most responsible for calling attention to the central place of eschatology in Jesus' teaching, regarded Jesus' ethical teaching as time-conditioned and transitory. According to Schweitzer the purpose of that teaching was to summon people to repentance and show them what they must do in order to enter the kingdom. It was, in Schweitzer's phrase, an "interim ethic" intended for only a relatively brief interval between the proclamation of the kingdom and its actual coming. Its content was conditioned by urgency, the need for an immediate response to the imminent end of the historical order. According to Schweitzer the interim ethic became impractical in changed circumstances when the end was no longer considered imminent.

In the eighty some years since Schweitzer published *The Quest of the Historical Jesus*, biblical scholars and theologians have continued to address the questions he raised. There is a broad consensus among them that the eschatological expectation was a significant factor in the presentation, if not the content, of Jesus' ethical teaching. Few if any, however, accept Schweitzer's concept of an interim ethic without putting it into a broader perspective. The fundamental issue is no longer whether there is an eschatological element to the Christian ethic, but what is the *meaning* of Jesus' proclamation of the kingdom and of the immediacy of the eschaton. Writers who recognize both the present and the future dimensions of the kingdom frequently make some distinctions, taking the sayings of Jesus one by one, but in general they acknowledge that his ethical teaching is not so time-conditioned as to be inapplicable in contemporary culture. Joseph Fitzmyer sums up the common view shared by practicing Christians in saying the Sermon on the Mount "is neither a perfectionist's code, nor an interim ethic, nor an expose of the impossible ideal, nor a utopian dream, nor a new Torah. It represents rather the Matthean Jesus' radical demands for the transformation of human life."[13]

Amos Wilder distinguishes a "discipleship-ethic" that made special claims upon Jesus' followers during the crisis associated with the coming of the kingdom.[14] Those claims were time-conditioned and transitory. But Wilder also emphasizes the permanent value of Jesus' ethical teaching. In so far as the kingdom lies in the future, it provides the motive for repentance, and the particular demands are looked on as conditions of entrance into it. In so far as the kingdom is already present, Jesus' ethical teaching points to new possibilities of life brought about by its presence. The tension between a "realized" eschatology and various forms of "anticipated" eschatology—that is, between the "already" and "not yet"—is blurred when it comes to the ethical demands of discipleship. The future reign of God is so near as already to affect the present.

The kingdom of God is central to soteriology and (as will become evident in succeeding chapters) is the starting point for ecclesiology. Like the other evangelists and Paul, Matthew portrayed the disciples both as the embodiment and the witnesses to the presence of the kingdom of God on earth. Jesus' parables of growth—the mustard seed, the leaven—image what the church is to become and do. Jesus' miracles displayed the power of God, and he promised that his disciples would do even greater things than he did. In explaining the significance of the miracles, John L. McKenzie once wrote:

Jesus fed five thousand; the church can feed the hungry in far greater numbers wherever the church meets the hungry. Jesus healed diseases and expelled demons; the church can heal diseases and comfort the afflicted wherever the church meets them. She can expel the demons of crime and violence by proclaiming the word of the Gospel (rather than the ethic of the just war) and by giving real hope to those who turn to crime and violence because they believe they have no other direction in which to turn. The church can even offer a new life to the guilty and the desperate. The church can do all these things because the church is the living and active presence of Christ in the world. The church does not do these things? Then let us not deplore the fact that we have cherished a naive belief in miracles which never happened, but bewail those miracles which did not happen because we did not have the faith the size of a grain of mustard seed. The miracle stories are among the most meaningful of the Gospel stories, and they deal with reality. They show the church what it can do.[15]

The church is the temporal and transient symbol of the kingdom in history. It is not the kingdom, for the KINGDOM WILL HAVE NO END. The kingdom is timeless in the sense that the now and the future dissolve into the eternal. At the end-time every creature will acknowledge the kingship of God. Meanwhile the church prays, "Our Father in heaven, . . . your kingdom come, your will be done on earth as it is in heaven." As we are reminded in the next chapter when we turn our attention to the third article in the Creed, it is by the power of the Spirit that we are children of God, heirs of the kingdom, and capable of crying out *Abba*—"Father."

Notes

1. *Catechetical Lectures* 15, 27. Quoted in Kelly, *Creeds*, p. 338.

2. Marcellus had attended the Council of Nicea, where he strongly opposed Arianism. His own troubles stem from his view that the Incarnation was only a transient phase. Marcellus admitted the eter-

nity of the Logos as such, but he also taught that at the consummation of the world Christ's reign would come to an end and he would abandon the human nature he had assumed for our sake. The Council of Constantinople also condemned Photinus of Sirmium, a disciple and ally of Marcellus, for the same teaching. See *NCE* 9:191.

3. From a feminist point of view the symbol of the kingdom is "potentially explosive" because it seems to carry with it the image of male dominance. See Sonya A. Quitslund, "A Feminist Perspective on Kings and Kingdom" *The Living Light* 19:2 (Summer 1982):134–139. Norman Perrin writes, "The Kingdom of God is the power of God expressed in deeds; it is that which God does wherein it becomes evident that he is king. It is not a place or community ruled by God; it is not even the abstract idea of reign or kingship of God. It is quite concretely the activity of God as king." *Jesus and the Language of the Kingdom* (Philadelphia: Fortress, 1976), p. 55.

4. Alan Richardson, *The Miracle-Stories of the Gospels* (London: SCM Press, 1941), pp. 38–45.

5. Ibid., pp. 16–17.

6. Much has been written on parables in recent years. Some of the more notable works available in English are C. H. Dodd, *The Parables of the Kingdom*, revised edition (London: James Nisbet, 1961); Joachim Jeremias, *The Parables of Jesus*, revised edition (New York: Charles Scribner's Sons, 1963); G. V. Jones, *The Art and Truth of the Parables* (London: S.P.C.K., 1964).

7. In *Parables: The Challenge of the Historical Jesus* (New York: Harper & Row, 1973), pp. 35–36. See Dermot Lane, *The Living Light* 19:2 (Summer 1982):107.

8. *JBC*, vol. 2, par. 102, p. 783.

9. Stendahl stresses the fact that the Our Father is another link to Israel. Krister Stendahl, "Your Kingdom: Notes for Bible Study" *Your Kingdom Come*. Report of the World Conference on Mission and Evangelism, Melbourne, Australia, 12–25 May 1980 (Geneva: World Council of Churches, 1980), p. 74.

10. The ending to the Lord's prayer, "For the kingdom, the power and the glory are yours, now and for ever," standard in Protestant books of worship for centuries and added to the Roman liturgy by Pope Paul VI, was already in use at the time of the *Didache* c. A.D.100. It comes from David's final prayer; see 1 Chron 29:11.

11. *JBC*, vol. 2, par. 51, p. 75.

12. *JBC*, vol. 2, par. 127, p. 95.

13. Joseph A. Fitzmyer, *A Christological Catechism: New Testament*

Answers (New York/Ramsey: Paulist Press, 1982), p. 34.

14. Amos N. Wilder, *Eschatology and Ethics in the Teaching of Jesus* (Westport, CT: Greenwood Press, 1978).

15. "The Demythologizing of Louis Evely," *Commonweal*, June 11, 1971, p. 308.

THE THIRD ARTICLE:

SPIRIT AND SANCTIFIER

We believe in the Holy Spirit, the Lord, the giver of life,
  who proceeds from the Father and the Son.
With the Father and the Son he is worshipped and
    glorified.
He has spoken through the Prophets.
We believe in one holy catholic and apostolic Church.
We acknowledge one baptism for the forgiveness of
    sins.
We look for the resurrection of the dead,
    and the life of the world to come. Amen.

15

The Holy Spirit
in Scripture and Experience

"The Holy Spirit, the Lord, the giver of life,
with the Father and the Son is worshipped and glorified"

Like the passage from one movement to another in a Beethoven symphony, the transition from one article of the Creed to another flows smoothly without a break in the melody. Strains of the Holy Spirit could be heard in the background during the movement of creation and redemption in the first and second articles, but now in the third they emerge crescendo in full volume and power. Jesus was filled with God's Spirit; he was conceived by the Holy Spirit (Lk 1:35); at his baptism the Spirit of God descended on him (Mt 3:16). Finally, Jesus promised to send the Spirit of truth, who will indict unbelievers for their lack of faith and lead the disciples on the way of truth (Jn 16:7-13).

Even before the early Christians recognized the Holy Spirit as a personal Being, they experienced the force of the divine presence in their lives. The New Testament account of the descent of the Spirit describes an experience of sound and fury "like a strong driving wind" and "tongues as of fire" that came to rest on each of the disciples (Acts 2:2-3). In describing the experience of the just who were transformed by the Holy Spirit, St. Paul says they find their behavior now characterized by love, joy, peace, patience, kindness, goodness, trustfulness, gentleness, and self-control (Gal 5:22). (Traditionally the qualities summarized under these headings have been known in Catholic theology as "fruits of the Holy Spirit.")

The beliefs grouped together in the third article of the Creed have an intrinsic unity. The simple confession of faith "in Holy Spirit" (found without an article in the most primitive creeds) was expanded to affirm the divine nature of the Spirit as well as the presence and activity of the Spirit in the church.[1] In later chapters we shall discuss the Spirit's role in the sanctification of the community and individuals, but here and in the next chapter we concentrate on the Holy Spirit in relationship to the Father and the Son. The third article of the Creed owes its form if not its substance to events surrounding the Council of Constantinople (381). It was Constantinople that shaped the definitive wording of the Creed: HOLY SPIRIT, THE LORD, THE GIVER OF LIFE . . . WITH THE FATHER AND THE SON HE IS WORSHIPED AND GLORIFIED. In order to appreciate how carefully these phrases were chosen it is necessary to recall the issues in the Arian controversy (see Chapter 4, above). In this chapter, therefore, we begin by examining the experience of the Holy Spirit as it is described in the Old and the New Testament; then we return to the events leading up to the Council of Constantinople.

THE SPIRIT OF GOD IN THE OLD TESTAMENT

The Bible speaks of the Holy Spirit in a variety of ways that defy systematization. The terminology is not fixed, and several metaphors and other images are used to describe the activity of the Holy Spirit in the world. In fact, "spirit" is itself a metaphor. "Like so many other religious terms," writes John Macquarrie, "this one began as an image rather than a concept."[2] Spirit translates the Greek term *pneuma*, which itself is a translation of the Semitic word *ruah*. *Pneuma*, like *ruah*, names invisible forces that are real without being tangible and, though intangible, are felt although people can neither see them nor control them. *Pneuma* is the word for wind—the fresh breeze of a spring day, the soft wind of an autumn evening, the awesome fury of tornadoes and hurricanes. *Pneuma* is also breath—the breath of life that enlivens and *inspires*. To cease breathing is to cease living. Whatever the image, spirit implies dynamism: energy, activity, life.

The biblical understanding of spirit should not be confused with notions of spirit in philosophy and the history of religions, though the two meanings are related. Ancient philosophers thought spirit to be like air: ethereal and invisible. It is common in religious studies to contrast spirit with matter; thus, to affirm that the Supreme Being is Spirit is to say that God is non-material, non-spatial, and timeless. Most philosophies and religions posit some kind of life principle—a "soul"—which though spiritual is not *pure* spirit in that it is permanently and necessarily tied to the physical. Much the same can be said of the human mind, which is "spiritual" and at the same time dependent on the brain. Without listing the many and diverse definitions of spirit, it is fair to say that philosophy and the history of religions generally emphasize the non-material quality of spirit while the Bible stresses its dynamic character.

In describing divine presence and activity in the world, the Old Testament often speaks of the "Spirit of God."[3] The divine power is evident in a special way in creation (see Pss 33:6; 104:30). Although modern translations of Genesis (e.g., the *New American Bible* and the *New English Bible*) speak of a "mighty wind" sweeping over the primeval waters (1:2), the text could also be rendered "the Spirit of God." The Spirit of God is the source of life (Gen 2:7; 6:3; Job 12:10; 27:3; 34:14; Ez 37:14). Specially chosen individuals, men and women assigned tasks that affect the course of history, are said to be temporarily endowed with the Spirit of God—e.g., Joseph (Gen 41:38), Moses (Num 11:17), Gideon (Jgs 6:34), Samson (Jgs 14:6), Saul (1 Sam 10:6; 16:14). The psalmist praises the Spirit of God as causing the salvation of Israel (51:12; 143:10). The Spirit of God has a special role in the coming of the Messiah, the prince of peace (Is 11:2; 42:1), and in the new Jerusalem the Spirit is given to all (Is 32:15-18; 44:3; Ez 11:19; 36:27; 39:29; Zec 12:10). Using apocalyptic imagery, the prophet Joel heralded the messianic age, saying that salvation would be accomplished with the out-pouring of the Spirit on all (Jl 3:1-5).

THE SPIRIT OF GOD IN THE NEW TESTAMENT:
THE POWER AND GIFTS OF THE SPIRIT

The significance of Joel's words was not lost on the early church. In his discourse on Pentecost, Peter quoted the text from Joel:

> It shall come to pass in the last days, says God, that I will pour out a portion of my spirit on all mankind: Your sons and daughters shall prophesy, your young men shall see visions and your old men shall dream dreams.
>
> Yes, even on my servants and handmaids I will pour out a portion of my spirit in those days, and they shall prophesy.
>
> I will work wonders in the heavens above and signs on the earth below: blood, fire, and a cloud of smoke.
>
> The sun shall be turned to darkness and the moon to blood before the coming of that great and glorious day of the Lord.
>
> Then shall everyone be saved who calls on the name of the Lord. (Acts 2:17-21).

The pentecostal outpouring of the Spirit inaugurated the new era. Jesus had promised that upon returning to the Father he would send the Holy Spirit. The Spirit dwells in the disciples and guides the destiny of the nascent Christian community. The Holy Spirit is the driving force of the church's missionary activity. It is the Spirit who elects Paul and Barnabas to preach to the Gentiles (Acts 13:2). The Holy Spirit leads Paul and his companions from Asia Minor to Europe (Acts 16:6-10). In his farewell discourse to the presbyters of Ephesus, Paul admonishes them, "Keep watch over yourselves, and over the whole flock the Holy Spirit has given you to guard" (Acts 20:28). The lie for which Ananaias and Saphira are so severely punished was regarded as particularly heinous precisely because it was seen as an offense against the Spirit (Acts 5:3,9).

Although warned by the Spirit that "chains and hardships" awaited him there, Paul is driven by the Holy Spirit to return to Jerusalem (Acts 20:22; 21:10-11). Jesus had anticipated that his disciples would be hauled into court, tried, and imprisoned. He told them that when that time came they need not worry about what to say or how to say it, because "the Spirit of your Father will be speaking in you" (Mt 10:16-20).

The Acts of the Apostles makes it clear that the Holy Spirit is the moving force within the church, directing its missionary activity and motivating its leaders, but we must look to the writings of Paul and John for a more detailed picture of the specific ways in which the Spirit operates within the community of the faithful. Paul's experience of the Spirit is directly related to the Easter event—the resurrection and the glorification of Jesus as Christ and Lord.[4] Paul proclaims "the gospel of God which he promised long ago through his prophets" and which has now become a reality. It is the gospel of God's Son "who was descended from David according to the flesh but was made Son of God in power according to the spirit of holiness, by his resurrection from the dead: Jesus Christ our Lord" (Rom 1:1-4). Elsewhere Paul is explicit in saying that it was the Spirit of God who raised Jesus from the dead (see Rom 8:11).[5]

The gift of the Spirit to the nations fulfilled the promise made to Abraham, the person of faith par excellence. In writing to the Galatians, Paul explains that the crucifixion took place "so that through Christ Jesus the blessing bestowed on Abraham might descend on the Gentiles in Christ Jesus, thereby making it possible for us to receive the promised Spirit through faith" (3:14). It is through the preaching of the gospel which inspires faith that the blessing of Abraham and the gift of the Spirit, promised by God, reach the Gentiles: "Our preaching of the gospel proved not a mere matter of words for you but one of power; it was carried on in the Holy Spirit. . ." (1 Thess 1:5; see 1 Cor 2:4-5,13). By faith and baptism Christians enter into a life in and through the Spirit. It is the life of the children of God, ("All who are led by the Spirit of God are sons of God") that enables us, by reason of adoption, to say "Abba." And when we cry out "Abba"—Father— it is the Spirit who "gives witness with our spirit that we are children of God" (Rom 8:14-17; Gal 4:6).

The Spirit plays a decisive role in building up the Body of Christ, the church. "It was in one Spirit that all of us, whether Jew or Greek, slave or free, were baptized into one body. All of us have been given to drink of the one Spirit" (1 Cor 12:13).[6] Paul emphasizes that the Spirit is the principle of unity within the Christian community and makes all its members one in Christ without destroying their individuality. Reconciled through the cross, the circumcised and uncircumcised overcome hostilities through the blood of Christ and "have access in one Spirit to the Father" (Eph 2:18). The Epistle to the Ephesians continues,

This means that you are strangers and aliens no longer. No, you are fellow citizens of the saints and members of the household of God. You form a building which rises on the foundation of the apostles and prophets, with Christ Jesus himself as the capstone. Through him the whole structure is fitted together and takes shape as a holy temple in the Lord; in him you are being built into this temple, to become a dwelling place for God in the Spirit.

Paul referred to both the Christian community and the individuals as "the temple of God" where the Spirit of God dwells, and he expressed concern lest anyone do anything to destroy that temple (1 Cor 3:16; 6:19). He was particularly alarmed with the behavior of members of the church at Corinth, where sometime about A.D. 50 he had spent eighteen months working among the Gentiles and had brought to the faith many poor and underprivileged. Factionalism, evident everywhere, was sapping the moral strength of the community so that it could not take appropriate action against those whose conduct was openly immoral or who had fallen back into pagan practices. Some questioned Paul's authority. The eucharistic assembly, the sign of Christian unity, had become an occasion for discrimination against the poor. Some were skeptical about the bodily resurrection, and some believed that, since they were living in the last age, they were beyond the difficult struggle between spirit and flesh (see 1 Cor 1:7; 4:8,10).

Factionalism and other problems developed in the church at Corinth because, while rejoicing in the gifts of the Spirit, the Christians there seemed unconcerned about the needs of the community as a whole. Paul charged them with showing more fascination with ecstatic phenomena than concern for charity (1 Cor 13:1-8,13). The Corinthians apparently attached more importance to gifts (charisms), which they freely ascribed to the Holy Spirit, than to the Spirit, the source of these gifts.

Paul takes up the problems one by one until he turns to a discussion of the gifts of the Holy Spirit. The Spirit is the very ground of the profession of faith. "No one can say, 'Jesus is Lord,' except by the Holy Spirit" (1 Cor 12:3). Paul had begun the Epistle by denying that Christ could be divided (1:13), and in chapters 12 and 14, while acknowledging diversity in the Body of Christ, the church, he emphasizes the power of the Spirit as a force of unity. All the variety of ministries and talents exercised by members of the community are doings of the Spirit.

> There are different gifts but the same Spirit; there are different ministries but the same Lord; there are different works but the same God who accomplishes all of them in everyone. To each person the manifestation of the Spirit is given for the common good. To one the Spirit gives wisdom in discourse, to another the power to express knowledge. Through the Spirit one receives faith; by the same Spirit another is given the gift of healing, and still another miraculous powers. Prophecy is given to one; to another power to distinguish one spirit from another. One receives the gift of tongues, another that of interpreting the tongues. But it is one and the same Spirit who produces all these gifts, distributing them to each as he wills. (12:4-11)

This list, one of several lists of Paul's gifts that illustrate the manifestation of the Spirit for the common good of the church, describes nine "charisms" (Greek = *charismata*).[7]

The first, "wisdom in discourse," recalls Paul's discussion in chapter 2 of the Epistle. Paul cites his own preaching of the gospel, which, he writes, did not rely on reasoned arguments but on "the convincing power of the Spirit." "As a consequence," he says to the Corinthians, "your faith rests not on the wisdom of men but on the power of God" (2:1-4). Paul acknowledges "a certain wisdom which we express among the spiritually mature," but it is radically different from worldly wisdom. It is God's wisdom, "a mysterious, a hidden wisdom," revealed through the Spirit. The Spirit enables us to interpret "spiritual things in spiritual terms," to gain insight into "all matters, even the deep things of God," and to know our inmost selves, recognizing the gifts the Spirit has given us (2:5-16).

Similarly *the second gift, "the power to express knowledge,"* recalls an earlier discussion in chapter 8 where Paul addresses the issue of eating food sacrificed to idols. The problem was a practical one for Christians in Greek city-states, where a considerable amount of meat sold in the open markets came from animals offered to the gods. Further, social conventions were such in Corinth that on occasion Christians joined pagan friends and relatives in celebrating family festivals, held often in the precincts of temples dedicated to a local deity.[8] Paul was asked to take sides between two factions. Apparently one group attributed a tangible impurity to sacrificial meats and felt that in eating such food they were defiled. A second group, secure in their *knowledge* that the pagan idols were in reality "non-gods" who could exercise no power over human affairs, did not hesitate to eat sacrificial meats (see also Rom 14:1—15:13). Paul allows that the knowledge of the one true God and of Christ distinguishes Christians from the pagans, but he also recognizes that unless it is joined to charity it leads to spiritual snobbishness. "Whereas 'knowledge' inflates, love up-builds" (8:1). Although he agrees that there is no intrinsic reason that prohibits a Christian from eating food offered to idols, even in the precincts of a temple, Paul says this knowledge of itself is not sufficient justification if it causes scandal. "If food causes my brother to sin I will never eat meat again, so that I may not be an occasion of sin to him" (8:13). Paul's point seems to be that whereas wisdom is divinely mediated through the Spirit, knowledge must be expressed in accordance with the Spirit—that is to say, in love.

Faith, the third gift, is one of the basic themes that permeate Pauline theology, but here in Corinthians he speaks of it as a particular gift that one receives "through the Spirit" (12:9). It inspires openness and confidence in God's power. In this context Paul associates faith—"faith great enough to move mountains" (13:2)— with *three other gifts of healing, miraculous powers, and prophecy*. The Spirit gives life and makes whole. Although Paul does not explain "miraculous powers," they would seem to include the ability to cast out demons. (It was in connection with a case of exorcism that Jesus chided his disciples, "If you had faith the size of a mustard seed, you would be able to say to this mountain, 'Move from here to there,' and it would move"— Mt 17:20.) Nor does he explain the gift of prophecy; but in biblical tradition prophets function as the voices of conscience for the community, reminding the members of their religious heritage, with its responsibilities and moral obligations before the Lord. Prophecy exhorts, corrects, and, in particular cases, announces the will of God. The text of Joel quoted by Peter on Pentecost implies that the gifts of the Spirit are given lavishly without discrimination to women and men, and Paul plainly indicates that both men and women prophesied in the church (1 Cor 11:4-5).[9]

Closely associated with the gift of prophecy is *a seventh gift: the gift of discernment of spirits*, and in fact there is some question whether the two are independent charisms.[10] Discernment provides a test for prophetic witness and a check against abuses. As if to keep prophesying in the assembly within bounds, Paul writes, "Let no more than two or three prophets speak, and the rest judge the worth of what they say" (1 Cor 14:29). Like all the gifts of the Spirit, charismatic prophecy and discernment are always gratuitously given and serendipitously received. The gift of discernment is characterized by a spiritual prudence which, while open to the movement of Spirit, causes one to stop and consider all other options before coming to a decision. Ethical criteria help discern the presence of the Spirit (Gal 15:19-31; Rom 11:17; 1 Cor 13). "Do not stifle the Spirit," Paul writes elsewhere. "Do not despise prophecies. Test everything; retain what is good. Avoid any semblance of evil" (1 Thes 5:19-22). Discernment steers a course along the border where reason and spontaneity meet.

The *eighth* and most striking gift, but also the most problematic phenomenon, the one that seemed to have held the most fascination for Corinthian Christians and that was proving to be a source of contention in the community, was the gift of tongues—*glossolalia*. Glossolalia were generally understood to be unintelligible stammerings in praise of God born of the enthusiasm and joy of faith.[11] Although Paul seems to have a higher regard for the gift of prophecy, he judges the phenomenon of tongues in a basically favorable light, but he demands that it be exercised in an orderly fashion in the assembly (1 Cor 14:4-5). The gift of tongues, at least as St. Paul describes it, is not a means of communication among the members of the community but a manifestation of the presence of the Spirit and an outward expression of a person's relationship with God (1 Cor 14:2). Speaking, praying, or singing in tongues seems more spontaneous than deliberate, and the audible sounds are unintelligible even to the speaker. It is only with the help of *the ninth gift* of the Spirit—*the gift of interpretation*—that one can make sense out of the prayer or hymn (1 Cor 14:6-13).

The gifts, though many and diverse, flow from a single source, God's grace (Rom 12:6). Unity and diversity. While Paul's natural preference seems to be for unity, even for uniformity and order, he recognizes that each person has his or her own gift from God (1 Cor 7:7). Although Christians are one in the Spirit, it is the same Spirit who empowers some as apostles, some as prophets, some as teachers, some as miracle workers, healers, helpers (as in helping ministries), and administrators as well as those who speak in tongues and those who interpret them (1 Cor 12:27-28). The gifts are not for one's personal well-being but for the building up of the community and the nurturing of life of the Body of Christ that is the church.

TRIADIC FORMULAS IN ST. PAUL

In addition to those charisms, St. Paul names the Spirit as the giver of life (Rom 8:2,11), a way of knowing (1 Cor 2:13-144),[12] and the one who brings about freedom—liberation from slavery to the law, sin, and death (Gal 5:16-21). "The Lord is the Spirit, and where the Spirit of the Lord is, there is freedom" (2 Cor 3:17).

The functions and attributes that Paul ascribes to the Holy Spirit are of such a variety that it is impossible to define exactly what he meant by spirit (*pneuma*).[13] Furthermore, there are a number of other texts— "triadic texts"—in Paul's Epistles that group the Spirit with God (or the Father) and Christ (or the Son). In a passage generally regarded as a reference to baptism he writes, "God is the one who firmly establishes us along with you in Christ; it is he who anointed us and has sealed us, thereby depositing the first payment, the Spirit, in our hearts" (2 Cor 2:21-22; see Eph 1:13-14). And he concludes his Second Letter to the Corinthians with a text that is often used as a greeting in the Roman liturgy: "The grace of the Lord Jesus Christ, and the love of God, and the fellowship of the Holy Spirit be with you all!" (13:13).[14]

A classic triadic text in the Epistle to the Ephesians is thought by many to echo the strains of a primitive creed:

> There is but one body and one Spirit, just as there is but one hope given all of you by your call. There is one Lord, one faith, one baptism; one God and Father of all, who is over all, and works through all, and is in all. (4:4-6)[15]

It is part of a longer passage concerned, like Chapter 12 of 1 Corinthians, with the dynamic tension between multiplicity and unity. If God were not in some sense three, there would be no point in insisting on the divine oneness. Paul then moves from the confession of God's oneness in 4:4-6 to a reflection on the many gifts, ministries, and members in the church (4:7ff). "Make every effort," he writes, "to preserve the unity which has the Spirit as its origin and peace as its binding force" (4:3).

Despite the fact that vestiges of primitive creeds such as the one in Ephesians indicate belief in the Trinity of divine persons, it took centuries before the identity of the Holy Spirit was clearly established. Although Jesus' instruction to the disciples to teach and baptize "in the name of the Father, and of the Son, and of the Holy Spirit" was clear enough, there remained a good deal of obscurity about how the Spirit related to the Father and Son, and how they in turn related to the Spirit. One reason why it took a long time to define the function and person of the Spirit is the want of some distinguishing personal characteristic. "Spirit" is not a proper name, nor does it name a relationship as do Father and Son. Moreover, the Father and Son are also spirit. Only when theologians found it necessary to explain the relationship of the Father to the Son and the Son to the Father in the fourth century against the Arians (see Chapter 4) did they begin to consider the position of the Holy Spirit in the equation.

PRELUDE TO THE COUNCIL OF CONSTANTINOPLE: CAPPADOCIANS VS. PNEUMATOMACHS

Although St. Athanasius, the dogged adversary of Arianism in all its forms, was principally concerned with defending the Nicene faith that the Son is one in Being with the Father (*homoousios*), he knew that the underlying issue was Trinitarian. He seemed aware that whatever was said of the Father-Son relationship had also to apply to the Holy Spirit. Plainly put, one does not have a Trinity unless all three persons are equal in every way. As with his defense of the divinity of the Logos, Athanasius also fell back on soteriology in his explanation of the divinity of the Spirit. He argued that only God could redeem the world and bring a new creation. First, it is only as incarnate Son of God that Christ brings about redemption. Similarly, it is only through the Spirit, through whom humanity is bonded to Christ, that the fruits of redemption are imparted to individuals and to the church. Within the framework of this reasoning the Spirit cannot be a creature any more than the Son can be. The work of redemption can be done only by a divine person.[16]

In the period between the Councils of Nicea (325) and Constantinople (381), before the Arian controversy had been fully resolved, the identity of the Holy Spirit became an issue—a problem within a problem. It broke into the open when a split occurred in the ranks of the homoeousian party, the so-called Semi-Arians. Although the homoeousians rejected the Nicean term *homoousios*, they were even more adamant in repudiating the Arian position (see Chapter 4). However, the homoeousians themselves were divided: one faction, led by Basil of Ancyra, stood near to Athanasius; another faction, led by Macedonius, bishop of Constantinople, was identified by its position regarding the Holy Spirit. Since the New Testament says nothing about the participation of the Spirit in the work of creation, members of this group denied that the Spirit is of the same nature or essence (*ousia*) as the Father and Son. In effect, they denied the divinity of the Holy Spirit. Saint Athanasius called them *pneumatomachoi*—enemies of the Spirit; in history they are also known as Macedonians, after the name of their principal spokesman. The majority of the homoeousians opposed the pneumatomachs, and eventually the latter were condemned by the Council of Constantinople.

After A.D.360 Athanasius and the generation of bishops who had been active participants in the Council of Nicea saw the leadership in the struggle against the Arians pass to younger men. Chief among them were three great Cappadocians, Basil the Great (330-379), his younger brother Gregory of Nyssa (d. after 394), and Basil's close friend, Gregory of Nazianzus (329?-389?). Basil and Gregory were born into a prominent Cappadocian family: their father was bishop of Caesarea; their oldest sister, famed as an ascetic and spiritual counselor, is known in history as St. Macrina the Younger to distinguish her from their grandmother, St. Macrina the Elder; and their youngest brother, Peter, became bishop of Sebasteia. When Basil was appointed bishop of Caesarea, the provincial capital of Cappadocia in 370, the prestige of the neo-Nicene party was considerably enhanced. The post gave him ecclesiastical jurisdiction over a large section of eastern Asia Minor, and Basil did not hesitate to use his authority and influence in the cause of orthodoxy. His brother, known in history as Gregory of Nyssa after the little Cappadocian town where he became bishop about 371, was highly regarded as both an orator and a theologian. The other Gregory in the troika is identified with Nazianzus, another small town in Cappadocia, where his father was bishop. Against his better judgment he allowed his friend Basil to install him as bishop of Sasima, hardly more than a watering-station, and for a short while in 381 he served as bishop of Constantinople. Gregory of Nazianzus was a renowned preacher and an even more outspoken foe of the pneumato-machs than the other two. All three Cappadocians, well versed in the writings of Origen, allied themselves with the homoeousians, who were in sympathy with Athanasius.

It was in the framework of their rather abstract theology of the Trinity that the Cappadocians worked out their pneumatology. In 374, acceding to the urging of a friend, Basil undertook a treatise on the Holy Spirit. He introduced the issues by recalling the doxology:

> Lately when praying with the people, and using the full doxology to God the Father in both forms, at one time *"with* the Son *together with* the Holy Ghost," and at another *"through* the Son *in* the Holy Ghost," I was attacked by some of those present on the ground that I was introducing novel and at the same time mutually contradictory terms.[17]

No fool, Basil knew the issue was not merely a quibble over his choice of words. He recognized that his adversaries pounced on the preposi-tions—words which define relationships—as a tactic in their "deep and covert design against true religion"; they cited the different preposi-tions used in the doxology to demonstrate that the Father, Son, and Holy Spirit are unlike one another in nature (*On the Spirit*, ch. 2). Relying on the rules of grammar and rhetoric and the simple example of the carpentry shop, the Arians and pneumatomachs argued that the nature of the cause (carpenter) is different from the nature of the means (tools) *with* which the carpenter did his work and from the nature of the time and place (the shop) *in* which he does his work. Basil chides them for reducing the work of the "Lord of all" to that of a carpenter and for "applying to the Creator of the universe language belonging to a hammer or a saw" (ch. 3). Then he proceeds to analyze the scriptural use of these prepositions to show that it does not suggest that the Father, Son, and Spirit are different according to their nature (chs. 4-8; chs. 25-27).

By chapter 9, when Basil begins to focus his remarks more explicitly on the Holy Spirit, his rhetoric heats up. Those who assert that the Holy Spirit cannot be ranked with the Father and Son on account of the difference of Spirit's nature and the inferiority of the Spirit's dig-nity, he writes, "shake down the foundation of the faith of Christ by levelling apostolic tradition with the ground, and utterly destroying it" (ch. 10). A major plank in Basil's reasoning is that in conformity with Christ's instruction, Christians are baptized in the name of the Father,

Son, and Spirit (chs. 10-15). Despite the claim of the "our opponents," who divide and rend asunder, and relegate the Spirit to role of a ministering angel, Basil writes, "in all things the Holy Spirit is inseparable and wholly incapable of being parted from the Father and Son" (ch. 10). In particular Basil is concerned to explain the role of the Spirit in creation, because in denying such a role the pneumatomachs also denied the divinity of the Spirit (ch. 16).

"Be it so," Basil quotes his opponents, "but glory is by no means so absolutely due to the Spirit as to require His exaltation by us in doxologies" (ch. 19). In answer the great Cappadocian collates the biblical texts that ascribe to the Holy Spirit coexistence and other attributes and functions that are prerogatives of the Godhead. Moreover, Basil shows where the New Testament speaks of the Spirit as "Lord." He argues that by recounting these same attributes and recalling the wonders they have worked, we glorify the Father and Son, and thus for the same reason and in the same way we give glory to the Spirit (chs. 21-24).

Despite the fact that Basil set out to discredit the position of the Arians and the Pneumatomachs, refuting their arguments one after the other, his own position regarding the Holy Spirit has been criticized for what he did not say. He was (and is) charged with being cautious and tentative in affirming the full divinity of the Holy Spirit. Thus Gregory of Nazianzus felt it necessary to give over part of his funeral oration to defend Basil against the charge of minimalism leveled against him already in the 370s.[18] It is true that Basil stopped short of saying that the Holy Spirit is God and that the Spirit is *homoousios* with the Father and Son, but his silence seems to have been dictated by two considerations: 1) he did not want to overstate his case by using terms that were not defined in Scripture; and 2) he hoped to win over sympathetic *homoiousians* and not further alienate the pneumatomachs. Since some peace was returning to the church after almost fifty years of controversy over Nicea's condemnation of Arianism, Basil was careful to let sleeping dogs lie. Although he did not insist on canonizing particular theological terms, there seems little doubt that his teaching on the Holy Trinity and specifically on the Spirit was entirely orthodox.

Basil died in 379, two years before the Council of Constantinople, convened in 381, and it fell to his brother Gregory of Nyssa to represent the neo-Nicene theology of the Cappadocians. Gregory's principal arguments for the divinity of the Holy Spirit were essentially the same as Basil's: 1) all the attributes and functions ascribed to the Spirit belong equally to the Father and the Son; 2) the Spirit is inseparable from the Father and Son; and 3) the Spirit is co-creative with Father and Son. With regard to the last, Gregory (influenced by Neo-platonic philosophy) is more insistent on the creative activity of the Spirit than is Basil.[19] Gregory played a leading role in the conciliar proceedings, and today it is generally conceded that the clarifications of the doctrine of the Holy Spirit in the Constantinopolitan Creed are largely an expression of the teaching of the two brothers.[20]

Although it has been known as the Nicene-Constantinopolitan Creed since the seventeenth century, the "Symbol of Constantinople" is in reality a revised version of the baptismal creed of the church of Salamis. (Of the 178 words in the Greek text of the Creed of Constantinople, only thirty-three, fewer than a fifth, are in the Nicene confession.)[21] The council was called to deal with the lingering vestiges of Arianism, particularly in the pneumatomachian variation that had emerged in the Macedonian wing of the homoeousian party. The third article of the Creed is plainly directed against the pneumatomachs, but again with the same prudence and caution that was characteristic of Basil's writings. To confess belief in the Holy Spirit THE LORD, THE GIVER OF LIFE, WHO PROCEEDS FROM THE FATHER [AND] WITH THE FATHER AND THE SON . . . IS WORSHIPPED AND GLORIFIED is a clear repudiation of the pneumatomachian position. The insistence that the Spirit is to be worshiped and glorified together with the Father and Son (the phrase is almost a direct quote from St. Athanasius)[22] clearly implies that the Spirit is one in being with the Father and Son, though it does not use the term *homoousios*. The doctrine was hard enough for many of the homoeousians to swallow without making it more unpalatable by coating it with unacceptable terminology.

Throughout the history of the Arian controversy, the Eastern fathers from Athanasius to the Cappadocians emphasized that the issue was not simply the matter of speaking accurately about the Godhead, but also the matter of affirming a truth about the nature and destiny of human beings. It was (and is) a question about our sanctification. Often with a reference to baptism, the Greek fathers argued that the Holy Spirit is God because only God can truly deify us.[23]

The irony—or better, the tragedy—in this pneumatomachian phase of the Arian controversy is that Holy Spirit whom St. Paul had presented as the principle of unity in the Christian community had become the cause of division and controversy. The irenic spirit behind the wording of the Symbol of Constantinople went a long way toward restoring unity in the church, but it was not long, as we shall see in the next chapter, before the third article of the Creed became itself the center of controversy and an occasion for the schism between Eastern Orthodoxy and Western Christendom that endures to the present.

Notes

1. Joseph Ratzinger, *Introduction to Christianity* (New York: Herder and Herder, 1970), p. 255.

2. Graymoor Lecture.

3. See *JBC*, vol. 2, pp. 742–743.

4. Yves Congar, *I Believe in the Holy Spirit* (New York: Seabury Press, 1983). I, p. 30. Henceforth *I Believe*.

5. He ascribes a variety of functions to the Holy Spirit that often stand in such sharp contrast to one another that it is impossible to define exactly what Spirit [*pneuma*] meant to Paul. "His lack of clarity," writes Joseph Fitzmyer, "should be respected for what it is and be regarded only as the starting point of the later development" (*JBC*, vol. 2, p. 814).

6. Jn 7:38–39 identifies the Spirit with "living water," which suggests that Paul's unique comparison to drink probably refers to baptism. William F. Orr and James A. Walther, *I Corinthians: Introduction with a Study of the Life of Paul, Notes, and Commentary*, The Anchor Bible, 32 (Garden City, NY: Doubleday and Co., 1976), p. 284.

7. Examples of other lists are 1 Cor 12:28–31; Rom 12:6–8; Eph 4:11–12. See also Eph 2:20 and 3:5.

8. *JBC*, vol. 2, par. 52, p. 266.

9. He later tries to restrict prophecy by women. See *JBC*, vol. 2, par. 81, p. 272; Anchor Bible, 32, p. 312–313.

10. Congar, *I Believe*, II, p. 180.

11. Kilian McDonnell considers this phenomenon at great length in *Charismatic Renewal and the Churches* (Garden City, NY: Doubleday and Co., 1976). See also Congar, *I Believe*, II, p. 173–177.

12. McDonnell, *Charismatic Renewal*, p. 223.

13. *Sacramentum Mundi* 3:55.

14. For other triadic texts in Paul, see 1 Cor 2:7–16; 6:10–11; Rom 5:1–5; 15:30; Eph 1:11–14,17.

15. Markus Barth, *Ephesians: Translation and Commentary on Chapters 4–6*, The Anchor Bible, 34A (Garden City, NY: Doubleday and Co., 1974), pp. 462–467.

16. McDonnell, *Charismatic Renewal*, pp. 199–200. See Charles Kannengiesser, "Athanasius of Alexandria and the Holy Spirit between Nicea I and Constantinople I," *Irish Theological Quarterly* 49:3 and 4 (1981):167–180.

17. *On the Spirit*, ch. 1 (*NPFN* 2nd Ser. VIII, p. 3).

18. Anthony Meredith, "The Pneumatology of the Cappadocian Fathers and the Creed of Constantinople," *Irish Theological Quarterly* 49:3 and 4 (1981):196–211.

19. Ibid., p. 206.

20. Reinhart Staats, "The Nicene-Constantinopolitan Creed as a Foundation for Church Unity?" *Irish Theological Quarterly* 49:3 and 4 (1981):213.

21. Ibid., p. 215.

22. Kelly, *Creeds*, p. 347.

23. Congar, *I Believe*. III, p. 75.

16

Principle of Unity,
Cause of Division:
the "Filioque"

"Who proceeds from the Father and the Son"

As we have seen throughout this work, the Symbol of Constantinople holds a unique place in Christendom. It is the Creed most widely regarded as *the* authoritative expression of the apostolic faith. In the Eastern Orthodox churches it came to displace all other creedal formulations, while in Western Christendom it is used regularly alongside the so-called Apostles' Creed. Despite its wide acceptance, however, the Creed of Constantinople has become not a basis for church unity but a cause of contention.

In addition to the clauses considered in the preceding chapter, Constantinople affirmed, "We believe in the Holy Spirit, . . . who proceeds from the Father." The procession of the Holy Spirit, long an integral part of the Nicene Faith, is based on the text in John's Gospel. "But when your advocate has come, whom I will send you from the Father—the Spirit of truth that issues from the Father—he will bear witness to me" (Jn 15:26, NEB). The Orthodox churches of the East

255

have remained fiercely attached to the language of the Constantinopolitan Creed, while the Latin church unilaterally inserted the term *filioque*, by which it affirmed that the Spirit PROCEEDS FROM THE FATHER *AND THE SON*, not simply from the Father.

Although we now see that the issues that brought about the schism between East and West are broader and deeper than the addition of a single word to the Creed, the *filioque* became the focal point for many of the differences that divide the churches. The controversy has been continuous since the ninth century when Photius, the Patriarch of Constantinople, accused the Latin church of heresy because of the *filioque*. Latins minimized the issue, claiming the difference between themselves and the Greeks was mainly one of terminology. Nonetheless, the *filioque* was and is a major obstacle to communion between the East and West, and it is for that reason that the Faith and Order Commission of the World Council of Churches organized a series of consultations to study the disputed term.[1]

Theologians currently engaged in ecumenical discussions on the *filioque* distinguish three issues: 1) the divergent approaches to the Trinity in the traditions of East and West; 2) the meaning of *filioque* and its significance in the Creed; and 3) the standing of the Creed of Constantinople as a witness to the apostolic faith. This last point will be the subject of Chapter 24. Here our concern is to provide some background for an understanding of points one and two. In the context of the third article of the Creed we attempt to summarize the circumstances and reasons that caused the Latin church to insert the term into the Creed in the first place. Next we summarize insofar as possible how the *filioque* became a bone of contention between Constantinople and Rome. Finally, we discuss the theology of "the double procession" in the context of the different ways in which Eastern and Western theologians approach the Trinity.

THE WEST ADDS "FILIOQUE" TO THE CREED

The *filioque* was probably added to the Creed in the last decade of the sixth century in Spain and Gaul, where the Creed had come to be recited in the Sunday Mass as a way of eradicating any lingering vestiges of Arianism.[2] According to the usual account, the Third Council of Toledo in A.D.589, with the express intention of repudiating the Arianism that still flourished among the Visigoths in Spain, introduced *filioque* into the Creed.[3] Although there is reason to doubt that the council made any change in the Symbol of Constantinople, it did state:

> Whoever does not believe in the Holy Spirit, or does not believe that He proceeds from the Father and the Son, and denies that He is coeternal and coequal with the Father and the Son, let him be anathema.[4]

However the term was introduced, it was accepted in good faith as an expression of the Nicene faith and did not become an issue until the time of Charlemagne, almost two centuries later.

The rule of Charlemagne spanned almost a half century (768-814) and extended over most of Western Europe. Very nearly deserving of the reputation that history and legend have since bestowed on him, Charlemagne was both servant and master of the church. He set himself up as "the pious overseer of the bishops" (as he was called by a medieval chronicler).[5] For reasons known only to himself and his advisers, he chose to make the *filioque* something of a personal cause, and he took every opportunity to flaunt it before representatives of the Eastern church.

In the 780s when Charlemagne was extending his power in the West, the effective ruler in Constantinople was the vice-regent Irene, who ruled in the name of her young son, Constantine VI (780-797). The Byzantine empire, which never managed to separate politics and theology, was again sharply divided, this time over the issue of icons. Constantine's immediate predecessors were aggressive iconoclasts: they outlawed images of Christ, Mary, and the saints, and destroyed icons wherever they appeared. Their policy, an affront to the devotional practices of ordinary Christians, angered the monks, stirred opposition in cities, especially in the capital, and strained relations with Rome.

Irene set herself to reversing imperial policy. Determined to resolve the iconoclast controversy at home and to restore normal diplomatic relations with the West, she summoned the Second Council of Nicea (787). Known in history as the seventh ecumenical council, Nicea II restored the cult of images, declaring:

> . . . the representations of the precious and life-giving cross, and the venerable and holy images as well . . . must be kept in the

holy Church of God . . ., in houses and on the roads, whether they be images of God our Lord and Saviour Jesus Christ or of our immaculate Lady the Mother of God, or of the holy angels and of all the saints and just. For the more frequently one contemplates these pictorial representations, the more gladly will he be led to remember the original subject whom they represent. . . .[6]

Of more immediate importance to the history of the *filioque*, Nicea II was also the occasion for the oath of the new Patriarch Tarasius, like Irene an iconodule. In the course of confessing the traditional faith, Tarasius professed that he believed "in the Holy Spirit, Lord and giver of life, proceeding from the Father through the Son." Upon learning of his declaration, Charlemagne protested to Pope Hadrian I (772-795) that "through" (*per*) does not have the same meaning as "from" (*ex*). Although Adrian assured him that Tarasius's formula conformed to the teaching of the church fathers, Charlemagne was not convinced. A short time later (790 or thereabouts) another Carolingian document accused the Greeks of having suppressed the *filioque*. In 794 Charlemagne convoked a provincial council at Frankfurt that condemned the workings of Nicea with its cult of images (which Frankfurt misrepresented) and proclaimed the *filioque* official teaching.

Leo III, who meanwhile had succeeded Hadrian as bishop of Rome (795-816), found himself in an awkward position between Constantinople and Aix-la-Chapelle. Despite pressure from Charlemagne he defended the actions of Nicea II and refused to insert *filioque* into the Creed in Rome. (In a note of some historical interest to students of the Creed, Leo added that it was not the custom of the Roman church to sing the Creed at Mass but to use it only for instructional purposes.)[7]

A few years later, toward the end of 808, the issue erupted again in an unlikely quarter. A Greek monk of the monastery of St. Sabas in Jerusalem noticed that liturgical books used in a Frankish monastery on the Mount of Olives included the *filioque*. Accused of heresy by the Greek monk, the Franks appealed to the pope in Rome, who in turn wrote to Charlemagne. The latter called on theologians to justify the Western teaching, and he summoned a council of his own bishops to legitimate the practice. Meeting at Aix-la-Chapelle in November of 809, the council decreed that the *filioque* expressed Catholic teaching and ordered it to be retained in the Creed sung at Mass. Charlemagne again tried to persuade Pope Leo III to insert the *filioque* into the

Creed, and again the pope refused. Although Pope Leo was in basic agreement with the theology of the two processions, he wanted to publicize his fidelity to the received text of the Creed. He had the Creed *without* the *filioque* engraved in Greek and Latin on two silver scrolls and hung on each side of the entrance to the *confessio* in St. Peter's Basilica.

It was another two centuries before the Creed, including the *filioque*, was introduced into the Mass in Rome during the pontificate of Pope Benedict VIII (1012-24). Benedict, an able warrior who thwarted Moslem incursions into Italy, was indifferent to church affairs. He paid lip service to reform to gain the support of the Germanic emperor, Henry II, who had inherited the title that had once belonged to Charlemagne. According to an eyewitness account, Henry was astonished to learn that Roman custom excluded the chanting of the Creed in the eucharistic liturgy. It was explained that the Roman church had no need to affirm its orthodoxy because it had never been tainted with heresy! Apparently the emperor was not convinced; Henry insisted, and Benedict complied in ordering the Creed (with the *filioque*) to be sung in public Masses.[8]

Charlemagne had made the *filioque* an issue in the Western church, where it was more a question of liturgical practice and uniformity than one of doctrine. His criticism of the Greeks, however, was more serious. In accusing them of heresy for having suppressed the *filioque*, Charlemagne exhibited a widespread and longstanding suspicion of the Greeks, born of ignorance of Eastern theology. Worse still, he had sown seeds of controversy and schism that were to bear bitter fruit a half century later when Photius became patriarch of Constantinople and that have been causing ecclesiastical indigestion ever since.

THE PHOTIAN SCHISM: CONSTANTINOPLE VS. ROME

The *filioque* controversy as it divides East and West dates from the time of Photius, patriarch of Constantinople (858-867 and 878-886), a man of great learning and problematic character, honored as a saint in the Orthodox church and for a long time denounced as schismatic in the West. Photius, a layman when he was appointed to the patriarchate, was never very secure in his position. His predecessor, Ignatius, had resigned under pressure, and political intrigue in the Byzantine capital twice caused Photius to be deposed. (Photius was living in a monastery when he died, probably in 891.) He found himself at odds with Pope Nicholas I (858-867) over the circumstances of his appointment and over the evangelization of the Bulgars. In fact, the Bulgarian confrontation was the immediate cause of the *filioque* controversy.

In an attempt to extend the Latin sphere of influence, Pope Nicholas sent two missionary bishops to Boris, the Bulgarian king. Finding themselves in competition with Greek missionaries, the Latins criticized certain customs of the Byzantine church and, to dramatize the differences between East and West, introduced the *filioque* into the Creed. The Byzantines, reacting vehemently to what they regarded as an encroachment into their territory, in turn denounced Latin practices and customs, including the *filioque*. Pope Nicholas himself fueled the controversy by sending a harsh letter to Photius that so infuriated the Byzantine patriarch that he convoked a synod in 867 to deal with the issues. It was in this atmosphere of conflict and personal affront that Photius wrote his famous encyclical denouncing Latin ignorance and errors, including his charge that the Latins had corrupted the Creed by adding the *filioque*.[9]

Some time after 886, when Photius had been deposed for the second time, he composed the work that became the primary source for ideas and arguments used by opponents of the doctrine of the two processions. He begins the *Mystagogy of the Holy Spirit* by quoting the classic text: "The Spirit of truth who comes from the Father . . . will bear witness on my behalf" (Jn 15:26). To say that the Spirit proceeds also from the Son, according to Photius, is to substitute personal opinion for divine revelation. One modern commentator says of the work,

> Photius' doctrine on the procession of the Holy Spirit being only from the Father is rigorous, comprehensive and convincing. It is a pity, however, that because of his strong polemical manner in discussing this issue, he was prevented from treating the subject thoroughly. Thus he does not fully discuss the procession of the Holy Spirit through the Son, even though it was a traditional teaching of the previous Greek Fathers.[10]

Given this oversight and neglect of his own tradition, it is indeed a pity that Photius' *Mystagogy* should have had such lasting influence upon the Byzantine attitude toward the *filioque*. In retrospect, his strongest argument upholding the procession of the Spirit "from the Father only" seems to be based more on dialectical reasoning than on biblical or patristic grounds.

The next major flare-up in the controversy came in the eleventh century during the patriarchate of Michael Cerularius (1043-58). Perhaps the most powerful ecclesiastic in the history of Byzantium, Cerularius claimed for Constantinople the primacy that was traditionally the prerogative of the Roman see. Papal legates sent to Constantinople by Leo IX (1049-54) excommunicated the patriarch, who in response convoked a synod. The synod met in July 1054, condemned the papal legates as imposters, and, following word for word Photius' encyclical of 867, repudiated the *filioque*. There was, however, one new element in the controversy. Whereas Photius noted with approval that the popes had resisted including the *filioque* in the Creed, the synod now criticized Rome for corrupting the Creed and teaching unsound doctrine because in the meantime, as we have seen, Benedict, succumbing to pressure from the German emperor, had added the *filioque* to the Creed used in the Eternal City. Contrary to legend, however, the incident did not mark the beginning of the schism between East and West. If anything, it awakened the Western church to the reality that schism was already a fact.[11]

Subsequent attempts to heal the breach provoked a bitter polemic over differences between Byzantine and Latin liturgy and theology. But of all the grievances, the *filioque* remained the principal complaint of the Greeks against the Latin church; it was the chief topic at the "reunion councils" of Lyons (1274) and Florence (1439). In both cases the Greek representatives, pressured by the Byzantine emperor, who needed to curry the favor of the West for military reasons, grudgingly accepted the Latin position as well intentioned if not entirely sound. In both cases, the agreement worked out at the top was not accepted by the majority of Greek clergy and people and therefore served more as temporary relief than as lasting remedy for the painful schism.

EASTERN AND WESTERN APPROACHES TO THE TRINITY

As long as the controversy over the procession of the Holy Spirit is unresolved, the *filioque* will remain an insurmountable obstacle on the road to church unity. Were it not for a shared faith in the workings of the Spirit, the history of the mistrust and bickerings between East and

West would be cause for despair. As ecumenical dialogue replaces polemical tracts, however, one sees a glimmer of hope in a new outlook on the issues. Today theologians recognize that the quarrel over the *filioque* is rooted in the different ways in which Greeks and Latins approached of the Tri-unity of the Godhead. Although they set out for the same destination on the journey to safeguard the mystery of the Holy Trinity, their points of departure took them along different paths.

The French theologian Theodore de Regnon (d. 1893) is credited with being first among the moderns to bring some fresh insight into the writings of the Latin and Greek Fathers. He said succinctly, "The Latin theologian says: 'three persons in God,' whereas the Greek says: 'one God in three persons.' "[12] As we shall see below, the Latins begin by emphasizing the unity of the divine nature (*ousia*) and then struggle to explain how the persons of the Blessed Triad differ among themselves. The Greeks, on the other hand, take as their point of departure the differentiation of the persons (*hypostases*) and then struggle to explain how they function together in perfect unison—how they form not simply a union but a unity. While each approach has its positive aspects, each also has inherent difficulties: there is in the Latin approach an inherent danger of modalism, while in the Greek approach there is the danger of subordinationism.

Arianism had forced theologians in the East to explore a different set of issues. Until the time of Nicea, Christian thinkers and preachers reflected on the Trinity almost exclusively in the context of the economy of salvation—revelation and redemption. After Arius they could no longer consider the "economic" Trinity apart from the related questions regarding the immanent Trinity. Because of the way the Arians posed the Trinitarian question, Greek theologians were forced to focus first on the identity of the Son vis-a-vis the Father and later, on the Holy Spirit vis-a-vis the Father and Son.

From the time of the Cappadocians onward, the Greek fathers were intent on affirming the irreducible distinctiveness of each of the divine hypostases of the Father, Son, and Holy Spirit and, at the same time, the uniqueness of the Father as the sole principle (*arche*), source (*pege*) and cause (*aitia*) of the divine nature.[13] While the Greeks could use such expressions as "from the Father through the Son" to describe the procession of the Holy Spirit, they could not accept the Western formula that this procession is "from the Father and Son." In their minds the *filioque* compromises the uniqueness of the Father by making the Son also principle, source, and cause of the Spirit's divinity.

In the ninth century Photius made reconciliation of the two approaches even more difficult when, not satisfied with reaffirming the procession of the Spirit from the Father, he effectively denied the Son's role by declaring, "The Spirit proceeds from the Father *alone*." Thus after Photius when the Greeks speak of the Holy Spirit as proceeding "through the Son," they refer to the "manifestation" of the Spirit, denying any causal mode of being. The Holy Spirit, they say, does not derive divine essence from the Father and Son but from the hypostasis of the Father, whose distinctive property is to "bring forth" the divine essence in the other persons.[14]

In the West, Trinitarian theology developed in a different direction that was largely unaffected by the issues raised at Nicea I. It followed along a path charted, though not originated, by St. Augustine. Already about 200, Tertullian, engaged in controversy with various forms of monarchianism, provided a basic Trinitarian vocabulary—*trinitas*, *substantia*, *persona*—that influenced even the East. Hilary of Poitiers (d. 367) and Ambrose of Milan (d. 397), in turn, transported important ideas of Eastern theology into the West—Hilary influenced by Athanasius, and Ambrose by the Cappadocians. Augustine had read Tertullian, Hilary, and Ambrose and was also familiar with the work of a lesser-known writer, C. Marius Victorinus (d. after 362), who, like himself and Tertullian, was of African origin. Victorinus, a neo-Platonist, had written an anti-Arian treatise that seems to have shaped Augustine's basic approach to Trinitarian theology. Despite his interest in the Trinity as an existential mystery closely linked to the working of grace in his life, Augustine, influenced by neo-Platonists such as Victorinus and by his own interest in philosophy, pursued the study of the Triune God apart from the Incarnation and the economy of salvation.[15] He addressed the issues raised by Sabellius in the third century and the Arians in the fourth, but his chief preoccupation was to explain how God, who is one in essence, is nevertheless identified with three distinct persons.

Ultimately, St. Augustine spent twenty years (399-419) writing and rewriting his treatise *De Trinitate*. He began by refuting the Arian position on the basis of the biblical texts[16] and then proceeded to use reason to disprove the arguments of "the heretics." Finally, in the latter half of the treatise (Books VIII-XV), Augustine described a number of images that he believed help us to understand the inner dynamic of the Trinity and the way the Persons relate to one another. He analyzed a series of triads structured in the human spirit that became classic images to illustrate the compatibility of threefold activity grounded in a single essence. One of the best known is Augustine's example of inseparable unity of the Lover, the One loved, and the Love that binds them. This unity is, he says, "the hinge" on which the rest of his discourse rests (Bk VIII, chs. 10, 14). Augustine identifies other ways in which the human spirit illustrates, in the unity of the same essence, a threefold distinction between one stable consciousness of self, one act of knowledge, and one movement of love that mirrors in some remote way the distinction between Father, Word, and Spirit.[17]

Augustine's pneumatology is contained in his Trinitarian theology and vice versa. He acknowledges that some who find it hard to accept the Catholic position regarding the Triune God have a particular difficulty as to the manner in which the Holy Spirit is in the Trinity, "whom neither the Father nor the Son, nor both, have begotten, although He is the Spirit both of the Father and the Son" (Bk I, ch. 5:8). He does not use the word *filioque*, but he clearly stakes out his position regarding the two processions from the Father. The Spirit is from the Father and the Son; thus, he concludes that if the Spirit proceeds from the Father as the Scriptures indicate (Jn 15:26),the Spirit must also be said to proceed from the Son (Bk IV, ch. 20:29; V, ch. 11:12; 14:15).

Almost as if to compensate for his neglect of the Holy Spirit in the early part of the work, Augustine again turns to the issue of the procession of the Holy Spirit toward the end of *De Trinitate*. He takes pains to insist that there are no intervals of time by which it could be said that the Son was born of the Father first, and then afterward the Holy Spirit proceeded from both. He is equally careful to stress that the property by which the Son is co-principle of the Spirit derives entirely from the Father (Bk XV, ch 26:45,47). Although in places Augustine's language indicates that the Spirit proceeds *per filium*, he says, "The Holy Spirit does not proceed from the Father into the Son, and from the Son proceed to sanctify the creature, but proceeds at once from both" (ch. 27:48). He cites the tradition by which the Son is said to be begotten—generated—by the Father, while the Spirit proceeds, and he acknowledges that it is most difficult to explain the difference between "generation" and "procession." In sum, Saint Augustine's *De Trinitate* marked a definite advance in the development of the Latin tradition. He not only affirmed the consubstantiality of God the Father, God the Son, and God the Spirit, but he clarified how the Holy Spirit is the Spirit of the Son as well as of the Father.

Although the teaching that the Spirit proceeds from the Father and the Son was not unknown in the East, it was not, as we have seen, generally accepted. Another idea uncommon among the Greeks but widely accepted in the West because of Augustine is the notion of the Holy Spirit as communion of Father and Son.[18]

> And the Holy Spirit, according to the Holy Scriptures, is neither of the Father alone, nor of the Son alone, but of both; and so intimates to us a mutual love, wherewith the Father and the Son reciprocally love one another.[19]

In the writings of the scholastics, Augustine's Trinitarian theology was crystalized into a formal system that became the standard teaching in the West. Medieval theologians from Anselm onward, though differing among themselves on some points, developed the theme identifying the mutual love that binds the Father and the Son as the distinctive property of the Spirit. Thomas Aquinas, for example, was one of many who spoke of the Spirit as *amor unitivus duorum*—"the love that unites the two." The formalized dialectic characteristic of medieval scholasticism brought the Augustinian tradition to a new level of refinement and, in the process, made dialogue with the East increasingly difficult.[20]

St. Augustine himself was aware that the Latin approach to the Trinity differed from that of the Greeks, but, like most Western theologians who do not have firsthand knowledge of the Eastern tradition, he seemed to think that the differences were merely verbal, not substantial. Modern theologians, brought together by ecumenical concerns rather than divided by polemical arguments, recognize that the protracted controversy that has swirled around the *filioque* is a tangled web of piety and politics, theology and suspicion. Pneumatology, inseparable from Trinitarian considerations, touches on every expression of Christian prayer and action, thought and feeling. The earliest witness to the Holy Trinity is found in baptismal formulas, and the first attempts at a Trinitarian theology are represented in the ancient doxologies that praise and bless the Father, Son, and Spirit. In the West the doxology is seen primarily as a prayer—a hymn of praise. In the East it is the expression *par excellence* of Christian life. Augustine's concern to emphasize that the Holy Spirit is the Spirit of the Son as well as of the Father was deeply rooted in Western spirituality—a spirituality that emphasizes the Incarnation. Eastern spirituality, having its consummate expression in the many forms of doxology, is always explicitly Trinitarian.[21]

THE "FILIOQUE" IN ECUMENICAL DIALOGUE TODAY

Is there a solution to the *filioque* controversy? The Anglican church, which began studying the issue in the nineteenth century, voted in 1985 to delete it from the text of the Creed. Theologians in other churches, including Roman Catholics, also favor deleting it as an ecumenical gesture.[22] If indeed the disputed phrase was simply the catalyst for different spiritualities and theologies of the Christian experience, both of which are legitimate, then the presence or absence of the *filioque* in the Creed will not heal the scandalous schism that separated Latins and Greeks. Is it too much to hope that the present ecumenical dialogue can re-create a climate of respect and trust like the one that existed in the time of the Athanasius and Hilary, the Cappadocians and Augustine, when, despite their differences, East and West maintained communion with each other?

Notes

1. Lukas Vischer, ed., *Spirit of God, Spirit of Christ. Ecumenical Reflections on the "Filioque" Controversy*. Faith and Order Paper No. 103 (Geneva: World Council of Churches, 1981). Henceforth *Spirit*.

2. Yves Congar, *I Believe in the Holy Spirit* (New York: Seabury Press, 1983), III, p. 53. Dietrich Ritschl says *filioque* was in liturgical use in Spain (against Priscillianism?) in the early fifth century. See Vischer, *Spirit*, p. 49.

3. Wulfila, a protege of Eusebius of Nicomedia, evangelized the Germanic peoples settled along the banks of the lower Danube. The "apostle of the Goths," as he is called, invented a Gothic alphabet,

translated the Bible, and introduced the Homoean Creed (360) among them. The Visigoths carried this homoean brand of Arianism with them as they moved westward and eventually established a Visigothic kingdom in Spain. St. Leander, bishop of Seville (c. 577–600), is credited with weaning the Visigoths away from Arianism. He presided at the Third Council of Toledo, where they formally embraced the Catholic faith expressed in the Symbol of Constantinople.

4. Quoted in Kelly, *Creeds*, pp. 361–362.

5. Henri Daniel-Rops, *The Church in the Dark Ages* II (Garden City, NY: Doubleday and Co., 1962), vol. II, p. 136.

6. J. Neuner and J. Dupuis, eds., *The Christian Faith in the Doctrinal Documents of the Catholic Church*, revised edition (Staten Island, NY: Alba House, 1982), nn. 1251–52, p. 359.

7. Kelly, *Creeds*, p. 366.

8. Ibid., p. 357.

9. Other examples of Latin ignorance and error cited by Photius were: Latins fast on Saturdays, they eat dairy products on the three days immediately preceding Ash Wednesday, they look down on married clergy, and they do not recognize confirmation given by a priest. See Jaroslav Pelikan, *The Spirit of Eastern Christendom (600–1700)* (Chicago: University of Chicago Press, 1974), pp. 170–172.

10. Markos Orphanos, "The Procession of the Holy Spirit According to Certain Later Greek Fathers," in Vischer, *Spirit*, p. 25.

11. *NCE* 2:945.

12. Quoted in Congar, *I Believe* III, p. xvi. Congar appreciates de Regnon's insight but warns against applying it uncritically—III, pp. 83–84.

13. Vischer, *Spirit*, p. 11; Pelikan, *Eastern Christendom*, pp. 183–199.

14. Vischer, *Spirit*, pp. 12, 27.

15. Congar, *I Believe*, I, pp. 77–80, III, pp. 80, 83.

16. Augustine used the old Latin version of the Scriptures; as a result his exegesis is frequently not substantiated by the original Greek. See *NPNF* 1st Ser. III, p. 14.

17. Congar, *I Believe*, III, p. 89, following Fulbert Cayré, lists eight such triads offered by Augustine.

18. Ibid., I, pp. 85–92; III, p. 88.

19. Bk XV, ch. 17:27, *NPNF*, III, p. 215.

20. Congar, *I Believe*, III, pp. 96–127.

21. The theology of grace illustrates from one aspect the different emphases in Western and Eastern spirituality, the former primarily christocentric, the latter Trinitarian.

22. Congar, *I Believe*, III, pp. 204–207.

17

The Inspired Word

"He has spoken through the prophets"

Montanus is an all-but-forgotten name in the pages of church history. He was overshadowed even in his own time by Marcion and Valentinus, who were more or less his contemporaries. According to some historians, if it were not for the fact that Montanism attracted to its ranks Tertullian, the foremost Latin writer of the early third century, Montanus would not be remembered at all. But this is to make light of one who, though he left no written work or lasting movement that bears his name, is a prototype of the charismatic prophet who appears over and over in the history of Christianity. His teaching differed greatly from gnosticism and from that of Marcion. The former corrupted the Christian mysteries by introducing foreign elements from Oriental cults; the later distorted the gospel by detaching it from, and even pitting it against, the Old Testament. Montanus—and the same can be said of Tertullian after him—was bent on holding to Christian doctrine in its entirety and on protecting its adherents from the corruption of the world.

In order to understand the appeal of Montanus and charismatic figures like him, it helps to recall the tradition of prophecy in the church. In his Pentecost sermon, Peter, appropriating a text from Joel, announced that a new era had arrived. "I will pour out a portion of my spirit on all mankind: your sons and daughters shall prophesy. . ." (Acts 2:17). St. Paul lists prophecy high among the gifts of the Spirit (see Chapter 15, above), and early writings from the *Didache* to St. Irenaeus testify to the prominence of prophets in the Christian community of the second century. St. Justin in his "dialogue" (which was in fact more a polemic) with the rabbi Trypho pointed to the prophetic charisms in the church as evidence that these gifts were transferred from the Jews to the Christians. The prestige of the prophets, who were endowed with the gift of interpreting the sacred mysteries of God, inevitably gave rise to false prophets—illusionaries and charlatans— who claimed powers they did not possess. Many of the same writings, notably the pastoral Epistles, the *Didache* and the *Shepherd of Hermas*, which exalted the role of prophecy, also warned against false prophets.

While the role of prophet as messenger and spokesman (in Hebrew, *nabi*) for God is familiar enough to Christians, we often overlook the fact that the prophet has traditionally provided the best analogy and chief model for biblical inspiration, which is attributed in a particular way to the Holy Spirit.[1] It is the latter truth as much as any other that is affirmed in the creedal phrase which characterized the Holy Spirit as the one who HAS SPOKEN THROUGH THE PROPHETS. J. N. D. Kelly cites 2 Peter 1:21 as an indication that the affirmation is rooted in the primitive kerygma; the words appear in the Apology of St. Justin, dated about A.D.150; and by the time of Cyril of Jersualem (c. A.D.350) they had a secure place in the baptismal creeds.[2] On the one hand the phrase conjures up the prophetic tradition in the church, and on the other it leads us to reflect on the Scriptures as the word of God.

> There is no prophecy contained in Scripture which is a personal interpretation. Prophecy has never been put forward by man's willing it. It is rather that men impelled by the Holy Spirit have spoken under God's influence. (2 Pet 1:20-21)

As this text suggests, from the beginning the church had to be vigilant in safeguarding the integrity of the gospel message. In this chapter we look at the role of the Old Testament prophets and how their messages came to be written down and regarded as the word of God par excellence. We also outline the formation of the biblical canon as one way the church defended the faith against misrepresentation. We conclude with a few notes about Montanus and Joachim of Fiore, who, each in his own way, distorted the gospel message and misrepresented the way the Holy Spirit speaks through the prophets.

PROPHETS AND PROPHECY

The Biblical Tradition   In the popular mind a prophet sees into the future and predicts what will happen. In the biblical tradition, however, the principal role of the prophet was to speak for God, to make known the divine will, and only secondarily, if at all, to foretell future events. It was not as a fortune-teller that the prophet predicted what was to come. Rather, God actually invested the prophetic word with a power that rendered it a dynamic element, first in Israel, later in the church. Backed by the Spirit of God, prophecy became a force in its own right that made it self-fulfilling; but, as John L. McKenzie remarks, "fulfillment" is more than seeing a prediction come true. "It is the fulfillment of a hope, a destiny, a plan, a reality."[3] Furthermore, the prophets seldom concerned themselves with detail; as messengers of God they looked to the grand design and dealt with specifics only in the light of God's plan of salvation.[4]

God spoke to the prophets and through them to the people of Israel. It was their task constantly to remind Israel that the nation was not just another political entity in the world of geopolitics, but that it had a special purpose and destiny as God's chosen people. The prophets served as the conscience of Israel, cajoling, threatening, and reprimanding the people and their leaders for the their lack of trust, for their frequent lapses into idolatry, and especially for their taking advantage of the helpless—orphans, widows, migrants. In the eyes of Israel's rulers the prophets were troublemakers; King Ahab, for example, looked upon Elijah as "the disturber of Israel" (1 Kgs 18:17). Nonetheless, one prophet after another arose to call the nation back to the terms of the covenant that Yahweh had made with Abraham, Israel, and David.

The prophets kept alive the stories of Israel's beginnings. They repeated the account of the Exodus, which engendered trust that Yahweh, who in times past had rescued them from slavery in Egypt, would continue to protect them. They pointed to the fate of the Caananites to show how God visits terrible destruction on Israel's enemies. During the period of the exile in Babylon, when the fortunes of the Jews were at their lowest and their hopes were shattered, the prophet Ezekiel romanticized the reign of King David—"the good old days"—and created the expectation that "the day of the Lord" would come with another king who would initiate a new era of peace and justice. Prophets were traditional, not in the sense that they desired to reconstruct the past, but in the sense that they used the primal traditions of Jewish history to explain the present.[5]

More concerned about current events than about events yet to happen, the prophets became agents of change. It was their charism to reinterpret history in such a way that tradition continued to provide the base on which to build for the future. Samuel moved Israel from tribalism to a kingship; at a time when Israel's royal line was threatened with extinction, Isaiah assured Ahaz that it would endure (albeit in a form that neither anticipated); when a small fragment of Jews was all that was left of once-mighty Israel, Ezekiel told of a new Jerusalem and another temple; at the height of Seleucid domination the Book of Daniel announced its demise and the emergence of a new kingdom not of human origin. The charism that distinguished the true from the false prophet, as in the case of Jeremiah and Hananiah, was the former's ability to discern which sacred traditions applied in a particular situation (see Jer 28).[6] From this, one infers that prophecy is the word of a living God who, as Lord of the present and future, cannot be boxed in by a rigid adherence to the past.

Jesus was in the tradition of the great prophets. Just as Moses designated Joshua to carry on his work and as the mantle of Elijah fell on Elisha, so Jesus took up where John the Baptist left off.[7] The Spirit of God was with him, and Jesus revealed the Father's will. Although he did not use prophetic formulas (e.g., "Thus speaks Yahweh") Jesus made known God's hidden purpose, determined before all ages, "to bring all things in the heavens and on earth into one under Christ's headship" (Eph 1:10). Jesus did not abolish the Law and prophets (Mt 5:17) but unveiled new levels of meaning in the traditions of Israel. More concerned about the spirit than the letter, he interpreted the Scriptures, applying them to circumstances and situations the original authors could not have anticipated. Like the prophets of old, Jesus was the voice of conscience. He reassured the troubled, but he troubled the complacent and the self-righteous. He promised mercy to those who would repent and retribution to those who would not.

The Compulsion to Write: Inspiration   The charism of the prophet was to *speak* the word of God. The Old Testament prophets employed every form of rhetoric imaginable: from lamentation to love song, from wise sayings to dialogue. They declaimed the word of God like orators, they announced it as messengers, they taught in the form of oracles. And when the spoken word would not do, they dramatized Yahweh's message with symbolic actions, as when Isaiah walked barefoot and naked as a portent of what was to befall Egypt and Ethiopia (Is 20:1ff) and when Ezekiel used a clay table to sketch a picture of Jerusalem under siege (Ez 4:1-8). Like Isaiah and Ezekiel, Jeremiah left a rather detailed description of his call, and all three make it clear that their mission was to *speak* on behalf of God to the people of God.

In describing their commission none of the prophets says anything about being told to commit Yahweh's message to writing. It was left to disciples of the prophets to collect the sayings of their mentors and preserve them for posterity. Nor did Jesus bequeath us any writings; the evangelists had the task of collecting his sayings and the stories about him. In a day when manuscripts were copied by hand and most people could not read, people "heard" the Scriptures. Paul, for example, in writing to the church at Thessalonica, asks that the letter be read to all the brethren (1 Thess 5:17). And similarly he requested that the letter he sent to the church at Colossae be read also to the congregation at Laodicea (Col 4:16). In the second century St. Justin confirmed that it was the practice in the Sunday liturgy to read passages from the Gospels—"the memoirs of the apostles"—and the writings of the prophets "as much as time permits."[8] The distinction between the so-called writing prophets, whose declarations we read in books that bear their names, and other prophets such as Nathan and Elijah, whom we can only read about, is not of itself a measure of their importance in the history of Israel. Whether or not they are recorded, the words of every true prophet are inspired of God. It was because the early Christians and, before them, the Jews regarded prophecy as the preeminent expression of the word of God that they referred to the Scriptures simply as the "law and the prophets." In the sense that they received the word of Yahweh and announced it to their people, even Abraham (Gen 2:7), Aaron (Ex 7:1), Miriam (Ex 15:20), many elders (Nm 12:6-8; Dt 34:10; 18:15-19) and Moses himself (Nm 11:16,24-26) are called prophets.

Moreover, when the Creed says that God in the person of the Holy Spirit SPOKE THROUGH THE PROPHETS it refers not only to Old Testament prophets but to members of the Christian community who had that charism. The significance of the preposition "through" should not be overlooked: prophets are messengers; their message is God's word, not their own. It is in this vein that the author of 2 Peter wrote, as we have seen, "There is no prophecy contained in Scripture which is a personal interpretation. Prophecy is not put forward by man's willing it. It is rather that men impelled by the Holy Spirit have spoken under God's influence" (1:20-21).

It was customary for medieval theologians to include in their treatment of prophecy some consideration of the Spirit's influence on the biblical authors. Although "inspiration" once applied to all promptings of the Holy Spirit, including grace, in contemporary theology it has taken on a technical meaning: inspiration denotes the special charism given to the authors of the Bible impelling them *to write*. They may have enjoyed other charisms: they may or may not have had the gift of prophecy; they may or may not have been given special revelations; but inspiration is the gift of the Spirit that influenced their literary effort.

Because of this movement of the Spirit we speak of "inspired writers" and "inspired writings." The Second Vatican Council in one of its most important documents, the Constitution on Divine Revelation (*Dei Verbum*), attributes everything asserted by the inspired writers to the authority of the Holy Spirit. Therefore, ". . . it follows that the books of Scripture must be acknowledged as teaching, firmly, faithfully, and without error that truth which God wanted put into the sacred writings for the sake of our salvation" (*Dei Verbum*, 11). By emphasizing "for our salvation" the Council wished to make it clear that biblical inspiration guarantees the accuracy of only those teachings that touch on the mystery of salvation. The Council echoes the words of St. Paul, who once reminded his protege Timothy,

> . . . from your infancy you have known the sacred Scriptures, the source of the wisdom which through faith in Jesus Chrsit leads to salvation. All Scripture is inspired by God and is useful for teaching—for reproof, correction, and training in holiness so that the man of God may be fully competent and equipped for every good work. (2 Tim 3:15-17)

Although the Holy Spirit impelled the sacred authors to write and even prompted them regarding the contents of what they wrote, the Spirit did not so override their natural talents as to make them robots. Just as their literary styles indicate the personal interests and abilities of the writers, so their reporting of facts betrays the culture of the times. Inspiration does not mean the biblical authors had access to some secret source of historical information and scientific data unknown to others of the time. In relying on historical records and folklore they were, as we know today, sometimes misinformed regarding the names of people and places, not to mention dates and other facts that have no direct bearing on our salvation.[9]

Furthermore, ". . . holy Scripture must be read and interpreted according to the same Spirit by whom it was written" (*DV*, 12). Since God speaks to us in a human fashion through the biblical authors, we must try to perceive what the inspired writers intended and what God wanted to teach by means of their words. From this understanding of biblical inspiration Vatican II drew several corollaries concerning the interpretation of sacred Scripture. 1) In searching out the intention of the biblical writers we must, among other things, identify the "literary forms" in which a particular book or text is written. Is the author writing history of one kind or another, prophecy, poetry, or using some other type of speech? 2) In interpreting a biblical passage we must pay due attention to "the customary and characteristic styles of perceiving, speaking, and narrating which prevailed" at the time when it was written. 3) We must examine the parts of the Bible in the context of the whole, and take into account the living tradition of the church "along with the harmony which exists between elements of the faith" (*ibid.*).

Paul's Epistles to Timothy are among his so-called pastoral Epistles—the letters that contain practical insights, counsels, directives, and doctrines useful to one charged with the care of a Christian community (in Timothy's case, Ephesus). But Paul's reflections on the part that Scripture played in Timothy's personal life apply to all Christians. The classic passage that put the Word at the cutting edge of a person's life is, however, found in the Epistle to the Hebrews:

> Indeed, God's word is living and effective, sharper than any two-edged sword. It penetrates and divides soul and spirit, joints and marrow; it judges the reflections and thoughts of the heart. (4:12)

SAFEGUARDING THE MESSAGE

"Canonizing" the Scriptures   Faced with an unending series of heretics who tried to legitimize their teachings by citing books of dubious origins, the Christian community found it necessary to compile an official list of sacred books—a "canon." In order to assure the pristine purity of the Gospel, the church began to be more precise as to which authors and writings give faithful witness to the traditional Gospel. There was precedent for this in the list of sacred writings recognized as authentic in Judaism. Until recently it was commonly held that the Jews had two such canons: a shorter one drawn up in Palestine by the rabbis at Jamnia, and a longer one in use in Alexandria, represented by the Septuagint (usually abbreviated LXX). It was this Alexandrian canon that was said to have to have been adopted by the early Christian community.[10]

The composition of the Old Testament was a slow process that took 1000 years and more. There was an accumulation of material into books and then into collections of books. The Hebrew Bible classifies the sacred books under three headings: the Law, the Prophets, and the Writings. Each division seems to represent a stage in the development of the canon. Until a few years ago scholars generally agreed that the Palestinian canon was given definitive form by a group of learned rabbis at Jamnia (a town west of Jerusalem, near the Mediterranean). With the discovery of the Dead Sea Scrolls and new interpretations of other evidence, however, it now seems that the Hebrew canon was not rigidly fixed until the end of the second century or early third century of the Christian era.

The name "Septuagint" refers to the Greek translation of the Old Testament. It is the form in which the Old Testament books were most widely known in the early church; it has been the liturgical text of Eastern Christians throughout the centuries. It takes its name from the Latin word for seventy (= *septuaginta*) because of an ancient legend that tells how a band of seventy-two scholars (six from each tribe) were sent to Egypt to make a Greek translation of the Jewish Law for the famous library at Alexandria.[11] It now seems that the Jews in Alexandria did not establish a canon of Hebrew writings on their own but that, like Jews elsewhere, they accepted the one fixed by the rabbinical schools in Palestine in the late second century. The Septuagint in so far as it represents an exclusive canon of Old Testament writings seems rather to have been the composition of the Christian community in Alexandria.[12]

Similarly the New Testament canon developed gradually, but over a shorter period of time.

The Muratorian Fragment, a mutilated piece of parchment of some eighty-five lines, gives an account of the sacred writings accepted by the church in Rome. Discovered by a scholarly Italian archivist, L. A. Muratori,[13] in 1740 in the Ambrosian Library at Milan, the work was thought until recently to date from the second century and thus to be the oldest witness to the New Testament canon that has survived the ravages of time. Although some would date the document as late at the fourth century, nonetheless it gives us some insight into why it was thought necessary to form an official list of books. After listing the Epistles of St. Paul, the Fragment continues,

> There is in circulation also one to the Laodicenes, another to the Alexandrians, both forged in Paul's name to suit the heresy of Marcion, and several others, which cannot be received into the Catholic Church; for it is not fitting that gall be mixed with honey.

The document cites "the Apocalypse of John" and makes a garbled reference to the Apocalypse of Peter, "which some of our friends will not have read in the Church." Then it concludes,

> But the Shepherd was written quite lately in our times in the city of Rome by Hermas, while his brother Pius, the bishop, was sitting in the chair of the church of the city of Rome; and therefore it ought indeed to be read, but it cannot to the end of time be publicly read in the Church to the people, either among the prophets, who are complete in number, or among the Apostles.

In conclusion it mentions the gnostic Valentinus, of whom "we receive nothing at all." Similarly, a new Book of Psalms composed for Marcion, and works by the gnostic Basileides and Montanus are rejected.[14]

From the Muratorian Fragment as well as from the writings of St. Irenaeus and others it appears that Marcion, in a negative way, was a principal cause of the compilation of the canon. His rejection of the Old Testament in favor of a truncated collection of Christian writings consisting of Luke's Gospel and ten Pauline Epistles represented a radical departure from the gospel. Thus an official list of accepted writings had the twofold function of ensuring the integrity of Christian teaching and rejecting others that distorted its meaning. According to the Fragment, the works of "the Asian founder of the Cataphrygians"—Montanus—could not be accepted because no addition could be made to the prophets, "who are complete in number, or among the Apostles."

Although the Muratorian Fragment does not explicitly state the criteria whereby a work is judged to be acceptable in and by the church, it suggests three rules of thumb: 1) orthodoxy; 2) liturgical usage; and 3) apostolic origin. In themselves these norms were neither rigid nor precise, but taken together they reenforced one another and justified acceptance of a book by the Christian community. Apostolic origin assured the Christian that a work reflects the faith and experience of the earliest disciples who witnessed to the death-resurrection of Jesus and had its meaning revealed to them. Today historians and biblical scholars assume the responsibility of ascertaining the date of composition of the New Testament books, but in the second century it was enough to link them to the names of particular apostles (though in fact it may have been their disciples who did the actual writing, as in the case of Matthew and John). Habitual usage, particularly in the liturgy, of certain writings helped secure a place for them in the canon. We have already noted that Paul recommended that his Epistles be circulated among the churches and read in their assemblies (Col. 4:16); and, according to St. Justin, by the middle of the second century writings of the apostles were being read in conjunction with the Old Testament in the Christian liturgy. As the Muratorian Fragment indicates, however, there existed writings which, though they carried the names of apostles, were not read in the liturgy because they were considered forged (e.g., Paul's epistles to the Laodicenes and the Alexandrians) or, in an obvious reference to their dubious orthodoxy, because "it is not fitting that gall be mixed with honey."

The New Testament canon was assembled by trial and error over a relatively long period of time. Some books that were accepted early on (e.g., the Epistle of Barnabas) were rejected later; other works, once excluded, were later accepted (e.g., the Book of Revelation). By the year 200 the four Gospels, thirteen Pauline Epistles, Acts of the Apostles, the First Epistle of Peter and the First Epistle of John were almost universally accepted; and by the end of the fourth century, all twenty-seven books that form today's New Testament canon were generally recognized. The official list of twenty-seven books was ultimately determined on the basis of the collective experience of the church (see *DV*, 8). The lists of St. Athanasius, St. Augustine, and the two African councils of Hippo (393) and Carthage (397) indicate that by the end of the fourth century the church was well on its way toward reaching a consensus regarding the New Testament canon. It was only in 1546, however, that the Council of Trent, in opposition to Protestant Reformers, solemnly stated the Catholic position regarding which books should be included in the Bible. It named as canonical forty-five books in the Old Testament (Lamentations, which brings the number to forty-six, was considered a part of Jeremiah) and twenty-seven books in the New Testament.

The main difference between the Catholic and Protestant Bibles is found in the make-up of the Old Testament canon. The Council of Trent in effect recognized the Alexandrian canon, while Protestant Reformers opted for the shorter (thirty-nine books) Palestinian canon. The latter contains only the earliest canonical ("protocanonical") works, while the former includes later writings (termed by Catholics "deuterocanonical" and by Protestants, "apocrypha"). Many Protestant versions of the Bible group the apocrypha or deuterocanonical books in a special section at the end of the Old Testament. Luther's translation of 1534 included the apocrypha with the note, "These are books which are not held equal to the Sacred Scriptures and yet are useful and good for reading."[15] These works are especially helpful in understanding late Judaism and the theological context for many New Testament teachings. Today Protestant and Catholic scholars alike discover that certain New Testament doctrines such as the resurrection of the dead, angelology, and the concept of retribution were latent in the deuterocanonical works or apocrypha.

The authority of the Bible in the church rests on the fact that its contents are inspired: that its authors were impelled by the Holy Spirit to write what they did. The norm of the biblical canon—the official list of writings assembled and accepted by the church—affirms their inspiration. Vatican II stated it this way:

> Those divinely revealed realities which are contained and presented in sacred Scripture have been committed to writing under the inspiration of the Holy Spirit. Holy Mother Church, relying on the belief of the apostles, holds that the books of both the Old and New Testament in their entirety, with all their parts, are sacred and canonical because, having been written under the inspiration of the Holy Spirit (cf. Jn 20:31; 2 Tim 3:16; 2 Pet

1:19-21; 3:15-16) they have God as their author and have been handed on as such to the Church herself. *(DV,* 11)

"Hold Fast to the Tradition"   From the beginning, the church was constrained to safeguard the integrity of the gospel message. Even before the gnostics and Montanus there were individuals who gave the Scriptures a "personal" interpretation, as the text from 2 Peter indicates. St. Paul felt it necessary to warn the Galatians about those "who wish to alter the gospel of Christ." Paul, by temperament and training given to strong language, directed his strongest rhetoric, not against sinners who because of weakness or confusion failed to live up to their calling, but against teachers who perverted the teaching of Christ.

> For even if we, or an angel from heaven, should preach to you a gospel not in accord with the one we delivered to you, let a curse be upon him! I repeat what I have just said: if anyone preaches a gospel to you other than the one you received, let a curse be upon upon him! (Gal 1:8–9)[16]

The gospel that he preached is not to be tampered with, says Paul, because it is "no mere human invention" but a "revelation from Jesus Christ" (Gal 1:11,12). Like the prophets before him, St. Paul was conscious that he was speaking the word of God: "We thank God constantly that in receiving his message from us you took it, not as the word of men, but as it truly is, the word of God at work within you who believe" (1 Th 12:13). Although the Epistle to the Hebrews refers to the Old Testament when saying God "spoke through the prophets," Ephesians clearly points to prophets of the New Testament: "I know," writes the author, "what I am talking about in speaking of the mystery of Christ, unknown to men in former ages but now revealed by the Spirit to the holy apostles and prophets" (3:14–15). The New Testament frequently pairs the apostles with the prophets. The Epistle to the Ephesians, for example, describes the church "as a building which rises on the foundation of the apostles and prophets, with Christ Jesus himself as the capstone (2:20).

Throughout his writings, Paul grounded his teaching on "the gospel of God which he promised long ago through his prophets, as the holy Scriptures record—the gospel concerning his Son. . ." (Rom. 1:1-3). He explained the mystery of salvation and its implications for Christian attitudes and behavior. The gospel message is not merely a report—a description—of the saving power of God; it is that power in action. The person who accepts the gospel—"the word of life" (Phil

2:16)—is saved. There is nothing mechanical or magical about it; it is a matter of allowing the Spirit to work within us. On the other hand, the gospel of which Paul speaks represents an accepted body of teachings. Apparently a corpus of distinctively Christian beliefs had begun to take shape very early, for already in one of his earliest Epistles Paul writes, "Hold fast to the traditions you received from us either by word or letter" (2 Thess 2:15).

In the later Epistles that bear his name, however, Paul sees a threat to the integrity of the gospel and shifts his emphasis to preserving the faith whole and intact as it was received from the apostles (1 Tim 1:3–5; 2 Tim 3:1–9; Tit 1:10–15; 3:10–11). Similarly the letters published under the names of Peter and Jude sound an alarm against false teachers. They reflect conditions in the church in the early part of the second century, more and more distant in time from Jesus and the apostles. The author of Second Peter, for example, writes:

> I am writing you this second letter dear friends, intending them both as reminders urging you to sincerity of outlook. Recall the teaching delivered long ago by the holy prophets, as well as the new command of the Lord and Savior preached to you by the apostles. Note this first of all: in the last days, mocking, sneering men who are ruled by their passions will arrive on the scene. (3:1–3)

The author wishes to strengthen the faithful against false teachers by reminding them of the instruction in his earlier letter:

> This is the salvation which the prophets carefully searched out and examined. They prophesied the divine favor that was destined to be yours. They investigated the time and the circumstances which the Spirit of Christ was pointing to, for he predicted the sufferings destined for Christ and the glories that would follow. They knew by revelation that they were providing, not for themselves but for you, what has now been proclaimed to you by those who preach the gospel to you, in the power of the Holy Spirit sent from heaven. (1 Pet 1:10–12)

The Paraclete   As the Christ, Jesus was at once the fulfillment of prophecy and the greatest of the prophets. In departing he promised, "I will ask the Father and he will give you another Paraclete—to be with you always. . ." (Jn 14:16). Jesus spoke several times of the Paraclete in his farewell discourse, and the condition for the coming of this new advocate seems to have been Jesus' own return to the Father (Jn 16:7). "Paraclete," a title peculiar to the Johannine writings, is close to the Greek *parakletos*, which has many meanings. "Paraclete" suggests a helper, friend, interpreter, consoler, witness for the defense, and advocate. Raymond E. Brown has compiled a list of all the texts where the word appears in John's Gospel and concludes that the Paraclete has two basic functions: 1) the Paraclete comes to the disciples and dwells with them, guiding and teaching them about Jesus; and 2) the Paraclete accuses the world and condemns it for its false values and sin—specifically, for unjustly sentencing Jesus to death.[17]

The portrait of the Paraclete in the Johannine Gospel bears a striking resemblance to Jesus. Virtually every quality ascribed to the Paraclete has a parallel in what was said of Jesus. Jesus himself says that the Father will send *another* Paraclete, thus clearly indicating that his own mission was that of a "paraclete," with all the complex connotations that this title carries. The Paraclete will come, sent forth by the Father just as Jesus came, sent into the world by the Father. It is said that the disciples will know the Paraclete and the Paraclete will remain with them, much as it was said that the disciples were privileged to know the Son, who will remain with them. The Paraclete will guide the disciples along the way of all truth; Jesus is the way of truth. The Paraclete will bear witness; Jesus bears witness (Jn 8:14). The reaction of the world to the Paraclete will be much the same as the world's reaction was to Jesus. The world does not know or accept the Paraclete, much as it remained ignorant of Jesus' true identity and rejected him (5:43; 12:48).

In many ways the Paraclete is to Jesus as Jesus is to the Father: just as the Paraclete is sent in Jesus' name, so Jesus came in the name of the Father. "Thus," writes Brown, "the one whom John calls 'another Paraclete' is another Jesus."[18] The Paraclete is the presence of God in the world when Jesus ascends to the Father. In his farewell discourse Jesus revealed that this Paraclete is in fact the Holy Spirit. He said, "The Paraclete, the Holy Spirit whom the Father will send in my name, will instruct you in everything, and remind you of all that I told you" (14:26). The Paraclete will not teach novel truths or a new revelation but will witness to the full meaning of Jesus' mission and revelation:

> When he comes, however, being the Spirit of truth he will guide you to all truth. He will not speak on his own, but will speak only what the hears, and will announce to you the things to come. In doing this he will give glory to me, because he will have received from me what he will announce to you. (Jn 16:13-14)

Thus the role of the Holy Spirit is twofold. Speaking through the Old Testament, the Spirit announces the coming of God's Anointed, the Christ, and then as Paraclete makes the presence and teaching of Christ a continuing reality in the world until Christ comes again in glory.[19]

MONTANUS AND JOACHIM OF FIORE

As we noted at the outset of this chapter, the prestige that prophets enjoyed in the early church, combined with the Jesus' promise to send the Paraclete into the world, helps explain the appeal and rapid spread of Montanism in the second century. Sometime about 170, Montanus, recently baptized, claimed the gift of prophecy and called Christians to withdraw from the world in preparation for the imminent Second Coming of the Lord. Two of his early followers, Priscilla and Maximilla, also given to ecstatic utterances and prophecy, separated from their husbands to prepare themselves for the parousia. (In the eyes of the Montanists, marriage is the strongest bond that ties men and women to the world.) Their prophecies stirred enthusiasm, and the reputations of the three—Montanus, Priscilla, and Maximilla—rapidly spread from their native Phrygia to other regions of Asia Minor, to Syria in the East, and as far west as Lyons and Carthage.[20]

At first the movement, seen as an outpouring of the Spirit, taught no new doctrine; but then Montanus began presenting himself as the Paraclete incarnate, the Holy Spirit promised by Jesus, who had come to guide the church to all truth and to prove the world wrong about sin, justice, and judgment (see Jn 16:8-13). The Montanists claimed new revelations that went beyond the teachings of Jesus, and they found themselves increasingly at odds with established Christian communities. The bishops realized the threat. Though tolerant toward the rigorous ascetical practices of the Montanists (intensive fasting, celibacy) and even toward their millennarianism, church leaders could not suffer a message that claimed to go beyond the gospel and to introduce a new hierarchy based on prophetism. The bishops of Asia Minor convoked a series of synods—the first in the history of the church—that condemned the "new prophecy," as the Montanist movement was called.

It is to Montanus' credit that, two centuries before the Council of Constantinople, he highlighted the role of the Holy Spirit. On the debit side, however, his pretending to be the Paraclete incarnate was crude and the teachings of the "new prophecy," exaggerated. In claiming new revelations he compromised the unique and central role of Christ in the mystery of salvation.

In some ways Montanus anticipated, by a thousand years, the work of Joachim of Fiore (c. 1132–1202), who proclaimed an Age of the Spirit. Dante describes Abbot Joachim as endowed with a prophetic spirit—*di spirito profetico dontato*. A native of Calabria in southern Italy, Joachim joined the Cistercian Order (a reformed branch of the Benedictines), became an abbot, and later founded a new monastery at Fiore, where he and his followers observed monastic life according to the strictest rules. During his lifetime Abbot Joachim had a reputation for preaching and sanctity, but after his death, when his writings began to circulate throughout Europe, he became known more for his apocalyptic ideas. Although he recognized a harmony in the texts of the Old and New Testaments, he held to a progressive notion of revelation. He believed that the two testaments would be succeeded by a third period, a new age with a new order of spiritual understanding. He linked each age to a particular person of the Trinity.

The first age, in which humanity lived under the Law until the end of the Old Testament dispensation, is the age of the Father. The second, the age of the Son, covers the New Testament dispensation, which is lived under grace. Joachim thought this second age would last for forty-two generations of thirty years each and then give way to the age of the Spirit, the age of the "eternal gospel" or the "gospel of the kingdom," characterized by "the New Law," freedom of the Spirit. The people and events featured in the New Testament prefigure realities in the age of the Spirit. In Joachim's triadic scheme of history, the first age was symbolized by the order of the laity—married couples; the second by the clergy; and the third by monks, contemplatives, and "spiritual men." According to Joachim, St. Benedict had inaugurated the third age, and other religious orders would arise to bring it to fulfillment with the establishment of the "spiritual church."

Joachim's doctrine of the Trinity was condemned by the Fourth Council of the Lateran (1215),[21] and his teaching on the three ages would probably have been forgotten were it not for the Franciscans. Friar Gherardo of Borgo San Donnino and a group of "spiritual Franciscans" interpreted Joachim's ideas to apply to their Order, which they saw as a sign of the spiritual church. They were condemned (and along with them, Joachim's teaching on the three ages) by popes and theologians alike, but the Joachimite doctrine held a great attraction for the followers of St. Francis, who saw in their founder the spiritual man par excellence. (Nor was it lost on the friars that Joachim's chronology for the apperance of the spiritual church coincided with the growth of the Order.) Thomas Aquinas was one of the theologians critical of Joachim. He condemned the good abbot on several points, including his view regarding the New Law. Aquinas argued that the regime of the New Testament is that of Christ and Spirit together. It is the final age, the definitive state, after which there can be no other.[22]

Like many before and after him, Joachim misunderstood the nature and purpose of the Book of Revelation. The writer of that book, much like Daniel (see Chapter 13) addresses his message to the oppressed and persecuted, people who need consolation and reassurance. It is not intended to "unveil" (the literal meaning of revelation) future events but to make known the significance of current happenings in light of the gospel. Implicit in the condemnation of Joachimite teaching was the guiding principle of Catholic, perhaps of all Christian theology, later made explicit by Vatican II: that the parts of the Bible are to be interpreted in the context of the whole. Thus the anticipated apocalypse must be interpreted in the light of the gospel, the Book of the Revelation in the context of the rest of Scripture, not vice versa.

Although it did not have Montanus and Joachim in mind, the Second Vatican Council reaffirmed the principle "The Christian dispensation (*oeconomia*), as the new and definitive covenant, will never pass away" (*DV*, 4). In Christ the work of salvation is complete. In him we have the fullness of revelation, the manifestation in the Word of God who is with us to free us from the darkness of sin and death. In that the Christ event represents the fulfillment of what was spoken through the prophets, it is an end, but that does not mean that at some point God arbitrarily ceased speaking and acting in history. It is true that after the incarnate Word there is nothing more to say or do, and it is precisely for this reason that nothing comes after him. The Christian dispensation is final. Subsequent history cannot pretend to surpass what has taken place in Christ. Jesus accomplished the plan of salvation "through His words and deeds, His signs and wonders, but especially through His death and glorious resurrection from the dead and final sending of the Spirit of truth" (*ibid*).[23]

The Holy Spirit, WHO HAS SPOKEN THROUGH THE PROPHETS, continues to witness to the Christ event in the pages of Scripture and in the Christian community, the church, out of which the Bible grew and for which it was written. It is to a consideration of the church that we turn in the next chapter.

Notes

1. Luis Alonso Schokel, *The Inspired Word: Scripture in the Light of Language and Literature* (New York: Herder and Herder, 1965), pp. 19–20; 91–97. Shokel (p. 91) reminds us that Thomas Aquinas, like other medieval scholastics, did not write a treatise on inspiration; rather, he treated the matter in his tract on prophecy.

2. Kelly, *Creeds*, pp. 72–73, 341.

3. John L. McKenzie, *Dictionary of the Bible* (New York: Macmillan Publishing Co., 1965), p. 698.

4. Schokel, *Inspired Word*, p. 354.

5. Paul J. Achtemeier, *The Inspiration of Scripture: Problems and Proposals* (Philadelphia: Westminster Press, 1980), pp. 124–131.

6. Achtemeier, ibid., pp. 86–87. J. L. McKenzie, *Dictionary*, p. 697.

7. Raymond E. Brown, *The Gospel According to John XIII–XXII*. The Anchor Bible, 29 A (Garden City, NY: Doubleday and Co., 1970), p. 1138.

8. *Apology* I, 66:3, 67:3.

9. Alois Grillmeier in Herbert Vorgrimler, ed., *Commentary on the Documents of Vatican II* (Montreal: Palm Publishers, 1968), vol. III, pp. 199–215.

10. Contemporary biblical scholars generally agree that the Old Testament canon was not fixed until the Christian era. In fact, some suggest that the rivalry offered by Christian writings caused the Jewish rabbis to compile a list of recognized writings. Others, however, suggest that the canon was drawn up because of disputes within

Judaism itself, particularly between the Pharisees and Jewish sects that were apocalyptically minded. *JBC*, vol. 2, 67:30, p. 521.

11. *JBC* vol. 2, 69:52–79, pp. 569–574.

12. *JBC*, vol. 2, 67:38–41, pp. 522–523.

13. The priest Lodovico Antonio Muratori (1672–1750) advocated freedom for historians and scientists in scholarly research, even in questions of religion. His moderately reformist ideas, especially with regard to the cult of the saints, provoked attacks on his orthodoxy, but he was protected by Pope Benedict XIV, with whom he corresponded. *NCE* 10:81.

14. The English translation quoted here is from J. Stevenson, *A New Eusebius: Documents Illustrative of the history of the Church to A.D. 337* (London: S.P.C.K., 1963), pp. 144–146.

15. Quoted in the *JBC*, vol. 2, 67:44.

16. "Let him be accursed" translates the Greek *anathema*, which becomes the standard formula used by church councils and ecclesiastical authorities to denounce heretics and error. The Greek suggests the idea of casting out, rejection. In medieval canon law anathematization was distinguished from excommunication: the latter meant exclusion from the sacraments and worship, whereas the former implied complete separation from the church body. *Oxford Dictionary of the Christian Church*, ed. F.L. Cross (London: Oxford University Press, 1966), p. 48.

17. *John*, pp. 1135–36; 1141.

18. Ibid., p. 1141.

19. Pope John Paul II describes the role of the Holy Spirit saying, the Paraclete "will help people to understand the correct meaning of the content of Christ's message . . . he will ensure continuity in the midst of changing conditions and circumstances. The Holy Spirit, then, will ensure that in the church there will always continue the same truth which the apostles heard from their master." Encyclical Letter, The Holy Spirit in the Church and the World, *Dominum et Vivificantem*, par. 4. (*Origins* 16:4 [June 12, 1986]:80).

20. Jules Lebreton and Jacques Zeiller, *Heresy and Orthodoxy* Book II of the History of the Early Church (New York: Collier Books, 1962), pp. 61–69; 263–265.

21. *DS* 803–807.

22. Congar, *I Believe*, I, pp. 128–129.

23. In commenting on par. 4 of *Dei Verbum*, Karl Rahner points out that the Council was more concerned to reaffirm that God's plan of salvation was fully revealed in the death and resurrection of Christ than in fixing the exact date for the close of public revelation. Thus Vatican II chose not to repeat the axiom that "revelation was completed with the death of the last Apostle"—a phrase that is often misunderstood. K. Rahner, "The Death of Jesus and the Closing of Revelation," *Theology Digest* 23:4 (Winter 1975):320–329.

18

From Community to Ecclesiology

"We believe in [the] church"

It is not by chance that Yves Congar, one of the most influential Catholic theologians of our time, crowned his career with a three-volume work entitled *I Believe in the Holy Spirit*. Congar, best known for his studies on the church, has been called "the most important ecclesiologist of this century."[1] When we examine even his earlier works we find that pneumatology is at the heart of Congar's ecclesiology: he sees the church first and foremost as the work of the Holy Spirit. For Congar, pneumatology is more than simply a dogmatic treatise on the Third Person of the Trinity. It is also more than, and, he says, "different from" an in-depth analysis of the indwelling and sanctifying activity of the Holy Spirit in individual souls. Pneumatology should, he writes,

> describe the impact, in the context of a vision of the Church, of the fact that the Spirit distributes the gifts as he wills and in this way builds up the Church. A study of this kind involves not simply a consideration of those gifts or charisms, but a theology of the Church.[2]

At the beginning of the second volume of his trilogy Congar writes, "However far we go back in the sequence of confessions of faith or creeds, we find the article on the Church linked to that on the Holy Spirit."[3] Thus we take our cue from the ancient creeds so that after reflecting on the Spirit in the previous chapter we now turn our attention to the church. In recent years ecclesiology, more than any other area of theology, has generated a vast corpus of literature—articles, surveys, monographs, official statements, etc. Even before the Second Vatican Council, the church had become a focal point for theology. Then with the Council, focused as it was on the nature and mission of the church, ecclesiology attracted the attention of all Catholic theologians, no matter what their speciality.

Within the space of this volume it is impossible to consider all aspects of the church, even in summary fashion. We limit ourselves first to a brief description of the primitive church and to an overview of the images used in patristic writings to describe the nature and mission of the church. These considerations are preliminary to a discussion of Vatican II and the conciliar documents. Our principal interest, as will become evident at the end of the chapter, is the church as the sphere of activity of the Holy Spirit. The influence of Yves Congar will be evident throughout this discussion.

THE PRIMITIVE CHURCH

The Jerusalem Community   From Easter Sunday onward, the disciples experienced the outpouring of the Holy Spirit (Jn 20:23). The coming of the Spirit transformed a band of men and women who honored the memory of Jesus of Nazareth into a community of believers who, in faith, were convinced that they were saved.

> When the kindness and love of God our Savior appeared, he saved us; not because of any righteous deeds we had done, but because of his mercy. He saved us through baptism of new birth and renewal by the Holy Spirit. This Spirit he lavished on us through Jesus Christ our Savior that we might be justified by his grace and become heirs, in hope, of eternal life. (Tit 3:4-6)

Although the first Christians banded together for prayer and shared their goods, in its early years the community in Jerusalem did not see itself as distinct from Judaism.

> They went to the temple area together every day, while in their homes they broke bread. With exultant and sincere hearts they took their meals in common, praising God and winning the approval of all the people. Day by day the Lord added to their number those who were being saved. (Acts 2:46-47)

The Christians, as they would come to be called, formed a community within the larger Jewish community. The Christian community represented a way of life. As Gentiles became members of the community, the new way gradually became an occasion of tension and division, separating Christians from the Jewish establishment.

The identity of the Christian community was most obvious to members and outsiders alike when, gathered for prayer, they saw themselves as an assembly (in Greek *ekklesia*) of the saved, the word that is etymologically and conceptually at the origin of "church." As we have seen (Chapter 14), "church" appears only twice in the synoptic Gospels (Mt 16:18; 18:17), but it is common in the Acts of the Apostles (twenty-three times) and even more common in the Pauline corpus (sixty-five times). In Acts, church refers to the Christian community in a particular place—a "local church"—and usually to the Jerusalem community. In Paul's Epistles *ekklesia* refers most often to local churches, but Paul also applies it to a specifically liturgical meeting (1 Cor 11:18; 14:23,24) and in the "captivity Epistles"—Ephesians and Colossians—he extends its meaning to cover the worldwide assembly of Christians.

The Greek word *ekklesia* embodies two meanings that are not self-evident in the English translation "church." First, as we shall see, it translates the Hebrew word *qahal* and thereby presents the church in continuity with the Old Testament notion of "People of God." It is not a restricted group—a sect—but a people, a concrete reality, formed not by agreement among its members but by the work of the Spirit. This is implicit in the second meaning, which links the reality of the assembly to the priority of the *call*. Men and women who hear the "good news" and give themselves to Christ respond to a call—a summons—from God. Thus the church is a *convocation* before it is a *congregation*.[4]

Church Offices and Ministries   In the eyes of Roman officials, Christianity was first a sect within Judaism and later another mystery religion from the East that undermined imperial authority and the moral fiber of the empire. From the outside the church looked like a secret society with its own organization and government. Although the organization of the local churches varied somewhat, early in the second century a uniform pattern was beginning to emerge. Presiding over the Christian community in each city was a supervisor (Greek = *episcopos*), whom we know in English as the "bishop." St. Ignatius of Antioch gives a vivid picture of the place of the bishop in the community about A.D. 100. Sentenced to be devoured by wild beasts in Rome, the bishop of Antioch was able to visit a number of the churches in Asia Minor—Ephesus, Magnesia, Tralles, Philadelphia, Smyrna—en route to his execution in the Eternal City. He wrote a series of "farewell" letters that are invaluable for the information they give about the internal conditions of the early Christian communities. To the church at Magnesia he said,

> I exhort you to strive to do all things in harmony with God: the bishop is to preside in the place of God, while the presbyters are to function as the council of the Apostles, and the deacons, who are most dear to me, are entrusted with the ministry of Jesus Christ.[5]

The bishop presides over the liturgy—baptism, agape, eucharist—sanctions marriages, and teaches the faithful. In short, the episcopal office is the focal point of the community, and to be in communion with the bishop is a safeguard against error and heresy and unites one to Christ, "the bishop of all" (*Magnesia* 3:1).

As time went on and the number and size of the churches increased, the priesthood took on increased importance. Although Christians remained a small minority in the Roman Empire until the time of Constantine, their numbers in large cities such as Rome necessitated the establishment of ecclesiastical centers under the care of priests. Known in Rome as *tituli* (presbyterial "titles"), these centers marked the beginning of parish churches. Furthermore, the third century was the time of the great persecutions. With the bishops forced into hiding, imprisoned, and executed, priests took a more direct role in church governance. In addition to their responsbilities for instructing the faithful and preparing the catechumens for baptism and penitents for reconciliation, priests presided at eucharistic celebrations, whereas previously they had only concelebrated with the bishop.[6]

The deacons, who, in the words of St. Ignatius, "were entrusted with the ministry of Jesus Christ," had a prominent part in the temporal administration of the church as assistants to the bishop. In the liturgy they read the Scriptures and baptized catechumens. By the third century they were delegated to watch over external discipline and manage the temporal affairs of the church, especially seeing that the poor were cared for. It was the custom even in the larger churches, Rome included, to limit the number of deacons to seven, doubtless in imitation of the seven "deacons" appointed to care for the Greek-speaking members of the Jerusalem church (see Acts 6:1-6).

Again, as the number of Christians increased and the demands of ministry became more time consuming, other ministries were given formal recognition. Among the earliest of these institutionalized ministries was the office of lector: individuals were singled out and charged with the public reading of the Scriptures. In large population centers the instruction of catechumens was entrusted to catechists (Latin = *doctores audientium*). The division of labor, however, differed from place to place. In the Latin-speaking church of the West, there were subdeacons and acolytes (neither of them were found in the Greek church) who shared in various ways in the ministry of the deacons. At one point in the West, burial of the dead, considered a particular ministry, was entrusted to a group called *fossores*—literally "gravediggers"—who also functioned as funeral directors. Two other ministries still recognized in Canon Law are the ministries of exorcists and porters; in the early church the former were charged with praying over those possessed by demons, and the latter, whose modern descendants function as ushers, guarded the doors of the church against intruders.[7]

Frequent mention is made of deaconesses in the early church, though they seem to have enjoyed more prominence in the churches of the East than in the West. St. Paul speaks of Phoebe, "our sister who is a deaconess of the church at Cenchreae" (Rom 16:1) and, in what is generally admitted as another reference to deaconesses, describes the qualifications they should have for their ministry (1 Tim 3:11). The ceremony in which they received their charge was similiar to that in which the deacons were ordained. The deaconesses instructed women catechumens and assisted at their baptism. They kept order in the women's section of the liturgical assembly and were present when bishops, priests, or deacons had reason to interview women. In monophysite and Nestorian communities deaconesses were known to have read the Scriptures in liturgical celebrations and to administer the eucharist to women.[8]

FROM IMAGES TO ECCLESIOLOGY

Images of the Church   To outsiders the church appeared simply as another religious movement, and it was regarded with suspicion by the Roman authorities. Insiders, however, never saw the church as a mere organization or social movement; they did not regard it simply as another mystery religion or even as a reform movement within Judaism. For Christians the church is a manifestation of *the People of God*; it is also the *Body of Christ* and the *temple of the Holy Spirit*. Other New Testament images fill out the picture of the church as the source and sustainer of life—the vine, the sheepfold, etc.—and early on, Christians began to speak of the church as *mother of the faithful*.

Jesus had reinterpreted the meaning and mission of Israel so that even Gentile Christians saw themselves as being of the elect of God and belonging to *the People of God*. The First Epistle of Peter, thought by many to incorporate an early baptismal liturgy (1:3—2:10), speaks to the faithful:

> You are "a chosen race, a royal priesthood, a holy nation, a
> people he claims for his own to proclaim the glorious works" of
> the One who called you from darkness into his marvelous light.
> Once you were no people, but now you are God's people; once
> there was no mercy for you, but now you have found mercy. (2:9-
> 10)

The New Testament clearly sees the baptized as the new Israel; it applies to the church the Old Testament refrain "I will dwell with them and walk among them. I will be their God and they shall be my people" (2 Cor 6:16). The church is the eschatological community, the fulfillment of the prophecy in Jeremiah which foretold a new covenant (Heb 8:8-12, note verse 10); it is also the sign of the New Jerusalem, where God shall dwell among the inhabitants, "and they shall be his people and he shall be their God who is always with them" (Rev 21:3).

As the People of God image links the church to Israel, *the Body of Christ* image relates the church to the Risen Lord. The metaphor is distinctively Pauline, and it is important to note that Paul uses the same word "body" (Greek = *soma*) when speaking of the *risen* body of Christ, of the church as the Body of Christ and of the eucharist as the Body of Christ (a point we shall discuss in Chapter 22).[9] The image of the Body of Christ, like the allegory of the vine in John's Gospel (15:1-18), implies that Christians as members of the body share the life of Christ. The body image pictures an organic unity that joins the members to one another and to Christ, the head. It is the image that Paul uses to emphasize that, though the offices and charisms in the church are many and diverse, the church is one (1 Cor 12:12). It is also the image he uses to remind Christians of their call to personal integrity in matters of sexual behavior: "You must know that your body (= *soma*) is a temple of the Holy Spirit, who is within—the Spirit you have received from God. You are not your own" (1 Cor 6:19).

Paul attributes the unity that exists in the Body of Christ—the members with one another and with Christ—to the Holy Spirit (1 Cor 12:4). "It was in one Spirit," he writes, "that all of us, whether Jew or Greek, slave or free, were baptized into one body" (1 Cor 12:13). Another of Paul's images for the church is a building—*a holy temple* of the Lord, a "dwelling place for God in the Spirit" (Eph 2:20-22). In reprimanding the church at Corinth for its immorality Paul wrote, "Are you not aware that you are the temple of God and that the Spirit of God dwells in you?" (1 Cor 3:16). Just as Jesus spoke of his body as a temple, the church is the temple where the presence of God is a reality visible to the eyes of faith.[10]

Mother Church   We cannot properly speak of an ecclesiology in the second and third centuries because Christian writers of the period did not reflect systematically on the church's nature and mission. For the faithful the church was an object of affection, a symbol of God's presence, a sign of divine acceptance, a community of men and women who shared a vision and a way of life. They looked on the church as *a loving mother* who nourishes life in the spirit. The church at Lyons, decimated by persecution in 177, spoke of the martyrs as children who went home in peace to God without saddening their mother. Tertullian's deep feeling for the church is evident especially in his pastoral writings. He speaks of "Lady Mother Church" (*domina mater ecclesia*), who with maternal care looked after the imprisoned. He describes how the newly baptized recited their first prayer, the Our Father, in common with their brothers and sisters in their mother's house, and he chides the heretics because they do not have a mother.[11]

"You cannot have God for your Father if you have not the Church for your Mother." These words of St. Cyprian of Carthage have become a Christian slogan. Cyprian, a teacher of rhetoric, described how he had wandered blindly about in darkness and confusion until "the Spirit coming from heaven changed me into a new man by a second birth."[12] Shortly after his baptism he was elected bishop of Carthage (249), the most important see in North Africa, and eight years later (257) he was beheaded by the Roman authorities. His short episcopate was a time of trial for the church, threatened from within by schism and from without by persecution. Cyprian has left a series of letters and a number or short tracts that describe Christians, including leaders, who had lost their sense of commitment, who compromised their faith when challenged by the government and who were at odds with their bishops over questions of discipline and of how to deal with apostates.

Two of the works, *The Lapsed* and *The Unity of the Catholic Church*, written in 251 while he was in hiding, address the problems. In the first, Cyprian tells of the joy of Mother Church because so many, despite threats of torture and banishment, confessed their faith openly and courageously (ch. 2). And he denounces those who "denied the Church to be our Mother, and God to be our Father" (ch. 9). He again speaks of the church as Mother in pleading for the unity of the church:

> So too Our Lord's Church is radiant with light and pours her rays over the whole world; but it is one and the same light which is spread everywhere, and the unity of her body suffers no division. She spreads her branches in generous growth over all the earth, she extends her abundant streams ever further; yet one is the head-spring, one the source, one the mother who is prolific in her offspring, generation after generation: of her womb are we born, of her milk are we fed, of her Spirit our souls draw their life-breath. (ch. 5)

It is in the next paragraph that Cyprian's axiom quoted above appears: *"Habere non potest deum patrem qui ecclesiam non habet matrem."*[13]

Issues in Ecclesiology   In the patristic period, it is evident, the church was both the context and the theme of theology. Though chiefly concerned with their local churches, the ancients nonetheless discussed the nature and mission of the worldwide church in connection with the heresies, schisms, and misunderstandings that beset them. Theirs was a crisis ecclesiology that evolved in response to specific problems and jurisdictional disputes. They were especially intolerant of schism because it blurred the image of the church as the mystery—the sacrament—of salvation. (The Latins translated the Greek word *mysterion* as *sacramentum*.) By reason of the Incarnation Jesus is the *sacramentum* of God, the visible embodiment of the divine presence in the world. By reason of its identification with the Body of Christ, the church is sacrament—the visible sign—of Christ's continued presence in the world.

For the most part the church fathers were careful not to affirm that the church, in so far as it is a visible reality, is the same as the kingdom of God and as the sacramental body of Christ. Nonetheless they used the notion of sacrament to explain that the church is an outward manifestation of the hidden reality of God's presence in the world. The Christian community, united in love, witnesses to the unity of all peoples and is the symbol of their union with God in Christ. In our own time the Second Vatican Council, taking its inspiration from the church fathers, adopted the notion of church as sacrament to emphasize that the church is both the visible manifestation of such unity and union and the instrument to achieve them. Carrying on the mission and ministry of Christ, the church is the means of salvation—"a necessary means, a divine means, but provisional as means always are."[14] The old axiom "Sacraments are for people, not people for the sacraments" applies also to the church.

Despite the rich imagery of the New Testament and the patristic portrayal of the church as sacrament, the treatise *De ecclesia* in seminary theology before Vatican II was narrowly conceived. It had been built up, as Henri de Lubac observed, in two main stages: the first in medieval controversies between papal jurists on the one side and imperial and royal jurists on the other; and the second in opposition to Protestant and Gallican doctrines of church polity in the sixteenth and seventeenth centuries. As a consequence the earliest tracts on the church were written by canon lawyers concerned either to vindicate the church's rights in relationship to civil authority or to defend the prerogatives of the papacy and hierarchy vis-a-vis one another and church councils. In the time of the Protestant Reformation, moreover, the organizational structure of the church itself became the center of controversy. Catholic apologists were intent on defending the hierarchical structure—pope, bishops, priests, deacons—as being of divine institution.

It is in this context that de Lubac laments that to learn the catechism *against* someone is to half learn it. Even if everything in the treatises written on the church between the Council of Trent and Vatican II were entirely accurate, does not, asks de Lubac, "the consequent narrowness of outlook and lack of proportion amount in practice to error?"[15]

THE ECCLESIOLOGY OF VATICAN II

The Second Vatican Council   The Second Vatican Council (1962-65), by sheer numbers, geographic distance, and cultural diversity was the most ecumenical—even the most Catholic—assembly of church leaders ever. Participants numbered almost 3,000: in addition to some 2,600 bishops there were hundreds of experts (*periti*)—biblical scholars, theologians, and canonists—who acted as advisers to individual bishops and served as staff to the various conciliar commissions. They came from every continent and, by the fourth session, included fifty-two men and women as "lay auditors." Almost every major Christian body was represented by official "observers" who were consulted on many points in the course of the deliberations. In addition, media coverage focused the attention of the whole Catholic world as well as that of many other Christians on the Council and stirred their interest in the issues discussed.

As important an event as the Second Vatican Council turned out to be, it is misleading to picture it as a break with the past. The foundations for the Council had been laid by the likes of Jesuits Henri de Lubac, Jean Danielou (both later named cardinals), and Karl Rahner, Dominicans Yves Congar and Edward Schillebeeckx, and less-known figures such as Frenchman Marie-Dominique Chenu, German Augustine Bea, Austrian Josef Andreas Jungmann, and Swiss Hans Urs von Balthasar. In one way or another these men were all linked to the "New Theology" and until vindicated by the Council were suspect in the eyes of establishment theologians. All shared a good grasp of history and deep respect for tradition; none saw himself as an innovator. In fact the New Theology (if indeed it is proper to speak of a return to the sources as if it were a fad) was intent on recovering the riches and diversity of the Catholic past. With Chenu they recognized the importance of grounding theology on experience. With de Lubac they found that theology born in controversy becomes misleading, even distorted; and with Rahner they saw it necessary to recover the spirit of inquiry of the great medieval scholastics and not be satisfied with reprinting their texts.

All had considerable knowledge of the Catholic theological tradition, but each had his own strength and particular interest. Yves Congar's, as we noted at the beginning of this chapter, was ecclesiology, and Congar, according to Richard McBrien, "perhaps did more than any other single theologian to prepare the way of the Second Vatican Council."[16] When he began teaching the course on the church to Dominican students in the 1930s Congar was struck by the pallid, two-dimensional image of the church presented in the seminary textbooks. In comparison with the picture of the church in patristic writings, textbook ecclesiology stood like a cartoon before a Michelangelo painting. The end result was that in the eyes of many Catholics, ecclesiology has been reduced to a description, cast in legal terms, of the church as a hierarchical society possessing authority to make laws and give pronouncements in matters governing the religious life of Christians. Congar gave himself to the life task of correcting this distorted view and of retrieving for the modern believer, actual and potential, the rich heritage of the past.

Congar was not alone in his efforts to renew ecclesiology, but more than others', his interests coincided with the fundamental issues and themes that were to dominate the discussions at Vatican II. In his many books and articles he presented the church as dependent on Christ—not, however, as an agency acting in his absence, but as a reality drawing its life and mission from the Lord who is made present in the church by the Holy Spirit. The church exists not for itself but to mediate salvation for all in the coming of the kingdom. Congar's view of the church was inclusive: it is a "people," the People of God, not a sectarian movement but a "structured community" in which all members share responsibility for its priestly, prophetic and pastoral mission in the world. Disunity among Christians is a scandal, and Catholics need to develop principles and a plan for ecumenism, beginning with an acknowledgment of past mistakes. These themes, together with Congar's emphasis on reform of the church in head and members, in structures and style of life, and his stress on the role of the laity, echo in the documents of Vatican II.

The Documents of Vatican II   The Second Vatican Council met from September-October to early December over a four-year period (1962-65), and in the course of its deliberations it issued sixteen formal statements—over 100,000 words—all of them touching in one way or another on the church's life and mission. They fall into three main categories: constitutions, decrees, and declarations.

The *constitutions* treat doctrinal matters that pertain to the very essence or "constitution" of the church. Four of the major documents fall into this category: the constitutions treating the nature and mission of the church (*Lumen Gentium*); the liturgy and prayer life of the church (*Sacrosanctum Concilium*); revelation and the word of God (*Dei Verbum*); and the pastoral responsibilities of the church in today's world (*Gaudium et Spes*).

The decrees and declarations are based on the doctrinal principles found in the constitutions, but they address specific issues and particular pastoral concerns. The nine *decrees* deal with such issues as the pastoral office of the bishops; the Catholic churches of the Oriental rites; the ministry, life, and education of priests; religious orders; the laity; missionary activity; and ecumenism. Finally, the Council promulgated three formal *declarations*; these outline principles governing religious freedom, the church's position toward non-Christian religions, and Christian education.[17]

In the sense that the Council relied on biblical images and metaphors to explain the nature and mission of the church, it represents a harking back to patristic times. It returned to the basic notion that the church is first and foremost a sacrament—a mysterious sign—that witnesses to the hidden presence of God. The very title of the dogmatic constitution on the church, *Lumen Gentium*, proclaims the church as a "light to the nations." It is the Body of Christ. It is both sheepfold and flock whose shepherd is Christ. It is the Temple of God, with Christ as the capstone. By elaborating on the image of the People of God, Vatican II has led Christians to see themselves once more as resembling ancient Israel: as a pilgrim people, a people with a mission, a holy people. By taking the image seriously the Council shifted the burden of being church from the hierarchy to all the People of God—pope, bishops, priests, deacons, and laity alike. The church is not an assembly of human origin but a creation of the Word of God. Everyone who hears the Word and is baptized belongs to the church.

The Council looked inward to examine every aspect of the church's life, organization, and spirit; and it looked outward to the world in which the church finds itself today. The decrees on missionary activity and the media reiterated the mission given by Christ to disseminate the gospel message among all peoples, recognizing both the opportunities and the obstacles opened to preaching and teaching by modern instruments of communication. The declarations on non-Christian religions and on religious freedom are both spin-offs from the decree on ecumenism. The first, *Nostra Aetate*, acknowledges that there is much that is true and beautiful in Hinduism, Buddhism, Islam, and other great world religions, and encourages dialogue and collaboration with them in order to promote common spiritual and moral values. It singles out the Jews, stressing the common spiritual ties that bond the church to "the stock of Abraham" (par. 4), and denounces every form of anti-Semitism.[18] The second, *Dignitatis Humanae*, affirms that every person, endowed by the Creator with dignity and freedom, should be immune from coercion of every kind in matters pertaining to conscience and the exercise of religion. Faith is both a gift from God and a free act on the part of the believer; consequently, it is improper to compel anyone to embrace Christianity, nor should anyone be penalized for not being a Christian.

The most comprehensive statement of the church's attitude toward the world is found in the longest and last document issued by Vatican II, *Gaudium et Spes*. From almost any point of view it is a singular document. It gives new meaning to the word "pastoral," expanding the notion of the church's call to service in the world. *Gaudium et Spes* is pastoral in the sense that it is programmatic, setting down principles, identifying specific modern issues, and calling for concrete action to safeguard the sanctity and quality of life for all human beings. (One example of concrete action traceable to *Gaudium et Spes*, and there are many, is the U.S. bishops' pastoral letter on nuclear armaments; see pars. 77-82.) Although its tone is positive and upbeat, it is also a realistic document in that it attempts to expose the sources of evil and discord that degrade and dehumanize people the world over. It represents a conscious effort to explain both "to all who invoke the name of Christ" and "to the whole of humanity" how the Council conceived "the presence and activity of the Church in the world of today." Paraphrasing the maxim of the ancient Roman Terence, *Nihil humana mihi aliena* ("Nothing human is alien to me"), *Gaudium et Spes* states that "nothing genuinely human fails to raise an echo" in the hearts of Christians (par. 1).

There is a great deal of repetition and overlap in the documents of Vatican II, but, given the great diversity of ideologies and interests represented at the Council, there is also surprising consistency. The bishops of Vatican II drew a picture of a servant-church which, like its founder, is in the world to minister, not to be ministered to. A constant theme running through everything the Council did and said was concern for the poor and oppressed, recognizing as it did that economic and educational deprivation often goes hand in hand with spiritual impoverishment. The bishops committed the church anew to work for justice and peace, human dignity and freedom, and to renew every aspect of its life. The Second Vatican Council did not formulate a systematic ecclesiology, but it recaptured the spirit and refurbished the image of the church, not as it once was but as it is called to be.

Vatican II and the Holy Spirit   In the course of the Council, Orthodox, Protestant, and Anglican observers frequently criticized the early drafts of the documents for their lack of pneumatology. Yves Congar admits that the criticism was justified but thinks the deficiency was largely remedied in the final text.[19] The Council stressed that the Holy Spirit is the Spirit of Christ: the Spirit carries out the work of Christ. In many places the conciliar documents call the Spirit the principle of life of that Body that is the church. *Dei Verbum*, the constitution on divine revelation, emphasizes that God's word was entrusted to the apostles by Christ the Lord and the Holy Spirit (par. 9) and that it is with the help of the Holy Spirit that the church "draws from this one deposit of faith everything which it presents for belief as divinely revealed" (par. 10).

Another way in which the conciliar documents reclaimed the pneumatological ecclesiology of Scripture and of the church fathers was in dealing with charisms. Though of human necessity the Christian community depends on institutional structures, including the sacraments, it relies principally on the infinite variety of gifts given to individuals.

> From the reception of these charisms or gifts . . . there arise for each believer the right and duty to use them in the Church and in the world for the good of mankind and for the upbuilding of the

Church. In so doing, believers need to enjoy the freedom of the Holy Spirit who "breathes where he wills" (Jn 3:8). At the same time, they must act in communion with their brothers in Christ, especially with their pastors. The latter must make a judgment about the true nature and proper use of these gifts, not in order to extinguish the Spirit, but to test all things and hold fast to what is good (cf. 1 Thes 5:12, 19, 21).[20]

It is evident from the foregoing text as well as from a statement in the decree on the church's missionary activity that the Council recognized that the Holy Spirit "often anticipates the action of those whose task it is to rule the life of the Church" (par. 29).

It is the Spirit who impels the church to open new avenues of approach to the world of today[21] and to renew itself ceaselessly if it is to remain faithful to its Lord.[22] The contemporary drive toward unity within the church—a drive embodied in the ecumenical movement—is, according to the decree on ecumenism, the work of the Spirit who is at work in other Christian communities (pars. 1; 4; 290).[23]

The Council speaks of church unity as a "sacred mystery" that has its "highest exemplar and source in the Trinity of Persons of one God, the Father and the Son *in* the Holy Spirit" (italics added). The unity of the church exists "in Christ and through Christ, with the Holy Spirit energizing a variety of functions."[24] As we shall see in the next chapter, it is because of the energizing power of the Spirit manifest in various ways in the church that an earlier council, the Council of Constantinople, confessed the church to be "one holy catholic and apostolic."

Notes

1. Richard P. McBrien, *Catholicism* (Minneapolis: Winston Press, 1980), p. 662.

2. Yves Congar, *I Believe in the Holy Spirit* (New York: Seabury Press, 1983), I, p. 156.

3. Ibid., II, p. 5.

4. Henri de Lubac, *Catholicism* (New York: Mentor-Omega Books, 1964), pp. 37–39.

5. *Magnesia* 6:1, *ACW* no. 1, pp. 70–71.

6. Jules Lebreton and Jacques Zeiller, *The Triumph of Christianity* Book IV of A History of the Early Church (New York: Collier Books, 1962), pp. 224–225, 226.

7. Paul VI, *Ministeria Quaedam* and *Ad Pascendum. NCE* 17:411–412.

8. *NCE* 4:668–669. *Oxford Dictionary of the Christian Church*, ed. F.L. Cross (London: Oxford University Press, 1966), p. 377.

9. John A. T. Robinson, *The Body: A Study in Pauline Theology* (London: SCM Press, 1952), p. 26–33.

10. Yves Congar, *The Mystery of the Temple* (Westminster, MD: Newman Press, 1962), pp. 150–235.

11. The classic study of this subject remains C. J. Plumpe *Mater Ecclesia: An Inquiry into the Concept of the Church as Mother in Early Christianity* (Washington, DC: Catholic University of America, 1943).

12. Cyprian left an autobiographical account of his conversion in his *Liber ad Donatum*. Quoted in Jules Lebreton and Jacques Zeiller, *Heresy and Orthodoxy* Book III of A History of the Early Church (New York: Collier Cooks, 1962), p. 268.

13. Ch. 6; see ch. 23. The quotes from Cyprian, unless otherwise noted, are from *Ancient Christian Writers*, vol. 25.

14. de Lubac, *Catholicism*, p. 40.

15. Ibid., p. 169.

16. *Catholicism*, p. 662.

17. There is no official English translation of the documents of Vatican II. The English versions most frequently cited are in *The Documents of Vatican II*, ed. Walter M. Abbott (New York: America Press, 1966), and *Vatican II: The Conciliar and Post Conciliar Documents*, ed. Austin Flannery (Northport, NY: Costello Publishing Co., 1975). Richard McBrien gives a good account of the Council's teaching on the church and an excellent summary of the documents in *Catholicism*, pp. 657–689.

18. See Chapter 8, note 15.

19. *I Believe*, I, p. 167.

20. Decree on the Apostolate of the Laity, par. 3.

21. Decree on Ministry and Life of Priests, par. 22.

22. *Lumen Gentium*, par. 9. *Gaudium et Spes*, pars. 21, 43.

23. See Congar, *I Believe* I, p. 171 and 173, n. 9. Also P. J. Rosato, "Called to God in the Holy Spirit: Pneumatological Insights into Ecumenism," *Ecumenical Review* 30 (1978):110–126.

24. Decree on Ecumenism, par. 2.

19

The Marks of the Church

"One holy catholic and apostolic"

To say as we did in the previous chapter that the early church did not develop a systematic ecclesiology does not mean that no effort was made to set forth its basic characteristics in an organized, coherent fashion. Given the number of groups—various gnostic schools, the Marcionites, the Montanists, and more obscure sects—catechumens as well as the faithful needed guidance in judging who represented the authentic gospel message. St. Cyprian complains about people who "still call themselves Christians after abandoning the Gospel of Christ and the observance of his law."[1] In the face of the confusion caused from without by rival claimants and from within by factionalism and schism, the church argued its case on the basis of its unity, holiness, universality, and apostolicity. These essential characteristics that distinguish the church from other groups have come to be known as "notes" or "marks" of the church. They served as a basis for catechesis that gave rise to a kind of rule of thumb expressed in the Creed of Constantinople as WE BELIEVE IN ONE HOLY CATHOLIC AND APOSTOLIC CHURCH.

In this chapter we examine the implications of the four marks of the church. Our theme is that unity, holiness, catholicity, and apostolicity are not only endowments given to the church by the Holy Spirit but

306

also tasks that challenge the church at every level, including the church of the Holy Trinity in Norfolk, Virginia, and the cathedral parish in Toronto, Ontario. Thus we survey the efforts of the modern ecumenical movement to make the unity of the church manifest in a divided world. In connection with apostolicity we discuss the special role of the apostle Peter and the Petrine office that was once the focus of church unity but is now an obstacle for many.

Before we deal directly with the marks of the church, however, we must make a distinction that will be developed more at length when we discuss the nature of faith (Chapter 23). Both the Nicene and the Apostles' Creeds affirm belief in the church: the briefer form of the latter states WE BELIEVE IN THE HOLY CATHOLIC CHURCH; the longer form of the Nicene Creed adds ONE and APOSTOLIC. The church is indeed an object of faith, but not in the same way that God is the object of faith. In commenting on this phrase, medieval theologians carefully explained that we believe in the Holy Spirit, not only *in se*, but as the one who makes the church one, holy, catholic, and apostolic.[2] The existence of the church in itself is not a matter of faith. Historians and sociologists of all religious traditions and no religious tradition accept the church as a social group made up of people who profess to be Christians. But the church as mystery eludes reason and is beyond empirical study; because of its origins, nature, and destiny the church demands faith. The Catechism of the Council of Trent, commenting on the Apostles' Creed, stated it this way:

> But with regard to the three Persons of the Trinity, the Father, the Son and the Holy Spirit, we believe in such a way that we place our faith in them. Here, however, the form of speech is changed and we profess to believe the Holy Catholic Church, and not *in* the Holy Catholic Church. This difference of expression distinguishes God, the author of all things, from created things and refers to the divine goodness all these exalted benefits which are gathered together for us in the Church.[3]

ONE AND UNDIVIDED

In the first article of the Creed we confess belief in *one* God by way of taking a stance against polytheism and idolatry; the unicity of God implies a unity within the Godhead, but the emphasis is on the uniqueness of God. In the third article we confess ONE CHURCH, but the emphasis here is on unity and only secondarily on the church's uniqueness. Unity implies both oneness and diversity: the church is one in that it presents a certain integrity or wholeness (which we shall see below means "catholic"). On the other hand, as St. Paul recognized in using the image of the body and its members, the church is made up of individuals of various backgrounds and diverse gifts. Despite differences they are one in confessing that Jesus Christ is Lord and in looking to him as their Savior. Nothing in the New Testament suggests that uniformity—the denial of diversity—is an ideal, and the history of the church is evidence that it has never been a reality.[4]

Unity in the Holy Spirit does not mean imposing on the church's life and thought a uniform pattern that ignores individual charisms and personal talents. Congar cites Jesus' allegory of the Good Shepherd, pointing out that while the church may be compared to the sheepfold or enclosure, the flock is made up of individual sheep, each of which the shepherd calls by name (Jn 10:1-3,16). In a passage that is doubly sad because it sounds autobiographical, Yves Congar laments the Catholic church's excessive reliance on authority to maintain unity. In the modern era there has been a tendency to confuse unity and uniformity, to reduce order to observance of imposed rules. It has led, he writes, "to the development of a system of supervision that has been effective in maintaining an orthodox line and framework, but this has been achieved at the price of marginalizing individuals who have had something to say, and often even reducing them to silence and inactivity."[5]

No less a power than the Spirit of God is necessary to bring the many diverse peoples and individuals who make up the church to a sense of solidarity. "It was in one Spirit that all of us, whether Jew or Greek, slave or free, were baptized into one body. All of us have been given to drink of the one Spirit" (1 Cor 12:13). It is important to keep in mind that the Holy Spirit is not the Spirit of the church but the Spirit of God, so that it is one and the same uncreated Spirit who is both in the head, Christ, and in his body, the church. In essence, unity in the Spirit is always *communion*—"union with." The Western church has traditionally ascribed to the Holy Spirit a unitive function within the Trinity, the bonding of Father and Son in love; similarly, the mission of the Holy Spirit in the world is seen as uniting believers to one another and to God in the Body of Christ. The Spirit, the principle of unity in the church, is also the source of the love that the members have for one another in their hearts.[6]

Jesus prayed to his heavenly Father that his disciples would be "one, even as we are one" (Jn 17:11). Ideally the church is called to mirror the tri-unity of God, the indivisible unity that binds Father, Son, and Spirit and at the same time acknowledges the distinctive properties of each. In describing the unity of the church, St. Cyprian uses the same language that Tertullian used in describing the Trinity:

> And the Church forms a unity, of which each holds his part in its totality. And the Church forms a unity, however far she spreads and multiplies by the progeny of her fecundity; just as the sun's rays are many, yet the light is one, and a tree's branches are many, the strength deriving from its sturdy root is one. So too, though many streams flow from a single spring, though its multiplicity seems scattered abroad by the copiousness of its welling waters, yet their oneness abides by reason of their starting point.[7]

The paragraph in *Lumen Gentium* that sets forth the special role of the Holy Spirit ends with another quotation from St. Cyprian to the effect that the church shines forth as "a people made one with the unity of the Father, the Son, and the Holy Spirit" (par. 4).[8]

The Ecumenical Movement   One of the chief concerns of the Second Vatican Council, as we noted in the previous chapter, was to restore unity among all Christians. The Decree on Ecumenism was emphatic in stating that without doubt a divided Christendom "openly contradicts the will of Christ, provides a stumbling block to the world, and inflicts damage on the most holy cause of proclaiming the good news to every creature" (par. 1). "Ecumenism" is a relatively new word to describe efforts to bring the churches into communion with one another, but ecumenism is not new. In medieval times repeated attempts were made to heal the breach between Eastern and Western churches, notably at the Councils of Lyons (1274) and Florence (1438-39), and in the early stages of the Protestant Reformation irenic-minded leaders made concerted efforts to mend differences and thereby forestall a breakup of Western Christendom. Over the years sporadic moves, especially among Protestants, continued to be made to negotiate working agreements and, thereby to establish some semblance of unity and cooperation among the various Christian bodies.

The modern ecumenical movement as it presently exists dates, for all practical purposes, from the Edinburgh Missionary Conference in 1910. Representatives of mission boards and mission societies of many

Protestant bodies came together to study their endeavors, especially in non-Christian lands, with an eye to making the work of evangelization more effective. A principal obstacle to effective evangelization, recognized by all, was the scandal caused by Christians' being divided among themselves and competing with one another. The Conference presented a vision of world Christianity and created a climate for greater cooperation among the churches. It was the forerunner of the Life and Work Conference that met for the first time in Stockholm in 1925. Dedicated to involving the churches in social, economic and political issues, it formulated the slogan "Doctrine divides, service unites," because it seemed easier to get the churches to work together on practical problems than to agree on points of doctrine. The slogan had an element of truth, but it was also simplistic insofar as it made it seem that doctrinal issues were unimportant or impractical. As a corrective, the first of the Faith and Order Conferences met in Lausanne (Switzerland) in 1927 to address theological and ecclesiastical questions with an eye to unity in faith and church structure.

These two groups laid the foundation for the World Council of Churches. Formally established at Amsterdam in 1948, the WCC describes itself as a "fellowship of Churches which accept our Lord Jesus Christ as God and Savior." Headquartered in Geneva, the WCC took the lead in fostering cooperation among Christian bodies and promoting the cause of ecumenism; its members are committed to close collaboration in Christian witness and service. Though it integrates and coordinates the tasks of the International Missionary Council, Life and Work and Faith and Order in a broader context, the older groups continue as commissions in the larger World Council. Beginning with the organizational meeting at Amsterdam, the World Council has held general assemblies every five years; and the Faith and Order Commission, meeting every few years, has contributed significantly to the goal of visible church unity.

Roman Catholic theologians enjoy full membership and have taken an active part in the deliberations of the Faith and Order Commission even though the Roman Catholic church does not belong to the World Council of Churches. The Faith and Order Commission has as its particular aim

> to proclaim the oneness of the Church of Jesus Christ and to call
> the churches to the goal of visible unity in one faith and one

eucharistic fellowship, expressed in worship and common life in
Christ, in order that the world might believe.[9]

The Faith and Order Commission describes its deliberations as "multi-
lateral conversations" because they involve representatives of "virtually
all the confessional traditions." Over the years it has held discussions
and has published a series of papers on some of the most divisive
theological issues in Christendom. We have already alluded to its study
of the *filioque* (Chapter 16), and in the next chapter we shall look the
so-called Lima Document, a position paper on baptism, eucharist, and
ministry. Here we note in passing that the Commission's continuing
effort to gain recognition for the Nicene-Constantinopolitan Creed,
"the church's common confession of faith," is in part the inspiration
for this book (we return to the topic again in the last chapter).

Ecumenical Dialogue and Bilateral Conversations   Despite the fact
that the Roman Catholic church does not participate as a full-fledged
member of the World Council, it follows the work of the Council very
closely and generally supports its endeavors. It was no accident, for
example, that Vatican II's constitution on the church is called *Lumen
Gentium*—"Light of the Nations." The Third General Assembly of
the WCC, which met at New Delhi in 1961, had as its theme "Jesus
Light of the World." Vatican II was careful not to give the impression
of inaugurating a separate Catholic movement but rather exhorted "all
the Catholic faithful to recognize the signs of the times and to take an
active and intelligent part in the work of ecumenism."[10] Shortly after
the promulgation of the decree on ecumenism, Cardinal Bea, then
president of the Vatican Secretariat for Promoting Christian Unity,[11]
officially welcomed an invitation from the WCC's Central Committee "to explore together the possibilities of dialogue and cooperation."[12]

One of the specific "activities" and "organized occasions" identified
in the Decree on Ecumenism as helpful in fostering unity was " 'dialogue' between competent experts from different Churches and Communities" (par. 4; see also 18). The purpose of dialogue is to create an
atmosphere of trust and respect in which Christians of different traditions may come to a genuine appreciation of one another's belief and
concerns. Dialogue takes many forms; the best known are the "bilateral conversations" (as distinct from the "multi-lateral conversations"
of the Faith and Order Commission) that have brought representatives

of the churches together to discuss theological issues. The Vatican Secretariat for Promoting Christian Unity sponsors ongoing dialogue with representatives of five world confessional families: the Orthodox Churches of the East, the Anglican Communion, the Lutheran World Federation, the World Methodist Council, and the World Alliance of Reformed Churches. Meanwhile churches of these other families have been in conversation with one another. Similar conversations are taking place at national and regional levels. The United States Bishops' Committee on Ecumenical and Interreligious Affairs, for example, sponsors bilateral conversations with the American Baptist Convention, the Christian Church (Disciples of Christ), the Episcopal church, Lutheran churches, the United Methodist church, Reformed and Presbyterian churches, and Orthodox and other Eastern churches. We have already (in Chapter 7) cited the study of Mary in the New Testament, a by-product of the United States Lutheran-Roman Catholic Dialogue, and later in this chapter we shall refer to another report from the same group, "Papal Primacy and the Universal Church."

The importance of these bilateral conversations and other, less formal, ecumenical efforts cannot be overemphasized, for the unity of the church grounds the other marks, and in the concrete the four marks of the church cannot be isolated from one another. Unity, as we shall see, cannot be isolated from catholicity, and catholicity implies apostolicity. Apostolicity, in turn, includes holiness in that it represents the continuity of a mission and a communion which begins in God.

A HOLY PEOPLE

The Holiness of the Church   However basic the notion of church unity, HOLY was the first note attributed to the church. About the middle of the second century, "holy" was on its way toward becoming a stock epithet to describe the church. St. Justin's *Dialogue* illustrates how it was used:

> We are not only a people, but we are a holy people, as we have already showed—"And they shall call them the holy people, redeemed by the Lord" (Is 62:12).[13]

In the third century, mention of HOLY is common in the baptismal creeds, usually in a context like that cited by St. Hippolytus, who quotes the third question addressed to the person being baptized: "Do you believe in the Holy Spirit in the *holy Church* for the resurrection of the flesh?"[14]

It is possible to approach the HOLY CHURCH by speaking either of the holiness *of* the church or holiness *in* the church. Since we deal with the latter—the sanctification of individuals—in the following chapters, we consider only the former here. The holiness *of* the church refers to the divine gift—the power of sanctification—that heals and justifies in the midst of human unholiness. In commenting on the Apostles' Creed, Albert the Great wrote:

> This article must therefore be traced back to the work of the Holy Spirit, that is, to "I believe in the Holy Spirit," not in himself alone, as the previous article states, but I believe in him also as far as his work is concerned, which is to make the Church holy. He communicates that holiness in the sacraments, the virtues and the gifts that he distributes in order to bring holiness about, and finally in the miracles and the graces of a charismatic type (*et donis gratis datis*) such as wisdom, knowledge, faith, the discernment of spirits, healings, prophecy and everything else that the Spirit gives in order to make the holiness of the Church manifest.[15]

Thus we do not claim that the church is HOLY because its members, collectively and individually, are holy, sinless people. The church's holiness is the expression of divine love which will not allow itself to be defeated by human willfulness and weakness. God's covenant is not a contractual arrangement that ceases when humans sin; God's grace abides despite everything.[16]

The image of the temple, which we noted in the previous chapter, suggests that the church is the house of the Lord, a dwelling or residence. The New Testament sees that the church is "fitted together and takes shape as a holy temple in the Lord; in him you are being built into this temple, to become a dwelling place for God in the Spirit" (Eph 2:21-22). The church as Body of Christ makes the holiness of the Lord a reality in the world. The church's holiness is inseparable from Jesus' holiness, and the way the church manifests its holiness is not unlike the way in which Jesus manifested his. Incarnate and living in the world, Jesus drew sinners—government officials, lawyers, prostitutes, thieves, and a few religious leaders—people who had either compromised themselves or who had been compromised by the society in which they moved. Though not always fully able to respond to Jesus' call for repentance, they were attracted to his promise of mercy and forgiveness. The taproot of the church's holiness is not to be found in its attempting to flee from the world to some never-never land untouched by impurity, compromise, and corruption, but in its embracing Jesus, through whom God embraced the world.

CATHOLIC AND ROMAN CATHOLIC

"Catholic": Many Meanings   The word "catholic" derives from the Greek adverbial phrase *kath' holou*, which means "on the whole." Although it was not until the fourth century that the creeds began to emphasize catholicity as a characteristic mark of the church, the first reference to the "Catholic" church is found in St.Ignatius of Antioch at the beginning of the second century: "Where the bishop appears, there let the people be, just as where Jesus Christ is, there is the Catholic Church."[17] Ignatius' point in this passage was that the local church community had reality, life, and power only to the extent that it formed part of the universal church in union with its spiritual head.[18] This is the sense in which another second-century writing speaks of St. Polycarp (d. 156) as "bishop of the Catholic church in Smyrna" and of Our Lord Jesus Christ as "Shepherd of the world-wide Catholic Church."[19] The Catholic church is at once local and universal, but not in the sense that the universal church is a conglomerate or confederation of local churches. The local church is "the church of God" in a particular place, Corinth (1 Cor 1:2), Smyrna, or New Ulm, Minnesota. For this reason it is not possible to speak of catholicity apart from the unity of the church; the church is one, not a union of parts but a unity of many in the sense of being a whole. (It is because catholicity implies wholeness and unity that the Apostles' Creed in confessing belief in the HOLY CATHOLIC CHURCH does not explicitly state it is also ONE.)

Already in the third century, "catholic" had come to be recognized as a characteristic mark that distinguished the church from sectarian, dissident, and heretical groups in the broader Christian community. During the Decian persecution (c. 250) the martyr Pionius, a priest of the church at Smyrna, identified himself to his judges as a Christian.

His judges then asked him, "To what church do you belong?" and he replied, "To the Catholic Church."[20] Pionius was referring to the worldwide church whose unity in faith was given visible witness by the bishops in communion with one another. It was in this sense that the Muratorian Fragment was understood when it enumerated the canon of sacred books that were received "in the Catholic church." Thus "Catholic faith" first signified the teaching commonly held worldwide and later came to indicate orthodoxy, a guarantee of the authentic doctrine "which comes to us from the apostles" (Eucharistic Prayer).

Catholicity, however, is not fundamentally a matter of geography. A striking passage in the catechetical lectures of St. Cyril of Jerusalem (c. 350) takes CATHOLIC to mean universal in every sense of the word. The church is called CATHOLIC, he says,

> because it extends over all the world, from one end of the earth to the other; and because it teaches universally and completely one and all the doctrines which ought to come to men's knowledge, concerning things both visible and invisible, heavenly and earthly; and because it brings into subjection to godliness the whole race of mankind, governors and governed, learned and unlearned; and because it universally treats and heals the whole class of sins, which are committed by soul or body, and possesses in itself every form of virtue which is named, both in deeds and words, and in every kind of spiritual gifts.[21]

Although it is said that St. Augustine's influence led medieval and later theologians to think of catholicity primarily from the standpoint of geography, in fact he understood CATHOLIC to mean whole, entire. Soon after he became bishop of Hippo in 396, Augustine found it necessary to deal with the Donatist schism. The Donatists (a dissident group about which more in a later chapter) had plagued the church in North Africa since the days of the Emperor Diocletian (c. 305). They claimed to be the one true church, a claim Augustine ridiculed because the Donatists were but a small sect in an out-of-the-way corner of the globe. The burden of his censure of the Donatists, however, was not their size nor that they were confined to a small territory, but that they were sectarian and narrow. He accused them of dealing with all problems as if they were African problems alone. In one of his homilies he said, "I don't know who restricted the limits of charity to Africa."[22] He went on to say that charity must extend over all the earth, for to love Christ is to love Christ's members everywhere. To love only a part is to be divided, separated from the head of the Body. Thus Augustine's admiration for the church Catholic was grounded on the fact that it brings human beings together, gathering them into a whole bonded by love and peace.

The Catholic Church and Catholic Churches   The history of CATH-OLIC as a description of the church and its faith is filled with anomalies. Although the Eastern creeds had incorporated the term long before it became a part of the Western creeds, it was the Western church that appropriated it as testimony to its own orthodoxy. Until the formal break between East and West in 1054, CATHOLIC continued to be used in the sense that it was understood by St. Ignatius and the Muratorian Fragment. In the East, however, the church in Constantinople and other churches in communion with it described themselves variously as the Orthodox Catholic Church, the Holy Orthodox Church, or with some designation such as the Russian Orthodox Church or the Greek Orthodox Church. It is a way of distinguishing the churches that accept the teachings of the seven ecumenical councils between Nicea I (325) and Nicea II (787) from other Christian bodies such as the Nestorians and the Jacobites, which reject Ephesus, Chalcedon, and subsequent councils.[23]

Another anomoly is that CATHOLIC, an adjective whose root meaning indicates something universal, general, and all-inclusive, has become in the eyes of many an exclusive term for a particular church. In some confessional documents of the Protestant Reformation, "Christian" was substituted for CATHOLIC in translations of the Apostles' Creed. In England, however, Reformers who regarded themselves catholic designated those who gave allegiance to the Pope as "Roman" Catholic.

The distinction between "Catholic" and "Protestant" is not as sharp as it once was. Many Protestant Christians, in so far as they lay claim to historic continuity with the faith and practice of the New Testament church, see themselves as Catholic. Others argue that CATHOLIC admits of degrees. It is like a musical tone that ideally sounds a perfect pitch, but in most instances when actually sung, the reality only approximates what it is supposed to be and many times is deplorably off-key. And finally, it should be said that while the church's catholicity is a guarantee of correct doctrine, correct doctrine does not of itself ensure catholicity. For example, a local church may be scrupulous about teaching the faith that has come down from the apostles, but it offends against catholicity because it excludes from its membership persons of different racial or cultural background.

APOSTOLIC: WITNESS AND MISSION

Apostolic in Beginning and End   Although it was the fourth century before the term "apostolic" is firmly ensconced in the creeds, the New Testament shows that from the beginning the church was conscious of being APOSTOLIC. "You form a building which rises on the foundation of the apostles and prophets, with Christ Jesus himself as the capstone" (Eph 2:20). The apostles were first and foremost called to be witnesses. Jesus' farewell message (emphasis added) in Luke's Gospel instructed them:

> Thus it is written that the Messiah must suffer and rise from the dead on the third day. In his name, penance for the remission of sins is to be preached to all nations, beginning at Jerusalem. *You are witnesses of this*. (Lk 24:46-48)

Luke picks up the same theme at the beginning of Acts when he quotes Jesus as saying, "You will receive power when the Holy Spirit comes down on you; then you are to be my witnesses in Jerusalem, throughout Judea and Samaria, yes, even to the ends of the earth" (Acts 1:8). The apostolic witness parallels and mediates the witness of the Paraclete:

> "When the Paraclete comes, the Spirit of truth who comes from the Father—and whom I myself will send from the Father—he will bear witness on my behalf."
>
> "You must bear witness as well, for you have been with me from the beginning." (Jn 15:26-27; see Acts 5:32)

In selecting Matthias as a replacement for Judas, Peter said it was entirely fitting that one of the company of disciples who had been with them from the time of Jesus' baptism onward "be named as witness with us to his resurrection" (Acts 1:22).

It must be stressed that apostolic witness is always directed forward in time. By the working of the Holy Spirit, Jesus remains active in and through the testimony of the apostles. In addition to testifying to Jesus' words and works, apostolic witness also proclaims their saving value in the present world and in the world to come. It is obvious that apostolic links the church to the origins of Christianity; less obvious, however, is the eschatological character of apostolicity. Just as the twelve sons of Israel formed the foundation of the People of God in the Old Testament, so "the Twelve" were called to be the foundation of the new People of God.[24] The Twelve who were witnesses at the beginning of the new Israel will also be witnesses at the end, judging the faithfulness of the People of God.

> Jesus said to them: "I give you my solemn word, in the new age when the Son of Man takes his seat upon a throne befitting his glory, you who have followed me shall likewise take your places on twelve thrones to judge the twelve tribes of Israel." (Mt 19:28)

Christ is Alpha and Omega, and it is the church's task, as it was the apostles', to witness to him as both the firstborn of every creature and the end of all creation.

But the apostles are not simply witnesses; they are sent into the world as the Son was *sent* into the world. "Go," Jesus said to them, "and make disciples of all the nations" (Mt 28:19). The Greek noun *apostolos* means "one who is sent"; and thus to affirm that the church is apostolic is to say that it is missionary. The church's task is that of the apostles: to *evangelize*, that is, to proclaim the good news of salvation to all the world (Mk 13:10), to announce it "to every creature under heaven" (Col 1:23). The proclamation is by way of witnessing, as we have just seen, and by way of teaching. "Teach them to carry out everything I have commanded you" (Mt. 28:20). In Jerusalem, Peter and John angered the Sadducees "because they were teaching the people and proclaiming the resurrection of the dead in the person of Jesus" (Acts 4:2; see also 4:18; 5:21,25,28; and *passim*). In Antioch Paul and Barnabas continued "along with many others, teaching and preaching the word of the Lord" (Acts 15:35).

Peter in the New Testament   The New Testament refers to several men as apostles but provides detailed information about only a few. Thanks both to the thirteen letters attributed to Paul and to the accounts supplied by the Book of Acts, we are best informed about Paul. Most of "the Twelve" are no more than names. Only Peter emerges from the pages of Scripture as a real life-and-blood figure, again because he is mentioned in Paul's Epistles to the Galatians and Corinthians, the Book of Acts, and in the Epistles attributed to his name.

It is one thing to acknowledge, as all biblical scholars do, Peter's leadership role in the New Testament; it is quite another to justify the Roman Catholic belief that the bishops of Rome—the popes—are endowed with a special charism of leadership in the church because they are successors to the Petrine office. A few years ago when papal primacy was the topic of discussion in the ongoing Lutheran-Catholic dialogue, an ecumenical task force of biblical scholars from different Christian traditions undertook a collaborative study of Peter in the New Testament. Their purpose was not to find evidence for or against the papacy as it has emerged in history, but simply to see if it is possible to come to some agreement about Peter's role in the apostolic church. The task force reported their conclusions under two headings: "first, the historical career of Simon Peter in the ministry of Jesus and in the early church; second, the images of Peter and the roles attributed to him in New Testament thought."[25] In brief, their findings were as follows.

Simon, one of the first called, was very prominent both in the group who were the steady companions of Jesus during his lifetime and among those who remained active disciples after his death and resurrection. In fact, the story of Jesus' ministry was not told without mention of Simon, though in the Gospel accounts his name is frequently associated with that of James and John and (sometimes) Andrew, who, in the synoptic tradition, formed an inner group of disciples. In the Johannine tradition he is associated with the Beloved Disciple. At some point in Jesus' ministry Simon probably asserted that Jesus was the fulfillment of Jewish expectations: according to the synoptic tradition, he is said to have confessed Jesus to be the Messiah; according to the Johannine account he confessed Jesus to be the holy one of God. Although it is difficult to be certain about all the details, the stories about Peter, taken as a whole—the tradition that Jesus rebuked him as Satan; Simon's misplaced enthusiasm; the story of his denials of Jesus—make it seem likely that before the resurrection Simon failed fully to understand Jesus.

In the early church Simon was known by the Greek name Cephas (translated into Latin as "Peter"), probably because Jesus himself gave him this name. (It should be noted, however, that the naming took place in different contexts in three Gospels: Mk 3:16; Mt 16:18; Jn 1:42.) The Risen Jesus made an appearance to Simon Peter. Probably it was Jesus' first appearance to an apostle, which may explain in part

Peter's prominence in the early church.[26] Not only did Peter witness to the Risen Lord, but he was a missionary among the circumcised and perhaps among Gentiles. With regard to the religious issues about which we are informed, specifically the observance of the Mosaic Law, Peter's stance seems to have been less rigid than that of James and more cautious than that of Paul.

The task force recognized that the minimal facts just summarized do not do justice to Peter's image in the New Testament, and therefore it sought to plot a *trajectory* of the New Testament images of Peter. Abandoning his career as a fisherman to follow Jesus, Peter became for the church a symbol of a fisher of men and women. His missionary activity suggests a fishing expedition that was phenomenally successful (Jn 21; Lk 5). Jesus commissioned Peter to strengthen his fellow Christians (Lk 22:32) through his missionary preaching. And if the first part of John 21 pictures Simon Peter as fisherman, the second part portrays him as shepherd of the sheep. The change in imagery "seems to reflect a shift in the concerns of church life" from initial concerns about the scope and manner of missionary activity to later concerns for the problems of established communities: local leadership, care of the faithful, difficulties caused by dangerous innovations, and so forth. Peter emerges as the model shepherd-pastor charged with feeding the sheep; his role and authority is based on his love for Jesus. When the presbyterate develops later in many churches, Peter is seen as the model for presbyters, instructing them on how to care for their flocks (see 1 Pet 5). With "the power of the keys" entrusted to him by Jesus, Peter's pastoral role is enhanced with the authority to bind and loose (Mt 16:19).[27]

Another point on the trajectory is the image of Peter as Christian martyr—the ultimate witness to the sufferings of Christ (1 Pet 5:1). We have "respectable evidence" that Peter died a martyr's death in Rome sometime in the sixties. The Johannine Gospel, in retrospect, recalls Jesus' words that predicted such an end (Jn 21:18); it is also the Fourth Gospel that recalls the example of the Good Shepherd who laid down his life for his sheep (Jn 10:11).

Then there is the image of "Peter the receiver of special revelation." It may have been the tradition that carried the story that Peter was the first of Jesus' companions to see the Lord after the resurrection that provided the context for much of the New Testament material about him. Thus, Peter was one of the three disciples who witnessed Jesus' transfiguration (Mk 9:2ff and parallels), an experience that is cited later to bring Petrine authority to bear on a particular situation in the church (1 Pet 1:16-18). The Book of Acts pictures Peter confronting Ananias and Sapphira (5:5:1ff), presumably because of knowledge revealed to him in a special way. Because of a vision he takes the initiative in the baptism of the Roman centurion Cornelius (Acts 10:9-16), and an angelic vision accomplishes his miraculous release from prison (12:7-9).

It is as a consequence of the special revelation associated with him that we have the image of "Peter the confessor of the true Christian faith" and "guardian of the faith against false teaching." Already during Jesus' ministry it is reported that Peter, guided by divine revelation, confessed Jesus to be the Messiah and Son of the living God (Mt 16:16-17). In the wake of the events of Easter, the Christian community recognized that because of this faith Peter is the rock (an obvious pun on his name; in Latin the word for rock is *petra*) on whom Jesus founded his church, which will withstand the powers of death. Implicit in the power of binding and loosing is the authority to act as guardian of the faith against false teaching. This power becomes explicit in the second Epistle that bears Peter's name where he "speaks as a magisterial voice that can interpret the prophecies of Scripture" (1:20-21) and corrects misinterpretations based on the teachings of Paul (3:15-16).

The Petrine Office   And finally there is the image of "Peter the weak and sinful man," but he is also the archetype of the repentant sinner. This person of little faith is saved from drowning by Jesus (Mt 14:28-31). Peter, the unworthy fisherman, is spiritually empowered by Jesus (Lk 5:8-10) and, truly repentant, becomes a source of strength for others (Lk 22:32). As we move from the portrayal of Peter in the New Testament to the portrayal found in the post-apostolic and patristic periods, we see the church, especially the church at Rome, consciously nurturing and developing what later comes to be known as the "Petrine office." The local churches, tenacious of their identity within the church catholic, assiduously cultivated unity and solidarity among themselves in the face of heresy, schism, and cultural diversity. They looked to the church at Rome for leadership, and Rome did not hesitate to intervene in the life of distant churches.[28]

It may have been, as the Eastern Orthodox hold, that the churches of Corinth and Lyons and Carthage and even Alexandria looked to

Rome for guidance because imperial Rome symbolized the unity of the Mediterranean world. The church at Rome, however, saw itself as heir to the role played by Peter: the ultimate witness to the sufferings of Jesus; shepherd-pastor entrusted with the task of confirming and strengthening the faith of the brethren; confessor of the true faith and bulwark against false teaching and teachers. In the fourth century St. Ambrose of Milan coined the phrase with reference to Rome, *Ubi Petrus, ibi ecclesia* ("Where Peter is, there is the Church"), and a short while later one of St. Augustine's sermons gave rise to the slogan *Roma locuta; causa finita* ("Rome has spoken, the matter is decided"). It was, however, in final analysis Pope Leo I, "the Great" (440-461), who gave consummate articulation to the notion of Roman primacy based on the Petrine office. The annual sermons preached by Leo on the feast of Sts. Peter and Paul and on the anniversary of his own ordination as bishop of Rome provided him the opportunity to reflect on prerogatives of the Roman see.[29]

Leo's pontificate (440-461) was remarkable for the way he advanced and consolidated the prestige of the Roman see under the most adverse circumstances. In the political sphere he was credited with saving Italy from Attila's Huns (452) and negotiating concessions from the Vandals when they overran Rome (455). His legates presided over the Council of Chalcedon; and Leo's *Tome*, a lengthy letter that outlined the traditional teaching of the church on christology, exercised a decisive influence on the conciliar fathers. According to the official Acts of the Council, after Leo's *Tome* was read "the most reverend bishops cried out: This is the faith of the fathers, this is the faith of the Apostles. . . . Peter has spoken through Leo."[30]

It is not possible in a work of this kind to trace the development of the papacy and of the Roman primacy from the patristic period to the present. Discounting exaggerated claims for the authority of the pope made at some periods in history, however, the trajectory beginning with Peter's multifaceted role in the New Testament can be charted, with some in-flight corrections, to Vatican II.

Indefectibility and Infallibility   Focusing as it does on both the origin and the goal of the Christian community, apostolicity means that God's intention and purpose for the church remains constant throughout history. It is a mark that identifies the church, but it is first of all a gift—*charism*—that ensures that the church ultimately remains faithful, despite setbacks, sinfulness, and temporary aberrations, to the messianic and eschatological way of living in community received from the Lord until he comes again. Apostolicity clearly implies "indefectibility" guaranteed by God's providence, which will prove stronger than all internal forces of dissolution and external threats to its existence combined. "The jaws of death shall not prevail against it" (Mt 16:18). The guidance of the Spirit does not allow the church to deviate fundamentally from the truth of the gospel or from the church's mission.

As a corollary of eschatology, indefectibility affirms that in the end the church will fulfill the destiny God intends for it. But more is at stake. To say all's well that ends well is not enough when people's lives—their hopes, values, and decisions—are at stake. En route to the eschaton the Holy Spirit also keeps the church faithful to apostolic teaching and to the spirit of the covenant. The Holy Spirit is present to the church so that when the Christian community is called on to confess, affirm, and explain the faith that has come down from the apostles, "it can do so in a confident, and we have to say," writes Congar, "an *infallible* way."[31]

Since the time of the first Vatican Council (1870), which affirmed infallibility to be a prerogative of the office of the bishop of Rome, successor of Peter, the word (Congar calls it a "disturbingly heavy term") as much as the concept has been a source of controversy. Much of the controversy is unfortunate because it obscures the fact that infallibility affirms a very positive doctrine and that it is not so much a personal attribute of the pope as a charism of the church.

Fortunately or unfortunately (according to one's temperament and outlook), papal infallibility is much more restricted than many Roman Catholics would like. There are those who would regard every papal utterance from the meditations of John XXIII to the instructions that John Paul II gives in his weekly audiences as infallible. In fact, however, Vatican I carefully qualified its definition, stating that

> the Roman Pontiff when he speaks *ex cathedra*, that is, when, acting in the office of shepherd and teacher of all Christians, he defines, by virtue of his supreme apostolic authority, a doctrine concerning faith or morals to be held by the universal Church, possesses through the divine assistance promised to him in the person of Blessed Peter, the infallibility which the divine Redeemer will His Church to be endowed. . . .[32]

As defined by Vatican I, papal infallibility is a *negative* gift; that is, it ensures that a particular teaching is not wrong. With most Catholic theologians, Richard McBrien explains that it "does not insure that a particular teaching is an *adequate* expression of a truth of faith or morals or even an *appropriate* formulation of that truth."[33] Papal infallibility, furthermore, is an extension of the church's infallibility and, as Vatican II makes clear, is always exercised in communion with the college of bishops and the whole church.

John Macquarrie, who expresses reservations about papal infallibility (at least, as it is popularly understood), nonetheless writes:

> For what is freedom from error if it is not penetration into truth? Could we say that just as a compass needle, when distracting influences have been removed, turns unfailingly toward the north, so the mind of the Church, when fully open to the Holy Spirit, turns unfailingly toward the truth? This would be the fulfillment of Christ's promise to the disciples, "When the Spirit of truth comes, he will guide you into all the truth" (Jn 16:13). This certainly does not mean that on any particular occasion there can be a verbal formulation that is totally free from error or that is delivered from the cultural and historical relativity that affects all verbalizations. Also, the relation to truth belongs to the whole Church, though clearly its leadership bears a special responsibility in this matter.[34]

Because infallibility is such a complex issue and the exercise of papal infallibility such a rare occurrence, more and more Catholic theologians, while emphasizing the positive dimension of infallibility alluded to by John Macquarrie and others, agree with Congar's assertion, "The concept which is most suitable to express the whole of the Church's attempt throughout history to profess the saving truth is, however, 'indefectibility.' "[35]

Apostolicity implies infallibility and indefectibility, but no more than the other notes—one, holy, catholic—does it mean that the church is not subject to the mischievousness and frailty of its members and leaders. The marks of the church are first of all gifts, but they need to be cultivated and nurtured. On the day of Pentecost, before it ever moved outside the gates of Jerusalem, the church was ONE, HOLY, CATHOLIC, and APOSTOLIC, much as a newborn is every inch a human being even before it begins to grow and develop its innate gifts. It is the Christian's task to make the marks visible and recognizable.

The marks are not gifts to some abstract, idealized, supra-national church that exists only in the vision of dreamers and ecumenists. Each local church that is truly church is of its nature ONE, HOLY, CATHOLIC AND APOSTOLIC. By reason of their baptism all Christians become members of the church, but their experience of church is fundamentally the community in which they worship, witness, and minister. In the next two chapters we look at baptism, eucharist, ministry, and other ways in which Christians struggle at the task of making the church appear as it really is ONE HOLY CATHOLIC AND APOSTOLIC.

Notes

1. *Unity of the Church*, ch. 3; *ACW*, p. 45.

2. Yves Congar, *I Believe in the Holy Spirit* (New York: Seabury Press, 1983), II, pp. 6–7. H. de Lubac, *La foi chrétienne*, chs. 4 to 6. J. P. L. Oulton, "The Apostles' Creed and Belief Concerning the Church," *Journal of Theological Studies* 39 (1938):239–243.

3. Article 9, n. 22. Bradley and Kevane, p. 111.

4. Yves Congar, *Diversity and Communion* (Mystic, CT: Twenty-Third Publications, 1985), pp. 9–43.

5. In February 1954, Congar was forbidden to teach. In 1956 he was given a limited assignment in Strasbourg. Despite suspicion and adversity, however, Congar continued to research and write. The concluding sentence to the paragraph just quoted reads: "Sometimes those persons have said what they have to say, but they have usually done so in irregular and unfavorable conditions." *Lumen Gentium*, the Constitution on the Church promulgated by Vatican II, incorporates many of Congar's insights and stands as a vindication of his lifelong efforts.

6. Congar, *I Believe*, II, p. 119.

7. *Unity of the Church*, ch. 5. *ACW*, no. 25, pp. 47–48.

8. The quotation is from St. Cyprian's treatise *On the Lord's Prayer*, 23. Congar calls attention to this passage, saying that this text from Cyprian inspired him in writing *Divided Christendom*. One also sus-

pects that Congar in turn inspired the passage in *Lumen Gentium*, par. 4.

9. By-Laws of the Faith and Order Commission quoted in *Baptism, Eucharist and Ministry* Faith and Order Paper No. 111 (Geneva: World Council of Churches, 1982), p. viii.

10. Decree on Ecumenism, par. 4. See Walter Abbot, ed. *Documents of Vatican II*, pp. 342, note 9, and p. 347, note 22. Also John T. Ford, s.v. "Ecumenical Movement" in *NCE* 18:140.

11. The Secretariat for Christian Unity was originally established as a preparatory committee for Vatican II and then in 1962 became a commission of the Council. In 1966 it became a permanent agency of the Roman Curia and continued to be headed by Cardinal Augustin Bea until his death in 1968.

12. See Walter Abbot, ed., *Documents of Vatican II*, p. 365, note 77.

13. Quoted in J.N.D. Kelly, *Creeds*, p. 159.

14. Congar, *I Believe*, II, p. 52.

15. *De sacrificio Missae* II, c. 9, art. 9. Quoted in Congar, *I Believe*, II, p. 6.

16. Joseph Ratzinger, *Introduction to Christianity* (New York: Herder and Herder, 1970), p. 263.

17. Smyrna, 8:2. *ACW*, p. 93.

18. Kelly, *Creeds*, p. 385.

19. *The Martyrdom of Polycarp*, 16:2; and see 8:1; *ACW*, No. 6, pp. 98, 99, 93.

20. Quoted in Kelly, *Creeds*, p. 385.

21. Catechetical Lecture 18:23; *NPNF* 2nd ser. VII, pp. 141–142. See Avery Dulles, "Representative Texts on the Church as Catholic," and "Meanings of the Word 'Catholic,' " in *The Catholicity of the Church* (Oxford: Clarendon Press, 1985), pp. 181–184, 185.

22. I Epistle of John, Homily X, quoted by de Lubac, *Catholicism* (New York: Mentor-Omega Books, 1964), p. 33. See *NPNF*, 1st ser., VII, p. 524.

23. *NCE* 10:789–801.

24. *JBC*, vol. 2, pp. 795–799.

25. Raymond E. Brown, Karl P. Donfried, John Reumann, eds., *Peter in the New Testament* (Paulist Press: New York, 1973) p. 158.

26. An editorial note explains that by "first appearance" the task force had in mind only those appearances of the Risen One "to those who would become official proclaimers of the resurrection." They do not discuss the question of previous appearances to the women followers of Jesus (p. 161, n. 340).

27. Pp. 163–164.

28. *Lutheran and Catholics in Dialog* V, p. 210.

29. For a selection of these sermons see J. Stevenson, *Creeds, Councils and Controversies* (London: SPCK, 1973), pp. 305–307. Also *NPNF* 2nd ser. XII.

30. *NPNF*, 2nd ser. XIV, p. 259. For the text of Leo's Tome, *ibid.*, pp. 251–258 and also in Stevenson, *Creeds, Councils and Controversies*, pp. 315–323.

31. Congar, *I Believe*, II, p. 46.

32. J. Neuner & J. Dupuis, *The Christian Faith*, n. 839, p. 234.

33. *Catholicism*, vol. II, p. 835.

34. *Principles*, p. 415.

35. *I Believe*, II, p. 46.

20

Sacraments of Initiation
and Sacramental Theology

"We acknowledge one baptism for the forgiveness of sins"

"There is a growing realization that the revised *Rite of Christian Initiation of Adults* (RCIA) is the most far-reaching and ambitious of all the post-Vatican liturgical reforms."[1] Some even go so far as to claim that the restoration of the ancient catechumenate—which is really at the heart of the RCIA—will prove in time to be the most significant of the changes inaugurated by the Second Vatican Council. The basis for these startling claims is that the RCIA put baptism once more at the front and center of the church's life. It unmasks a long series of cherished but mistaken understandings of what it means to be Christian. By involving the whole Christian community in all the steps that lead to membership in the church, it corrects the prevalent notion that baptism is a private matter. By emphasizing the adult aspects of the rite, the RCIA makes its clear that even the baptism of infants is not a childish affair. Based on the premise that baptism represents a complete reorientation of one's life, the catechumenate requires a prolonged period of reflection and preparation lasting a year or more. (In the early church the time of probation lasted several years!)

Although we shall say something about the restored rite, our interest here is not in the RCIA and the catechumenate as such. Rather, we use the ritual as a window through which to view the multiple meanings baptism had for Christians in the time of the New Testament and the patristic period. We consider baptism in the context of sacramental theology as a gift of the Holy Spirit. First we describe the rites of initiation, especially baptism and confirmation, in relationship to one another. (A fuller treatment of the eucharist, also an essential element in the initiation rite, will be given in the next chapter.) We review the Donatist controversy by way of introducing a consideration of the nature and effectiveness of sacraments. In the context of these general reflections on sacramental theology we then point up the significance of infant baptism.

Understandably, the full significance of baptism is obscured when only one or the other aspect of the sacrament is emphasized. If indeed many Christians have come to have a narrow understanding of baptism, seeing it primarily, if not solely, as a water-bath that washes away sins, it may have been that the Creed itself contributed to it because of the clause, WE ACKNOWLEDGE ONE BAPTISM FOR THE FORGIVENESS OF SINS. In proper context, however—that is, as explained and celebrated in the catechumenate and through the various steps that constitute the baptismal ritual—THE FORGIVENESS OF SINS is seen not to be so simple as a literal interpretation of the words first makes it appear.

BAPTISM AND CONFIRMATION

Baptism and the Forgiveness of Sins   The wording of the Apostles' Creed and of the Creed of Constantinople is representative of Western and Eastern forms. Both Creeds mention THE FORGIVENESS OF SINS in connection with the action of the Holy Spirit in the church, but in the Western creeds this phrase is simply one of the five clauses that make up the third article, while in the Eastern creeds it is routinely linked to baptism. Although the most primitive forms of the Creed often did not affirm the remission of sins, we have Peter's dramatic words in response to those who, upon hearing the proclamation on the first Pentecost, asked, "What are we to do, brothers?" He answered: "You must reform and be baptized, each one of you, in the name of Jesus Christ, that your sins may be forgiven; then you will receive the gift of the Holy Spirit" (Acts 2:38).

Several second-century writers pick up the theme found also in Paul (see 1 Cor 6:11) that linked washing with sanctification. The Epistle of Barnabas states, "We descend in the water, laden with sins and filth, and then emerge from it bearing fruit, with the fear (of God) in the heart and the hope of Jesus in the soul."[2] Justin tells us that candidates for initiation were instructed during their novitiate to pray specifically for the forgiveness of their sins, and that their prayers were supported by the intercession of the community. By the beginning of the third century there is such great emphasis on the remission of sins that in the *Apostolic Tradition* of Saint Hippolytus it is all but synonymous with baptism itself. The catechumenate, which had taken definite shape by this time, is said to have been "a vast sacramental dominated by the idea of exorcism," with elaborate rites designed to impress on catechumens the power of the devil and their need to separate themselves from a sinful world.[3]

The remission of sins referred to in connection with baptism is once and for all, not in the sense that future sins are forgiven but in the sense that baptism makes one a member of the church forever and ever. The rite of Christian baptism is never to be repeated. Later, in connection with other forms of penance and sacramental practice that developed in the early church, we shall consider remedies for sin committed after baptism. For the moment, however, we concentrate on baptism as the rite of Christian initiation.

Baptism as Initiation   Although writers extend the meaning of baptism to include "baptism of blood" (martyrdom), "baptism of desire" (as, for example, in the case of catechumens), and "baptism in the Spirit" (about which more later), baptism in its root meaning implies water. Why water? First of all, the Greek *baptizesthai* quite literally means "to be drowned." Furthermore, the primitive Christian community in Jerusalem, still very much attached to the Temple, was steeped in the Jewish custom of ritual washings, including proselyte baptism. A rite of washing was used by the Qumran community—a kind of monastic group located on the shores of the Dead Sea, some twenty kilometers from Jerusalem—to initiate new members. The example of John the Baptist, who baptized in the Jordan, had particular significance for Christians. Although John disclaimed that he was the Messiah, he appeared as a prophet preaching penance and announcing the imminent judgment of God. He stationed himself near a river crossing on the banks of the Jordan and made baptism in the river the hallmark of his ministry. He preached *metanoia*—repentance and conversion to a new way of living. John did not proclaim the kingdom of God, but he did call his listeners to face up to the coming judgment and take responsibility for their lives.

It is significant that Jesus allowed John to baptize him. In Mark's Gospel the event dates the beginning of Jesus' public ministry. Edward Schillebeeckx sees it as a "prophetic act"—an example of the kind of symbolic actions whereby Old Testament prophets dramatized the message they spoke in words.[4] Thus Jesus' baptism is revelatory. We see Jesus as a prophet sent by God to preach repentance and to proclaim the coming of the kingdom. All four Gospels note that when Jesus was baptized by John, "coming out of the water" he saw the Spirit descending on him like a dove from the sky (Mk 1:10; Mt 3:16; Lk 3:22; Jn 1:32). Many texts in the Old Testament use water imagery in describing the communication of God's spirit (Is 32:15; Joel 2:28-29; Ez 36:25-26). The Fourth Gospel quotes a saying of Jesus, "I assure you, no one can enter into God's kingdom without being begotten of water and Spirit" (Jn 3:4).[5]

The earliest instruction on baptism that we have, in the *Didache*, dates from about A.D.100:

> Baptize as follows: after first explaining all these points ["the way of death" vs. "the way of life"], baptize in the name of the Father and of the Son and of the Holy Spirit, in running water. But if you have no running water, baptize in other water; and if you cannot in cold, then in warm. But if you have neither, pour water on the head three times. . . .[6]

The preference for running water—the water of streams, springs, and fountains—stems from the fact that it better captures the spirit of life than does stagnant water of pools and cisterns. Furthermore, water from streams and fountains, because it is generally cool, refreshes and invigorates in a way that tepid water does not.

In many cultures, water rituals are used in *rites of passage*. Rites of passage are ceremonies that mark an individual's transition from one status to another—for example, from puberty to adulthood, from the single state to marriage. Anthropologists customarily distinguish three successive phases in such rites: separation, transition, and incorporation.[7] In their eyes, baptism as practiced in the ancient church and as it is now being revived in the RCIA is a typical example of a rite of passage: separation from previous life-style and behaviors; transition during the period of the catechumenate; and incorporation into full membership in the Christian community—an incorporation marked by the pouring of water and the confession of faith. In traditional religious terms the three phases of passage are referred to as "conversion": a turning away from evil, a turning toward God, and finally a commitment.

Christian baptism, moreover, is a rite of passage in another sense. It is not simply a pun to say that it represents the passage of the Israelites through the Red Sea. For the church, baptism *symbolizes*—that is, both represents and makes present—the sequence of events that constitute the Passover-Exodus theme and the basis of Christian life. The baptismal rites recall the experience of the Israelites: at the beginning of the formal catechumenate the brows of the candidates are anointed just as the houses of the Israelites were marked with the blood of the Passover lamb, a signal that they were to be exempted from the punishment due to sin. The Israelites fled Egypt, abandoning a way of life they had known for generations, leaving behind most of their possessions. The forty days of lenten penance correspond to the forty days Jesus spent in the desert and in turn to the years the Israelites spent in the Sinai, for Lent also is a time of trial, of inner conflict when the powers of darkness vie with the Spirit of light in the soul. The scrutinies, the exorcisms, and the blessings expose the devil and strengthen the candidates in overcoming the demons that beset them from within and without.

The baptismal ritual is a fabric of symbolic actions, gestures whose significance is inherent in the rite itself, beginning with the day itself: Easter is the most appropriate time for it recalls the Passover and commemorates Jesus' own death and resurrection. Ideally the Easter liturgy is scheduled at night, as it was in ancient times, to bring out the contrast between the darkness that envelops the earth and the light that emanates from the Paschal candle representing Christ, the light of world. By professing the Creed, the candidates for baptism once again renounce Satan and confess the saving work of the Triune God for all to hear. Baptism by immersion dramatizes how one dies to sin and is buried with Christ and is raised to a new life in him. (It should be noted that even though the new rite allows the practice of merely pouring water on the head of the baptizand, it also states, "The washing is not merely a rite of purification, but a sacrament of union with

Christ" (par. 32). Baptism typifies the reality of the paschal mystery, Christ's passover from death to life. By the power of the Trinity, made real by the action of the Holy Spirit, the baptizands experience in faith death and resurrection—in the words of St. Ambrose, a "passing over from sin to life, from guilt to grace, from defilement to sanctification."[8] This sacramental resurrection constitutes rebirth as children of God. "At the new birth of each one of us," said Leo the Great in one of his sermons, "the baptismal water becomes the mother's womb. For the same Holy Spirit which filled the Virgin fills the font as well, so that sin, which in her case was eliminated by her sacred conception, is here blotted out by a mystical washing."[9]

The meaning of baptism is further dramatized by three "explanatory rites" (RCIA 223): the newly baptized are anointed with holy oil, clothed with a white garment, and presented with a lighted candle. The anointing "is a sign of the royal priesthood of the baptized and their enrollment in the fellowship of people of God" (RCIA 33, 224). The white garment "is a symbol of their new dignity" (RCIA 33), clothed as they are in the new life in Christ that they are called upon to live until his return. And the candle, lighted from the paschal candle that represents Christ, "shows their vocation of living as befits the children of light" (RCIA 33) so they may one day enter into his heavenly kingdom (RCIA 226).

Confirmation   In order to gain a richer understanding of the rites of Christian initiation, we need to see confirmation, which has become in the Western church a separate sacrament, in its original context. In the early Church it was an integral part of the baptismal rite, and the RCIA tries to recapture something of the spirit of the ancient rites by adapting many of the former practices. St. Hippolytus gives a rather detailed account of baptism as it was celebrated in Rome about 215.[10] With a little imagination it is easy to picture the scene he describes.

The Christian community is gathered for the celebration of the Easter Vigil. The people spend the night reading the Scriptures that tell how God created the universe, sent the flood to purge the world of wickedness, rescued Israel from slavery in Egypt, and led them safely through the Red Sea and trials in the desert to a land flowing with milk and honey. All the while the paschal candle, symbolizing Christ the light of the nations, burns bright in their midst.

About daybreak ("at the hour when the cock crows") the newly converted ("neophytes") are led to the baptistry or perhaps to the banks of the nearby Tiber River, where one of the priests bids them renounce Satan and then anoints each of them with the oil of exorcism. A deacon leads them down into the water, where another priest asks them to affirm the church's profession of faith, the Creed, and thereupon baptizes them. When they come out of the water they are again anointed by the priest, this time with the fragrant oil of thanksgiving. They dry themselves, put on their clothes, and return to the assembly, where they are greeted by the bishop, who stretches out his hand and prays over them in Greek:

> O Lord God, who didst count these [*Thy servants*] worthy of deserving the forgiveness of sins by the laver of regeneration, make them worthy to be filled with Thy Holy Spirit and send up on them Thy grace, that they may serve Thee according to Thy will; [*for*] to Thee [*is*] the glory, to the Father and to the Son with [*the*] Holy Ghost in the holy Church, both now and ever and world without end. Amen.

The bishop, pouring oil and laying his hand on each of the newly baptized, says, "I anoint thee with holy oil in God the Father Almighty and Christ Jesus and the Holy Ghost." Thus "sealing" them on the forehead, the bishop gives each the kiss of peace saying, "The Lord be with you." The rest of the community then welcomes them with a kiss of peace, and for the first time they remain to celebrate the eucharist. As he goes along, the bishop explains the symbolism of the ceremonies so that the newly baptized can enter more fully into the celebration.

From Hippolytus' account it is evident that at Rome the initiation rites lasted through the night into the morning. By his time it was the established practice to move immediately from baptism to the celebration of the eucharist, which is an important part, in fact the highlight, of the initiation rites. The initiation process forms an integral whole whose meaning is blurred when the parts are separated from one another and their essential unity destroyed. The anointing within the baptismal rite is the "sealing" with the Holy Spirit that signals the incorporation of the baptized into the unity of the Body of Christ. The anointing, in fact, makes each Christian another *christus*—"one who is anointed," and a sharer in Christ's royal priesthood. It is precisely because the anointing rite came to stand alone, apart from the water rite and eucharist, that the meaning and purpose of confirmation has been for centuries one of the most controversial, not to say confused, issues in sacramental theology.

Given the fact that it was the bishop's prerogative to perform this post-baptismal chrismation—anointing with chrism—it is understandable how circumstances conspired to separate confirmation from the celebration of the Easter Vigil and from the context of Christian initiation itself. Pope Innocent I stated, "The right of bishops alone to seal and to deliver the Spirit the Paraclete is proved not only by the custom of the Church but also by that reading in the Acts of the Apostles which tells how Peter and John were directed to deliver the Holy Spirit to people who were already baptized."[11] The absence of the bishop because of illness, difficulty of travel, or simply because the see was vacant forced postponement of the confirmation rite. In large cities such as Rome, where it was necessary to establish "presbyteral titles" (that is to say, parish churches; see above, Chapter 18), each with its own liturgy, the bishop could not be present at more than one Easter celebration. During the Middle Ages, especially north of the Alps, where the church was less urban and more rural, the bishop was even more inaccessible.[12] Gradually the confirmation rite, whereby the bishop ratified a person's initiation into the Christian community, took on a life of its own.

Following the mandate of Vatican II, Pope Paul VI revised the rite of confirmation so "that the intimate connection of this sacrament with the whole of Christian initiation [would] stand out more clearly."[13] The best and easiest way to maintain the proper relationship of the sacraments of initiation to one another is, first, to respect the traditional order of baptism, confirmation, and eucharist; and second, to celebrate them together, as is done in the Rite of Christian Initiation of Adults. The RCIA (34) explains the unity of the sacraments of initiation as follows:

> This connection signifies the unity of the paschal mystery, the close relationship between the mission of the Son and the pouring out of the Holy Spirit, and the joint celebration of the sacraments by which the Son and the Spirit come with the Father upon those who are baptized. (n. 34)

The revised rite of confirmation was inspired in large part by the tradition of the Eastern churches, with its emphasis on the working of the Holy Spirit. As the minister anoints the confirmand with the oil of chrism he says, "Be sealed with the Gift of the Holy Spirit." The formula blends two New Testament texts: Ephesians 1:13, where Paul says that in Christ "you were sealed with the Holy Spirit who had been promised," and Acts 2:38, where Peter urges his hearers to be baptized "that your sins may be forgiven; then you will receive the gift of the Holy Spirit."[14] For the most part the Eastern churches managed to safeguard the integrity of Christian initiation rites better than the West so that with them the sacrament of confirmation or, as they prefer to call it, chrismation, does not have a separate identity. The priest who baptizes also anoints. A vestige of the bishop's role remains, however, in that it is he who consecrates the oil of chrism.

The very essence of the rite of confirmation is the gift of the Spirit, whose seal marks the baptized as Christians. In the ancient world one's seal was like a modern person's signature. Impressed on wax, it identified the author of an official document or letter; a seal tattooed on the forearms of soldiers identified them with a particular legion; branded on animals, the seal indicated ownership. Thus the outpouring of the Holy Spirit seals Christians with the sign of the cross—the insignia of their allegiance, the mark of their salvation.[15]

THE NATURE AND EFFECTIVENESS OF SACRAMENTS

Church and Sacrament   It is evident that the significance of these rites of initiation, individually and collectively, within the overall baptismal ritual is multivalent. They make subtle allusions to the People of God in the Old Testament, the paschal mystery exemplified in the death and resurrection of Jesus, and the church as both the eschatological community of the saved and the gift of the Spirit in the lives of the baptized. The baptism ritual simultaneously embodies elements of a rite of purification FOR THE FORGIVENESS OF SINS, a sacramental enactment of dying and being born again, incorporation into the Body of Christ, and the receiving of the Holy Spirit. Although these various aspects of baptism are related, it is impossible to force them into a tidy synthesis. Only when baptism is seen as an initiation rite that incorporates one into the Christian community do the pieces fit together.[16] The basic meaning of baptism derives from the reality of the church, which itself is many things: People of God, Body of Christ, temple of the Holy Spirit, reconciling community, symbol of the eschatological kingdom. Baptism is *a* sacrament—even, in the words of Vatican II, a *fundamental* sacrament, but the church is *the* sacrament in which all other sacraments are grounded.

Donatism, Ecclesiology, and Sacramental Theology   Baptism and eucharist (the latter is the other *fundamental* sacrament), both essential to the very notion of church, were celebrated from the earliest days of the Christian community. It was only over the course of time, however, that a theology of sacraments emerged. St. Justin, St. Hippolytus, and others describe the rites, but it took until the fourth century, with the peace of Constantine, before the church found itself engaged in a full-blown discussion about the meaning, nature, and function of sacraments. At the same time that controversy over theology of the Trinity and christology raged in the eastern half of the Empire, the church in North Africa found itself divided over issues of episcopal ordination and baptism. Underlying the dispute, as we shall see, was the question of what it means for the church to be holy and catholic. The dispute in Africa was triggered by Donatism, a complex movement fueled by nationalistic and socio-economic factors as well as by religious and theological issues. The Donatist movement conditioned St. Augustine's reflections on the nature of sacrament and thereby proved to be the crucible in which were forged the ecclesiology and sacramental theology of the West (and indirectly of the East) to the present day.

North Africa's ties with the Roman Empire predate Christianity, but its populace was never entirely Latinized. Although the irradicable vestiges of the native Berber culture are often overlooked in church history because the earliest Christian authors of North Africa—Tertullian and Cyprian—wrote in Latin, they were an important element in the spread of the Donatist schism, which was in large part a populist reaction against the Roman establishment.[17] Apart from the theological issues, St. Augustine's sympathies and strategies, especially in the later phases of the dispute, were conditioned in large part by his loyalty to the empire. Tertullian and Cyprian, intransigent in the face of the dominant culture, each in his own way had differences at times with Rome, while Augustine, totally Latinized, looked to Rome for leadership and approval.

The immediate occasion of the Donatist schism was the election and ordination of the unpopular archdeacon Caecilian as bishop of Carthage in 312. There was first of all a jurisdictional dispute: Caecilian took possession of the see, disregarding the primate of neighboring Numidia (eastern Algeria), who claimed the right to consecrate each new bishop of Carthage. But more importantly, there was a theological issue: according to rumor (later proved false), one of the bishops who had ordained Caecilian had been a *traditor*—that is, an individual who, in compliance with an anti-Christian edict of 303 during the reign of Emperor Diocletian, handed over copies of the Christian Scriptures to Roman authorities. Thus it was charged that Caecilian's ordination was invalid. An ecclesiastical council controlled by his adversaries declared the see vacant and a short time later in 315 (after its first nominee died) installed Donatus, a Numidian cleric, as bishop of Carthage. The action created in the African church a schism which, despite papal and imperial interventions, endured more than a century.[18] The Catholic world remained in communion with Caecilian and his successors, but in the provinces of North Africa Donatism had strong popular support, especially among the Berber population in rural areas.

Although the Donatist doctrine regarding the sacraments was shaped by the circumstances that gave rise to the schism, its roots ran deeper. Inspired by the noble tradition of African martyrs, the Donatists saw every accommodation to the contemporary world and human weakness as compromise. To them, the church was an exclusive caste separated from a sinful world. Their understanding of holiness meant that the church's ministers must be holy and that the efficacy of sacraments depended on the worthiness of the ministers. The Donatists regarded Caecilian's ordination to the episcopate as invalid because, they alleged, one of the ordaining prelates was a *traditor* and therefore the sacraments dispensed by Caecilian, his followers, and successors were likewise invalid.

By the time Augustine returned to North Africa in 388 and became active in the church, Donatism was well established. Augustine's native Numidia was its stronghold, and a number of his relatives were adherents. From 392, that is, even before he was a bishop, until the close of his life in 430, Augustine addressed the Donatists in his sermons, correspondence, biblical commentaries, and formal theological treatises. For the most part his approach was irenic, debating them as schismatics rather than heretics. Augustine showed little tolerance, however, for their practice of rebaptizing converts from the Catholic church, who in the eyes of the Donatists were heretics. For him it was a monstrous distortion of both baptism and church.

Augustine faulted the Donatist church on two counts. First, it was not Catholic, because it had cut itself off from communion with the apostolic sees in the rest of Christendom. Second, its insistence that the church be without spot or blemish could not be sustained either on scriptural grounds or in reality. Parables such as that of the wheat and tares (Mt 13:24-29) and that of the dragnet (Mt 13:47-50) make it clear that in this world the church is a mixed body; its true members would be recognized only on the last day, not "in the time of Donatus."

Augustine illustrated his fundamental difficulty with the Donatists by referring again and again to their practice of rebaptizing everyone who was not baptized by one of their own ministers. For their part, Catholics accepted Donatist baptism because the sacrament, regardless of whether the minister is in good standing in the church, is valid as long as it is administered in the name of Christ. We have already noted that the Western creeds, like that in use in North Africa, did not explicitly mention baptism. In all likelihood, however, the confession of ONE BAPTISM in the Creed of Constantinople was intended to reaffirm the church's ban on rebaptizing heretics. Raymond Brown suggests that the Epistle to the Hebrews may be insisting on the once-only aspect of baptism when it says: "For when men have once been enlightened and have tasted the heavenly gift and become sharers in the Holy Spirit . . . and then have fallen away, it is impossible to make them repent again" (6:4). It is significant that the one time the phrase occurs in the New Testament it is in a Trinitarian context:

> There is but one body and one Spirit, just as there is but one hope given all of you by your call. There is one Lord, one faith, ONE BAPTISM; one God and Father of all, who is over all, and works through all, and is in all." (Eph 4: 4-5; emphasis added)

The focus of this passage, according to Brown, is not on the one-time-only aspect of baptism but on the fact that the oneness of baptism comes from the oneness of the Lord into whom all are baptized. He interprets the foregoing in light of another passage in Ephesians which says that Christ gave himself up for the church "to make her holy, purifying her in the bath of water by the power of the word" (5:25-26).

Thus through ONE BAPTISM Christians are initiated into the death and resurrection of Jesus—the saving event that is *eph hapax*, "once for all."[19]

Word and Sacrament   In criticizing the Donatist practice of rebaptizing Catholics, Augustine wrote:

> In the question of baptism we have to consider, not who gives, but what he gives; not who receives, but what he receives; not who has, but what he has.[20]

Thus he attributed an objective power to the sacramental rites themselves that transcends the moral dispostions of both the minister and the recipient. It is this power that theologians have in mind when they use the phrase *ex opere operato* ("by power of the work done").

Consequently Augustine and theologians after him are able to distinguish two ways in which a sacrament is effective: it can be valid but, because of the disposition of the recipient, unfruitful regarding sanctification; or it can be (as it should be) both valid and fruitful. Although the moral disposition—the holiness—of the minister is not essential to the efficacy of the sacrament, the moral disposition of the recipient has a bearing on its fruitfulness. At a minimum, as in the case of an infant being initiated into the church, the sacrament is both valid and fruitful with regard to salvation as long as the recipient does not thwart its power by putting an obstacle in its way. On the other hand, an adult who tenaciously remains unreconciled with an erstwhile friend or willfully continues unrepentant for some other serious sin may be validly baptized yet not have his or her sins remitted.

It is important to stress that it is God who makes the divine presence a reality in the sacraments. Sacramental rites such as washing in water, anointing with oil, or breaking bread together have a power that transcends the activities themselves, but their effectiveness does not inhere in the actions as if those actions were some kind of magic. An essential part of every sacramental act is the spoken word. The word evokes the Word of God and situates the sacrament in the context of the believing community, the church. It is the word that gives the washing, anointing, and eating their special significance and distinguishes them from ordinary human activities. Word and sacrament are necessary to each other. Word gives meaning to the sacramental action; the sacramental action gives substance to the word. The proclamation of the word calls the church into being; the church, the sign of God's presence, exists to mediate the Word in the world. The church as sacrament signals to men and women of faith what God has done and continues to do for the salvation of humanity in and through Christ and the Holy Spirit. Baptism, eucharist, and other sacraments proclaim by word and action the reality of the atonement, reconciliation and pledge of future glory for individual believers.

INFANT BAPTISM

Although his mother Monica saw to it that baby Augustine was "marked with the sign of the cross and purified with the salt" as a catechumen, he was almost thirty-three years old when he asked to be baptized. Given the fact that Augustine himself was already an adult when he was baptized, his frequent references to the practice of baptizing infants are significant. His position regarding infant baptism becomes even more intriguing in light of the following passage from his commentary on the "enlightenment" of the man born blind (John 9). The man blind from birth, according to Augustine, is the embodiment of the human race. Augustine recounts how Jesus first anointed the man's eyes with mud made of spittle and then sent him off to wash in the pool of Siloam, a symbol of baptism. Augustine continues:

> Ask a man, Are you a Christian? His answer to you is, I am not, if he is a pagan or a Jew. But if he says, I am; you inquire again of him, Are you a catechumen or a believer? If he reply, A catechumen; he has been anointed, but not yet washed. But how anointed? Inquire, and he will answer you. Inquire of him in whom he believes. In that very respect in which he is a catechumen he says, In Christ. See, I am speaking in a way both to the faithful and to catechumens. What have I said of the spittle and clay? That the Word was made flesh. This even catechumens hear; but that to which they have been anointed is not all they need; let them hasten to the font if they are in search of enlightenment.[21]

Augustine's audience, which evidently included catechumens, could not have missed his point. Catechumens were "hearers" (Latin, *audientes*), and though they confessed belief in Christ, their eyes were not yet opened to the fullness of the sacred mysteries. His admonition that they hasten to the font was an implicit criticism of the current fashion that led many "Christians" to postpone baptism unduly. Even prominent figures such as St. Basil the Great, St. Gregory Nazienzus, St.

Ambrose, St. Jerome, and St. John Chrysostom, born into Christian families and anointed as catechumens in infancy, postponed baptism to their adult years.[22]

Although infant baptism gradually became the prevalent practice in the church, the New Testament makes no specific mention of it. Many scholars, however, find implicit evidence for the practice in a number of biblical texts. In using the example of circumcision to explain the significance of baptism, St. Paul seems to imply that baptism, like circumcision, could be administered to infants (Col 2:11ff). Elsewhere the apostle says the children of Christian parents are "holy" (1 Cor 7:14), and he exhorts them to obey their parents "in the Lord" (Col 3:30; Eph 6:11). At no time does Paul (or any of the other New Testament writers) suggest that these children will have to seek baptism at some later date as they grow into adulthood. In Mark's Gospel Jesus is pictured as putting his arms around a child and saying, "Whoever welcomes a child such as this for my sake welcomes me" (Mk 9:37). Some scholars read into this passage a justification for infant baptism. When, as in the case of Lydia's (Acts 16:15), an entire "household" was baptized, children are presumed to have been included along with the adults (see Acts 16:33; 18:8; 1 Cor 1:16).

By the second century, evidence for the practice of infant baptism is more definite. St. Justin speaks of Christians sixty or seventy years old who had "from childhood been made disciples" (*Apol.* I, 15). St. Irenaeus speaks of Christ as giving salvation to people of every age, and he expressly includes "infants and little children" (*Adv. Haer.* ii, 39). In the third century, Tertullian voices opposition to infant baptism (the protest itself witnesses to the practice). He urged that the baptism of children be deferred until they can "know Christ." As he grew older, Tertullian became even more strict. His principal reason for postponing baptism was that he felt the remission of sins committed after baptism was difficult if not impossible.

Although the catechumens' habit of postponing baptism until adulthood was widespread, by the time of Augustine at the end of the fourth and the beginning of the fifth century, the practice of infant baptism was in the ascendent. Even before dust had settled on the Donatist controversy, Augustine took up his pen against the Pelagians who held that infants were innocent until, corrupted by bad example, they fell into sin. By way of refutation Augustine cites the practice of infant baptism as evidence for original sin: baptism is for the remission of sin; the church baptizes infants who are incapable of personal sin; therefore it must follow that sin is rooted in some way in human nature. (It should be noted that when Augustine and other church writers of the early period speak of infant baptism they take it for granted that the initiation rite includes the anointing, laying on of hands, and eucharist—in the case of small babies, Communion consisting of a few drops of the consecrated wine.

Inspired by Augustine's reasoning in his debates against both the Donatists and Pelagians, theologians frequently use infant baptism to illustrate the essential nature of Christian sacraments. Infant baptism dramatizes in a way that adult baptism does not the special favor of God's election. The child, incapable of doing anything toward her or his own salvation, is adopted as a child of God, to share by grace in the divine life that the eternally begotten Son possesses by nature. Arthur Carl Piepkorn describes the worst possible scenario:

> As the child is carried to the font, it is incapable of meeting any precondition. It does not have contrition; it does not have faith; it does not have the intention of receiving a sacrament; it cannot comprehend or respond to a proclamation of the gospel. What is more, the minister of the sacrament may be immoral and unrepentant. The sponsors that represent the church may be members of the holy community *nomine tantum non re* ["nominally but not in practice"]. Whatever happens in baptism must be God's work.[23]

Unworthy minister, lackadaisical godparents, and (perhaps) indifferent parents notwithstanding, the baptism of a newborn infant, an entirely gratuitous gift, is the paradigm of God's saving grace bestowed on human beings.[24]

Infant baptism became controversial with the Reformation. On the one side were the Catholics, Lutherans, and Calvinists, who staunchly defended the traditional practice. On the other side were the "anabaptists," so nicknamed because of their practice of rebaptizing persons who had been baptized as infants. The anabaptists include a number of disparate groups, sometimes referred to as "the left wing of the Reformation," who insisted on a personal confession of faith as a requisite for true baptism. Among their modern descendants are the Mennonites (after Menno Simons, an early leader) and the Baptists. The latter trace their origins to John Smyth, who, influenced by the Mennonites, recognized only "the baptism of believers" as the basis for fellowship in the church.

The need to reconcile these divergent traditions has been a major task of the Faith and Order Commission of the World Council of Churches. In its so-called Lima document it states:

> Both the baptism of believers and the baptism of infants take place in the Church as the community of faith. When one who can answer for himself or herself is baptized, the personal response will be offered at a later moment in life. In both cases, the baptized person will have to grow in the understanding of faith. . . In the case of infants, personal confession is expected later, and Christian nurture is directed to the eliciting of this confession. All baptism is rooted in and declares Christ's faithfulness unto death. It has its setting within the life and faith of the Church and, through the witness of the whole Church, points to the faithfulness of God, the ground of all life in faith. At every baptism the whole congregation reaffirms its faith in God and pledges itself to provide an environment of witness and service. Baptism should, therefore, always be celebrated and developed in the setting of the Christian community.[25]

PASSING ON THE STORY

In addition to the RCIA—"believer's baptism"—a new ritual was prepared for the baptism of children. Like the former, it emphasizes that the rite should be celebrated in the setting of the Christian community, preferably during the Easter vigil but in lieu of that, in the context of the Sunday liturgy. The People of God, the church, made present in the local community, has an important part in the baptism of both infants and adults. Before and after the celebration of the sacrament, the baptized has a right to the love and support of the community. The faith that the baptized confesses is not the private possession of individuals or of one's family but is the common treasure of the whole church of Christ.[26]

In the rite of initiation the sharing of common faith is symbolized by the community's "handing over" the Creed to the catechumens shortly before they present themselves for baptism. We have mentioned this rite earlier in explaining that the Creed is a synopsis of the Christian story—the account of God's saving action in the world. It is a story that needs to be told over and over, but it is also a mystery that transcends mere words. In the next chapter we shall see how the *communio sanctorum*, which is the context of the Creed, provides substance for the words.

Notes

1. Michael Dujarier, *The Rites of Christian Initiation* (New York: W. H. Sadlier, 1979); in the foreword by Charles W. Gusmer, p. 14.

2. Ch. 11, 9. *ACW* no. 6, p. 54.

3. *Apostolic Tradition* xxii:1. Other texts for this period are cited in J. N. D. Kelly, *Creeds*, pp. 161, 162.

4. *Jesus: An Experiment in Christology* (New York: Crossroad, 1981), p. 138.

5. See Raymond E. Brown, in *One Baptism for the Remission of Sins: Lutherans and Catholics in Dialogue II*, ed. Paul C. Empie and T. Austin Murphy (Minneapolis: Augsburg Publishing House, 1967), pp. 12–13.

6. Ch. 7. *ACW*, no. 6, p. 19.

7. In 1909 Charles-Arnold Kurr van Gennep (d. 1957) published *The Rites of Passage*. It opened a whole new approach to the study of religion and ritual. *International Encyclopedia of the Social Sciences* 6:113–114.

8. *De Sacramentis* I, 4, 12; quoted in Burkhard Neunheuser, *Baptism and Confirmation* (New York: Herder and Herder, 1964), p. 115.

9. *Sermo* 24, 3; quoted in Neunheuser, ibid., p. 132.

10. Gregory Dix, ed., *The Apostolic Tradition of St. Hippolytus of Rome* (London: SPCK, 1937), pp. 30–43.

11. E. C. Whitaker, *Documents of the Baptismal Liturgy* (London: SPCK, 1970), p. 229.

12. J. D. C. Fisher, *Christian Initiation: Baptism in the Medieval West* (London: SPCK, 1965) pp. 22–24; 47–77.

13. *Sacrosanctum Concilium*, n. 71.

14. Gerard Austin, *Anointing with the Spirit* (New York: Pueblo Publishing Co., 1985), pp. 42–46.

15. G. W. H. Lampe, *The Seal of the Spirit* (London: Longmans, Green and Co., 1951).

16. Krister Stendahl, "The Focal Point of the New Testament Baptismal Teachings," in *Lutherans and Catholics in Dialogue II*, p. 24.

17. W. H. C. Frend argues this thesis in *The Donatist Church*, 2d ed. (Oxford: Oxford University Press, 1971), and in an abridged form in *Saints and Sinners in the Early Church* (Wilmington, DE: Michael Glazier, 1985), pp. 94–117.

18. Constantine's action was a precedent for his intervention a short time later in the Arian controversy, and it influenced church-state relations into modern times.

19. Brown, *One Baptism*, pp. 17–18.

20. *De baptismo contra Donatistas*, IV, 10:17.

21. Tract. XLIV, 1; *NPNF*, VIII, p. 245.

22. By the end of the fourth century the catechumenate was no longer for a fixed period. Basil and Gregory Nazianzus lived for a number of years as monks before their baptism at 26 and 28 respectively. Jerome was 19 when he was baptized, and Ambrose was baptized only after he was acclaimed bishop of Milan at the age of 35. St. John Chrysostom, under the tutelage of monks from a very early age, was nearly 20 before he received baptism.

23. Paul C. Empie and T. Austin Murphy eds., *Lutherans and Catholics in Dialogue I–III* (Minneapolis: Augsburg Publishing House, n.d.), II, pp. 51–52.

24. The worthiness of the minister, it must be noted, is not a matter of indifference. See Karl Rahner, *The Church and the Sacraments* (New York: Herder and Herder, 1963), pp. 98–99.

25. *Baptism, Eucharist and Ministry*. Faith and Order Paper No. 111 (Geneva: World Council of Churches, 1982), par. 12, p. 4.

26. *Rite of Baptism for Children*, n. 5.

21

Holy Things
for Holy People

"The communion of saints"

We concluded the last chapter stressing that baptism is a social event that should always be celebrated and witnessed by the Christian community. The first effect of baptism, we saw, is to initiate individuals into the *visible* church and thereby incorporate them into a network of mystical relationships. In Latin we call this network the *communio sanctorum*. The term appears in the Apostles' Creed and is routinely translated as COMMUNION OF SAINTS though it can be rendered—perhaps more accurately—as "a sharing in, or partaking of, holy things." It is evident that these translations lead to very different understandings of *communio sanctorum*. The first and more familiar translation, COMMUNION OF SAINTS, interprets the Latin *sanctorum* as referring to persons (*sancti*)—the martyrs and confessors, living and dead, and all who constitute the body of Christ. The second interprets *sanctorum* as a neuter noun referring to "holy things" (*sancta*), a traditional term for the elements of the eucharist.

As different as these two translations of *communio sanctorum* are, they are not mutually exclusive. In this chapter we begin by taking

347

communio sanctorum to mean "partaking of holy things," a reference to the eucharist and, in an extended sense, to all the sacraments and other benefits that members of the church share. Next we turn from the "holy things" that are shared by the "saints," to the holy people, who share sacred gifts and comprise the community. Before we attempt to reconcile these two points of view, however, and come to an understanding of what is intended by the confession of belief in the *communio sanctorum*, it will be helpful to say a word about the first appearance of the phrase and its setting in the Apostles' Creed. Its origins provide a clue to its meaning.

There is no mention of the *communio sanctorum* in the Creed of Constantinople or in the old Roman Creed that was the core of most of the baptismal creeds—including the Apostles' Creed—in the Latin West. Among the surviving examples of the Creed, the earliest mention of *communio sanctorum* is found in a fourth-century commentary by one Nicetas, a missionary bishop of Remesiana (the site of the modern Yugoslavian village of Bela Palanka, southeast of Nish). About the same time, the phrase appeared in an imperial rescript of 388 banning the Apollinarians from the *communio sanctorum* and in a canon of a synod at Nimes about 394. Subsequently, mention of the *communio sanctorum* begins to occur as a regular feature in the creeds of South Gaul.

During the lifetime of Nicetas (c. 335-414), there seems to have been a strong current of influence that flowed from the East to South Gaul through his Balkan homeland. Nicetas himself is known to have been inspired by Eastern writings as is indicated by his dependence on the Catechetical Lectures of St. Cyril of Jerusalem. Moreover, there are, in J. N. D. Kelly's words, "persuasive pointers" that the phrase was an import from the East.

> While the expression SANCTORUM COMMUNIO was rare and its meaning fluctuating in the West, the Greek equivalent, viz. *koinonia ton agion*, and related phrases were firmly established in the East and bore the clear-cut sense of "participation in the holy things," i.e. the eucharistic elements.[1]

The provenance of the phrase is important in interpreting its meaning. If, as more and more contemporary scholars are persuaded, *communio sanctorum* translates the Greek phrase *koinonia ton agion*, it is, as Kelly says, a clear-cut reference to the eucharist.[2] If, however, the phrase was coined in South Gaul or in some other Latin-speaking region, its original meaning might well have been a reference to the "saints."[3]

THE PARTAKING OF THE HOLY THINGS (SANCTA)

The Eucharist   Christians incorporated into Christ—made members of the Body of Christ—once and for all by baptism, identify with him in his suffering and death (Phil 3:10; 1 Pet 4:13) and his risen glory (1 Pet 5:1; Rom 6:3-11). It is a communion sealed with the gift that is the Spirit of Christ (2 Cor 13:13; Phil 2:1; Gal 4:6; Rom 8:14-17). But their union with Christ continues to be most dramatically represented by partaking of the Lord's body and blood in the eucharist (1 Cor 10:16-17).

The journey of two disciples to Emmaus was the preview of every eucharist. The eucharist, combining as it does the liturgy of the word with action, recalls the church's past, reflects on its present mission, and looks forward to its destiny. The readings from Scripture narrate God's saving action in history: the story of the People of God rescued from bondage and brought into the promised land; St. Paul's constant reminders of the dignity and responsibility that come with baptism; and Jesus' miracles and proclamation of the kingdom. The sharing of a meal in obedience to Jesus' injunction "Do this in memory of me" recalls how he celebrated the Passover with his disciples on that fateful night before he was executed. The breaking of the bread and the partaking of the cup, symbolic of the life that Christians share with one another, recall how Jesus laid down his life for others.

The eucharist celebrates the divine presence in the Word. Jesus as Word of God is the fullest expression of that presence. The presence of the Word is proclaimed in the assembly of the faithful and made real in the written word—the Scriptures inspired by the Holy Spirit. And wherever two or three are gathered together in his name, Jesus is in their midst. Jesus identified himself with the bread as he broke it to share it with his disciples; as he poured out the wine so that they could partake of it, he anticipated the shedding of his own blood. To the faithful there is no doubt about Jesus' presence in the eucharist. They look about them and see people who like themselves were baptized—made members of Christ's Body—and who like themselves carry the marks of his sufferings in their person. To emphasize that the divine presence is an objective reality and not simply tokenism or some kind of group delusion, it is spoken of as "real" presence (though the wording seems redundant because not to be *really* present is to be absent!).

In ordinary parlance the eucharist has acquired many names, each highlighting one or other of the elements that make it up. Among the more common ways of referring to it are the Lord's Supper, the breaking of the bread, Holy Communion, the divine liturgy, and sacrifice of the Mass, or simply the Mass. The eucharist, essentially a one-act drama, comprises several themes; we single out three for particular consideration: *thanksgiving to the Father, memorial of Christ, invocation of the Spirit.* Each of these three themes traditionally carried a Greek label—*eucharistia, anamnesis, epiklesis*—and each gives an insight into the inexhaustible richness of the eucharist. Taken together they indicate the bond between the eucharistic celebration and the Triune God and at the same time demonstrate why the eucharist is described as the sacrament that contains the whole mystery of our salvation. After examining these three themes, we shall briefly discuss two other revealing descriptions for the eucharist: sacrament of unity and *sacramentum sacramentorum.*

Thanksgiving: Of all the names used to describe the assembly of faithful gathered in worship, "eucharist" is the oldest and most widely used. "Eucharist" is at root a Greek word meaning "to give thanks." Literally and in the original sense it is the thanks of people who have received "goodly gifts" (*eu*, good; *charis*, gift). The eucharist is the great thanksgiving to the Father, in Jesus' name, for everything God has done in creation, redemption, and sanctification. In the words of the Lima statement, "The eucharist is the great sacrifice of praise by which the Church speaks on behalf of the whole creation."[4] Christ, united with the faithful, offers himself in intercession, to reconcile sinners with God and all human beings with one another. Bread and wine, fruits of the earth and of human labor, are presented in thanksgiving and, like the priestly people who offer them, are transformed into the body of Christ. In the Roman liturgy the Mass brings this prayer of thanksgiving to a climax that addresses the heavenly Father:

> Through Christ our Lord, you give us all these gifts. You fill them with life and goodness, you bless them and make them holy.

> Through him, with him, in him, in the unity of the Holy
> Spirit, all glory and honor is yours, almighty Father, for ever and
> ever. Amen (Eucharistic Prayer I)

Memorial: The eucharist is the memorial (Greek, *anamnesis*) of the
death and resurrection of Christ, "the living and effective sign of his
sacrifice, accomplished once and for all on the cross and still operative
on behalf of all humankind."[5] The words and acts of Christ at the
institution of the eucharist stand at the heart of the eucharistic prayer.
They recall Jesus' last Passover celebration with his disciples, and
through them we are renewed in the covenant sealed by the blood of
Christ. We remember that it was by the blood of the lamb that the
ancient Israelites were saved from the avenging angel of death, and we
recall visions in the Book of Revelation where the saved, marked with
the blood of the Lamb (14:1), sing a "new hymn":

> With your blood you purchased for God men of every race and
> tongue, of every people and nation. You made of them a king-
> dom, and priests to serve our God, and they shall reign on earth.
> (5:9-10)

Invocation of the Spirit: Epiclesis (Greek, *epiklesis*) simply means
"invocation," but in theology, where it has acquired a more technical
meaning, it refers specifically to the invocation of the Holy Spirit in the
liturgy.[6] In the liturgies of the Eastern churches it has always held a
prominent part, and the epiclesis is the most noteworthy feature of the
new Eucharistic Prayers introduced into the Roman liturgy after Vatican II.

> . . . Father, we bring you these gifts. We ask you to make them
> holy by the power of your Spirit that they may become the body
> and blood of your Son, our Lord Jesus Christ, at whose com-
> mand we celebrate this eucharist. (Eucharistic Prayer III)

The other forms of the Eucharistic Prayer incorporate a similar invocation. By the power of the Holy Spirit the words of the priest, who is
cast as another Christ and presides over the eucharist, are rendered
efficacious. It is a mistake, however, to concentrate exclusively on one
or the other prayer formula because the whole action of the eucharist
has an "epicletic" character. Not only are gifts changed; all who share
them are changed and transfigured into the Body of Christ by the
power of the Spirit.

The church, as the community of the new covenant, invokes the
Spirit, in order that it may be sanctified and renewed, led into all
justice, truth and unity, and empowered to fulfill its mission.[7]

Sacrament of Unity   Jesus' prayer to his heavenly Father for the
disciples, "that they may be one, even as we are one" (Jn 17:11),
presents the ideal church and the goal of the ecumenical movement.
Prompted in part by ecumenical concerns and in part by the desire to
retrieve the ancient tradition that pictured the eucharist as both the
symbol of church unity and the supreme means to achieve it, contemporary authors emphasize its unitive force. St. Paul's reference to sharing the body of Christ, "Because the loaf of bread is one, we, many
though we are, are one body, for we all partake of the one loaf" (1 Cor
10:17), gave rise to a literary tradition that elaborated on the metaphor
of the loaf. The Eucharistic Prayer reported in the *Didache*, for example, implores "As the broken bread was scattered over the hills and
then, when gathered became one mass, so may Thy Church be gathered from the ends of the earth into Thy Kingdom" (9:4). The image
of kernels of wheat becoming one in a loaf of bread also evoked the
metaphor of wine-making. Speaking to the newly baptized, St. Augustine declared:

> "The Body of Christ," you are told, and you answer "Amen."
> Be members then of the Body of Christ that your Amen may be
> true. Why is this mystery accomplished with bread? We shall say
> nothing of our own about it; rather let us hear the Apostle, who
> speaking of this sacrament says: "We being many are one body,
> one bread." Understand and rejoice. Unity, devotion, charity!
> One bread: and what is this one bread? One body made up of
> many. Consider that the bread is not made of one grain alone,
> but of many. During the time of exorcism, you were, so to say, in
> the mill. At baptism you were wetted with water. Then the Holy
> Spirit came into you like the fire which bakes the dough. Be then
> what you see and receive what you are.
>
> Now for the Chalice, my brethren. Remember how wine is
> made. Many grapes hang on the bunch, but the liquid which
> runs out of them mingles together in unity. So has the Lord
> willed that we should belong to him and he has consecrated on
> his altar the mystery of our peace and unity.[8]

The eucharistic meal, the consummate expression of communion, "union with" Christ, in essence means sharing the "holy things"—the one bread and the common cup. The eucharistic meal is the sacrament of unity par excellence in that it draws the participants—or better, "the celebrants"—into union with one another and with Christ.

Sacramentum Sacramentorum   In linking all the other sacraments to the eucharist, Vatican II said it "is the fount and apex of the whole Christian life" (*Lumen Gentium*, n. 11). The eucharist, writes Karl Rahner, "cannot simply be put on a level with the other sacraments and listed along with them." In discussing the seven sacraments in his small but important tract *The Church and the Sacraments*, Rahner declares, "We begin not with baptism, as the usual treatises on the sacraments do, but the eucharist."[9] When the rites of initiation—baptism, confirmation and eucharist—are taken as a unit, baptism incorporates one into Christ's Body, but the Body is seen whole only when gathered in celebration of the eucharist. Thus baptism-confirmation points toward the eucharist as the richest form of the church's self-expression, and all other sacraments are in a sense further actualizations of it. The eucharist is, as Henri de Lubac has said, "sacrament in the highest sense of the word—*sacramentum sacramentorum*," the sacrament which embodies the whole mystery of our salvation.[10]

Penance and Reconciliation   It is in the eucharist that the community of God's people, the church, is most fully visible. The church's ancient penitential discipline illustrated this sacramental relationship between eucharist and church most dramatically. To be banned from the Christian community because of public and serious sin—e.g., apostasy, adulterous relationship, murder—meant exclusion—"excommunication"—from the eucharist. On the other hand, readmission to the sacraments signaled one's good standing in the community and before God. "The whole aparatus of public penance and pardon," writes Henri de Lubac, "made it clear that the reconciliation of the sinner is in the first place a reconciliation with the Church, the latter constituting an efficacious sign of reconciliation with God."[11] Just as in the rites of initiation, where the social integration of the catechumen into the Christian community signals the forgiveness of sins, the penitential rites, culminating in the return to the *communio sanctorum*, are at once the means and the sign of reconciliation with the church.

The church stands as the sacrament of God's love for the world. Since its mission is to announce both Christ's victory over the forces of evil and the coming of the kingdom, it cannot remain indifferent to sin. Sins committed by members of the community compromise the church and contradict its very reason for being. Nonetheless, already in New Testament times the Christian community had to face up to the fact that not all its members were living up to the gospel ideals. The parables taught that in this world wheat and weeds, the grain and the chaff, sheep and goats would coexist until the time came for a final sorting out. St. Paul found it necessary to denounce Corinthian Christians for their lapses, and the Epistle of James advised his readers, "Declare your sins to one another" (5:16). Although we know few details about the penitential rites in the early church, its policy regarding notorious sinners was relatively clear. They needed to confess their wrongdoing and give public evidence of repentance. The policy regarding persons whose occasional lapses, serious though they were, were more a matter of weakness than pride and contempt tended to be more lenient. It was many hundreds of years, however, before the penitential discipline took final shape, but even then many of the rites continued to change. The earliest descriptions of the penitential rites add little to the text of James' Epistle. The *Didache*, for example, speaks in two places of a public confession of sins. Both are in connection with prayer: the first, at the end of its recital of the virtues that constitute "the way of life," states simply, "In church confess your sins, and do not come to your prayer with a guilty conscience" (4:14); and the second, in the context of the eucharist, says, "On the Lord's own day, assemble in common to break bread and offer thanks; but first confess your sins, so that your sacrifice may be pure" (14:1).

But confession is simply one aspect of repentance; a change of heart is another. The sinner is further admonished to *do* penance, that is, to undertake some good work that will overcome evil habits and wipe away sin.

> Almsgiving is good, as is penance for sins. Fasting is better than prayer, but almsgiving better than both. And *love covers a multitude of sins* (Rom 12:16), but the prayer of one with a good conscience delivers from death. Blessed is everyman who is full of these works. For almsgiving lightens the burden of sin.[12]

Everyone was encouraged to do penance, but it was *required* of notorious sinners. Individuals known as public sinners had to give evidence of repentance and be on their good behavior for a protracted period before they were readmitted to the eucharist. Sometime in the early Middle Ages a more flexible practice was introduced (probably influenced by Irish monks whose presence on the Continent seemed ubiquitous in the seventh century). It permitted readmission to the eucharist with the understanding that penance—fasting, alms, prayer— of some sort would be performed. (The change had as great an impact on Christian life-style of the time as the shift from cash purchases to a buy-now-pay-later economy has had on the contemporary American way of life.)

Another medieval development was a clarification of the role of the priest in the penitential rites. According to the earliest documents we have, mostly from the third century, it fell to the bishop acting in the name of the church to reconcile penitents, just as it was his prerogative to preside over the rites of initiation. But many of the same reasons that gave rise to parish churches presided over by priests also made it necessary for the bishop to delegate "power of the keys" to pastors and eventually to other priests. However, when no priest was available Christians continued to confess their sins to one another a la James 5:6; but canon law made it clear that formal reconciliation with the church came only with absolution by a duly authorized priest.

In 1215 the Fourth Council of the Lateran, as much a landmark in the medieval church as Vatican II has been in the modern, decreed:

> Let everyone of the faithful of either sex, after reaching the age
> of discretion, faithfully confess in secret to his own priest all his
> sins, at least once a year, and diligently strive to fufill the penance
> imposed on him, receiving reverently, at least during Paschal
> time, the sacrament of the Eucharist. . . otherwise, while living
> let him be denied entrance into the church and when dead let him
> be deprived of Christian burial. . . ."[13]

Although the primary intent of the decree was to remedy abuses and neglect of the sacraments, its linking of confession of sins and eucharist is hardly in the spirit of the ancient *Didache*. The decree of Lateran IV formally introducing the "Easter duty"—the obligation of Catholic to receive Holy Communion annually sometime between Ash Wednesday and Trinity Sunday—is hardly more than a token recognition of the eucharist as a celebration of the paschal mystery.

Later in the sixteenth century, Protestant Reformers, also concerned about abuses in the penitential rites, raised a number of practical and theoretical questions about the sacrament of penance. In response the Council of Trent (1551) issued a major decree that is in fact a comprehensive theological tract dealing with the origins, matter and form, minister, and other aspects of the sacrament that were being debated.[14] It may be, however, that the decree of Trent did less to shape the popular mindset regarding the rites of penance than did the introduction of the confessional. Through the Middles Ages it was the custom to confess in the open, often in front of an altar, as is the custom in many of the Eastern rites today. St. Charles Borromeo, the great reform bishop of Milan, seems to have popularized the use of a closet-like structure that would function much like a modern telephone booth, shielding penitent and confessor from the distraction of outside noises and in turn keeping their conversation from being overheard by others. It also served as a safeguard against other abuses, as is suggested by Borromeo's diocesan statutes that forbade priests to hear women's confessions "outside the confessional unless there is a divider between them."[15] Although the origin of the confessional is not to be found, as is sometimes thought, in a desire for anonymity, the design of confessionals, especially in the United States, where many were dark and constricted, created a wrong impression of the sacrament (though, some might argue, a correct impression of sin!). They led to the very individualistic notions that sin was a private matter between a person's conscience and God and that reconciliation was entirely a matter between the penitent and confessor. The idea that both sin and reconciliation had a social and specifically ecclesial dimension was deemphasized if not entirely forgotten.

It was in the light of these and other misshapen notions that Vatican II decreed, "The rite and formulas of penance are to be revised in such a way that they may more clearly express the nature and effects of this sacrament" (*Liturgy,* 72). Although the new rite of penance, published in 1973, does not offer a blueprint for the place where the sacrament is to be celebrated, it introduces new forms that cannot be implemented in the narrow confines of the confessional box. The new rite retains the traditional elements—contrition, confession, absolution, and satisfaction (i.e., penance)—but it outlines various forms and options for celebrating the sacrament. The three basic forms are: 1) the rite for the reconciliation of individual penitents; 2) the rite for several penitents with individual confession and absolution; and 3) reconciliation of several penitents with general confession and absolution.

The new forms of the rite encourage the reading of appropriate passages from Holy Scripture by way of preparing for the sacrament, and they seek in various ways to underline that sin and its forgiveness have a social aspect (nn. 17, 18). The second and third forms effectively show the ecclesial nature of penance by incorporating communal celebrations.

> The Church exercises the ministry of the sacrament of penance through bishops and priests. By preaching God's word they call the faithful to conversion; in the name of Christ and by the power of the Holy Spirit they declare and grant the forgiveness of sins.[16]

The new rites attempt to recapture a spirit of penance and ongoing conversion which, abetted by the Holy Spirit, transforms sinful individuals into a holy people.

Healing the Sick   In the abstract, sin is evil that in existential terms is translated into pain and suffering. In the social context sin is divisive: it extols selfishness and thereby undermines the trust necessary if individuals and groups are to live in peace. Insofar as the sacrament of penance reconciles individuals with one another and with the community, and insofar as it restores trust built on justice and love, it heals divisions among peoples. But individuals also need healing. Sinners wound themselves. They become mortally ill because sin is a social disease. People are driven by demons bent on destroying them. Everyone needs healing, and when individuals, feverish and racked with pain, cry out in anguish, the Christian community remembers how Jesus made the disabled whole, cured diseases, and drove out demons. The Epistle of James says,

> Is there anyone sick among you? He should ask for the presbyters of the church. They in turn are to pray over him, anointing him with oil in the Name of the of the Lord. This prayer uttered in faith will reclaim the one who is ill, and the Lord will restore him to health. If he has committed any sins, forgiveness will be his. (5:14-15)

The Council of Trent, dwelling on the forgivenss of sin and health of the soul, interpreted the anointing of the sick as complementary to the sacrament of penance. Vatican II also sees it as a sacrament of healing, but it better captures the spirit of James in emphasizing that it heals the whole person.[17] The anointing of the sick, symbolizing as it does the massage so effective in many cases for relaxing muscles and alleviating pain, attends to the physical well-being of the patient; it soothes and brings comfort as well as serving as a tangible sign of inner healing and solace.

The anointing of the sick, like penance and all the sacraments, manifests in a visible way the operation and organic structure of the priestly community. Vatican II declares:

> By the sacred anointing of the sick and the prayer of her priests, the whole Church commends those who are ill to the suffering and glorified Lord, asking that He may lighten their suffering and save them (cf. Jas 5:14-16). She exhorts them, moreover, to contribute to the welfare of the whole People of God by associating themselves freely with the passion and death of Christ (cf. Rom 8:17; Col 1:24; 2 Tim 2:11-12; 1 Pet 4:13).[18]

We have just seen in discussing penance and the anointing of the sick how the eucharist, the *communio sanctorum*, stands as symbol of the church and witnesses to its communal ministry of healing. Now we shall say a brief word as to how this also applies to holy orders and marriage, sometimes referred to as sacraments of vocation.

Holy Orders   The church is charismatic in the sense that it is endowed with gifts of the Spirit for the common good of the whole People of God. The Holy Spirit bestows on the community of believers diverse and complementary gifts that enable the church to carry on the mission of Christ as the visible sign of salvation in and for the world. Anointed in baptism, Christians form a priestly people (1 Pet 2:9), though not all are apostles, nor prophets nor teachers nor miracle workers nor healers (see 1 Cor 12:29-30). The church continues to exist not just because it once possessed these gifts, but because it is also endowed with the power to transmit them; that is how it keeps on reconstituting itself anew.

There has never been a time when the church was without persons holding specific authority and responsibility. The apostles, by definition, are sent to witness to the Lord's life and resurrection. The New Testament describes the role of the Twelve within the communities of the first generation: they lead the disciples in prayer, teaching, the breaking of bread, proclamation and service (Acts 2:42-47; 6:2-6; e.g.).

Early on, the increase in the size of the community meant involving others in their ministry. So the Jerusalem community presented seven of their number to the apostles, "who first prayed over them and then imposed hands on them" (Acts 6: 6). Whatever their original tasks, two of these new associates, Stephen and Philip, were soon proclaiming the gospel to all who would listen. Acts tells us about "certain prophets and teachers" in the church at Antioch.

> On one occasion, while they were engaged in the liturgy of the Lord and were fasting, the Holy Spirit spoke to them: "Set apart Barnabas and Saul for me to do the work for which I have called them." Then after they had fasted and prayed, they imposed hands on them and sent them off. (Acts 13:2-3)

Saul, who soon was to become Paul, in turn delegated others to help him. He put Timothy in charge of the Christian community at Ephesus and later wrote, "I remind you to stir into flame the gift of God bestowed when my hands were laid on you" (2 Tim 1:6; see 1 Tim 4:14). Timothy had the responsibility of organizing the community, including the selection of men for the offices of bishop and deacon (3:1-13). Paul entrusted Titus with a similar charge for the island of Crete. Titus was to appoint bishop-presbyters "in every town" (Tit 1:5-9).

The New Testament indicates a certain evolution in the way the forms of ministry evolved. It does not describe a single pattern that might serve as a blueprint, normative for all future times in the church. As we have seen (Chapter 18), however, during the second and third centuries the threefold office of bishop, presbyter and deacon became the established pattern. The bishop, the leader of the community, had the primary responsibility for proclaiming the word and presided over the liturgy. With the increase in numbers, especially in metropolitan areas such as Rome, it became necessary to establish *tituli presbyterali*—the beginnings of parish churches, where a presbyter became the leader of the local eucharistic community. Others with various charisms were—and still are—charged with responsibility for a specific ministry in the church, but the episcopacy, presbyterate, and diaconate are the three principal offices. Individuals were commissioned—ordained—to these offices by the invocation of the Holy Spirit and the laying on of hands.

According to Catholic tradition, reaffirmed in the documents of Vatican II, it is Christ who proclaims the word, presides over the eucharist and guides the People of God on their pilgrim way. He acts in the person of bishops, assisted by priests and deacons, who inherited their role from the apostles. The apostles, energized by the outpouring of the Holy Spirit (Acts 1:8; 2:4; Jn 20:22-23), took up Jesus' mantle and in turn passed it on to their helpers, a new generation of ministers in the church. The sacrament of holy orders, which has its fullest (though not exclusive) expression in the ordination of bishops, ensures that the fundamental functions of the church, those most important to the building up of the Body of Christ, namely, preaching the word and ministering the sacraments, will be perpetuated.

> . . . by means of the imposition of hands and the words of consecration, the grace of the Holy Spirit is so conferred, and the sacred character so impressed, that bishops in an eminent and visible way undertake Christ's own role as Teacher, Shepherd, and High Priest, and that they act in His person.[19]

Ordination is a call to ministry. It empowers individuals with particular charisms, not for their personal aggrandizement but for the benefit and well-being of the *communio sanctorum*. The bishop's ministry, aided by that of priests and deacons, is the focus of unity within the Christian community.

Marriage   As with many other aspects of Christian life, the marriage rites of the primitive church are shrouded in silence. The earliest non-biblical reference is found in the oft-quoted letter of Ignatius of Antioch (d. 107): "It is right for men and women who marry to contract their union with the advice of their bishop, so that their marriage is made in the Lord, and not for the sake of passion."[20] It strains the text to cite it as proof that marriages between Christians were celebrated by the bishop in accordance with some established ritual. It does indicate, however, that the bishop, representing the Christian community, was pastorally involved, perhaps to the point of giving his approval to the union. The marriage ceremony itself was probably a Christianized form of the Jewish Talmudic rite, centered around a festive meal (the eucharist?), with the bridegroom pronouncing the blessing.

Christian tradition is of one voice in defending the divine origin of Christian marriage (Gen 2:18-24). Catholics number it as one of the seven sacraments, and it has even been argued that marriage illustrates the sacramental principle better than any other rite with the possible exception of the eucharist.[21] In its broadest form the principle of sacramentality means that the visible and the tangible, the historical and the human, mediate the presence of God in the world. In other words, the invisible and numinous are experienced and revealed in and through the world of matter, and in this sense everything has the potential of being *sacrament*. In a related but restricted sense, a sacrament is commonly understood as an outward sign that mediates grace, the visible symbol of an invisible reality. A sacrament is always more than meets the eye; it reveals mystery. It is of the nature of sacrament to express a truth deeper than the words convey, which to the person of faith is like reading between the lines to get beyond the obvious meaning of the text to what the author really intends.

In marriage the wedding vows, a public statement of intention, commit the spouses to an unconditioned sharing of their lives. To marry is to do what comes naturally. In the eyes of the casual observer it is a human act, the noblest of human acts, but the person of faith finds in it a deeper meaning. The Epistle to the Ephesians sees in marriage a symbol of the relationship of Christ to members of the church. It quotes Genesis: "For this reason a man must leave his father and mother and be joined to his wife, and the two will become one body," and then adds, "This mystery has many implications; but I am saying it applies to Christ and the Church" (Eph 5:31-32, JB). The covenant that husband and wife make with each other is an effective sign of the covenant that God has made with the chosen people. God's love and fidelity is reflected in the love and fidelity they show to each other.

The love of one human being for another excites altruism and generosity. The most spiritual of experiences, it is also capable of exciting passion and physical desire that permeates a person's whole being. In marriage two persons come together, not as opposites but as complements so that the physical becomes an expression of the spiritual and the spiritual brings a new dimension to the physical. It was not by chance that marriage became the target of movements that attacked the church's fundamental vision of life and reality—not just differing with it over some fine point of doctrine. The gnostics and Manichees, for example, objected to the sacramental system as being materialistic. They so contrasted the physical and spiritual, making one the principle of evil and the other the principle of good, that they came to regard marriage as the invention of the devil. Crass materialists, on the other hand, object to the sacramental principle because they deny any deeper dimension to reality than what is obvious to the senses. The best they can say for marriage is that it is a social institution, invented by human ingenuity to ensure stable relationships and the perpetuation of the human species.

It was at the wedding feast of Cana that Jesus "performed [the] first of his signs" (Jn 2:11). The dramatic gesture by which the water used for Jewish purification was transformed into the choicest of wines signaled the beginning of a new era.[22] In the Old Testament the wedding symbolized messianic days (Is 54:4-8; 62:4-5), and on several occasions Jesus used wedding customs to illustrate his own teaching about the messianic kingdom. In the parable of the ten virgins, for example, he instructed the disciples to be patient in their watchfulness so to be prepared for the coming of the bridegroom (Mt 25:1-12; see Lk 12:36-37). Eschatological expectation—waiting for the coming of the Lord—is an essential element of Christian life. Given the fact that it "proclaims the death of the Lord until he comes" (1 Cor 11:26), it is easy to see why the faithful regard the eucharist as the joyful anticipation of the wedding feast that a king prepared for his son (Mt 22:1-14; Lk 14:16-24). Weddings and eucharists are festive occasions; they celebrate love—the love of Christ for his church, the universal love of God for the all peoples, and the love that bonds the members of Christ's Body to one another. In bonding people to one another, marriage like the eucharist, creates unity and thereby becomes an expression of what it signifies. Each of these sacraments in its own way, while bringing the kingdom into being, anticipates the coming of that kingdom, when love will be boundless and ecstasy endless.[23]

FELLOWSHIP WITH THE SAINTS (*SANCTI*)

The Assembly of Believers   In his commentary on the Apostles' Creed, Wolfhart Pannenberg reports that since the sixteenth century "the prevailing view" in Protestant churches has been to interpret the phrase *communio sanctorum* in the personal sense, namely, to read as a reference to Christians themselves (*sancti*).[24] This interpretation corresponds to New Testament usage, especially in the Pauline corpus, in which members of the churches at Rome, Corinth, and elsewhere "dedicated to Christ" (Rom 1:7, NEB) are thought of as "saints" (in the older translations—see Rom 1:7; 1 Cor 1:2; 2 Cor 1:1; Eph 1:1; Phil 1:1; Col. 1:2). This interpretation, prevalent also in Catholic circles, is traceable to Nicetas of Remesiana (c. A.D.400) whose commentary, as we have already noted, contains the earliest witness to a mention of the *communio sanctorum* in the Creed. It is clear that Nicetas understood the phrase to refer to the community of all blessed men and women who make up the church, including those who have gone before and those yet to come:

> What is the Church but the congregation of all saints? From the beginning of the world patriarchs, prophets, martyrs, and all other righteous men who have lived or are now alive, or shall live in time to come, comprise the Church, since they have been sanctified by one faith and manner of life, and sealed by one Spirit and so made one body, of which Christ is declared to be head, as the Scripture says. Moreover, the angels, and the heavenly virtues and powers too, are banded together in this Church. . . . So you believe that in this Church you will attain to the communion of saints.[25]

On the basis of this passage in Nicetas, it appears that even in Gaul, where *sanctorum* was generally understood in a personal sense, *communio sanctorum* originally referred not so much to the *assembly* of believers who came together for fellowship as to their *solidarity* with the holy martyrs who already had found salvation and thus were the "co-guarantors of the future participation in salvation of all Christians."[26] This interpretation seems to find confirmation in Faustus of Riez, the fifth-century monk-bishop who wrote, "Let us believe in the communion of saints. . . . they deserve to be venerated worthily, forasmuch as they infuse into us, through their contempt of death, the worship of God and the yearning for the life to come."[27] Although Faustus seems to have had only the martyrs in mind, another Gallican author of about the same period interprets the communion of saints to refer to the fellowship of the living with all the blessed who have passed away in faith. There is a tendency in some of the commentaries, even in those that assert a solidarity in faith of all Christians, to transfer the full realization of the communion of saints to the future life.

Though the weight of scholarly opinion seems to be shifting in favor of a sacramental meaning of the communion of saints, there are those who insist that the two interpretations of *sanctorum*, the one referring to fellowship with the martyrs and confessors (*sancti*) and the other to sharing the sacraments (*sancta*), have "equally primal force."[28] Whether it referred originally to "holy people" or to "holy things," in fact, makes little difference because *communio sanctorum* came to be interpreted in such a way as to link the two. Although it was for the purpose of sharing the eucharistic elements that Christians came together as a community, it was not very long before they understood the *communio sanctorum* to include themselves as members of Christ's Body united and sanctified by God's holy gifts. Medieval theologians were aware of the two interpretations of the phrase. Some, like Alexander of Hales, merely juxtaposed the two views; some like St. Thomas Aquinas attempted to synthesize them.[29]

In a short essay on the Apostles' Creed, Aquinas wrote, "Because all the faithful form one body, the benefits belonging to one are communicated to the others. There is thus a sharing of benefits (*communio bonorum*) in the Church, and this is what we mean by *sanctorum communio*."[30] Thomas explained that the goods shared include everything worthwhile done on earth by the saints, and in particular the seven sacraments, which convey to us the power of Christ's passion, he being the head of the body. Today, a return to an older, wider, and fuller vision of *sanctorum* leads commentators to include in it all the tangible signs of the infinite benefits of Christ's work: the word of God, the sacraments, even the Creed itself—everything that culminates and finds its center of gravity in the eucharist.[31]

Solidarity of the Living with the Dead   St. Thomas provides the inspiration for the text in the Roman Catechism which says there is "another communion in the Church, which demands attention: every pious and holy action, done by one, belongs to and becomes profitable to all, through charity. . . ."[32] The gift of charity, with its radical principle, the Holy Spirit, says Congar, "is present in all the members of the communicational Body of Christ and therefore allows an intercommunion of spiritual energy to take place between them." He quotes St. Thomas again: "Not only are the merits of the passion and the life of Christ communicated to us, but also all the good that the saints have done is communicated to those who live in charity, since all are one."[33]

Since all who live in charity are one, the communion of saints extends to those who have passed from this life. The eucharist, which celebrates the memory of the Lord in eschatological expectation, bonds the living with all who have died in Christ. The custom of celebrating the eucharist in memory of the faithful departed began in the earliest days of the church. Pictures and graffiti in the early Christian cemeteries tell of the funeral meal (Latin, *refrigerium* = "refreshment") that was held near the tomb or mausoleum on the day of burial and, in the case of martyrs and other prominent "saints," on the anniversary of their death. The Lord's Supper, not without some difficulty, replaced the pagan custom of holding a funeral banquet to honor the dead. Christians adapted the practice, distributing food and alms to the poor and celebrating the eucharist in anticipation of the heavenly banquet when the saints of all ages will celebrate together.

According to Thomas, prayer for the dead is based on the fact that even death "cannot separate us from the love of God in Christ Jesus our Lord" (Rom 8:38-39). Charity is the bond that unites all the members of the communion of saints—those on earth and those beyond the veil that hides them from our sight. Thomas applies the "pneumatological theology of the communion of saints" even to the baptism of babies. Although infants do not personally possess faith, the faith of the whole church profits them through the activity of the Holy Spirit, who unites the church and distributes its spiritual goods among the members.

The fellowship that Christians experience in their local communities can be easily projected to a feeling of corporate solidarity with all "who have died and gone before us marked with the sign of faith" (Eucharistic Prayer I). Because the lives of the heroic martyrs and ordinary confessors are sometimes dramatic and always inspiring, the personal interpretation dominates catechetical materials and is reinforced by the annual celebration of All Saints and All Souls days. When this view of the communion of saints totally eclipses the full understanding of *sanctorum*, however, the church becomes merely an assembly of more or less good people—a support group for saints and sinners struggling to resolve the conflicts in their lives. The solidarity of the saints with one another rests on their communion with Jesus, the Lord. It is his presence that transforms a thanksgiving meal into a eucharist. It is his communion with the Godhead that makes the COMMUNION OF SAINTS, in spite of human sinfulness, the source and sacrament of holiness in the world.

From the vantage point of the eucharistic table, Christians have a cosmic vision. The *communio sanctorum* extends beyond the frontiers of death. The liturgy calls on those gathered around the altar to join in the hymn of praise of the saints and of all the choirs of heaven. In the eucharist the fellowship effected by the communal sharing in the benefits of Christ's death and resurrection is visible to all. We shall return to this last topic in the next chapter.

Notes

1. J. N. D. Kelly, pp. 174–175; 388–391. It is interesting to note that this passage represents a change on the part of the author, whose classic study of the early Christian creeds has shaped the views of many students of the Creed. In the first edition (1950), he defended the "personal" interpretation of COMMUNIO SANCTORUM; whereas in the third edition (1972), after reexamining the evidence, he seems to favor the "realist" interpretation.

2. See Henri de Lubac, *Corpus Mysticum*. 2d ed. (Paris: Aubier, 1948), pp. 27–34.

3. Gaius J. Slosser, *The Communion of Saints*. Report No. 2 Prepared for the World Conference on Faith and Order. Edinburg, 1937 (New York: Harper & Brothers, 1937), pp. 10–12.

4. *Baptism, Eucharist and Ministry*. Faith and Order Paper No. 111 (Geneva: World Council of Churches, 1982), n. 4 (p. 10).

5. *Baptism, Eucharist and Ministry*, no. 5, p. 11.

6. Yves Congar, *I Believe in the Holy Spirit* (New York: Seabury Press, 1983), III, pp. 228–257.

7. *Baptism, Eucharist and Ministry*, n. 17, p. 13.

8. Sermons 272 and 234, quoted in H. de Lubac, *Catholicism* (New York: New American Library, 1964), p. 53. Parallels can be found in sermons 227 and 229.

9. New York: Herder and Herder, 1963, p. 82.

10. *Catholicism*, p. 51.

11. *Catholicism*, p. 50.

12. *Second Letter of Clement*, 16, quoted in Paul Palmer (ed.), *Sacraments and Forgiveness* (Westminster, MD: Newman Press, 1959), p. 16.

13. Palmer, pp. 197–198. It should be noted that the obligation to make one's "Easter duty" is incumbent on all the faithful; but according to canon law the duty to confess once a year obliges only those who have committed serious sin.

14. Palmer, ibid., pp. 239–254.

15. Quoted in *Commentary on the Rite of Penance* Study Test IV (Washington, DC: United States Catholic Conference, 1975), p. 23.

16. *The Rite of Penance*, n. 9a, in *The Rites of the Catholic Church as revised by Decree of the Second Vatican Council and Published by Authority of Pope Paul VI* (New York: Pueblo, 1976), p. 348.

17. Alexandre Ganoczy, *An Introduction to Catholic Sacramental Theology* (New York: Paulist Press, 1984), pp. 122–124. Vatican II discouraged calling this sacrament "extreme unction" lest people be misled into thinking that the rite is only for those who are at "the *point* of death" (Constitution on the Sacred Liturgy, n. 73).

18. *Lumen Gentium*, n. 11.

19. *The Church*, n. 21. The Lima document describes ordination in the section on Ministry: "The act of ordination by those who are appointed for this ministry attests the bond of the Church with Jesus Christ and the apostolic witness, recalling that it is the risen Lord who is the true ordainer and bestows the gift. In ordaining, the Church, under the inspiration of the Holy Spirit, provides for the faithful proclamation of the Gospel and humble service in the name of Christ. The laying on of hands is the sign of the gift of the Spirit, rendering visible the fact that the ministry was instituted in the revelation accomplished in Christ. . ." *Baptism, Eucharist and Ministry*, Faith and Order Paper no. 111 (Geneva: World Council of Churches, 1982), par. 39, p. 30.

20. *To Polycarp*, 5:2, quoted by Kenneth Stevenson, *Nuptial Blessing: A Study of Christian Marriage Rites* (New York: Oxford University Press, 1983), p. 13.

21. Ronald A. Knox, *Hidden Stream* (New York: Sheed and Ward, 1953), p. 219.

22. Raymond E. Brown, *Gospel According to John I–XII* The Anchor Bible, 29 (Garden City, NY: Doubleday and Co., 1966), pp. 104–105.

23. Geoffrey Wainwright, *Eucharist and Eschatology* (New York: Oxford University Press, 1981), *passim*.

24. *The Apostles' Creed in the Light of Today's Questions* (Philadelphia: Westminster, 1972), p. 149.

25. Quoted in J. N. D. Kelly, *Creeds*, p. 391.

26. Pannenberg, *Apostles' Creed*, p. 149.

27. Quoted in Kelly, *Creeds*, p. 391.

28. Pannenberg, *Apostoles' Creed*, p. 149.

29. See F. X. Lawlor who gives citations to their works in *NCE*, s.v. "Communion of Saints," 4:43.

30. Quoted in Kelly, *Creeds*, p. 394.

31. Pierre-Yves Emery, *The Communion of Saints* (London: The Faith Press, 1966), p. 185.

32. Congar, *I Believe*, II, p. 80. See, *The Catechetical Instructions of St. Thomas Aquinas*, Ed. and trans. Jos. B. Collins (New York: Joseph F. Wagner, 1939), art. X, pp. 53–54.

33. Congar, *I Believe* II, p. 60.

22

Immortality
and/or Resurrection?

"We look for the resurrection of the dead,
and the life of the world to come"

Not too many years ago Krister Stendahl, then professor of biblical studies at Harvard University, edited a book with the subtitle *Death in the Western World: Two Conflicting Currents of Thought*. The book's main title, *Immortality and Resurrection*, identifies the two currents that are said to conflict with one another.[1] In none of the four studies that make up the collection is the tension between immortality and resurrection more starkly evident than in the lecture by another renowned biblical scholar, Oscar Cullmann. Cullmann, in the tradition of classic Protestant thought, posits a radical distinction between reason and revelation, between the philosophy of the Greeks and the post-Easter witness of the New Testament, and ultimately between the immortality of the soul and the resurrection of the body.[2]

Although most Catholics and many Protestants think that Cullmann exaggerates the differences, they nonetheless admit that some tension exists. It is a tension that, recognized already in the early church, is reflected in the statement of the Ecumenical Creed WE LOOK

369

FOR THE RESURRECTION OF THE DEAD AND THE LIFE OF THE WORLD TO COME and in the Apostles' Creed THE RESURRECTION OF THE BODY AND LIFE EVERLASTING. We shall explain the variation in wording in due course, but for now we note that the first half of this wording is traceable back to the earliest forms of the Creed, but that the second makes its appearance only some time later, perhaps in the fourth century. After explaining briefly the two principal reasons why the Creed mentions the resurrection of the body, we consider the immortality of the soul and, next, the biblical understanding of the resurrection, first in the Old Testament and then in the New, with a special emphasis on the writings of St. Paul. Finally we reflect on the meaning of death and everlasting life in the Christian tradition.

RESURRECTION AS AN ESCHATOLOGICAL SIGN

There are at least two reasons why the Creed mentions the bodily resurrection almost from the beginning. Mention of the resurrection appeared at the end of the second century because the Creed confronted and implicitly rejected the gnostic tenet that physical matter was the principle of evil and irredeemable. Whether described as OF THE FLESH or in the more wholistic term OF THE DEAD, the resurrection reaffirmed the goodness of all creation—the seen and unseen, the material and spiritual—and the essential unity of the human person, body and soul, flesh and spirit. The writings of St. Irenaeus and especially of Tertullian emphasized the resurrection of the flesh as a repudiation of gnosticism's view of creation. In one of his earliest tracts (c. 200), for example, Tertullian extols the faith that the Roman church held in common with the African. A passage that sounds like a paraphrase of the baptismal creed states that the Roman church "acknowledges one Lord God, creator of the universe, and Christ Jesus, Son of God the creator from the Virgin Mary, and the resurrection of the flesh."[3] In this and similar texts Tertullian underscores the principal issues that separated the gnostics from the church: the oneness of God, the genuine humanity of Jesus, and the basic worth of matter (flesh).

If proof were needed that this was indeed the faith of the Roman church, we could once again cite the *Apostolic Tradition* of St. Hippolytus of Rome, a contemporary of Tertullian. Hippolytus' account of baptism reported that the neophyte, upon being immersed for the third time, was asked, "Do you believe in the Holy Spirit and the holy church and the resurrection of the flesh?"

The second and principal reason why the Creed mentions the bodily resurrection is eschatological. Resurrection reaffirms a truth fundamental to apostolic preaching. The core of the primitive kerygma—the proclamation of the gospel—was the Easter message. In its original Jewish setting the primary significance of Jesus' resurrection was understood both by the disciples who proclaimed it and by those who heard it to mean that the last times, "the age to come," was at hand. Regardless of the apprehension and *angst* that individuals experienced in the face of death, Jewish eschatology was preoccupied less with personal immortality—what is going to happen to *me* after death—than with the fulfillment of God's promises to Israel, the vindication of the Israelites fidelity to the covenant, and the ultimate victory of justice over evil. The Jews knew of and expected the resurrection of the dead at the end of time, and therefore they regarded Jesus' resurrection as an eschatological sign, an indication that final judgment was at hand.

But it was not simply a message for the Jews. Paul, speaking to the Greeks in the Areopagus in Athens, concluded his discourse saying,

> God may well have overlooked bygone periods when men did not know him; but now he calls on all men everywhere to reform their lives. He has set the day on which he is going to 'judge the world with justice' through a man he has appointed—one whom he has endorsed in the sight of all by raising him from the dead." (Acts 17:30-31)

Although a few Athenians did join Paul "to become believers," the majority sneered when they heard about the raising of the dead, "while others said, 'We must hear you on this topic some other time' " (v. 32).

IMMORTALITY OF THE SOUL: FROM PLATO TO DESCARTES

It is not surprising that the Athenians did not give Paul a sympathetic hearing, because the resurrection of the dead simply did not fit the categories of Greek philosophy. The Greeks were concerned with life after death in terms of personal survival or, as the question was debated by the philosophers, in terms of the immortality of the soul.

The crown of Plato's philosophy is the reflections on the soul interlaced through his dialogues, especially the *Phaedo*, in which Socrates, faced with imminent death, discourses on immortality. As Plato has

Socrates explain it, we are essentially composite beings; in addition to the corporeal element—the body—there is also another element, different in kind: the soul, which is incorporeal and immaterial. In the Platonic system, body and soul are essentially alien to each other. Although it is immaterial, the soul is nonetheless a substance that existed prior to becoming somehow attached to, incorporated into— Plato even suggests "imprisoned" in—a body. The soul is the principle of life and movement in the universe, and in one text Plato makes the soul one with a person's identity.[4]

Plato's arguments for the immortality of the soul are grounded in his philosophy of being and his theory of knowledge, topics too vast to summarize here. Basic to his cosmogony, however, is the idea of a world soul. The soul's immortality follows from the cyclic character of nature: the soul existed prior to the body and will survive the body's dissolution. The soul, since it is simple—that is, not constituted of parts—is indissoluble; since it is incorporeal and immaterial, it is indestructible—immortal. Since it grasps the ideal forms of the True, the Good, and the Beautiful, which are eternal, the soul, like these forms, must be eternal.

The soul belongs to the eternal world, but as long as it is confined within the body its movement is restricted, and thus it is unable to live fully in accord with its own nature. Plato, therefore, regarded death as the great liberator because it looses the bonds that chain the soul to the body. Death frees the soul to return to its natural habitat in the world of ideas, where Truth, Goodness, and Beauty are eternal. The body, being material and corruptible, has no place in the eternal world. The dissolution of the body, according to Plato, does not mean the annihilation of the soul any more than the destruction of an instrument causes the destruction of a musical composition.

The early church fathers were greatly influenced by Plato's thought, especially in the form of the neo-Platonism popular in the Hellenistic period. While they generally—Origen is an interesting exception—rejected the preexistence of souls, they nonetheless found the dualism of the Platonic world very congenial to their way of thought. They accepted the basic idea that the human being is a composite of matter and spirit and that the two elements—body and soul—live in tension with each other. Though the fathers sometimes state that the soul is by nature immortal, their explanation differs from Plato's. The soul is created by God; it is immortal because it partakes of God's own spiritual being.[5]

In the West it was again St. Augustine whose teaching on the soul dominated Latin theology until the end of the twelfth century. Although Augustine stressed the unity of body and soul, he never managed to escape the dualism inherent in the Platonic view of the universe. He defined the soul as "a substance endowed with reason and fitted to the body," but he saw the soul as clearly the dominant element in the composite; the relationship between soul and body is a relationship between ruler and the ruled. To demonstrate the immortality of the soul, Augustine used arguments reminiscent of those of Plato and Plotinus. Like Plato, he pointed to the soul's capacity to grasp eternal truth as evidence of immortality, and he reinforced his position with arguments based on moral grounds—reward and punishment—and biblical texts.[6] In the Augustinian synthesis both the tension between body and soul and the cause of death were rooted in sin—the sin inherited from our first parents and the sins we commit on our own.

There was, however, another tradition in Greek philosophy, one associated with the name of Aristotle, but it took until the time of St. Thomas Aquinas in the thirteenth century before it became assimilated into Christian thought. Aristotle began as a pupil of Plato, but in his mature years he abandoned almost every vestige of Platonic dualism. The declared aim of Aristotle's great treatise De anima was "to ascertain the nature and essence of the soul" as "the principle of life." By insisting on a substantial union between form and matter, Aristotle overcame Plato's dualism, but at the same time he undermined the arguments for the immortality of the soul. According to Aristotle the soul is the "form" that animates the body and while they can be distinguished from each other, they cannot exist apart. Death of the body means that the soul too ceases to exist. Only the suprapersonal intellect (Greek, nous) is immortal, which is to say that Aristotle precluded personal immortality because he denied that after death the nous could have any recollection of previous experiences in the body.

Thomas Aquinas' great achievement was that he was able, starting from the Aristotelian position, to explain the soul in a manner consonant with Christian doctrine. Aristotle provided him the basic categories to overcome Platonic dualism. The soul and the intellect are one. While the rational soul is the unique, substantial form of the body, it transcends the body in intellectual power. Aquinas argued from the capability and activity of the human intellect to the immortality of the soul. In the Thomistic synthesis the human experience of tension, inner conflict, and even death, is ascribed entirely to our sinful condition and not to the fact that body and soul, matter and spirit, are alien to one another.

St. Thomas' position has never entirely succeeded in overcoming the dualistic view of the universe that seems to have perennial appeal because its categories—matter and spirit—seem easier to explain than the subtle distinctions of Aquinas. In contrasting the spiritual and the physical, soul and body, popular Catholic works tend to propagate ideas that are closer to Cartesian philosophy than to Christian theology. Frenchman Rene Descartes, the founder of modern philosophy, was in many respects a revolutionary thinker, but with regard to the soul he followed the path of the Platonic tradition. Descartes says the nature of the soul is to think, to be conscious. ("I think; therefore, I am.") Conversely, the body excludes consciousness. While he would maintain a substantial union of the body and soul, Descartes does not clearly explain how the two substances unite.

Using an argument that echoes Qoheleth (Eccl 3:19), Descartes argued for the immortality of the soul on moral grounds: unless there is some retribution in the afterlife, there is no difference between humans and beasts. Were it true that "after this life we have nothing to fear or to hope for," added Descartes, many "feeble spirits" would have little incentive for virtue. He concluded that "our soul is in its nature entirely independent of the body, and in consequence that it is not liable to die with it. And then, inasmuch as we observe no other causes capable of destroying it, we are naturally inclined to judge that it is immortal."[7] By positing, as it were, a soul capable of existence apart from the body, the Cartesian system, like almost all dualistic systems, regards the body as the only real victim of death. Upon separation from the soul the corporeal element dissolves, disintegrates, while the incorruptible soul endures.

THE ANTHROPOLOGY OF THE BIBLE

Although there is a confluence of the two traditions in Christianity, the doctrines of the immortality of the soul and of the resurrection of the body are rooted in very different anthropologies. As we have seen throughout this work, Greek philosophy and the Bible expound widely different views concerning the origin, nature, and destiny of human beings. Even though biblical writings after the Exile—the Hellenistic period in secular history—show some influence of Greek thought, one must be cautious because verbal similarity—especially in translation—does not always indicate affinity of concepts.[8] Biblical anthropology, for example, used more categories than people conditioned to think in the categories of body and soul are accustomed to. Although it speaks of *basar* (flesh), *nephesh* (living soul), and *ruah* (spirit), the Old Testament regards the human being as one. In simply translating these terms, as is generally done, by "flesh," "soul," and "spirit," there is a degree of equivocation because they do not correspond to the philosophical categories the English words represent.

Basar, the biblical word for "flesh," connotes much more than the carnal pulp formed by blood and tissue. It is visible, limited, powerless, and carries within itself the seed of corruption; it stands in stark contrast to the God who saves; to God who is spirit, infinite, all powerful, and eternal. *Basar* not only designates each individual but humanity as such. The frequent reference in the bible to *kol basar*—"all flesh"—clearly refers to humanity taken as a whole.

Nephesh, misleadingly translated "soul," designates a "living being"; it connotes vitality in the broadest sense. Etymologically *nephesh* is associated with breathing, and hence it came to mean life or an individual's life and even an individual self. The *nephesh*, however, is not immune from death and in no way guarantees the survival of the human person after death. At death the *nephesh* simply goes out, draining away with the blood. The dead are said to continue a tenuous existence in Sheol as little more than shadows of their former selves (Is 14:9; 1 Sam 28:14).

The Old Testament has another word, *ruah*, which we have mentioned above in connection with "Lord, Giver of life"; it is translated "spirit." It too has a broad range of meanings and at times seems to be synonymous with *nephesh*. There is, however, a difference, and it seems that *nephesh* is used to suggest a human property, while *ruah* connotes a divine gift. *Ruah* describes the life force as it comes from God, and life continues only so long as God's breath remains to animate the individual.

One would expect at this point a fourth Hebrew term, a word for "body," but despite the fact that the Old Testament names about eighty parts of the human organism, it has no word for the conglomerate other than *adam*, "man." In fact, almost any part—head, eye, hand, blood—was used to designate the whole. The powers and functions, physical as well as psychic, of an individual are attributed somewhat indifferently to various organs. The absence of a Semitic word for "body" becomes an important consideration, as we shall see, in trying to understand St. Paul's theology of the resurrection.

But before moving on to consider the resurrection in the New Testament, it must be said in final analysis that the Old Testament, taken by itself, leaves the question of human destiny unresolved.

RESURRECTION OF THE BODY

From the time of the Babylonian exile onward, the idea of the resurrection of the dead becomes a recurring theme in the canonical and intertestamental writings. Originally intended as a metaphor for the restoration of Israel as a people, the resuscitation of the dead bones (Ez 37) certainly pointed to "corporate" rather than to a mere individual spiritual survival. A new era is promised which will be a day of awakening for Israel. In the period of the Maccabees there was thought of a resurrection, not only of the just but of the wicked as well. The prophet Daniel, for example, in one of his apocalyptic visions, speaks of a day of reckoning: "Many of those who sleep in the dust of the earth shall awake; some shall live forever, others shall be an everlasting horror and disgrace" (12:2). The author is refering to the martyrs who suffered death under Antiochus IV Epiphanes and their other persecutors, not to a general resurrection of the dead. The Book of Daniel, moreover, makes it clear that by raising the dead to life God exhibits not only divine power but retributive justice. The chosen will rise again. They will enter into eternal life while others are destined for everlasting torment. Another work of about the same period, the Second Book of Maccabees, expresses a belief in the resurrection and, as in Daniel, links it with retribution (7:9,11,14). It was in this context that Judas Maccabeus, motivated by belief in the resurrection, promoted the practice of praying and offering expiatory sacrifices for the dead, "for if he were not expecting the fallen to rise again, it would have been useless and foolish to pray for them in death" (2 Mc 12:44).

In the time of Jesus, the Pharisees were known for their belief in the resurrection, and it is probably through their influence that the doctrine prevailed in Palestine. On the other hand, the Sadducees actively opposed the teaching, as is attested by the Jewish historian Josephus and the New Testament itself (see Mk 12:18; Acts 4:1-2; 23:6-8).[9] In defending himself before the Sanhedrin, Paul cleverly played the Pharisees off against the Sadducees:

> Brothers, I am a Pharisee and was born a Pharisee. I find myself on trial now because of my hope in the resurrection of the dead. At these words, a dispute arose between Pharisees and Sadducees which divided the whole assembly. (The Sadducees, of course, maintain that there is no resurrection and that there are neither angels nor spirits, while the Pharisees believe in all these things.) (Acts 23:6-8)

Even the Pharisees and other Jews who held to the notion of the resurrection did not agree whether everyone would be raised: some would have limited the resurrection to Israel, some only to the just. The just would be raised so they could continue to live; for, as we have seen, there is no true life without the body. Those who taught that sinners would also be raised linked the resurrection to eschatological judgment. In either case, the wicked—enemies and persecutors of Israel—and the unjust would be condemned to punishment in the shadowy existence of the nether world.[10]

The New Testament takes up where the Old leaves off. It is clear from Jesus' dialogue with the Sadducees that he tried to correct the popular notion that resurrection means a return to the conditions of earthly life; the life of the risen is more like that of the angels in heaven (Mk 12:25). The Epistle to the Hebrews lists the "resurrection of the dead and judgment" among the elementary teachings of the church (6:2). In the tradition of late Judaism, Luke's Gospel links the reward of the just to resurrection. Although none of the synoptic Gospels mentions the resurrection of sinners, Paul, charged with inciting riots, defends himself before Felix, the Roman governor, by confronting his Jewish accusers and saying, "I have the same hope in God as these men have that there is to be a resurrection of the good and wicked alike" (Acts 24:13).

PAUL'S THEOLOGY OF THE RESURRECTION

In the kerygma and in the catechesis of the apostolic church, Christ's resurrection is seen as heralding a new era. The day of the Lord has arrived! But it was not enough to proclaim the good news and simply repeat elementary teachings; it was found necessary, as the Epistle to the Hebrews stated, to "go beyond the initial teaching about Christ and advance to maturity" (6:1). It fell to St. Paul to develop a theology of the resurrection of the body. The church at Corinth, under the influence of Greek philosophy or perhaps of gnosticism, raised doubts about the resurrection of the body. Though Paul found some of the questions "nonsensical" (1 Cor 15:34), he felt obliged to answer them.

For Paul, as for most Jews of the time, life without a body is not true human life; consequently redemption does not consist, as the Greeks and gnostics taught, in liberation of the soul from the body. Fundamental to Pauline theology is the connection between Christ's resurrection and redemption, between his resurrection and that of all Christians. Paul writes,

> Christ is now raised from the dead, the first fruits of those who have fallen asleep. Death came through a man; hence the resurrection of the dead comes through a man also. Just as in Adam all die, so in Christ all will come to life again. . . . (1 Cor 15:20-22)

Thus he explains the importance of the resurrection of Jesus as the cause and basis of our own hope to share a similar experience. The apostle also sees Jesus' resurrection as the exemplar that gives us some insight into the manner of our resurrection.[11] Though Paul examines the question from many sides, we concentrate in these reflections on only one aspect: How are we to think of the resurrection of the body? "How are the dead to be raised up? What kind of body will they have?" (1 Cor 15:35).

Today it is widely conceded that though Paul wrote in Greek and at times borrowed from Hellenistic sources, his anthropology is grounded in that of the Old Testament. He did, however, make one terminological innovation. Following the Septuagint, Paul used two Greek words to render *basar*; in some places he speaks of *sarx* ("flesh") and in others of *soma* ("body"). Modern interpreters of Pauline thought agree that they represent two quite different aspects of the human being. The classic English study by J. A. T. Robinson emphasizes that *sarx* is not a component of the *soma*.[12]

Sarx is the person viewed, as it were, from the outside. It represents the physical, the "materialistic" element in human nature. It speaks of the humans' solidarity with creation and of their limitations, weakness, and mortality. To make matters worse, *sarx* has fallen into the grip of sin and is under the sentence of death. Thus when Paul speaks of the flesh lusting against the spirit and the spirit against the flesh (Gal 5:17), he is describing the struggle of the force of death against the force of life and vice versa. Nonetheless, Paul's view of matter is radically different from that of the gnostics, who, as we have seen, regarded flesh and everything connected with it as inherently evil and for that reason in mortal conflict with the spirit, the principle of good. His classic description of *sarx* is found in Romans:

> The tendency of the flesh is toward death but that of the spirit toward life and peace. The flesh in its tendency is at enmity with God; it is not subject to God's law. Indeed, it cannot be; those who are in the flesh cannot please God. (8:6-7)

For Paul *sarx* is in itself neutral, but he saw a person "living according to the flesh" as living for himself or herself, for the world. When Paul describes such a person as being "carnal," that person's sin extends beyond mere sensuality; it is comprehensively "selfish" in that it engulfs the whole being.

Paul uses *sarx* primarily to explain a person's otherness from God, the weakness and mortality of the individual. The main theme of his anthropology, however, is the notion of *soma*. It is the common thread running through his view of human destiny, of the Gospel message, the church, and everlasting life. Although the *soma* is an accomplice in one's sin and corruption, it is also the carrier of the resurrection.

In many Pauline texts, *soma* and *sarx* seem almost interchangeable. Both describe the make-up of individuals not in terms of what they have, but in terms of what they are. (The Greek *has* a body; the Jew *is* his or her *soma*.) *Soma* represents the whole person, one's external as well as innermost being. Moderns use the word "psychosomatic" when discussing the intimate relationship between mind and body, a relationship that Paul had in mind when speaking simply of the *soma*. In fact there are authors who try to capture the full meaning of *soma* by using the neologism "body-person."[13]

Robinson sums up the differences between *sarx* and *soma* in an italicized passage as follows:

> . . . however much the two may come, through the Fall, to describe the same thing, in essence *sarx* and *soma* designate different aspects of the human relationship to God. *While sarx stands for man, in the solidarity of creation, in his distance from God, soma stands for man, in the solidarity of creation, as made for God.*[14]

Because it came to represent a person's distance from God, *sarx* has no place in the kingdom and for that reason is not redeemable. Given the way he understood *sarx* in contradistinction to *soma*, Paul could never use the phrase "resurrection of the flesh." He is explicit: "This is what I mean, brothers: flesh and blood cannot inherit the kingdom of God; no more can corruption inherit incorruption" (1 Cor 15:50). In Paul's writings (and this is true of the New Testament in general), whenever he mentions the resurrection he speaks of the "resurrection of the dead." The first references to resurrection of the flesh (body) appear in the second century in writings that understand *sarx* in its classical sense, quite apart from Paul's use of the term.[15]

Unlike the *sarx*, the *soma* can look forward to the resurrection, but there is a condition. The body-person must be radically changed, fashioned anew. It must be purified of sin and corruption. Though the carnal self cannot know God, the body is for the Lord. In speaking of Christ's resurrection as the cause and exemplar of our own, Oscar Cullmann expounds Paul's thought in this way: "Deliverance consists not in a release of soul from body but in a release of both from flesh. We are not released from the body; rather the body itself is set free."[16]

Paul himself stresses the change that must take place if we are to enter into the kingdom. Still thinking that an apocalyptic end of the world was imminent, he wrote:

> Now I am going to tell you a mystery. Not all of us shall fall asleep, but all of us are to be changed—in an instant, in the twinkling of an eye, at the sound of the last trumpet. The trumpet will sound and the dead will be raised incorruptible, and we shall be changed. This corruptible body must be clothed with incorruptibility, this mortal body with immortality. (1 Cor 15:51-53)

In discussing Jesus' resurrection we emphasized that it signaled a radical change in his appearance (Chapter 11), but that there is also continuity. The risen and glorified Lord is the same body-person as the earthly Jesus.[17] This is the value of the apostles' witness; it is the basis of our faith. The mystery and meaning of the resurrection of the body far exceeds the philosophical implications of the immortality of the soul. Philosophers speak of a "substantial change" at death, but for most of them the human story ends with one's passing from this world. For Christians, life in this world is but the beginning. The resurrection represents New Being, a New Creation, not merely survival after death.

Furthermore, the moral dimension of the resurrection transcends the argument for the immortality of the soul, an argument based on retribution. To put off the old and become "the new man" in Christ Jesus implies a metamorphosis that begins already with baptism. It is not simply a matter of punishment or reward for what one does or does not do, but a question of rising to a new level of life. As Paul describes it, to "put to death whatever in your nature is rooted in earth" (Col 3:5) means to repudiate a style of life that tolerates—even values— various forms of subhuman to antisocial behavior from fornication to lying, from anger to foul language. To the Christians at Colossae Paul says:

> Clothe yourselves with heartfelt mercy, with kindness, humility, meekness, and patience. Bear with one another; forgive whatever grievances you have against one another. Forgive as the Lord has forgiven you. Over all these virtues put on love, which binds the rest together and makes them perfect. Christ's peace must reign in your hearts, since as members of the one body you have been called to that peace. (Col 3: 12-15)

Writing to the church in Rome, Paul describes the resurrection of the dead as a work of the Trinity. The significance of being baptized in the name of the Father, Son, and Spirit is:

> You are not in the flesh; you are in the spirit, since the Spirit of God dwells in you. If anyone does not have the Spirit of Christ, he does not belong to Christ. If Christ is in you the body is dead because of sin, while the spirit lives because of justice. If the Spirit of him who raised Jesus from the dead dwells in you, then he who raised Christ from the dead will bring your mortal bodies to life also, through his Spirit dwelling in you. (Rom 8:9-11)

In his more mature writings Paul makes it clear that Christians experience a life-giving death already in baptism, a destruction of the old so that new life can be nurtured and flourish. In Romans he writes:

> If we have been united with him through likeness to his death, so shall we be through a like resurrection. This we know: our old self was crucified with him so that the sinful body might be destroyed and we might be slaves to sin no longer. A man who is dead has been freed from sin. If we have died with Christ, we believe that we are also to live with him. (6:5-8)

In Ephesians he says God "brought us to life with Christ when we were dead in sin. By this favor you were saved. Both with and in Christ Jesus he raised us up and gave us a place in the heavens" (2:4-6). The linking of baptism to the Lord's death and resurrection, once dramatized in the liturgy by immersing the baptizands under water as if burying them in a tomb, gets it meaning not from the ritual but from the reality. Jesus spoke of his own death as a "baptism" that would cause him no little anguish (Lk 12:50). It is in this context that Jesus also warns his disciples that they too "will be baptized in the same bath of pain as I" (Mk 10:38-39).[18] Thus it was that a martyr's death, a "blood baptism," was regarded as efficacious and even more esteemed than water baptism (see 1 Jn 5:6-8).

THE CHRISTIAN TRADITION:
LIFE IS CHANGED, NOT ENDED

Despite belief in the resurrection, the Christian attitude toward death remains ambiguous. The Gospels even present Jesus as so thoroughly human that he shook with fear at the thought of death (Mk 14:34-36). Death contradicts the biblical image of God as the God of the living. It is a destructive force that threatens the very existence of creation. In Jesus' Jewish eyes, to die meant to be abandoned by God: "My God, my God, why have you forsaken me?" (Mk 15:34). The evangelists glossed over none of the details in describing Jesus' grisly death. Human in mind as well as in body, he felt the anguish of helplessness, and the pain that pierced to the inner fiber of his being. The Gospel writers make no distinction between body and soul: the whole person experiences death. And yet it is precisely because of Jesus' death that Christians have hope. His victory over death was not (as some early gnostics would have had it) that he escaped death but that he confronted it in all its horror. In the mysterious (and paradoxical) plan of God, the innocent Jesus suffered the death penality so that the guilty might escape it! (Rom 4:25; 2 Cor 5:21).

In the light of Christ's death and resurrection, Christians view death as a metamorphosis, a substantial change in the form of life. Death opens new, unexpected possibilities. Speaking of his own death, Jesus says, "Unless the grain of wheat falls to the earth and dies, it remains a grain of wheat. But if it dies it produces much fruit" (Jn 12:24). St. Paul elaborates on the same metaphor in describing the transformation that occurs in the resurrection:

> When you sow, you do not sow the full-blown plant, but a kernel of wheat or some other grain. God gives body to it as he pleases. . . . So is it with the resurrection of the dead. What is sown in the earth is subject to decay, what rises is incorruptible. What is sown is ignoble, what rises is glorious. Weakness is sown, strength rises up. A natural body is put down and a spiritual body comes up. (1 Cor 15:37-38,42-44)

It is this outlook that the Catholic liturgy expresses in the preface for Masses for the dead: *vita mutatur, non tollitur*—"life is changed, not ended."

Despite St. Paul's clear teaching on the resurrection, it was not enough for some people—Christians, no less—to be assured that they will one day rise from the dead! Apparently, no one had explained to them the radical difference between the resuscitation of Lazarus and the resurrection of Jesus (though the Fourth Gospel carefully contrasts them). Lazarus, like the Old Testament personages and the "saints" who came out of the graves at the time of the crucifixion (Mt 27: 52-53), lived to die again. Thus in an effort to clarify the meaning and bring out the full significance of the RESURRECTION OF THE BODY, LIFE EVERLASTING secured a place in the Creed—probably in the fourth century. A sermon addressed to catechumens and attributed to St. Augustine acknowledges in so many words that the phrase LIFE EVERLASTING was added to make it clear that the resurrection of believers would be like that of Jesus rather than like the resuscitation of Lazarus.[19]

Taking LIFE EVERLASTING as a point of departure, St. Cyril of Jerusalem explained in his famed catechetical instructions on the Creed that the phrase implies far more than the mere continuance of life. It points, he said, "to the real, veritable life," which is the very being of

God.[20] Thus in the course of time, emphasis shifts from the affirmation of endless existence to the blessed quality of life in the world to come.

Faith in the resurrection is not a mere appendage to the gospel message; it is integral to that message. It is what makes the Christian story different from that of other religions. Jesus not only teaches and preaches victory over sin and death: he embodies it in his person. Christians become identified with the Risen Lord through dying and rising with him in baptism, the sacrament that makes real what it symbolizes. And like the figure who appeared to Thomas (Jn 21:24-29), they, though raised from the dead by the power of God, continue to bear the marks of suffering in their bodies. The crucified Jesus is the Risen Christ; and like their Savior, baptized Christians are at once both victims and victors; they live on the fine edge between the already and the not-yet.

As we come to the end of the Creed we are ready to begin reading it anew. The resurrection takes us back to affirming the power of God, MAKER OF HEAVEN AND EARTH, OF ALL THAT IS SEEN AND UNSEEN. To confess, as we do in the first article of the Apostles' Creed, that God is MAKER OF HEAVEN AND EARTH, is not simply to affirm that God brought the universe into being. Creation is not a finished product; rather, it marks the beginning of a dynamic process that flows and ebbs between existence and annihilation, order and chaos, life and death, wholeness and fragmentation. The New Testament describes the resurrection as the ultimate vindication of good over evil, life over death.

The three articles of the Creed do not deal with three separate and distinct chapters of faith. Speaking for his fellow Christians, Paul says, "For us there is one God, the Father, *from* whom all things come and for whom we live; and one Lord Jesus Christ, *through* whom everything was made and through whom we live" (1 Cor 8:6; emphasis added). And of the Spirit, THE LORD AND THE GIVER OF LIFE, we pray, "When you send forth your Spirit, they are created and you renew the face of the earth" (Ps 104:3). Creation, culminating in the resurrection of the dead, is the work of the Triune God: "If the Spirit of him who raised Jesus from the dead dwells in you, then he who raised Christ from the dead will bring your mortal bodies to life also, through his Spirit dwelling in you" (Rom 8:11). The three moments of creation, reconciliation, and re-creation, represented successively in the narrative of salvation and attributed respectively to Father, Son, and Spirit, are in fact one as God is one.

Notes

1. New York: Macmillan, 1965. The work consists of four Ingersoll lectures given at Harvard University 1955–59; Stendahl's introduction attentuates the conflict.

2. "Immortality of the Soul or Resurrection of the Dead," in Stendahl, *Immorality and Resurrection*, pp. 9–53.

3. *De praescriptione*, ch. 36; quoted in Kelly, *Creeds*, p. 85.

4. *Alcibaides*, 129e, 130c.

5. H. A. Wolfson, "Immortality and Resurrection in the Philosophy of the Church Fathers," in Stendahl, pp. 54–96. See Jaroslav Pelikan, *The Shape of Death: Life, Death and Immortality in the Early Church Fathers* (New York: Abingdon, 1961).

6. Augustine treats the immortality of the soul in several works, chiefly *Soliloquia* and *De immortalitate animarum*. He discoursed on the reverence due the body in *De cura pro mortuis*.

7. Quoted in *Encyclopedia of Philosophy*, 4:146.

8. A. M. Dubarle, "Belief in Immortality in the Old Testament and Judaism," in Pierre Benoit and Roland Murphy, ed., *Immortality and Resurrection*, Concilium 60 (New York: Herder and Herder, 1970), pp. 34–45. J. A. T. Robinson, *The Body: A Study in Pauline Theology* (London: SCM Press, 1952), pp. 111–116.

9. Josephus, *Jewish Wars*, II, 8, 14. *Antiquities*, XVIII, 1, 4. The Sadducees, less numerous than the Pharisees, nonetheless wielded a great deal of influence. Although their role in the trial and crucifixion of Jesus was not very prominent, they led the opposition against the apostles because the latter were proclaiming the resurrection of the dead in the person of Jesus (Acts 4:1–2).

10. *Sacramentum Mundi* 5:335–336.

11. J. Kremer, "Paul: The Resurrection of Jesus, the Cause and Exemplar of Our Resurrection," in Benoit and Murphy, *Immortality*, p. 78–91.

12. Robinson, *The Body*, pp. 26–33. M. Carrez, "With What Body Do the Dead Rise Again?" in Benoit and Murphy, *Immortality*, pp. 92–102.

13. "Body-person" is a term favored by the Chardin school. See C. F. Mooney, *Teilhard de Chardin and the Mystery of Christ* (New York: Harper & Row, 1965), pp. 71–74, 90, and passim. In 1979 the Congregation for the Doctrine of the Faith issued a statement summarizing the church's teaching about the resurrection of the dead. Among other points it stated, "The church understands this resurrection as referring to the whole person," and then it continues: "The church affirms that a spiritual element survives and subsists after death. . . To designate this element, the church uses the word 'soul,' the accepted term in the usage of scripture and tradition. Although not unaware that this term has various meanings in the Bible, the church thinks that there is no valid reason for rejecting it; moreover, she considers that the use of some word as a vehicle is absolutely indispensable in order to support the faith of Christians." *Origins*, 9 (Aug. 2, 1979):132.

14. *The Body*, p. 31.

15. *Sacramentum Mundi* 5:339.

16. In Stendahl, *Immortality and Resurrection*, p. 27.

17. O. Cullmann in Stendahl, *Immortality and Resurrection*, p. 27.

18. See O. Cullmann, *Baptism in the New Testament*. Studies in Biblical Theology 1 (London: SCM, 1950), pp. 9–22.

19. *Sermo ad catechumenos*, 9, and *Ep.* 102. Kelly, *Creeds*, discusses this at some length, pp. 387–388.

20. Kelly, *Creeds*, p. 388.

WE BELIEVE IN . . .

23

From Belief to Faith

"We believe, I believe." What does this mean?

Religious and theological language, as we pointed out in our commentary on the first article at the beginning of this book, needs to be taken with the proverbial grain of salt. When speaking of God, the Truth who transcends the limitations of our intellects, our words do not mean what they seem. FATHER and ALMIGHTY, as we indicated, cover a range of human experience that is both more than and different from what we know in everyday life.

Another problem that compounds the difficulty of interpretation is that language changes with the passage of time. Conditioned by culture and usage, words come to have different connotations in different periods. We noted how the biblical phrase son of God rang differently in the polytheistic culture of the Roman Empire from what it does today. "Spirit" and "flesh" are examples of everyday words that took on technical meanings in the Christian glossary.

Translation always implies interpretation, and as a language evolves, new translations must be made. By way of example, we cite "credo." No word, no phrase in the Creed has undergone a greater metamorphosis in translation than the opening word itself, "credo." It is in the first instance itself a translation of the Greek *pisteuo*, which, for Christians, had a distinctive meaning. The English translation, "I believe," first used in the High Middle Ages, attempted to capture the biblical idea of faith—a notion something quite other than what "I believe" has come to signify in current speech. The term "believe" is so deeply imbedded in the life and thought of the English-speaking world that such a major shift in its meaning could not but have far-reaching ramifications in religious attitudes and Christians' understanding of "faith."

Before we can even discuss the biblical notion of faith or what a Christian means when he or she, reciting the Creed, says "I *believe*," it is necessary to come to some understanding of terms or at least to recognize the ambiguity of the English phrase. Since the substance of the commentary to this point has been the *contents* of faith (*fides quae creditur*), a topic we return to in the next and final chapter, the emphasis here is on the *act* of faith (*fides qua creditur*). This chapter begins with a word study; relying on the now classical research of Wilfred Cantwell Smith, it traces the etymology of "belief," "creed," and "faith," and relates them to one another. The middle section explains faith primarily in the Augustinian sense as believing in *someone* (God), and analyzes various aspects of faith in relationship to love, to prayer, and to being human. The final section briefly explains the Danish philosopher Søren Kierkegaard's "leap of faith," and the way faith was presented at the First and Second Vatican Councils. The theme that runs through the chapter is that faith represents a certain way of apprehending reality, a way of looking at the totality of one's relationships, actions, and attitudes toward God and the world in which a person finds himself or herself. Not everyone who makes an act of faith is Christian, but as Kierkegaard argued, the absence of faith is despair.

THE METAMORPHOSIS OF "BELIEF"

Literally and originally, "to believe" means "to hold dear." This is the meaning that the German equivalent *belieben* still has in the sense of "prefer" or "give allegiance to." Etymologically, "believe" is related to a broad range of familiar words, some archaic, like *lief* (dear, willing), some still in use, like "beloved" and "love." The history of "believe" in its various forms ranging from Old English *be loef* to the early modern English synonym "beloved," through the seventeenth-century misspelling that gave us "believe" instead of "beleeve" is a chronicle of its gradual change in meaning. It is in this sense that one of the earliest examples of the word "belief" is used in a medieval homily where the preacher warns that Christians should not set their hearts, as we might say today, on worldly goods. The actual phrase is "should not set their belief" on them.

In the fourteenth century, about the time of John Wycliffe (1330-84), important changes began to take place that mark the transition from Middle to Modern English. A new word, "faith," was coming into use as the English form of the Latin *fides*. Early evidence of the transition can be seen in the two versions of the English Bible attributed to Wycliffe, both based on the Latin Vulgate. In the first, *bilefe* translates *fides*, whereas in the second, "faith" appears in a number of places. By the seventeenth century the transition was virtually complete. The 1611 King James Authorized Version used the word "faith" 246 times, "belief" once. The *Oxford English Dictionary*, which describes this evolution (s.v. *belief*), states,

> . . . the word *faith* being, through O[ld] F[rench] *fei*, *faith*, the etymological representative of the L[atin] *fides*, it began in the 14th c[entury] to be used to translate the latter, and in course of time almost superseded 'belief' esp[ecially] in theological language, leaving 'belief' in great measure to the merely intellectual process or state. . . . Thus "belief in God" no longer means as much as 'faith in God."

This change was true only for the noun. Unlike Greek and biblical Hebrew, however, English never developed a verb form associated with "faith." Translators, therefore, used "believe," which continued to have the meaning it had in the medieval period: to hold dear, to cherish. Until very recent times "I believe" clearly implied (as it still does for some) to entrust oneself, to give one's heart, to be loyal, to make a commitment.

The idea of commitment, it should be noted, is also at the root memory of the original Latin. Etymologically *credo*, it seems, is a compound of two other Latin words, *cor*, *cordis*, "heart" (as in the English derivatives "cordial," "concord," and "accord") and an archaic verb *-do*, "put, place, set" (of which a trace is seen in such English words as "tradition" and "condominium"). The primary meaning of *credo* in classical Latin was "to entrust," "to commit," "to trust something to someone," for example, money (as suggested by the cognate "credit").

There seems little doubt that in the early days of the Latin church, a person about to be baptized, in saying *credo*, meant "I herein give my heart to God the Father, . . . to Jesus Christ his only son, . . . to the Holy Spirit." At the crucial moment in the liturgical rite, the spokesman for the Christian community asks, "*Credis*?" "Do you believe?" The baptizand declares *credo*—"I give my heart," "I commit myself," and in doing so makes a solemn act of self-dedication. Everywhere in the ancient church—in Rome (according to the *Apostolic Tradition* of St. Hippolytus), in the instructions of St. Cyril in Jerusalem, St. Ambrose in Milan, and St. Augustine in Africa—the tone of the baptismal rite, whether in Greek or Latin, marks a change in one's allegiance from Satan to God, from darkness to light, from sin to purity, from worldly attachments to attachment to the kingdom of God. Baptism is not merely a "head trip," a question of moving from disbelief to belief, as the terms are currently understood, but a conversion—a change of heart.

BELIEF AS UNCERTAINTY

But what does the assertion "I believe in" mean to the modern Christian? Do we mean the Creed to be an act of self-dedication, a loyalty oath, that signals a commitment that has transformed our life? Or are we more tentative? When we say "I believe," do we mean that we are less than confident—that we are really not certain? Wilfred Cantwell Smith, to whom I am indebted for much of the foregoing history of terms, says that the metamorphosis of the meaning of "I believe" may be dramatically characterized by the following contrast:

> There was a time when "I believe" as a ceremonial declaration of faith meant, and was heard as meaning: "Given the reality of God, as a fact of the universe, I hereby proclaim that I align my life accordingly, pledging love and loyalty." A statement about a person's believing has now come to mean, rather, something of this sort: "Given the uncertainty of God, as a fact of modern life, so-and-so reports that the idea of God is part of the furniture of the mind."[1]

The change in meaning that took place over a period of time, has in the end proven drastic. Whereas to believe originally meant to hold dear and clearly implied a strong personal commitment based on trust, it now connotes an element of uncertainty, and even when addressed to a person—"I believe you"—it signals a minimum of trust and does not imply commitment. More often than not, "believe" in the modern sense implies doubt. To illustrate the point, Smith cites the *Random*

House Dictionary. The first entry under the word "belief" defines it as "an opinion or conviction" and offers by way of example *the belief that the world is flat*! Thus the user of this popular dictionary comes away from it associating belief with a notion that is antiquated and false.[2]

"Faith" and "belief," as defined in our modern dictionaries, are not synonymous. Given the distinction, moreover, it must be emphasized that the Creed is a confession of faith before it is a listing of beliefs. "Believing in God" in the modern, problematic sense—that God exists—is not an article of faith; at least it is not the main focus of the Creed. One may also "believe" something in lieu of firsthand evidence, accepting the truth of a statement on the word of someone regarded as trustworthy; but strictly speaking one has faith—believes—only in a person. This is the classic distinction of St. Augustine: *credere Deo* (to believe on God's authority), *credere Deum [esse]* (to believe that God exists), and *credere in Deum* (to believe in God). St. Thomas says that all three are aspects of the single act of faith.[3]

The verbal form "I believe in" must be taken in the sense it had into the seventeenth century; and the preposition *in* needs to be duly stressed, for it points up the difference between saying "I believe you" and "I have faith in you." Like the Latin CREDO IN which it translates, "I believe in" signals an avowal, a firm commitment to the Triune God. Faustus of Riez (d. 490/500), in a passage that continues to be quoted, said it is not enough to believe that God exists (one also believes that the devil exists), but one must believe *in* God.

> To believe in God is to seek Him in faith, to hope piously in Him, and to pass into Him by a movement of choice. When I say that I believe in Him, I confess Him, offer Him worship, adore Him, give myself over to Him wholly and transfer to Him all my affection.[4]

In reciting the Creed, Christians declare their faith before both God and the world. Thus the purpose of their confession is twofold: before God it is doxology, an act of praise and thanks giving whereby we applaud all that God has done in creation. Before their fellow human beings, Christians declare publicly that God continues to act in the world in Christ and in the Holy Spirit. The Creed echoes the faith of the New Testament church. By it the individual Christian follows in the centuries-old tradition of the baptized who began confessing their faith by *protesting* in the original sense of the word—that is, "witnessing for"—"Jesus is Lord!"

THE ACT OF FAITH

The Creed presupposes an *act of faith* that is highly personal and antecedent to any verbal formulation. Before saying out loud, "I believe in God," I must say in my heart, "My Lord and my God, I believe in *You*" in order to say it sincerely.[5] For Christians "the act of faith" is one's personal response to God who calls, a commitment to divine being revealed in Jesus Christ.

The Old and New Testaments witness to one fundamental fact. It is God who calls human beings, addresses each by name and manifests love and care for them. According to the Scriptures God encounters us in much the way we encounter other persons. It is true, the Creator and creatures are not equals; God is not "person" in the way humans are (see Chapter 1). On the other hand, the Bible makes it clear that neither is God an "impersonal" being, neither in the sense of one who is distant and disinterested, nor in the sense of a cosmic force.

God is mystery, beyond human capacity and categories. Individuals can ultimately *know* God only in faith and can understand the divine self-revelation only in response to God's prior call. The Christian doctrine of grace is based on the fact that God takes the initiative. Even when individuals seem to discover God, perhaps after a long and tortuous search, they are successful because God has first found them. It seems that when humans pretend to have found God on their own, without the Scriptures, without the church, they misrepresent the divine essence. At best, God becomes a creature of human ingenuity, a mental construct or hypothesis demanded by some theorem that explains the universe; at worst, a caricature no better than the idols of whom the Psalmist said,

> They have mouths but speak not;
> they have eyes but see not;
> They have ears but hear not;
> they have noses but smell not;
> They have hands but feel not;
> they have feet but walk not;
> they utter no sound from their throat.

Their makers shall be like them,
    everyone that trusts in them. (Ps 115:4-8)

The believer responds to God as a person, speaks to and of God with personal pronouns—"Thou" rather than "it." As inadequate as the category is, we have no better adjective than "personal" to capture the testimony of Scripture.

The act of faith thus establishes a bond between persons. Faith tells us that we are accepted; it is the ground of love. The act of faith implies mutual trust that goes beyond objective reasons. Like love, it is not something we can force. Like love, faith is not something we deserve because of our achievements or because of our moral integrity, our generosity, or our education. Simply put, faith responds to faith. This is the line of reasoning behind the Credo in Leonard Bernstein and Stephen Schwartz's musical work, *Mass*:

I believe in God,
But does God believe in me?
. . .
I believe in one God,
But then I believe in three.
I'll believe in twenty gods
If they'll believe in me.
. . .
Who created my life?
Made it come to be?
Who accepts this awful
Responsibility?
. . .

Faith tells us that Another loves us for ourselves. We respond tentatively, cautiously. At first we do not know the Other's name. We do not ask. We are secure for the moment in the knowledge that Someone trusts us, takes responsibility for us. Paradoxically, in finding the Other we discover ourselves. In faith and love we come to see our own worth. We may have doubts, but doubts do not destroy faith any more than intellectual difficulties destroy love. It is neglect and lack of trust that undermine faith and love. One displays but cannot verify faith any more than a person can prove his or her love. Faith, like love, is expressed in myriad ways ("How do I love thee? Let me count the ways . . .") but proves elusive when analyzed and subjected to the scrutiny of rational arguments.

FAITH AND PRAYER

The act of faith is essentially a prayer addressed directly to God. It is the human response in the dialogue instituted by God, and it is from that initial "I believe in You," that every other prayer arises. Prayer acknowledges one's dependence. Praying means opening oneself to another. "The Other" becomes intimate with us and touches us at the depth of our existence.

One of the better insights of contemporary theologians is found in the parallels they draw between faith and prayer. They note that objections raised against the latter are similar to those raised against the former. One objection alleges that prayer (and by implication faith) stands apart from everyday experience. In normal situations, so the reasoning goes, we deal with problems ourselves; in crisis and emergency situations, when we cannot cope, we have recourse to prayer. If indeed this were the case, the implications are far-reaching: God becomes "God-of-the-gaps," the *deus ex machina* who descends out of the blue to rescue us when all else fails. The clear insinuation is that God stands aloof from the everyday world. To have recourse to prayer is to rely on a higher power; in effect, as the argument goes, this means a "pray-er" does not take the world seriously. Human endeavors of all kinds—political activity, struggles for freedom, economic development, scientific research—may be regarded as important to a greater or less degree, but not as ultimately significant. Thus the further insinuation is that one uses faith as an excuse to avoid making a firm commitment to the human enterprise.

These misrepresentations of the nature of prayer reflect much of the contemporary misunderstanding of the nature of faith. An act of faith that does not take the world and the human condition seriously does not, in effect, accept God as the ground of all being. It implies that God is finite and an entity apart from the created universe. The locus of faith, like the proper place for prayer, is not a niche in a corner of one's life, a space, however small or large, where "religious" activity and *perhaps* ethical decisions take place. Faith is more like the atmosphere, fresh air that permeates and enlivens every hour of individual and communal life, waking and sleeping, work and leisure, production and consumption. Where faith is concerned, there are no gaps. The faith response to God's self-revelation implies a reverence for all that

God has made, an acceptance of the inherent goodness of creation. Christian faith implies a readiness to assent to God as both the ground and goal of human existence.

THE HUMAN FACE OF FAITH

Faith is essential to human life. No one lives, at least for long, entirely without faith, because it is intricately bound up with the meaning of human existence. Even non-believers—people who do not have faith in the Christian sense—adopt a basic stance toward life. In making an act of faith a person exercises a fundamental choice that defines one's views about reality, about what is important and what is not, about what is moral and immoral. Faith is not an optional accessory one adds like a fireplace in a house or air-conditioning in an automobile. "A person," writes Wilfred Cantwell Smith, "is not a human being and then also a Jew, or also a Christian, or a Muslim. One is a human being by being one or the other of them."[6] Smith explains his point by taking the Hindu as an example. Hindu simply means "Indian." The people of India who speak Hindi think of themselves as Hindus; the distinction between Indian and Hindu is, in origin, a foreign invention. Endemic to their culture is the Indians' desire to be human, to discern as best they can how to live properly. To be authentically human in a world where matter and spirit converge and vie with each other for preeminence is not an easy task. The enterprise of becoming human is something that must be worked at in the context of cosmic forces. It cannot simply be left to chance or circumstance or fate. Outsiders view the lifestyle that Indians have developed over the centuries in religious terms and thus consider "Hinduism" as one of the world's great religions. In India, however, to be Hindu represents nothing more than the effort to be human.

Likewise, Buddhists set themselves not "Buddhist" ideals, but human ones. The individual they call the Buddha—"the Enlightened One"—disclosed how human beings may best live. There are no Buddhist truths, no Buddhist ideals, no Buddhist values apart from the cosmic truth, human ideals, absolute values that are inherent in the universe. Enlightenment like that experienced by the Buddha should be everyone's goal, though in Buddhist eyes, only the Buddha himself attained it perfectly.

Each of the great religions of the world, in that it takes a fundamental stance toward reality and what it means to be human, represents a different faith. Thus it is for Christians who proclaim that Jesus revealed not only who God is, but what it means to be human. And more. By reason of the Incarnation, the very fact that God "came down from heaven" and became one of us opened the possibility for us to become one with God. Jesus the Christ, Savior and Lord, not only reveals in the sense of discloses, but also enables us to be what we are called to be. The Christian faith does not—should not—stand in contrast to authentic human existence. As for Buddhists, for Christians there are no Christian truths, values, ideals, but only Truth, Goodness and Life exemplified by the One who said "I am the way, the truth and the life." All human beings are called to the same destiny.

To insist on the human quality of Christian faith does not mean that reason and the secular world are the sole criteria for a correct interpretation of the gospel, but it does mean that there is no salvation apart from the struggle to be human in the fullest sense. On the other hand, while faith, like prayer, cannot be defined apart from a societal context, the social aspects do not exhaust it meaning. Modern theologians emphasize that faith is multi-dimensional: it extends vertically to the heights and depths of existence as well as horizontally across the full range of human experience, individual and corporate.

FAITH IN DISPUTE

According to popular accounts of the sixteenth-century Reformation, the issue that divided the theologians, generally along Protestant-Catholic lines, was whether faith is basically trust in God's mercy and forgiveness or whether it is essentially a matter of content—what is believed. In retrospect it seems as if the opposing camps were so intent on expounding their own point of view that they were not listening to each other. The disputants, in fact, held more in common than they realized. Most accepted Augustine's threefold *credere* — *credere Deo*, *credere Deum (esse)*, *credere in Deum*—and in the tradition of medieval theology regarded them as representing three different facets of the single act of faith. Luther's quest for a merciful God led him to emphasize *credere in Deum*—the trust and confidence on which faith is grounded. Catholics, uneasy about the Reform movement as a whole, wanted something more definite and less individualistic than what would come to be called "a personal relationship." None of the disputants, however, questioned the existence of God—*credere Deum (esse)*.

Although the sixteenth-century controversies helped clarify the Christian understanding of faith, they had deleterious (and for a long while undetected) consequences. Once the Reformation became established, the Protestant-Catholic debate centered not on the act of faith, but on the contents of faith—"revealed truths." Catholic theologians were wont to compile lists of truths that Christians were obliged to accept because they were grounded on revelation—doctrines, practical truths (e.g., the Ten Commandments), and the means of salvation (e.g., the Lord's Prayer, the sacraments of baptism, penance, and eucharist). More often than not the doctrines were a paraphrase of the Apostles' Creed (the argument ran that these truths were obligatory, as evidenced from the constant practice of the church in requiring that Christians profess them as a condition for baptism).[7] Many points that Catholics considered "revealed" were disputed by Protestants. In the eyes of non-theologians, the end result was that theology took on the tone of polemics and apologetics. The discussion no longer centered on transcendent realities basic to the act of faith, but had shifted to particulars, the differences that separated the churches. Or to state it in the categories we have used through much of this chapter, theologians focused their attention on *what* must be believed on divine authority (*credere Deo revelante*), to the neglect of faith as personal commitment (*credere in Deum*).

The Enlightenment, in part a reaction against theological disputes, confessional rivalries, and wars of religion, forced the churches to focus their attention once more on basics. Avowed rationalists in the movement exalted reason to the exclusion of revelation. They regarded faith as defective knowledge, little more than ill-founded opinion or, at best, a means of legitimating religious and ethical teaching until society advances or individuals mature to the point where reason and science liberate them. Many not only rejected faith in revelation and faith in a personal God, but many questioned the very existence of God (*credere Deum esse*) (see Chapter 1). Thus in nineteenth-century Europe, Christians were once again made to ask themselves what they meant when they said, WE BELIEVE IN . . . .

It is impossible in a few pages to summarize or even name the many ways in which theologians, Protestant and Catholic, attempted to respond to the Enlightenment. We single out two approaches which, because of their lasting influence, are of more than historical interest. The one is associated with the father of modern existentialism, Søren Kierkegaard (1813-55); the other with the First Vatican Council (1869-70). Taken together they illustrate the paradox of Christian faith, which is at once decision and grace, human and divine action converging in the personal dimensions of life.

"THE LEAP OF FAITH"

Among Protestants one of the most vehement critics of the Enlightenment was the melancholic Dane Søren Kierkegaard. Kierkegaard described "the leap of faith" that embodied his views of choice and truth. Reacting in particular against what he considered the cosmic determinism and impersonal collectivism of Hegel, Kierkegaard set out to vindicate the individual. His starting point was the insecurity—the anxiety and alienation—that people experience in their everyday lives. He had little patience with philosophers who raised theoretical doubts about the certainty of religious and ethical truths but stopped short of asking the kind of question that exposes even more radical doubt about the purpose and meaning of human existence. Existential doubt brings one face to face with despair. Intellectual doubt is partial; despair engulfs one's whole being. It is possible to live with the former, not with the latter. As Kierkegaard intended, the title of one his most famous books, *Either/Or*, illustrates the fundamental option that confronts the individual: one is faced with the choice "either" to despair "or" to risk a leap into the unknown—a leap of faith.[8]

In opposition to Hegel's tendency to generalize and deal with humans in the abstract, Kierkegaard focused on concrete existence, personal freedom, and the act rather than the contents of faith. In his existentialist view, individuals define themselves not in terms of what they understand, but in terms of the choices they make. An individual constitutes himself or herself as individual by choosing one mode of existence rather than another.

Much like Blaise Pascal two centuries earlier, Kierkegaard was impatient with speculative philosophy and theology that made no difference in people's lives. He emphasized that truth must be defined as much by the way it is apprehended as in terms of what is apprehended. One chooses truths (others might say "values") by making a subjective commitment to a particular (in the sense of concrete) style of life. For Kierkegaard truth is subjectivity. It comes also to be called "existential truth," a lived truth rather a mere verbal truth. According to Kierkegaard truth consists not in the correspondence of thought with things, "not in knowing the truth, but in being truth." Although truth rests on the life choices one makes, there are no criteria to guide the decision or to say that it is correct or incorrect except that the choice be honestly made.

One's quest for authentic existence leads to making a basic choice regarding ultimate reality. This fundamental option is essentially a leap of faith, a plunge into the unknown. Kierkegaard accepts the Old Testament patriarch Abraham as the archetype of the person of faith. Called by Yahweh, Abraham had the courage to depart the land of his kinfolk and the familiar surroundings of his father's house to live the uncertain existence of a nomad and journey to an unknown land. In one of his more important works, *Fear and Trembling* (1843), Kierkegaard reflects on how God, who had promised Abraham that he would have descendants as numerous as the stars in the sky and the sands on the seashore, instructs the patriarch to sacrifice his only son. Although Abraham could see no other way in which God's promises were to be fulfilled except through Isaac, he proceeded dutifully up Mount Moriah. Further, in demanding the life of Isaac, God asks for human sacrifice, something that from an ethical standpoint is absolutely forbidden. Abraham must make a leap of faith, accept the absurd, do something that in human terms makes no sense. According to the Dane's analysis, faith is grounded in an existential attitude of being open to all possibilities of human existence. In the existential moment—now—one accepts the past and makes a commitment to fulfilling one's potentialities. The opposite, "unbelief," means being closed, shut-in against the limitless possibilities that human existence offers. (One of Kierkegaard's complaints against Hegel was "his work is full of syntheses, while life is full of choices."[9])

The Kierkegaardian leap of faith is often misrepresented as merely "the will to believe" and sheer subjectivism. In fact, the Danish thinker recognized Christianity's claim to be objectively true, independent of anyone's subjective commitment. He raged against the established church precisely because it so institutionalized and systematized the gospel that Christian faith no longer made a difference in one's life.

THE FIRST VATICAN COUNCIL

The First Vatican Council also represented a reaction against the Enlightenment or, more precisely, against theological tendencies in the church that were shaped by it. Two opposing trends dominated theology in the nineteenth century: rationalism and fideism. Rationalism in its various forms, as we have seen, considered reason as the only valid source of human knowledge. Fideism held that divine revelation is the sole basis for certainty in the arena of religious and ethical truth; fideists manifested distrust of human reason. The church had on several occasions cautioned theologians against dangers inherent in the two extreme positions, and finally the struggle against them reached a climax when both tendencies were condemned by Vatican I.[10]

The Constitution *Dei Filius* set forth in four chapters the Council's teaching on revelation and faith. Chapters 1 and 2 affirm the existence of God, known first in creation and then revealed in God's word in varied ways to the prophets and "in this, the final age . . . through his Son" (Heb 1:2). Chapter 3 treats of faith, and Chapter 4 enters into the complex problems of the relation between faith and reason. The Constitution must be read in the context of nineteenth-century theology. For example, it presents revelation primarily as the communication of supernatural truth inaccessible to natural reason, and faith as the acceptance of revealed truth. The Council had to chart a path between fideism and rationalism. *Dei Filius* affirmed in Chapter 1 that the existence of God can be known by the light of natural reason, and then in Chapter 3 described faith as follows:

> . . . faith, which is the "beginning of man's salvation," is a supernatural virtue whereby, inspired and assisted by the grace of God, we believe that what He has revealed is true, not because the intrinsic truth of things is recognised by the natural light of reason, but because of the authority of God Himself who reveals them, who can neither err nor deceive. For faith, as the apostle testifies, is "the assurance of things hoped for, the conviction of things not seen" (Heb 11:1).[11]

Dei Filius outlined a position that described the preambles to faith as consisting in the acceptance of God's existence, established by philosophical proofs, biblical revelation, and the authority of the living church as the divinely appointed guardian of revelation. The credibility of the Scriptures and of the church is authenticated by a variety of visible signs such as miracles, prophecies fulfilled, the exemplary lives of holy men and women, and the growth and durability of the church itself. These preambles speak to reason: "The use of reason precedes faith and must lead to it." The preambles do not prove the truth of faith, but they indicate that the omniscient God is the ultimate authority for what Christians believe. Although Vatican I was careful to present faith as made plausible by rational arguments, faith in origin and content is a "supernatural virtue," which is to say a gift—grace.

VATICAN II

From the Catholic standpoint the declarations of the First Vatican Council regarding faith brought a resolution to the nineteenth-century debates. But unlike Kierkegaard, something of a prophet crying out in the wilderness who used his own categories to attack at random the philosophy and philosophers of his time, Vatican I was constrained to address the issues in the theological framework of the period. Concerned with the dangers of anti-intellectualism inherent in fideism, it stressed that revelation, inaccessible to reason by itself, is nonetheless communicated in terms—words—intelligible to the human mind. If it seemed that Vatican I put too much emphasis on the intellectual and rational dimensions of faith, the Second Vatican Council corrected the imbalance. Vatican II, reflecting the theology of the twentieth century, adopted a more personalist approach. In the Constitution on Divine Revelation, revelation is presented as the self-communication of God and faith as the free, human response in the commitment of one's whole person.

Vatican I had distinguished two kinds of knowledge—knowledge that one gains by reason, and knowledge that comes with faith. It is common among theologians interpreting the work of the First Vatican Council to describe these two as natural and supernatural knowledge respectively. There is another way, however, of interpreting these two forms of knowledge, a way that illustrates the diverse approaches of the two Vatican councils. The Enlightenment defined knowledge (and it might be said, human experience in general) in terms of intellectual apprehension. Thus when Vatican I spoke of knowledge of God it centered on the cognitive—the perception and affirmation of truth in the mind. By contrast Vatican II made a conscious effort to stay as close as possible to biblical language and imagery; its understanding of knowledge was more existential and experiential.

The ancient Israelites had no word that corresponds exactly to "intellect." For them knowledge was as much a matter of the heart as of the mind. To know meant to experience, to possess as, for example, when the Bible uses "know" to describe the intimacy of sexual intercourse (Gen 4:1,17, 25; Lk 1:34). One who has firsthand experience of another knows a person (Ex 1:8; Dt 9:2, 24). This kind of knowing involves one's whole being. It is a matter of the sensible and intellectual appetites as well as of perception. It connotes not only awareness that the other person exists, but an understanding of who that person is. By the same token, to make known is to acquaint another with, to make another experience someone or something.[12] It is in this sense that God's self-revelation and the knowledge of God that results become the basis of faith. To say I BELIEVE IN presupposes that one knows in an experiential way—has existential knowledge—of God.

Vatican II emphasized that through divine revelation

> the invisible God out of the abundance of His love speaks to
> human beings as friends and lives among them, so that He may
> invite and take them into fellowship with Himself. This plan of
> revelation is realized by deeds and words having an inner unity:
> the deeds wrought by God in the history of salvation manifest
> and confirm the teaching and realities signified by the words,
> while the words proclaim the deeds and clarify the mystery con-
> tained in them. By this revelation then, the deepest truth about
> God and the salvation of humanity is made clear to us in Christ,
> who is the Mediator and at the same time the fullness of all
> revelation. (*DV*, 2)

The human response to God's self-revelation is faith, which Vatican II describes as "an obedience by which a person entrusts his [or her] whole self freely to God."[13]

THE NEW TESTAMENT UNDERSTANDING OF FAITH

The specifically Christian meaning of faith as found in the New Testament adapts a Greek vocabulary to express the Old Testament notion of faith. The verb "believe" and the noun "faith" in our English Bibles translate the Greek words *pisteuein* and *pistis*, which in classic Greek connote assurance and conviction. In the New Testament, *pistis* is made to incorporate the meaning of several Hebrew words that suggest the trust and confidence one puts in a person or a person's word because that person is judged trustworthy and dependable. Old Testament faith meant that the Israelites committed themselves to Yahweh and accepted with full confidence that the word spoken by God would be fulfilled.

In the Gospels, faith connotes the trust and confidence that arise from accepting the person of Jesus and his claims. The faith that moves mountains clearly implies belief in the power he exhibited in his own person. In the Johannine Gospel the object of faith is made more explicit: it is faith that Jesus is the holy one of God (6:69), that he came from God (16:30), that he is the Messiah (11:27). Faith in Jesus means faith in his words (Jn 2:22; 5:47; 8:45). To become a Christian is to put faith in the Lord Jesus Christ (Acts 5:14; 9:42; 11:17), and to believe that one is saved by the power of his grace (Acts 15: 11).[14]

After his conversion Paul wrote, "The life I live now is not my own; Christ is living in me. I still live my human life, but it is a life of faith in the Son of God, who loved me and gave himself for me" (Gal 2:20). Faith joined with baptism renders a person righteous (Rom 1:17; 3:22, 26, 28, 30; 4:5; 9:30; Gal 2:16; 3:8, 24) and makes Christians children of God in Christ (Gal 3:26). In his Epistles to the Galatians and Romans, particularly in Chapter 4 of the latter, Paul points up the antithesis between faith and the Law; and in other passages where he opposes faith and works, he also implies the contrast faith and the Law. Those who think they can be saved by the works of the Law without faith in the Lord Jesus are no better than unbelieving Gentiles.

St. Paul emphasizes that faith is a grace—an undeserved gift. After his discussion of the gifts of the Spirit (see above, Chapter 18), which the apostle implies are transitory or certainly not as central to Christian life as the "three things that last: faith, hope, and love" (1 Cor 13: 3).[15] In the New Testament the concepts of faith and hope are closely linked, and to a certain extent, interchangeable.[16] Thus 1 Peter says, "Should anyone ask you the reason for your hope," the explanation to be given "gently and respectfully" is an interpretation of the death, resurrection, and exaltation of Jesus at God's right hand (3:15,18-22). The Epistle to the Hebrews, after a passing reference to baptism—"our bodies washed in pure water"—says that the Christian's profession of faith "gives us hope, for he who made the promise deserves our trust" (10:22, 23). The confidence that drives Christians to persevere in their calling despite suffering, insults, and persecution is like that of Abraham, who "never questioned or doubted God's promise." Christian hope rests on the fidelity and power of God, "who raised Jesus our Lord from the dead" (Rom 4:20,24). In these passages hope is not to be confused with sheer optimism of the kind that looks to human ingenuity, technology, and economic development to build a bright new world. Christian hope, the expectation of the unseen (Rom 8:24. Heb 3:6; 11:1), is sustained by faith in God's promises. Faith, grounded as it is in the revelation of God's presence and activity in Christ, who is the alpha and omega of all creation, looks to the future as well as to the past.

Christian faith and hope are both eschatological in the sense that they are future oriented, focused on things not yet seen. With the consummation of the world, the fulfillment of God's plan for creation, they will pass away, and only love will remain. The earnest Christian is like the seeker after romantic love described by Kierkegaard in *Either/Or*. His romantic lover looks to the future and longs for the day announced by the prophets.

> O God, you are my God whom I seek.
> For you my flesh pines and soul thirsts.
> Like the earth parched, lifeless and without water. (Ps 62)

Like the romantic in pursuit of his beloved, the person of faith moves forward in hope. Word and promise spur the romantic on, but he encounters his beloved only at the end of the quest. He struggles to remain faithful until the moment in which his love will be consummated. Like the romance of the roundtable, faith tells a tale of longing and expectancy; and like the medieval stories of chivalry and courtship, it ends abruptly in the moment of fulfillment. But conjugal love remains. Married love—union—begins when one possesses and is possessed by the beloved. There is no past, no future; married love (like all true love) is lived in the present. The consummation of love makes the now eternal.[17]

Until the eschaton, however, we live by faith. For the Christian no less than for St. Paul, faith is not a mere sentiment; it has a built-in imperative that demands to be expressed. One witnesses to faith by lifestyle and public confession: more than once Paul sums up the obligations of the law in the single commandment of love of neighbor (Rom 13:8-10; Gal 5:6,14). And elsewhere he says that Christians who believe in their hearts must also confess with their lips (Rom 10:9). This will be the subject of the next chapter.

Notes

1. Smith, *Faith and Belief* (Princeton: Princeton University Press, 1979). p. 118.

2. Smith, ibid., p. 120.

3. *S. Th.* 2a 2ae, 2, 2.

4. *De Spiritu Sancto*, bk. 1, ch. 1. Quoted by Henri de Lubac in *The Splendour of the Church* (Glen Rock, NJ: Deus Books, 1963), p. 24; for the Latin text see p. 241, no. 65.

5. Henri de Lubac, *La foi chrétienne: Essai sur la structure du Symbole des Apôtres* (Paris: Aubier-Montaigne, 1970), p. 371.

6. Smith, *Faith and Belief*, p. 138.

7. *NCE* 5:804.

8. The notion of a "leap" is a fundamental category in Kierkegaard's thought. It appears in his earliest published work *Either/Or* (1843), and becomes more developed in his later writings, notably *The Concept of Dread* (1844), and his *Unscientific Postscript* (1846). See T.H. Croxall, (trans.), *Johannes Climacus and A Sermon* (Stanford, CA: Stanford University Press, 1958), pp. 28, 78–81.

9. Quoted in Martin Marty, *Varieties of Unbelief* (New York: Holt, Rinehart and Winston, 1964), p. 76.

10. Pope Pius IX had addressed both Rationalism and Fideism in the encyclical *Qui pluribus* (1846). Georg Hermes (1775–1831) and L. E. Bautain (1796–1867), both greatly influenced by Immanuel Kant, were the principal Catholic representatives of Rationalism and Fideism respectively. Closely akin to Fideism in its distrust of reason was Traditionalism. According to the traditionalists, God communicated a general revelation to our earliest ancestors which was then kept alive by tradition handed on from one generation to the next.

See J. Neuner & J. Dupuis (eds.), *The Christian Faith in the Doctrinal Documents of the Catholic Church* (Staten Island, NY: Alba House, 1982), pp. 35–40.

11. Neuner and Dupuis, no. 118 (p. 42). Denzinger-Schonmetzer 3008.

12. See J.L. McKenzie, *Dictionary of the Bible*, s.v. "Know, knowledge" (pp. 485–488).

13. The Council emphasized in several places that the act of faith implies a free assent. The Declaration on Religious Freedom states: "It is one of the major tenets of Catholic doctrine" that one's response to God in faith must be free. No one is to be forced to embrace the Christian faith against his (or her) own will. . . "The act of faith is of its very nature a free act" (*Dignitatis Humanae*, 10).

14. McKenzie, *Dictionary*, s.v. "Faith" (pp. 267–271).

15. Faith, hope, and love are traditionally called the theological virtues to distinguish them from the natural virtues—prudence, justice, temperance and fortitude. They are not virtues in the ordinary sense of moral philosophy, but rather the opening up of a new vision of reality. Faith, hope, and charity are *infused*, which is to say they are interior graces whereby human potentialities are caught up and given a new dimension by God acting on the person.

16. Joseph Ratzinger, "On Hope," in *Communio* 12 (Spring 1985):75.

17. See *Either/Or*, vol. II; quoted in Robert Bretall, *A Kierkegaard Anthology* (New York: The Modern Library, 1959), pp. 83–91.

24

One Faith,
Many Creeds?

Two tendencies pulling in opposite directions in today's church puzzle observers. On the one hand there is the drive toward a "common confession of faith," and on the other a burgeoning number of new creeds. The first tendency, inspired by the quest for church unity, has come to center, as we noted in the introduction, on the Ecumenical Creed of Nicea-Constantinople.

The creeds of the early church, especially the Creed of Constantinople, have a privileged place in the tradition common to all Christians. Although the various churches differ in their regard for creeds in general, these ancient formulations represent an enduring point of reference which binds the churches together. In speaking of these early creeds, Lukas Visher, director of the secretariat of the Faith and Order Commission of the World Council of Churches, stated a position which is the underlying premise of this commentary:

> They recall those first centuries in which decisions were taken with far-reaching implications for the teaching and structure of the Church. No Church can come unscathed out of a confrontation with that formative period. The creeds must also be taken seriously as testimonies because they were taken seriously by all the generations which preceded us, which means that a commu-

nity through the ages is inconceivable without respect for the creeds.[1]

Meanwhile as ecumenical discussions focus on the Ecumenical Creed, the number of creedal formulations increases. These new statements differ greatly from the classic creeds and from one another in purpose, structure, length, and content. Few if any of these confessions of faith, however, are intended to replace the Creed of Constantinople or the Apostles' Creed in the church's repertoire of creedal statements. The authors of most of these confessions see them as making explicit teachings which have always been part of Christian tradition. Although they are clearly meant to express the faith professed by groups and individuals, few have found their way into regular liturgical use. The new creeds, as will be pointed out below, also differ in several respects from the confessional statements of the sixteenth and seventeenth centuries which served as tests of orthodoxy in the various churches.

NEW CREEDS

In order to sort them out for discussion, Avery Dulles, with his usual clarity, has classified these new creeds in four categories according to authorship:[2]

1. Individuals, including a number of prominent Catholic theologians, have published short professions of faith. The purpose of the authors is first of all to express their personal credos, and secondly to witness to the Christian faith in language that is more readily understood by people of today.

In writing their own confessions of faith some individuals seem intent on trying to clarify their own beliefs. Examples are likely to be found in works of fiction as in personal journals which describe the paths that led the protagonists to a religious conversion and sometimes to Christian faith. Creedal statements of this kind display a marked tendency to highlight the human predicament. Many take their point of departure not from traditional Christian doctrines (which, as Dulles notes, would imply prior acceptance of "the faith of the church"), but from the malaise, anxiety, and confusion which seem to characterize life in the twentieth century. They express a need to affirm God in order to find self.

Many responsible for creedal affirmations of this kind are driven by the disquiet described by Dietrich Bonhoeffer:

> What do we really believe? I mean, believe in such a way that we stake our lives on it? The problem of the Apostles Creed? 'What *must* I believe?' is the wrong question; antiquated controversies, especially those between the different sects: the Lutheran versus Reformed, and to some extent the Roman Catholic versus Protestant, are now unreal. . . .[3]

People today, probably like people in every age, want to find out not what someone else believes, nor even what the church believes, but what we ourselves really believe. We want to know what, if anything, is important enough for us to fight and die for, and even more, to live for.

Theologians sensitive to pastoral needs had come to realize that for many Christians the gospel message is overgrown with explanations and customs like ivy on a country church so that the shape of the original structure can hardly be recognized. Karl Rahner argued that it should be possible to express what the Christian faith stands for in short formulas and everyday language. He felt that by concentrating on essentials it is possible to achieve the delicate balance between simplicity and simplification.[4] A number of Catholic theologians accepted the challenge; Piet Schoonenberg, P. Smulders, and Edward Schillebeeckx in Holland, Hans Küng and Walter Kasper in Germany, and Avery Dulles and Monika Hellweg in the United States are among the prominent names who have published personal credos.

2. Groups and coalitions drawn together, often across denominational lines, by a common cause have found it useful to dramatize their social concerns and legitimize their action programs in the context of the gospel and the church. Peace groups, conservationists, feminists, and others interpret their Christian heritage in the light of their shared interest.

Conservationist groups have reaffirmed their faith in God as creator with a call to accountability for the earth's resources.[5] At least one group of women in the United States has published a statement which women and men can use to give common witness.[6] Similar confessions of faith by student groups assert belief in the unity and dignity of all peoples, responsibility for the world, and, often, a pacifist refrain.[7]

The efforts of these interest groups to apply Christian principles to particular issues, praiseworthy as they are, point up *the* major obstacle in drafting a common confession of faith. Until recently, disputes over the Creed have centered on specific phrases and words ("born of the Virgin Mary," "descended into hell"), but today the challenge is to find expressions that speak to and for people of widely different backgrounds and concerns. Given the pluralism in contemporary society, one is taxed to identify experiences that everybody shares and can agree on in an objective ordering of values. In some parts of the world the issue is survival—food, water, shelter—whereas elsewhere the overriding issues are freedom of speech and the opportunity to work. In one segment of society, the emphasis is on the right to life; in another, the dignity of life. A creed like that composed by a youth group in the German Democratic Republic (East Germany) illustrates how Christians living in a socialistic system that threatens the rights and dignity of individuals respond by witnessing to the importance and integrity of a person precisely as an individual.

I Believe in God.
By this, I mean
I believe I am wanted.
> I know, therefore, I shall be used
> for the many small steps of the great love of God.

I am of value.
I therefore have courage to allow myself to be used.

I Believe in Jesus.
By this, I mean
I believe I am loved.
> I know, therefore, I shall not be discarded or cast off,
> but preserved—
> in sorrow and pain, in weakness and failure,
> in disaster and death, I shall not perish.

I am irreplaceable.
I therefore have courage to live and love to the utmost.

I Believe in the Spirit.
By this, I mean
No one can shake my faith.
> For I know Jesus is close to me and I am close to him!
> His victory even in and through death is my victory too.

I am indestructible.
I therefore have courage to renew my faith over and over again.[8]

Affirmations of faith by groups and coalitions of this kind reflect the universal anguish and hope of the human heart, but they are shaped by diverse circumstances. Implicitly they incorporate the same principles for social action that are found in the gospel itself. Although few of these confessions explicitly mention sin, most make some reference to the powers of destruction and division that threaten human existence, but they name them differently. Each formulation arises from a different experience of life. In final analysis, the evidence seems to indicate that it is no longer possible to agree on a short formula which speaks for all segments of society.

3. Churches, in an effort to make the Christian message more readily accessible to their members, have given formal approval to confessions which dress the traditional Creed in contemporary garb. Many go beyond the ancient creeds in that they proclaim the gospel as a the source of new life and the pattern of holiness.

Although the creedal statements in this third category do not at first glance appear appreciably distinct from those of unofficial groups and coalitions, they differ generally in two important respects.

First of all, they have been endorsed by some official body within the church.

Second, these church-endorsed creeds, unlike many personal confessions and creeds of unofficial groups, make a conscious effort to affirm the apostolic faith transmitted in baptism. The language, often non-biblical, is intended to be readily intelligible to members of the congregation. Their contents highlight certain aspects of the Christian tradition which, because of contemporary conditions, have taken on greater importance and therefore need to be emphasized; in general, they express an ethical imperative not found in the classic creeds. The confession of Jesus Christ as Lord and Savior, however it is stated, affirms the connection between salvation and the advent of peace and justice in the world, and the elimination of all forms of oppression and exploitation. Though it is often only implicit, the phrase "for us and for our salvation" takes on fresh, not new, meaning in these creeds.

One example of this kind is the confession of faith approved by the Catholic bishops of West Germany meeting in Würzburg in 1975.[9] The bishops, intending to produce a comprehensive statement of Catholic beliefs relevant to the times, were careful to make it a unified, balanced whole. At the outset they manifested an awareness of the contemporary world religious situation, acknowledging the God of Abraham,

Isaac, and Jacob who created heaven and earth and whom we publicly confess along with the Jewish people and people of Islam. Their concern for Catholic orthodoxy surfaces in allusions to specific teachings, as for example, the sacrament of penance; and they are even more emphatic that the social gospel is at the core of Christian faith.

A characteristic of faith statements in this genre is the importance they put on hope. The creed produced by the Würzburg synod, for example, begins with "God our hope," speaks of the "many bearers of our hope," and wants its witness to be an "invitation to hope." Christian hope is grounded on faith in the mystery of Christ, who suffered, died, and rose from the dead. Faith in the resurrection makes Christianity relevant. The life of Jesus inspires people to generosity and love of neighbor, but he is not simply a model from the past; because of the resurrection, he continues to be a force of freedom and life in the world today.

The confession of the German bishops is remarkably similar in tone and vision to the document produced at the Faith and Order conference held at Accra (Ghana) in 1974. Because of its origins it has a strong African accent, but essentially the Accra statement is also a summons to hope. Hope in the resurrection and longing for God, grounded on faith in the mystery of Christ, do not mean abandoning the world to death. On the contrary, faith and hope oblige Christians to vindicate God's rights over creation and to transform this world into a more human dwelling place.[10]

Another creed that belongs in this category is the one drafted in the 1960s by the United Church of Canada. Unlike the two previous examples, this one is brief. Consisting of less than 100 words, it is only half as long as the Ecumenical Creed and slightly shorter than the Apostles' Creed. Because of its brevity it leaves much unsaid (notably, it makes no clear reference to the power of sin that threatens human life, nor does it witness to Jesus' death and resurrection), but it is in the tradition of the ancient creeds in so far as it was designed for use in worship. It is at once a doxology, an expression of faith, and a prayer of hope.[11]

4. Groups of churches or their representatives, impelled by ecumenical concerns, have drafted agreements expressing their common faith that are intended to serve primarily as a basis for mutual recognition and cooperation. They are statements in the tradition of the great creedal confessions of the Reformation, with one significant differ-

ence. Whereas documents such as the Augsburg Confession (1529), the Thirty-nine Articles (1563), and, in its own way, the Profession of Faith of the Council of Trent (1564) were written to describe the positions of their respective churches; they stressed teachings which made them distinct from one another. By contrast, confessional statements drawn up by interdenominational groups today, and even those published by believers of a single tradition, are more likely to center on doctrines of the apostolic faith held in common by a majority of Christians: Protestant, Catholic, and Orthodox. Their purpose is to identify elements which can serve as the basis for agreement and collaboration and ultimately as a stepping stone on the way to full communion with one another.

Creedal statements of this fourth kind outline principles and common assumptions. By reason of style and length, their language does not suit them to liturgical use. Although they generally include a summary statement which has the ring of a confession of faith, they are more "constitutions" than creeds in the traditional sense. One example that illustrates this approach was published a decade ago as the "Proposed Constitution for the Church of Christ in India." It explains faith in the triune God, the significance of the one, holy, catholic, and apostolic church, Christian ministry, the sacraments, and the church's hope. The section subtitled "The Faith of the Church" affirms the authority of the canonical Scriptures and the value of the confessional statements of the Reformation for interpreting them. It acknowledges both the Apostles' and the Nicene Creed "as a true response and witness to the Word of God and as safeguards to the faith of the Church" and makes it clear that they do not have meaning apart from Scripture. The church, it says,

> also acknowledges its responsibility to confess its faith in the context in which God places it and under the guidance of the Holy Spirit, always conscious of the fact that all creeds and confessions are subordinate to the authority of the Scripture.[12]

THE NEED FOR NEW CREEDS

It is clear to anyone who had persevered through the pages of this commentary that the creeds of the early church were shaped by particular needs at given moments in history. The Ecumenical Creed is, as we have seen, a fourth-century witness of the time when the councils of

Nicea and Constantinople found it necessary to clarify and defend the apostolic faith against Arius and others who were interpreting the Trinity to the point of distortion. Like the Apostles' Creed, the Creed of Constantinople is a *timeless* summary of the faith only in so far as it embodies the kerygma which is at the heart of the gospel message. It enjoys a privileged place because at a critical moment in history it reaffirmed the apostolic teaching regarding the God who is one and three, who is at once transcendent and incarnate. Reinforced by long usage, the Ecumenical Creed has served the Christian community well as the classic expression of its belief in the Holy Trinity and the Incarnation, the mysteries basic to Jesus' revelation.

But why the present compulsion to write creeds? What are the needs of our time that cause individuals and groups to set their hand at redoing the ancient formulas?

Pope Paul VI took the occasion of the nineteenth centenary of the martyrdom of Saints Peter and Paul in 1967 to commit the Catholic church anew to the apostolic faith. He took note of "the disquiet which agitates certain modern quarters with regard to faith" and allowed that the church "has always the duty . . . to study more deeply and to present in a manner ever better adapted to successive generations the unfathomable mysteries of God, rich for all in fruits of salvation." Seeing his task to be that of Peter, namely, to confirm the other disciples in faith, Paul VI promulgated the "Credo of the People of God."

> We shall accordingly make a profession of faith, pronounce a creed which without being, strictly speaking, a dogmatic definition, repeats in substance, with some developments called for by the spiritual condition of our time, the Creed of Nicea, the creed of the immortal tradition of the holy Church of God.[13]

A year or so later Paul VI offered a further explanation for promulgating the Credo. He noted the challenges arising from contemporary philosophy, psychology, and historical studies, including exegesis, which for many prove to be obstacles to faith. The pope had no intention of writing a new creed, but like many others he recognized the need to relate the apostolic tradition to today's problems. "The Credo of the People of God" represents a paraphrase of the traditional text, interpolating phrases by way of explanation and application to current issues.

Each of the four types outlined above answers a different need. The last, most clearly, responds to an institutional need: the church's obligation to confess Jesus as Lord and Savior with one heart and one voice, and thus to overcome the division which is a scandal to believers and nonbelievers alike.

The confessions composed by the churches—the third type—represent a desire on the part of the Christian community to reach out to its members, especially those who find the language of the ancient creeds off-putting. In a consumer culture very conscious of the way things (and yes, ideas) are packaged, it is recognized that even vintage wine must be bottled in an appealing way (which is quite the opposite of putting new wine into old wineskins). The intent of the churches is to present the gospel message as something alive—ever fresh, ever new.

Churches' efforts to rewrite the creed are inspired by much the same motive that prompted individual theologians to compose short formulas of faith. Although they speak as individuals, theologians claim that their confessions of faith echo the faith of the church. In giving witness to their personal faith, the theologians make a statement about their allegiance to a tradition and their commitment to a faith community. Just as the churches want to make it clear that the gospel message is separable from the language in which it is expressed, so theologians are saying it is possible to update the theological idiom: one Lord, one faith, one baptism, but there are many ways to confess them.

The creeds composed by groups and coalitions drawn together by common concerns tend to be action oriented. Their immediate purpose is not to reaffirm the Christian message as a whole but to relate it to a particular cause or issue. Many examples, despite the God-language they employ, have the ring of social manifestos. They clearly imply commitment on the part of individuals. Taken together, these creeds witness less to historical Christianity than to the continued relevance of the gospel in today's world.

The way a particular church can appropriate the substance and spirit of the apostolic faith, and express it in language different from the ancient formulas, is dramatically exemplified in a creed used by the Masai people of East Africa:

We believe in the one High God,
>who out of love created the beautiful world
>and everything good in it.

He created people and wanted them to be happy in the world.

God loves the world and every nation and tribe on the earth.

We have known this High God in the darkness,
>and now we know Him in the light.

God promised in the book of his word, the Bible,
>that He would save the world and all nations and tribes.

We believe that God made good his promise
>by sending his Son Jesus Christ:
>A man in the flesh,
>A Jew by tribe,
>Born poor in a little village,
>Who left his home and was always on safari doing good,
>Curing people by the power of God,
>Teaching them about God and humanity,
>Showing that the meaning of religion is love.

He was rejected by his people,
>tortured, and nailed hands and feet to a cross,
>and died.

He was buried in the grave,
>but the hyenas did not touch Him,
>and on the third day He rose from the grave.
>He ascended to the skies.
>He is the Lord.

We believe that all our sins are forgiven through Him.

All who have faith in Him must be sorry for their sins,
>be baptized in the Holy Spirit of God,
>live by the rules of love,
>and share the Bread together in love,
>to announce the good news to others
>until Jesus comes again.

We are waiting for Him.

He is alive. He lives.

This we believe. Amen.[14]

The Masai creed illustrates another dynamic involved in the formulation of new creeds that we alluded to in the Introduction, but have not yet touched on in this chapter. Missionary activity in the far East and Africa has greatly enlarged the Christian world. Christians in the young churches of these continents, however, find themselves separated by denominational differences they have inherited but do not fully understand. The Reformation and the ensuing wars of religion that divided Christendom is a chapter in European history foreign to the heritage and experience of Asia and Africa. Where the ancient creeds have proved an obstacle in the young churches, the cause is less theological than cultural. Like the Masai, Christians in many of the young churches feel the need to express their faith using familiar images and idioms.

The personal confessions, other than those by theologians with a pastoral purpose, address still another need. They respond to the *felt* need, experienced by many, to do things in their own way. Dulles opines that post-Enlightenment Christians feel that, if they are to achieve a personal authenticity, they must express their deepest convictions in their own words. It is hard for some persons to appropriate the traditional formulas of the Christian community because simply to repeat the words of others is to compromise personal integrity by thwarting one's individuality and evoking a commitment on terms not of one's own making.

LESSONS FROM ANTIQUITY

Historically the church has seen itself as an agent, even the principal agent, of the Holy Spirit in assisting individuals and entire peoples in their quest for meaning and purpose, which is to say, faith. The church mediates the wisdom of the Christian tradition embodied in Word and Sacrament. In every age the Christian community is challenged to educate new generations to a living faith and personal commitment. It is not enough for its members to conform outwardly to accepted norms and merely parrot beliefs which they cannot truly affirm because they do not understand them. The dialogue between Philip and the Ethiopian eunuch continues in the modern world.

> Philip ran ahead and heard the man reading the prophet Isaiah. He said to him, "Do you really grasp what you are reading?"
>
> "How can I," the man replied, "unless someone explains it to me?" (Acts 8:30-31)

The attempts of churches and theologians to rewrite the Christian creed in ordinary language is a way of explaining it.

But do the new creeds, widely diverse in purpose, style and emphasis, represent a sign of health and hope in the church? Or are they the products of a centrifugal force spinning off in all directions and thereby negating the struggle of church leaders to focus attention on the Ecumenical Creed of Constantinople as a point of convergence and unity? We can only speculate on answers to these questions, but reflection on the experience of the early church puts them in context. The history of the creeds, an underlying theme in this book, suggests that if there was a period which has any lessons for today's church it was the beginning of the age of the councils. The fourth century rivaled our own in the proliferation of creeds.

We have had occasion to point out that the Council of Nicea did not produce a confession of faith *ab ovo* (Chapter 4). It took a baptismal creed from one of the local churches—probably of Syro-Palestinian origin—and edited it to address the particular issues of Arianism. The Council of Constantinople followed a similar procedure and formulated the Ecumenical Creed. In reaffirming the Nicene faith, "the hundred and fifty fathers" took still another local creed and amended it to clarify the person and nature of the Holy Spirit. Although the Ecumenical Creed of Constantinople gradually won the day, there had been previous attempts to resolve the disputes and heal the divisions caused by Arianism. J. N. D. Kelly chronicles the "large number of controversial assemblies" between Nicea and Constantinople, many of which published formularies of faith.[15] Among the most important were the four creeds associated with the Dedication Council held in Antioch in 341, the "Western Creed of Serdica" (modern Sofia), the *Ecthesis Macrostichos* (the "Long-lined Creed"), the First, Second, and Third Creeds of Sirmium, and the Fourth Formula of Sirmium, also known as the "Dated Creed" (see Chapter 13). In addition there were other conciliar creeds, encyclical letters of individual bishops and parties of bishops containing theological manifestos, and uncounted baptismal creeds in use in local churches.

And even though the Creed of Constantinople won gradual acceptance in the universal church, it did not put an end to the writing of creedal statements. In the Introduction we described the Athanasian Creed, and in connection with the christological controversies of the fifth century we mentioned the creed of the Council of Chalcedon. And there were other creeds too obscure to merit our attention except as evidence that the church has had a continual, if not continuous, history of creed writing. The modern creeds, though different in content and emphasis from most of the ancient and medieval formularies, have precedents in tradition. The church and its members must constantly restate the apostolic faith in the idiom and in the context of issues and problems of the day.

Another lesson one learns from reflecting on the history of the Ecumenical and Apostles' Creeds is that in substance they were "owned" by the Christian community as a whole. The bishops and their theological advisors amended and edited them to safeguard orthodoxy, but the basic text of the classic creeds was known to the Christian faithful through the catechesis they had received in preparation for baptism. The ecumenical councils were—*are*—not theological congresses; they were assemblies of bishops, pastoral leaders, concerned to mend divisions and schisms which threatened the unity of the church. One speculates that the reason other creeds drafted by councils and synods, despite their precision and careful distinctions, never took root was that they were theological compositions rather than popular confessions of faith.

The classic creeds, on the other hand, were always more than theological statements. They were doxologies, prayers of praise and thanksgiving for all that God has done. By making the Ecumenical Creed one's own, an individual identifies with the Christian community which extends backward in time and outward through the world. As a confession of faith a creed is spontaneous; it comes from the heart—the heart of the community and the hearts of its members. For a creed to capture the imagination, to be a rallying cry, a marching song for Christians, it must swell up from a shared experience and acclaim common beliefs and values. The issue today is to find such a creed that brings to the lips the faith that is in Christians' hearts.

A creedal statement must pulsate with the faith of the Christian community. The modern ecumenical movement confirms this lesson from the age of councils. A common confession of faith is not the starting point of church unity, but the result of it. The image which comes to mind is that of an infant learning to walk (though in the case of the church a more apt comparison would be an invalid whose handicap is attitudinal as well as physical). First one foot, then the other, a step at a time until confidence is built up. First some sharing, then a creedal statement; more sharing, then another affirmation of common beliefs. With each new step comes a provisional creed until a time when full unity is achieved.

Unity of the church, however, cannot be programmed. If another creed is to gain the stature and acceptance of the ancient Ecumenical Creed it will have to address a compelling need and arise from the heartfelt faith of the church at large. But who is to say that with the church and the world so deeply divided a compelling need does not already exist? Lukas Visher, the director of the Commission on Faith and Order, whom we quoted at the beginning of this chapter, has written:

> A new creed cannot be planned. It cannot be drafted and composed by a commission on the basis of theoretical discussions. The compelling occasion is required. Only when they are faced by an inescapable challenge will those who have to speak find the courage to speak in binding terms. Only then will they speak with authority. Only then will they find a common language. Only then will the Church really listen to them. Correct though these observations are, they can be taken too far. They can be misused to evade the task the Church faces . . . Truth and unity are already endangered . . . Of course, a new creed will be a gift of the Spirit. It cannot be programmed. But neither will it appear automatically one day without any preparation. That is why we need a constant common effort to express the meaning of the Gospel. Only when the possibility of a new creed is constantly before our eyes may it one day be granted to us. A stress on the need for a compelling occasion may be an expression of blindness and idleness.[16]

PREFERENCE FOR THE ECUMENICAL CREED OF NICEA-CONSTANTINOPLE

No creed, ancient or modern, represents a complete statement of Christian doctrine; therefore, none can be considered normative for every aspect of Christian life. Given that even the ancient creeds have only limited use as a norm of orthodoxy, why is the Faith and Order Commission of the World Council of Churches pushing to have the Ecumenical creed of Nicea-Constantinople accepted as the common confession of faith in the church? Why this preference for the Nicene Creed and not for a new one?

There are two answers, one negative, one positive. On the negative side, the task of drawing up a new creedal formula and gaining acceptance for it throughout Christendom seems, in human terms, impossible. The variety of new creeds outlined above illustrates the degree to which pluralism—cultural, social, and political, not to mention religious and theological—shapes the priorities of Christians even when they manage to agree on basic doctrines. Furthermore, there is no structure to sanction such a move. The World Council of Churches disclaims authority; and another Vatican council, even as broadly representative as Vatican II, would be recognized only by Roman Catholics.

On the positive side, the Nicene Creed's continuous use over many centuries and its wide recognition in the Christian world today make it more prestigious than any other formula of faith including the Apostles' Creed.

In the past century or two biblical scholars, historians, liturgiologists, and theologians have collaborated with anthropologists and other social scientists in clarifying the nature and function of creeds. Their research has contributed to a better understanding of the place of creeds in church life. Although these scholars point out the limitations inherent in all creedal statements, they also emphasize the utility and importance of creeds both to individuals and to the church as a whole. This modern scholarship has abetted ecumenism in two important ways:

First, the position of the Creed vis-à-vis Scripture, at one time thought to be an issue that divided Protestants and Roman Catholics, no longer appears to be an insurmountable obstacle. Although some may want additional clarification, the statement in the "Proposed Constitution for the Church of Christ in India" cited above is commonly accepted; today there is general consensus that "all creeds and confessions are subordinate to the authority of Scripture."

Second, by emphasizing that the Creed is first and foremost a confession of faith that originated in the baptismal liturgy, we are reminded of its prime purpose. The credo—"I place my heart"—represents a commitment made in love and hope; it is a response to God's initiative experienced as grace and known by revelation. In the context of the liturgy, the Creed stands as it did originally: a doxology applauding the work of the Triune God in our lives and in the world. It calls to mind the mystery of salvation, and in the context of worship, Christian doctrines become statements of enlightenment, truth, and praise. The old axiom *lex orandi, lex credendi*—"prayer is the norm of belief"—is still valid. As has been evident throughout these pages, doxology precedes doctrine; practice comes before theory; the church, before ecclesiology. The current agenda of the ecumenical movement seems to be on the right road: first baptism, eucharist, and ministry, and then will come the common confession of the apostolic faith.[17]

Notes

1. Lukas Visher, "An Ecumenical Creed? An Attempt at a Synthesis," in H. Küng and J. Moltmann, eds., *An Ecumenical Confession of Faith?* Concilium 118 (New York: Seabury Press, 1979), p. 105.

2. Avery Dulles, "Foundation Documents of the Faith X: Modern Credal Affirmations," in *Expository Times* 91 (1980):291–299.

3. *Letters and Papers from Prison*, enlarged edition (London: SCM Press, 1972), p. 382. Quoted in Dulles, *Expository Times*, p. 296.

4. "The Need for a 'Short Formula' of Christian Faith," in *Theological Investigations* IX (New York: Herder and Herder, 1972), pp. 117–126. "Reflections on the Problems Involved in Devising a Short Formula of the Faith," *Theological Investigations* XI (New York: Seabury Press, 1974), pp. 230–244. Also see the "Epilogue" to Rahner's *Foundations of the Christian Faith* (New York: Seabury Press, 1978), pp. 448–459.

5. *Confessing our Faith Around the World*. Faith and Order Paper No. 104 (Geneva: World Council of Churches, 1980), p. 25.

6. *Around the World*, p. 75.

7. Ibid., p. 32.

8. Ibid., p. 31.

9. René Marle, "Giving an Account of the Hope That Is in Us," in H. Küng and J. Moltmann, eds., *An Ecumenical Confession of Faith?*

10. Marle, ibid., p. 98.

11. See Gregory Baum, "A New Creed," in *The Ecumenist* 6 (July–August 1968):164–167. Other examples of church-endorsed creeds are the Statement of Faith of the United Church of Christ (USA); the

Confession of the United Presbyterian Church of the USA (1967); and the Confession of the Faith of the Presbyterian-Reformed Church in Cuba (1977).

12. *Around the World*, p. 14.

13. Pope Paul VI, *The Credo of the People of God: A Theological Commentary*, Candido Pozo, ed. (Chicago: Franciscan Herald Press, 1980), pp. 7–8.

14. The translation is by Vincent Donovan in his book, *Christianity Rediscovered* (Maryknoll, NY: Orbis Books, 1982), p. 200.

15. *Creeds*, p. 263.

16. In Küng and Moltmann, pp. 108–109.

17. E. Glenn Hinson, "Towards a Common Confession of Apostolic Faith," in *Ecumenical Trends* 12 (July–August 1983):110.

Epilogue

"Amen"

The Creed ends as it began, with an act of commitment. The significance of AMEN is much like that of *credo*—"I set my heart on. . ." In the original Hebrew form, *amen* is a way of saying "yes." It affirms trust, fidelity, and other meanings that imply conviction and commitment. By ending the Creed with a resounding "amen," the individual believer and the church as a whole witness to the substance of the creed and ratify everything it contains. It has been said that one can no more speak "amen" softly or with restraint than one can say "hurrah" in a whisper or without excitement.[1] St. Jerome described the fervor of Christians in fourth-century Rome, saying their "amen" sounds so loudly, "like spiritual thunder," as to "shake the temples of the idols."[2]

The Book of Revelation makes Amen a divine title which it attributes to Christ, who is "the faithful Witness and true" (3:14). Like St. Paul, Christians cannot be vacillating or uncertain about what God has done for them because their faith is founded in the person of Christ Jesus. God's promises have been fulfilled in Jesus and "therefore it is through him that we address our Amen to God when we worship together." Paul describes three effects of our initiation into the Christian life. In baptism Christ "anointed us and has sealed us, thereby depositing the first payment, the Spirit, in our hearts" (2 Cor 1:20, 21-22). The Holy Spirit is the guarantee of our inheritance in the messianic kingdom until such a time that we shall come into full possession of it (see Eph 1:13-14; Rom 8:23).

425

It was the custom in the ancient Mozarabic liturgy of old Spain to inject "amen" after each sentence of the Creed. Much can be said for the practice as a spontaneous expression of faith as long as it does not splinter the Creed into bits and pieces. Christian beliefs, as we have tried to show throughout the foregoing pages, are not simply a compilation of opinions agreed upon by the church. The parts of the Creed stand together as a whole; they lose their significance when they are isolated from one another. The Creed narrates the story of salvation, a story grounded in history that focuses on a point beyond time.

THE ECONOMIC TRINITY

This commentary on the Creed was substantially complete when Pope John Paul II published his encyclical letter *Dominum et Vivificantem*—"Lord and Giver of Life."[3] One wishes that space permitted the publication of the entire text of the encyclical because it would be an appropriate epilogue to this book. In a relatively brief compass, Pope John Paul recapitulates the main themes of the Ecumenical Creed and of this book.

Dominum et Vivificantem emphasizes that salvation is the work of the triune God present in the world. Although the title evokes the image of the Holy Spirit, the encyclical taken as a whole is a meditation on the economic trinity, that is, the relationship of the Father, Son and Spirit to each other and their distinctive roles in the redemption and sanctification of the world. Pope John Paul took as his starting point Jesus' farewell discourse at the Last Supper in which, said the pope, "the highest point of the revelation of the Trinity is reached" (par. 9). Ironically it is the very departure of Jesus through the cross and resurrection that insures the coming of the Paraclete who will remain until the end of time. The moment marks a new beginning of God's self-communication to humanity in the Holy Spirit:

> While it is through creation that God is he in whom we all "live and move and have our being" (Acts 17:28), in its turn the power of the redemption endures and develops in the history of man and the world in a double "rhythm" as it were, the source of which is found in the eternal Father. On the one hand there is the rhythm of the mission of the Son, who came into the world and was born of the Virgin Mary by the power of the Holy Spirit; and on the other hand there is also the rhythm of the mission of the Holy Spirit, as he was revealed definitively by Christ. Through

the "departure" of the Son, the Holy Spirit came and continues to come as Counselor and Spirit of truth. And in the context of his mission, as it were within the indivisible presence of the Holy Spirit, the Son, who "had gone away" in the pascal mystery, "comes" and is continuously present in the mystery of the church, at times concealing himself and at times revealing himself in her history, and always directing her steps. . . .(par. 63)

Pentecost inaugurated the era of the church with the descent of the Holy Spirit on the apostles. In fact, Pope John Paul's avowed purpose in writing *Dominum et Vivificantem* is to foster the awareness that the church, in the words of Vatican II, "is compelled by the Holy Spirit to do her part toward the full realization of the will of God, who established Christ as the source of salvation for the whole world" (par. 2). The church, constituted by word and sacrament, is not made by human hands. In the Spirit it is the symbol and means of solidarity of humans with God. The Holy Spirit is the unitive force that draws Christians into union with one another and with the triune God.

A common confession of faith in the triune God will be the means and sign of reconciliation of Christians with one another. Although a divided Christendom may not yet be ready to agree on the doctrinal implications of every phrase and strophe in the traditional Creed, Christians more and more are praying it together. The Creed in origin and purpose is a doxology that acclaims God's glory, a confession of praise and thanksgiving for all that God has done for us and our salvation. To this synopsis of the story of salvation proclaimed in the Scriptures, Christians can but respond with a grateful "Amen."

Notes

1. Gilbert Roxburgh, "The Great Amen," *The Bible Today* 25 (Oct. 1966):1785. For more on *amen*, see Mary Charles Bryce, "The Interrelationship of Liturgy and Catechesis," *American Benedictine Review* 28 (March, 1977):1–40.

2. Preface to Book II of his Commentary on Galatians. *NPNF*, 2nd ser., VI, p. 497.

3. *Origins*, June 12, 1986.

Abbreviations and Reference Works

Unless otherwise noted, the Scripture texts used in this work are taken from the *New American Bible*, copyright 1970 by the Confraternity of Christian Doctrine, Washington, D.C., and are used by license of said copyright owner. No part of the *New American Bible* may be reproduced in any form without permission in writing. All rights reserved.

The quotations from the documents of Vatican II, unless otherwise noted, are from Walter M. Abbot, ed., *The Documents of Vatican II*. New York: Guild Press, 1966.

ACW	*Ancient Christian Writers*. The works of the Fathers in translation edited by Johannes Quasten and Joseph C. Plumpe. Westminster, MD: The Newman Bookshop, 1946 ff.
DS	*Enchiridion Symbolorum: Definitionum et declarationum, de rebus fidei et morum.* Henricus Denzinger et Adolphus Schönmetzer, eds. 33rd ed. Freiburg im Br.: Herder, 1965.
Congar, *I Believe*	Yves M. J. Congar, *I Believe in the Holy Spirit*. 3 vols. New York: Seabury Press, 1983.

429

JBC	*The Jerome Biblical Commentary*. Edited by Raymond E. Brown, Joseph A. Fitzmyer, and Roland E. Murphy. 2 vols. Englewood Cliffs, NJ: Prentice-Hall, Inc., 1968.
Kelly, *Creeds*	J. N. D. Kelly, *Early Christian Creeds*. 3rd ed. Essex, UK: Longman Group Ltd., 1981.
McKenzie, *Dictionary*	John L. McKenzie, *Dictionary of the Bible*. New York: Macmillan Publishing Co., 1965.
NCE	*New Catholic Encyclopedia*. 17 vols. New York: McGraw-Hill Book Co., 1967ff.
Sacramentum Mundi	*Sacramentum Mundi*. An Encyclopedia of Theology. Edited by Karl Rahner, *et al*. 6 vols. New York: Herder and Herder, 1968.
NPNF	*A Select Library of the Nicene and Post-Nicene Fathers of the Christian Church*. Edited by Philp Schaff. 14 vols. Reprint. Grand Rapids: Wm B. Eerdmans Publishing Co., 1956.
NPNF 2nd ser.	*A Select Library of Nicene and Post-Nicene Fathers of the Christian Church*. Edited by Philip Schaff and Henry Wace. 14 vols. Reprint. Grand Rapids: Wm B. Eerdmans Publishing Co., 1961.

Index of Names

Index of Subjects